They Knew Marilyn Monroe

MW01285100

ALSO BY LES HARDING
AND FROM MCFARLAND

The Newfoundland Railway, 1898–1969: A History (2012)

*Holy Bingo, the Lingo of Eden, Jumpin' Jehosophat
and the Land of Nod: A Dictionary of the
Names, Expressions and Folklore of Christianity* (2008)

*Elephant Story: Jumbo and P.T. Barnum
Under the Big Top* (2000)

*A Book in Hand Is Worth Two in the Library:
Quotations on Books and Librarianship* (1994)

They Knew Marilyn Monroe

Famous Persons in the Life of the Hollywood Icon

LES HARDING

McFarland & Company, Inc., Publishers
Jefferson, North Carolina, and London

LIBRARY OF CONGRESS CATALOGUING-IN-PUBLICATION DATA

Harding, Les, 1950–
They knew Marilyn Monroe : famous persons in the life
of the Hollywood icon / Les Harding.
p.   cm.
Includes bibliographical references and index.

ISBN 978-0-7864-6637-5
softcover : acid free paper ∞

1. Monroe, Marilyn, 1926–1962—Friends and associates—Dictionaries.
2. Actors—United States—20th century—Biography—Dictionaries.
I. Title.
PN2287.M69H33   2012   791.4302' 8092—dc23   2012029410

BRITISH LIBRARY CATALOGUING DATA ARE AVAILABLE

© 2012 Les Harding. All rights reserved

*No part of this book may be reproduced or transmitted in any form
or by any means, electronic or mechanical, including photocopying
or recording, or by any information storage and retrieval system,
without permission in writing from the publisher.*

On the cover: A 1950s publicity shot of Marylin Monroe (Photofest)
Front cover design by Mark Berry (www.hot-cherry.co.uk)

Manufactured in the United States of America

*McFarland & Company, Inc., Publishers
Box 611, Jefferson, North Carolina 28640
www.mcfarlandpub.com*

Table of Contents

Preface

Who doesn't love Marilyn Monroe? This may surprise you, but I do not. I'll admit to carrying a torch for the early Marilyn, when she was fresh, sparkling, and almost ethereally beautiful. But when I think of the second half of her adult life—with the drinking, the pills, and the psychoanalysts—she was still beautiful but I feel angry and annoyed with her. Marilyn came to depend on pretentious pseudointellectual parasites and poseurs. Poor Marilyn. She lacked the emotional stability, the self-confidence, and educational depth to distinguish the genuine from the phony. That was the source of her tragedy. I just want to shake some sense into her and warn her off those people.

I am an old movie buff, and that is the genesis of this project. I started watching, re-watching and collecting Marilyn Monroe films. *The Seven Year Itch* is my personal favorite. But as is my nature, I wanted more information. So I hit the libraries, made an impressive number of interlibrary loans, visited the bookstores and the second-hand bookstores wherever I went, searched the internet, put the photocopier to good use, and it just spiraled out of control.

This is not a biography of Marilyn Monroe. There are literally hundreds of those and I did not feel the need to add to the heap. Instead, I have done something which I think is unique. I have found 618 famous names (famous to me, anyway) and have briefly summarized the relationship Marilyn Monroe had with each. The arrangement is alphabetical. The range is as immense as it is unexpected—Sir Laurence Olivier to The Three Stooges, Nikita Khrushchev to Dylan Thomas, Brigitte Bardot to Eleanor Roosevelt. Of course, the Kennedys, Joe DiMaggio, and Arthur Miller are included.

It has become politically correct to spell that popular golden hair color as "blond" without an "e," even when referring to a woman. But somehow, I feel that "blonde" with an "e" is more appropriate for Marilyn Monroe and I have spelled it that way throughout. After all, who but Marilyn could get away with saying, "I like to feel blonde all over."

A thank you is in order for the staff at the St. John's Public Library and the Queen Elizabeth II Library at the Memorial University of Newfoundland for tolerating my many requests for interlibrary loans. Dianne Taylor-Harding gets a special thank you for her suggestions, knowledge of research sources and resolving the inevitable computer issues.

Introduction

The woman who continues to electrify the world as Marilyn Monroe, a half century after her death, was born Norma Jeane Mortensen at 9:30 a.m. on June 1, 1926, in the Charity Ward of the Los Angeles General Hospital. Her mother, Gladys Pearl Monroe, worked as a film cutter at Consolidated Film Industries, a Hollywood film processing lab. Gladys was 26 when her daughter was born and, by all accounts, she was a beautiful woman who bore a passing resemblance to silent screen star Norma Talmadge. She was also a woman suffering from deep mental and emotional disturbances. Although the birth certificate listed the baby's father as one Martin Edward Mortensen, it also lists him as being of unknown residence. Norma Jeane never met him and he was certainly not her biological father. Mortensen, a feckless immigrant from Norway, was legally married to Gladys at the time but had hit the road prior to Gladys becoming pregnant.[1] Before Mortensen, Gladys had married and divorced Jack Baker. Norma Jeane never met him either, but just to complicate matters, Gladys and her daughter often used the Baker surname. At the baptism on December 6, 1926, the baby's name was recorded as Norma Jeane Baker.

It will never be known for sure who Norma Jeane's father was, but the most likely candidate is Charles Stanley Gifford, Gladys's shift foreman at Consolidated Film Industries. Marilyn Monroe believed this to be the case. She made several attempts to contact Gifford, but was harshly rebuffed each time. Throughout her life, Marilyn was to feel an aching loss for never having had a father.

Gladys Baker, as she was calling herself, liked the fast life and found the responsibilities of single motherhood too much to handle. When Norma Jeane was less than two weeks old she was boarded with a foster family, the Bolenders, for $5 per week. The Bolenders were kind to the children in their care, but they were strict and very religious. Gladys never missed a payment and visited her child when she could. Norma Jeane, however, remembered the visitor not as her mother but as "the woman with the red hair" (Spoto 1993, 20).

In 1933, after seven years of this arrangement, Gladys took her daughter back as she had secured enough for a down payment on a modest bungalow near the Hollywood Bowl. Norma Jeane and her mother became regular moviegoers. At Grauman's Chinese Theater Norma Jeane placed her feet in the concrete footprints of Gloria Swanson and Clara Bow. But the good times were all too brief. In January 1935, Gladys suffered a breakdown and was diagnosed as a paranoid schizophrenic. She was committed to a state mental hospital and, apart from brief interludes, was institutionalized for the rest of her life.[2] Marilyn Monroe was thereafter to have a morbid terror of genetic insanity.

An English couple, the Atkinsons, who worked as bit players in the film industry, were renting rooms in Gladys's house. They stayed on and looked after Norma Jeane. But eventually they returned to England. The little girl was then placed under the guardianship of Gladys's best friend, Grace McKee, a film librarian. Grace was a frustrated actress and transferred her ambitions to her ward. She would say, "Don't worry, Norma Jeane. You're going to be a beautiful girl when you get big—an important woman—a movie star" (Spoto 1993, 34). Grace was not well off and it was necessary for Norma Jeane to be passed through a succession of foster homes. Several of the families wanted to adopt her but Gladys, who still exercised the ultimate legal authority over her daughter, refused to consider such a thing. On September 13, 1935, Norma Jeane was placed in the Los Angeles Orphans Home. She was devastated. In a 1962 interview, Marilyn said of that time, "I began to cry, 'Please, please don't make me go inside. I'm not an orphan, my mother's not dead. I'm not an orphan—it's just that she's sick in the hospital and can't take care of me. Please don't make me live in an orphan's home.'" (Steinem & Barris 36).

Marilyn Monroe made much of her supposed Dickensian childhood—how she was given mere pennies to wash mountains of dishes in the orphanage, was molested by a foster parent and raped by a rogue policeman. Marilyn's childhood was difficult but the horror stories were probably figments of her overheated imagination and an attempt to gain sympathy from the listener.

The orphanage was actually a well-run and enlightened place. Even so, it was still an institution, and Norma Jeane's feelings of abandonment and loneliness were intensified. The Los Angeles Orphans Home was only a block away from the RKO Studio. Norma Jeane could look out her window and see the brightly lit water tower on the RKO Radio Pictures lot. She remembered that her mother had worked on RKO films and began to dream that someday she would be a movie star herself.[3] At Christmas, the children were invited to a party and a movie at the studio. The film industry ran through every part of Marilyn Monroe's life.

Grace McKee took Norma Jeane out of the orphanage in the summer of 1937. More foster homes followed until Norma Jeane went to live with Grace's aunt, Ana Lower. Aunt Ana was a kind woman and provided Norma Jeane with the most stable home environment she would ever know. The older woman was a devout Christian Scientist and introduced her ward to that faith. Norma Jeane was a Christian Scientist for about eight years; this would remain her strongest religious influence.

Norma Jeane started Emerson Junior High School in September 1939. Her fully developed body soon made her very popular with the boys. She attended Van Nuys High School in September 1941, but dropped out of the tenth grade. Grace McKee and her husband were moving to West Virginia and it was decided that Aunt Ana was too old and unwell to care for Norma Jeane any longer. The obvious solution was to marry the 16-year-old schoolgirl off to the handsome neighbor boy, 21-year-old James Dougherty. The alternative would have been for Norma Jeane to be sent back to the orphanage. Dougherty had a steady job at Lockheed Aviation and Norma Jeane already had a crush on him. The wedding took place on June 19, 1942, less than three weeks after Norma Jeane's 16th birthday.

Whether or not the marriage was happy depends on whom you believe. After the fact, Marilyn Monroe would claim that she was forced into a loveless marriage. Dougherty said that it was a good union based on love. In the fall of 1943, with World War II raging, Jim Dougherty joined the Merchant Marine as a physical-training instructor. He was posted to Catalina Island off the Southern California coast, and his beautiful young bride went with him. Much to her husband's chagrin, Norma Jeane caused something of a sensation with the young men based on the island. The following year, Dougherty was posted overseas. Norma Jeane moved in with her husband's parents and began working at the Radio Plane factory in Burbank.

In the spring of 1945, Corporal David Conover, an Army photographer, came to Radio Plane to shoot some morale-boosting pictures of women doing war work. Conover spotted the stunning 18-year-old in her overalls and knew he had found the ideal model. The resulting photographs received wide distribution and Norma Jeane's career as a cover girl was underway. She was a natural before the camera. In the summer of that year, Norma Jeane registered with the Blue Book Modeling Agency in Los Angeles. The director, Emmeline Snively, started coaching her and she soon quit the defense plant and began getting work as a photographer's model. On the advice of Miss Snively, Norma Jeane increased her employment prospects by changing her light brown hair to a golden honey-blonde.

When Dougherty came home on leave, he realized that things had changed. His wife's focus was no longer on him but on her career as a photo model. Norma Jeane was not the tall willowy type suited for fashion modeling. Instead, she made her mark in pinup magazines such as *Cheesecake, U.S. Camera, Laff, See,* and *Peek.* This was a traditional way to get the attention of movie producers. Norma Jeane pursued her career with a single-minded determination, appearing on 33 magazine covers in her first six months as a professional model.

When Jim Dougherty shipped out again, he received a letter from a Las Vegas attorney. Norma Jeane had established residency in Nevada and had filed for divorce. She had decided to take things to the next level and become a movie actress. The film studios did not want their starlets tied down to husbands. They invested some serious money in their girls and were not about to have a pregnancy put their investment at risk.

In 1946, shortly after her 20th birthday, Norma Jeane had an interview with Ben Lyon, a former actor who was now the casting director at Twentieth Century–Fox. Lyon was impressed with Norma Jeane, thinking she resembled Jean Harlow, with whom he had worked in *Hell's Angels* in 1930. A screen test was scheduled and, on the strength of it, Norma Jeane was signed to a six-month contract at $75 per week. But the name Norma Jeane Dougherty had to go. Lyon suggested "Marilyn" and Norma Jeane added "Monroe," her mother's family name. Lyon liked the alliteration and "Marilyn Monroe" was born.[4]

As a lowly contract player, Marilyn spent her days at Fox taking dancing, singing and pantomime classes, as well as posing for seemingly endless rounds of publicity photo sessions. Marilyn worked hard and began to get noticed. She landed her first speaking role in 1947. The film was a forgettable comedy entitled *Scudda Hoo! Scudda Hay!* "Hi, Rad" was all she was given to say. The rest of the scenes Marilyn filmed ended up on the cutting-room floor.

One day, as she walked across the Fox lot, Marilyn caught the eye of Joseph M. Schenck. Nearly 70 years of age, Schenck was an executive producer. He had a lively interest in pretty girls (he had been married to Norma Talmadge, the actress Marilyn's mother resembled) and invited Marilyn to a dinner party at his house. The unknown starlet immediately became a regular at Schenck's parties. Did Marilyn become the old man's mistress as some have alleged? Probably not, as her career did not suddenly take off. But Schenck remained Marilyn's friend and mentor until his death in 1961. Schenck probably did help her get a small part (and 14th billing) in *Dangerous Years.* Shot in May 1947, it was a film about juvenile delinquents.[5] Marilyn played a waitress in a teen hangout and was given her first close-up. But a few days after completing the picture, Fox decided not to renew her contract.

In March 1948, after more pinup photos and modeling jobs, Marilyn signed a six-month contract, at $125 per week, with Columbia Pictures. Columbia raised Marilyn's hairline using electrolysis and changed her hair color from ash blonde to platinum blonde. Marilyn was given second billing in *Ladies of the Chorus,* a low-budget musical in which she was a burlesque star who falls in love with the scion of a prominent family. She got to sing two songs in the movie. She also fell in love with Fred Karger, the film's musical director. Marilyn wanted to marry Karger but he didn't think she was suitable mother material for his young children. Although he was not about to marry her, Karger introduced Marilyn to serious music and good books. He also gave her valuable voice coaching and wardrobe advice and took her to an orthodontist to have a slight overbite corrected. Columbia's head drama coach, Natasha Lytess, was asked to help Marilyn with her acting technique. Lytess was so impressed with Marilyn's natural talent and drive to succeed that she quit her job at Columbia and devoted herself exclusively to Marilyn for the next seven years! Columbia was ruled with an iron hand by Harry Cohn, and despite the studio's investment in their newest starlet, her contract was allowed to expire in September 1948. The story is that Marilyn refused Cohn's sexual advances.

After a few lean months, Marilyn landed a tiny part in a Marx Brothers comedy, *Love Happy*. The film was not very good but Marilyn's walk-on generated a lot of attention, so much so that she was sent across the country on a promotional tour. Next up for Marilyn was a small role in a musical, *A Ticket to Tomahawk*. Between the production of *Love Happy* in 1949 and its release in the spring of 1950, Marilyn posed for her famous nude calendar shots. The calendar went on to earn millions but all Marilyn got out of it was $50.

Marilyn now attracted the attention of Johnny Hyde, a top Hollywood agent. Hyde, who was 53, immediately fell in love with the 22-year-old starlet and did everything he could to promote her career. Thanks to him, Marilyn was cast by John Huston in her first "A" picture, a gritty film noir, *The Asphalt Jungle*.[6] Marilyn then appeared in three minor films, *Right Cross, Hometown Story* and *The Fireball*, a roller skating epic with Mickey Rooney. Again, thanks to Hyde, Marilyn got a small but important part in her most prestigious film to date, *All About Eve*. She shared scenes with the likes of Bette Davis, Anne Baxter and George Sanders. In December 1950 Marilyn was signed to a seven-year contract by Fox. She would be paid $500 per week in the first year, gradually rising to $3,500 per week in the final year. The contract was the last thing Hyde was able to do for her. He died of a heart attack just days after it was signed.

Fox was quick to put their newest property to work in three minor comedies: *As Young As You Feel, Love Nest* and *Let's Make It Legal*. Still reliant on Natasha Lytess, Marilyn, on loan to RKO, was coached on the set of *Clash by Night,* a drama based on a Clifford Odets play, directed by Fritz Lang. The story of Marilyn's nude calendar came out at this time. The studio was nervous and wanted her to deny everything. Marilyn did the opposite.

She admitted everything, saying she had done nothing wrong. The public agreed.

The public also learned that her mother was not dead (as they had been led to believe) but was in a state mental hospital. Marilyn had her mother moved to a private sanitarium. Although she only visited her mother occasionally, she took care of all the expenses.

Increasingly, Marilyn yearned for what she never had, a normal family life. And she desperately wanted to be a mother. In May 1952, she had her appendix removed. As he prepared to operate, the surgeon found a handwritten note on Marilyn's stomach. "*Cut as little as possible ... no ovaries* removed ... do whatever you can to prevent large *scars*" (Banner 177). By now Marilyn Monroe had appeared in *Time* and *Life* magazines and soldiers in the Arctic had voted her "The Girl Most Likely to Thaw Alaska" (Riese & Hitchens 28). Next for her were comedy roles in *We're Not Married, O'Henry's Full House* (opposite Charles Laughton) and *Monkey Business* (opposite Cary Grant and Ginger Rogers).

Marilyn finally got the opportunity for a major dramatic part when she played a psychotic babysitter in *Don't Bother to Knock*. But it was her next picture, *Niagara*, which propelled her to stardom. The tag line on the movie posters was: "Marilyn Monroe and *Niagara*—a raging torrent of emotion that even nature can't control!" (Victor 214).

In the summer of 1952 Marilyn began seeing the legendary baseball player Joe DiMaggio. They married in 1954 and, after a tempestuous union, they divorced less than a year later. Thereafter, DiMaggio became the person upon whom she could rely more than any other.

Gentlemen Prefer Blondes was released in 1953. Even though Marilyn was now a star she was scandalously underpaid. She was under contract for $1,500 per week while co-star Jane Russell was getting between $100,000 and $200,000 for the movie. Understandably, Marilyn complained: "I *am* the blonde, and it is *Gentlemen Prefer Blondes*" (Riese & Hitchens 174). Her next movie, *How to Marry a Millionaire*, teamed her with Lauren Bacall and

Betty Grable. After three hits in a row, Marilyn got stuck in what she called a grade-Z western, *River of No Return*. There was no love lost between her and the film's authoritarian director, Otto Preminger.

By this time, Marilyn was worrying about the quality of the films she was given. Seeking control of her future, her reputation and a better salary, Marilyn endeavored to renegotiate her contract. Fox refused and put her on suspension. Eventually, Twentieth Century–Fox relented and Marilyn was cast in *There's No Business Like Show Business*. She agreed to do the film because she was promised *The Seven Year Itch*. That film, with its famous skirt billowing scene, became the image most associated with Marilyn Monroe. At the end of 1954, Marilyn defied Hollywood convention by establishing her own production company with photographer Milton Greene.

Marilyn had begun a romance with playwright Arthur Miller and began attending classes at the famed Actors Studio in New York. Natasha Lytess, her devoted acting coach, was out and Lee and Paula Strasberg were in. It got to the point where Marilyn Monroe would not appear anywhere near a movie camera unless Paula Strasberg was at her side. This arrangement was none too popular with most film directors. In 1956, Marilyn made the well-regarded drama *Bus Stop*. To this day there are those who feel it was an injustice that her performance was not nominated for an Academy Award. After marrying Miller, the newlyweds were off to England where Marilyn filmed *The Prince and the Showgirl* with Sir Laurence Olivier. The two stars clashed, and the production was a troubled one, Marilyn gave a scintillating performance.

To her legion of fans all was well but by this time in her life Marilyn was overcome with self-doubt and suicidal despair. She self-medicated with an ever-increasing intake of alcohol and pills. In November 1956, unhappy and exhausted, Marilyn flew back to America. Already, there were signs that her marriage to Arthur Miller was in trouble. Marilyn took a two-year break from filming to repair her marriage and have a child. But her joy at becoming pregnant turned to despair. It was a tubal pregnancy and had to be terminated.

In 1959, Marilyn Monroe came roaring back to the screen, appearing with Tony Curtis and Jack Lemmon in one of her most famous films, *Some Like It Hot*. During the filming, Marilyn became pregnant again but suffered a miscarriage. Next up for her was a mediocre musical comedy, *Let's Make Love*. During its production Marilyn conducted a passionate affair with her French co-star, Yves Montand.

As a last gift to his wife, Arthur Miller had written a screenplay about modern-day cowboys and the woman they all love. *The Misfits*, shot in the 100-degree heat of the Nevada desert, was a nightmare for Marilyn. Her marriage was over and her life was spinning out of control. Yet somehow, she turned in one of her greatest performances. She was having daily sessions with a psychiatrist and was washing down a bewildering pharmacopoeia of prescription drugs with booze.

During her last year, Marilyn Monroe began her famous involvement with the Kennedy brothers and started work on *Something's Got to Give*. The movie would never be completed. On May 19, 1962, Marilyn took an unauthorized leave of absence from the film set to sing "Happy Birthday, Mr. President" before John F. Kennedy in Madison Square Garden. Shortly after, Marilyn was fired from *Something's Got to Give*. On August 5, 1962, Marilyn Monroe was found dead in her bedroom, clutching the telephone in her hand, an empty vial of sleeping pills beside her. [7]

Sorry to disappoint the conspiracy enthusiasts, but there was no plot to kill her. Marilyn Monroe was not murdered. The Kennedy family did not orchestrate her passing. The CIA did not kill her, nor did the Mob nor anyone else. Marilyn Monroe killed herself. As on many other occasions, Marilyn took too many pills and ended up in a semi-comatose state. But this time she forgot and took some more pills. No one, none of her friends, her husbands or her lovers, certainly no one from the movie industry, staged an intervention. Marilyn Monroe was abandoned to her fate, a true Hollywood tragedy.

Chronology

1926

June 1—Norma Jeane Mortensen is born to Gladys Pearl Baker (née Monroe) and an unknown father, in Los Angeles General Hospital. Mortensen appeared on the birth certificate because Gladys was married to a Norwegian immigrant of that name, although she had not seen him for more than a year.

June 11—Norma Jeane is placed with the Bollenders, a foster family. Her mother, Gladys, visits when she can.

December 6—Norma Jeane is baptized at evangelist Aimee Semple McPherson's Angelus Temple in Los Angeles.

1927

July—Norma Jeane is purposefully nearly smothered by her mentally ill grandmother, Della Monroe, who is soon committed to a hospital.

1933

October 1933—January 1934—Norma Jeane briefly moves in with her mother, Gladys Baker.

1934

January—Gladys Baker is diagnosed as a paranoid schizophrenic and is institutionalized.
—Norma Jeane lives with an English couple for a few months.

June 1—Family friend Grace McKee becomes Norma Jeane's legal guardian on her eighth birthday.

Late 1934—Early 1935—Norma Jeane lives with the Giffens, a foster family.

1935

September 13—Grace McKee places Norma Jeane in the orphanage of the Los Angeles Orphans Society. Norma Jeane becomes orphan no. 3463.

1937

June 26—Norma Jeane leaves orphanage to live with Grace McKee.

June 1937—Early 1938—Norma Jeane lives with two foster families.

1938

January or February—After marrying Erwin "Doc" Goddard, Grace McKee takes Norma Jeane to live with her.

September—Norma Jeane enrolls at Emerson Junior High School in Los Angeles.

November—Norma Jeane moves in with family friend, "Aunt" Ana Lower.

1941

June 27—Norma Jeane graduates from Emerson Junior High School.

1942

June 19—At age 16, Norma Jeane marries a neighbor, James Dougherty.

1944

April—Norma Jeane Dougherty starts working as a spray painter and parachute packer at the Radio Plane factory in Burbank, CA.

1945

June 26—Army photographer David Conover photographs Norma Jeane for *Yank* and *Stars and Stripes* magazines.

Summer—More photo sessions with Conover.

August 2—Norma Jeane joins the Blue Book Modeling Agency.

November—Photo shoot with André de Dienes.

1946

April 26—Norma Jeane appears on her first national magazine cover—*Family Circle*.

June—She files for divorce from James Dougherty and dyes her brown hair blonde.

July 19—Norma Jeane gets her first screen test at Twentieth Century–Fox.

July 24—Twentieth Century–Fox changes Norma Jeane's name to Marilyn Monroe and signs her to a six-month contract. Still a minor, she had to have her guardian, Grace Goddard, co-sign.

July 29—Hedda Hopper gives Marilyn Monroe her first mention in a Hollywood gossip column.

September 13—Marilyn's petition for divorce from James Dougherty is granted.

1947

January—Contract with Twentieth Century–Fox is extended for six months.

January 4—Release of *The Shocking Miss Pilgrim*. Although not usually included in Marilyn's filmography, the film marked her first screen role, although her performance ended up on the cutting-room floor.

February—Marilyn makes her first recognized film appearance in *Scudda Hoo! Scudda Hay!* although the film is not immediately released.

Summer—*The Dangerous Years*, which includes Marilyn's first speaking role, begins filming.

August 25—Twentieth Century–Fox drops her.

October 12–November 2—Appears in *Glamour Preferred* at the Bliss-Hayden Theater in Beverly Hills.

December 9—Her first released film is *Dangerous Years*.

1948

February—Befriends elderly mogul Joseph M. Schenck.

February 20—Wins the title of Miss California Artichoke Queen.

March 4—*Scudda Hoo! Scudda Hay!* Is released.

March 9—Signs a six-month contract with Columbia Pictures.

April—Meets Natasha Lytess who becomes her personal drama coach.

August–September—Appears in *Stage Door* at the Bliss-Hayden Theatre.

September 8—Columbia drops Marilyn.

December 31—Meets agent Johnny Hyde who offers to promote her.

1949

February—Groucho Marx selects Marilyn for a small part in *Love Happy*.

March—*Ladies of the Chorus* is released.

May 27—For $50 Marilyn poses for what would become the most famous nude calendar of all time.

July 24—Interviewed for the first time by columnist Earl Wilson.

August—Has an uncredited part in *Right Cross*.

August 15—Starts filming *A Ticket to Tomahawk*.

October—Signs a contract with MGM to appear in *The Asphalt Jungle*.

October 10—Featured in a *Life* magazine feature on aspiring stars.

1950

January 5—Begins filming *The Fireball*.
March 8—*Love Happy* is released.
April—Films *All About Eve*.
April 21—*A Ticket to Tomahawk* is released.
May 11—New seven-year contract with Twentieth Century–Fox comes into effect.
June 26—*The Asphalt Jungle* is released.
October 7—*The Fireball* is released.
November 14—*Right Cross* is released.
November 22—*All About Eve* is released.
December—Films *As Young As You Feel*.
December 10—Signs a contract with Twentieth Century–Fox.
December 18—Death of Johnny Hyde, the man who negotiated Marilyn's contract.

1951

January 1—Marilyn makes her first cover appearance on *Life* magazine.
Early January—Marilyn meets Arthur Miller.
Spring—Starts acting lessons with Michael Chekhov.
March 29—Marilyn presents an Oscar at the Academy Awards ceremony.
April 18—Began work on *Love Nest*.
May 11—Marilyn's contract with Twentieth Century–Fox is upgraded to seven years.
June 14—Does a screen test with Robert Wagner for *Let's Make It Legal*.
June 15—*As Young as You Feel* is released.
July 18—*Hometown Story* is released.
September 8—*Colliers* does the first full-length national magazine feature on Marilyn titled "1951's Model Blonde."
November 14—*Love Nest* is released.
October 31—*Let's Make It Legal* is released.

1952

March 5—Shooting begins on *Monkey Business*.
March 13—The story of Marilyn's nude calendar photos becomes public.
March 15—Goes on a blind date with baseball superstar Joe DiMaggio.

March 17—Watches Joe DiMaggio play baseball for the only time. It was at Gilmore Field, on behalf of the Kiwanas Club for Children.
April 7—Marilyn appears on the cover of *Life* magazine for the first time.
June—Starts work on *Niagara*.
June 1—On her 26th birthday Marilyn is given the part of Lorelei Lee in *Gentlemen Prefer Blondes*.
June 16—*Clash by Night* is released.
July 23—*We're Not Married* is released.
July 30—*Don't Bother to Knock* is released.
August 31—Marilyn makes her live radio debut.
September 2—Acts as grand marshal at the Miss America parade and is criticized for wearing a dress which is too revealing.
September 18—*O'Henry's Full House* is released.
October 1—*Monkey Business* is released.
October 4—Allegedly marries Robert Slatzer (the marriage is said to have lasted for three days).
October 18—Guests on *The Charlie McCarthy Show* on radio.
November 17—*Gentlemen Prefer Blondes* goes into production.

1953

January 23—*Niagara* has its premiere; Marilyn Monroe becomes a star.
February 9—At the *Photoplay* Awards, Marilyn is named the "Fastest Rising Star of 1952."
March—Marilyn wins the *Redbook* magazine award for "Best Young Box-Office Personality."
March 6—*Gentlemen Prefer Blondes* is completed.
March 9—*Photoplay* magazine names Marilyn "Fastest Rising Star of 1952."
April—Filming begins on *How to Marry a Millionaire*.
June 26—Marilyn leaves her hand- and footprints in cement at the forecourt of Grauman's Chinese Theater.

July 31—*Gentlemen Prefer Blondes* is released.

August-September—*River of No Return* begins filming in Canada.

September 13—Marilyn makes her television debut on *The Jack Benny Show*.

October 31—At a party at Gene Kelly's house, Marilyn meets future business partner Milton Greene.

November 5—*How to Marry a Millionaire* is released.

December—Begins interviews with Ben Hecht for her autobiography, *My Story*.

December—Marilyn's famous nude calendar photo appears in *Playboy* magazine's inaugural issue as its first centerfold.

December 15—Feeling she is being undervalued, Marilyn does not show up to film *The Girl in Pink Tights*.

1954

January 4—Twentieth Century–Fox suspends Marilyn.

January 14—Marries Joe DiMaggio in San Francisco.

February 2—Arrives in Japan on her honeymoon.

February 17—21—Marilyn goes to Korea to entertain troops on a ten-concert tour.

March 9—At the *Photoplay* Awards, Marilyn wins the gold medal for *How to Marry a Millionaire*.

May 5—*River of No Return* is released.

May 28—Marilyn starts work on *There's No Business Like Show Business*.

August 10—Marilyn begins work on *The Seven Year Itch*.

September 10—Shoots the famous skirt blowing scene from *The Seven Year Itch*.

October 5—Separates from Joe DiMaggio.

October 27—Files for divorce from Joe DiMaggio on the grounds of mental cruelty.

November—Broke the color bar at the Mocambo nightclub by securing a booking for Ella Fitzgerald.

November 4—Filming on *The Seven Year Itch* finishes.

November 5—"Wrong Door Raid" takes place with Joe DiMaggio and Frank Sinatra.

November 6—Honored at a party at Romanoff's by Hollywood's elite.

December 25—*There's No Business Like Show Business* is released.

December 31—With Milton Greene, she forms Marilyn Monroe Productions.

December 1954—February 1955—Marilyn lives with Milton Greene's family in Weston, Connecticut.

1955

January-February—Begins a relationship with Arthur Miller.

January 7—Announces the launch of Marilyn Monroe Productions at a press conference.

January 15—Marilyn is suspended again by Twentieth Century–Fox. By this time she has moved to New York.

February—Meets acting coach Lee Strasberg and begins taking classes at the Actors Studio.

March 30—Rides a pink elephant at Madison Square Garden at a benefit for the Arthritis and Rheumatism Foundation.

April 8—In a live television broadcast, Marilyn is interviewed by Edward R. Murrow on *Person to Person*.

June 15—*The Seven Year Itch* is released.

November 1—Divorce granted from Joe DiMaggio.

December 31—Marilyn signs a new Contract with Twentieth Century–Fox.

1956

January 4—Agreement between Twentieth Century–Fox and Marilyn Monroe Productions is announced.

February 9—Press conference in New York with Laurence Olivier to announce the production of *The Prince and the Showgirl*.

February 17—Performs a scene from *Anna Christie* at the Actors Studio.

February 22—At the Ambassador Hotel in New York, Marilyn poses for photographer Cecil Beaton.

February 23—Legally changes her name to Marilyn Monroe.

February 26—Marilyn returns to Hollywood after living in New York for more than a year.

March 3—Starts work on *Bus Stop*.

April—Meets Israeli foreign minister Abba Eban at Yankee Stadium

May 14—*Time* magazine has a cover story on Marilyn.

May 31—Marilyn meets visiting President Sukarno of Indonesia.

June 3—Returns to New York after finishing *Bus Stop*.

June 29—Marries Arthur Miller in a civil ceremony.

July 1—Marries Arthur Miller in a Jewish ceremony.

July 14—Arrives in London for another press conference with Laurence Olivier to announce the production of *The Prince and the Showgirl*.

July 26—Marilyn is the guest of honor at playwright Terence Rattigan's home; it is said to be the social event of the year.

August—Becomes pregnant but suffers a miscarriage.

August 7—Starts filming *The Prince and the Showgirl* in England.

August 15—*Bus Stop* is released.

October 29—Meets Queen Elizabeth II at a Royal Command film performance.

November 20—Leaves England, returns to the U.S.A.

December 18—Marilyn does a radio show from the Waldorf-Astoria in New York.

1957

January—Marilyn and Arthur Miller vacation in Jamaica.

April—Partnership with Milton Greene comes apart.

July 3—*The Prince and the Showgirl* is released.

August 1—Tubal pregnancy is terminated.

1958

August 4—Starts filming *Some Like It Hot*.

September 19—Hospitalized for "nervous exhaustion."

October—Marilyn becomes pregnant.

November 6—Finishes work on *Some Like It Hot*.

December 17—Marilyn suffers another miscarriage.

December 28—Richard Avedon's photos of Marilyn impersonating screen goddesses of the past appear in *Life* magazine.

1959

April 8—*Some Like It Hot* is released.

May 13—Marilyn receives the David Di Donatelo, Italy's top award for acting.

June—Marilyn undergoes surgery to facilitate pregnancy.

September 18—Meets Nikita Khrushchev at a reception at Twentieth Century–Fox.

1960

February—Marilyn starts work on *Let's Make Love*.

—Begins affair with co-star Yves Montand.

March 8—Receives a Golden Globe for her performance in *Some Like It Hot*.

June—Starts daily sessions with psychoanalyst Ralph Greenson.

—Finishes work on *Let's Make Love*.

July 18—Starts filming *The Misfits* in Nevada.

August 6—Marilyn suffers a nervous breakdown and spends ten days in a Los Angeles hospital.

August 24—*Let's Make Love* is released.

September 5—Returns to the set of *The Misfits*.

November 4—Finishes work on *The Misfits*.

November 10—Marilyn announces that her marriage to Arthur Miller is over.

1961

January 20—Divorce from Arthur Miller becomes final.

February 1—*The Misfits* is released.

February 7—Admitted to the Payne Whitney Psychiatric Clinic in New York.

February 11—Joe DiMaggio gets Marilyn

released from the clinic and admitted to the less-restrictive Columbia Presbyterian Hospital.

March 5—Released from Columbia Presbyterian Hospital.

March 6–20—Vacations in Florida with Joe DiMaggio.

October 4—Meets Robert Kennedy at a dinner party at Peter Lawford's beach house.

November 19—Meets President John F. Kennedy at Peter Lawford's house.

1962

February—Moves into her last home, in Brentwood, CA.

February 1—Attends a dinner in honor of Robert Kennedy.

March 5—Marilyn is awarded a Golden Globe award as "World's Film Favorite 1961."

March 24—Marilyn spends a weekend with JFK in Palm Springs.

April 30—Starts filming *Something's Got to Give*.

May 16—Marilyn may have been introduced to LSD by Timothy Leary.

May 19—Sings "Happy Birthday" at a gala for President Kennedy at Madison Square Garden.

May 28—Nude pool sequence filmed for *Something's Got to Give*.

June 1—Final day at Twentieth Century–Fox (Marilyn's last public appearance).

June 8—Fired by Twentieth Century–Fox for unreliability. Production of *Something's Got to Give* is halted.

June 23—"The Last Sitting" photo session with Bert Stern.

June 28—Marilyn meets with Twentieth Century–Fox executives concerning *Something's Got to Give*.

June 29—Photo session for *Cosmopolitan* magazine.

July 4—Marilyn gives her last extensive interview.

July 6—Photo shoot for *Life* magazine.

July 12—Marilyn has another meeting with Twentieth Century–Fox executives.

July 20—Enters Cedars of Lebanon Hospital for treatment of endometriosis.

July 28—Spends a weekend at CAL-NEVA Lodge with Frank Sinatra.

August 1—Marilyn signs a new contract with Twentieth Century–Fox at twice her usual salary. *Something's Got to Give* to be restarted.

August 3—Marilyn appears on the cover of *Life* magazine.

August 4—Last day alive. Marilyn has a six-hour session with her psychoanalyst, Dr. Ralph Greenson.

August 5—Marilyn is found dead in her bedroom, nude, with a telephone in her hand. An autopsy is performed.

August 8—Marilyn's funeral is held at Westwood Memorial Park Cemetery in Los Angeles.

August 18—An announcement is made that Marilyn died of a drug overdose.

August 28—Marilyn's death certificate is signed.

Marilyn Monroe Filmography

The Shocking Miss Pilgrim (1947) Twentieth Century–Fox (uncredited extra)

You Were Meant for Me (1948) Twentieth Century–Fox (uncredited extra)

Green Grass of Wyoming (1948) Twentieth Century–Fox (uncredited extra)

Scudda Hoo! Scudda Hay! (1948) Twentieth Century–Fox

Dangerous Years (1948) Twentieth Century–Fox

Ladies of the Chorus (1948) Columbia Pictures

Love Happy (1950) United Artists

A Ticket to Tomahawk (1950) Twentieth Century–Fox

The Asphalt Jungle (1950) Metro-Goldwyn-Mayer

All About Eve (1950) Twentieth Century–Fox

The Fireball (1950) Twentieth Century–Fox

Right Cross (1950) Metro-Goldwyn-Mayer

Hometown Story (1951) Metro-Goldwyn-Mayer

As Young as You Feel (1951) Twentieth Century–Fox

Love Nest (1951) Twentieth Century–Fox

Let's Make It Legal (1951) Twentieth Century–Fox

Clash by Night (1952) RKO Radio Pictures

We're Not Married (1952) Twentieth Century–Fox

Don't Bother to Knock (1952) Twentieth Century–Fox

Monkey Business (1952) Twentieth Century–Fox

O'Henry's Full House (1952) Twentieth Century–Fox

Niagara (1953) Twentieth Century–Fox

Gentlemen Prefer Blondes (1953) Twentieth Century–Fox

How to Marry a Millionaire (1953) Twentieth Century–Fox

River of No Return (1954) Twentieth Century–Fox

There's No Business Like Show Business (1954) Twentieth Century–Fox

The Seven Year Itch (1955) Twentieth Century–Fox

Bus Stop (1956) Twentieth Century–Fox

The Prince and the Showgirl (1957) Warner Bros.

Some Like It Hot (1959) United Artists

Let's Make Love (1960) Twentieth Century–Fox

The Misfits (1961) United Artists

Something's Got to Give (uncompleted) (1962) Twentieth Century–Fox

In addition, Marilyn's "Every Baby Needs a Da-Da-Daddy" song from *Ladies of the Chorus* (1948) was recycled in *Okinawa* (1952). She also appeared in a photograph in a Gene Autry western, *Riders of the Whistling Pines* (1949).

The Dictionary

-A-

CASEY ADAMS (a.k.a.: Max Showalter) Actor and friend who appeared with Marilyn Monroe in *Niagara* (1953) and *Bus Stop* (1956). He was to experience firsthand Marilyn's casual attitude toward nudity. In *Niagara* Adams played a nerdy honeymooner. Adams remembered how, during a break in the location shooting, Marilyn appeared nude at her hotel window in Niagara Falls, Ontario, and was genuinely surprised by the commotion she was causing in the street below. Adams had to tell Marilyn that maybe it was because "you haven't got a stitch of clothing on" (Schwarz 357). Adams and Marilyn had adjoining rooms at the General Brock Hotel. Marilyn insisted that the connecting door between the rooms be kept unlocked to form a suite. You can imagine Adams's surprise when, on the night before the first day of filming, a nude Marilyn Monroe came into his room and crawled into bed with him. She said: "Don't do anything but just hold me" (Victor 6). No sex was involved. Marilyn was frightened about what the next day would bring and wanted Adams to help her practice her lines.

EDIE ADAMS Comedienne, Broadway, film and television actress who was married to the zany and innovative comedian Ernie Kovacs. At private parties, Adams occasionally did hilarious impressions of MM[1] improbably singing 19th century German lieder. Soon, complete with heavy red lipstick, a blonde wig and fur stole, Adams was appearing on *The Jack Paar Show*[2] and her husband's television program, *The Ernie Kovacs Show*. Adams added more Marilyn impressions to her act and depicted her breathlessly reciting Shakespeare. Adams did her MM impersonation during a month-long engagement at the Persian Room in the Plaza Hotel in New York in March 1956 and that led to television appearances on *The Ed Sullivan Show*. As she recalled, "Ed Sullivan came to the Plaza and saw me and asked me to do Marilyn on his Sunday–night show. It was on the Sullivan show that it became really big. It brought so much mail I had to repeat it two weeks later." At the time, Al Capp's popular cartoon strip, *Li'l Abner*, was being turned into a Broadway musical. The producers wanted Marilyn for the lead role of Daisy Mae but she was not interested. Adams thought: "If they want Marilyn, maybe they'll take a first-string Monroe imitator." She told the producers to watch her on the Sullivan show. They did and Adams got the part, for which she earned a Tony Award (Ricco 191–3). Adams was ten months younger than Marilyn and survived her by 46 years.

Marilyn came to believe that the movie star called Marilyn Monroe was just an act she was obliged to perform. She said, "All my life I've played Marilyn Monroe, Marilyn Monroe, Marilyn Monroe. I've tried to do a little better and find myself doing an imitation of Edie Adams doing an imitation of me. I try to do a little better, but then I do an exaggeration of myself doing the same thing. I want to do something different" (Schwarz 530).

FRED ALLEN Tired-looking radio comedian and wit, who made an occasional film. In 1952, Allen made his last two movies, *We're Not Married* and *O. Henry's Full House*. In both of these Allen co-starred with MM but did not share screen time with her. Allen died on March 17, 1956 while Marilyn was working on *Bus Stop* (Victor 224, 322; *www.imdb.com*).

STEVE ALLEN Comedian, musician, and songwriter who pioneered the talk show format

15

on television. Allen wrote 54 books[3], nearly eight thousand songs and originated the phrase, "Is it bigger than a breadbox?" He also acted in a few movies, among them was MM's unfinished *Something's Got to Give*, in which Allen was cast as a psychiatrist. On March 5, 1962, Marilyn received the Golden Globe "World Film Favorite of 1961" award. Allen was on hand as master of ceremonies. On August 5 of that year, just hours after Marilyn was found dead in bed from an overdose of barbiturates, there was a black-tie gala at the Ambassador Hotel[4] in honor of Nat King Cole. Steve Allen was again the master of ceremonies, and Marilyn's passing was on everyone's mind. Allen delicately raised the subject when he said that, with regard to Cole, they had not waited too long to demonstrate their affection (Epstein 1999, 323–5; Schwarz 575; *www.imdb.com*; *www.cursumperficio.net* /files/ awards).

JUNE ALLYSON   Film and television actress, most popular in the 1940s and 1950s. Allyson's wholesome girl-next-door screen image was the mirror opposite of MM's overt sexuality. In 1950, Allyson was one of the stars of *Right Cross*, an MGM picture which featured starlet MM in an uncredited part opposite Allyson's real-life husband, Dick Powell. Marilyn played a bar girl named Dusky Ledoux and had fewer than 20 words in the film. In her autobiography, Allyson recalled how she and her husband "reminisced about Marilyn Monroe and how we'd been floored, both of us, the day that Marilyn, then a young starlet, an unknown, had arrived, wiggling, on the *Right Cross* set, and how neither of us had predicted she'd be a star" (Allyson 217). Allyson was nearly nine years Marilyn Monroe's senior, but outlived her by 44 years (Riese & Hitchens 11; *www.imdb.com*).

HOLLIS ALPERT   Film critic and writer. In 1959, Marilyn's publicist, Joe Wohlander[5], and Alpert assisted her in nothing so ordinary as moving a big television set from her New York apartment to her home in Roxbury, Connecticut. The TV was too large for their car and other arrangements had to be made to move it (Morgan 218–19). It was surprising that Marilyn and Alpert were on such good terms considering what he said about *Gentlemen Prefer Blondes* (1953): "It is an empty and graceless remake of a fair-to-middling Broadway musical that only comes alive when Marilyn Monroe and her partner, Jane Russell, stop talking and start wiggling" (*Saturday Review*, v. 36 #2, 27).

HARDY AMIES   British fashion designer and dressmaker for Queen Elizabeth II. Amies and MM were introduced on July 26, 1956, at the playwright Terence Rattigan's house in Berkshire, near London. The event, an after-theater supper dance, hosted by Rattigan, Sir Laurence Olivier and Vivien Leigh in honor of Marilyn and her husband, Arthur Miller, was the social event of the season. Marilyn was in England to film Rattigan's *The Prince and the Showgirl* with Olivier. Amies was knighted in 1989, 27 years after Marilyn's death (Gottfried 2003, 301).

EDDIE ANDERSON *see* **ROCHESTER**

KEITH ANDES   Handsome actor who played MM's love interest in the gritty melodrama *Clash by Night* (1952). Andes was six years older than Marilyn and survived her by 43 years. "Here was a pinup cutie everyone was getting nuts about," recalled Andes. "The studio had a box-office back-up because men wanted to see Marilyn's tits and her ass, and the women would go to get annoyed with seeing what they haven't got" (Gilmore 139).

Clash by Night was released just as the sensational story of Marilyn's nude calendar emerged. On location in Monterey, California, Marilyn and Andes discussed the situation. Because of what she had done, Marilyn was worried that the studio would have the weapon they needed to exercise total control over her. Andes suggested that visits to her lawyer and her agent were in order. He thought Marilyn was talking crazily when she threatened to run away and hide. The studio had spies everywhere and would eventually track her down. Marilyn reasoned that it would not be worth the studio's time to sue her. Because of her ironclad contract, she had no money. What were they going to do, she joked, shoot her?

"'Marilyn for Christ's sake, what are you talking about?'" recalled Andes. "She just clammed up at that, wouldn't say any more. But she was right, this fuzzy, blonde bunny that had all these conflicts going on. She called it right because the studio tried to shoot her legally—to punish her. She outfoxed them, though, and each subsequent time she outfoxed them she became more important to the industry. No one was going to argue with the grosses tallying up because of Marilyn, and she knew it. She had it in her mind, which incidentally wasn't any empty-headedness by a long shot, that she was going to get their *butts* over the barrel for a change. 'Ring their gongs,' is what she said" (Gilmore 140–41).

DANA ANDREWS   Dependable leading man of the 1940s and 1950s. On October 29, 1956, Dana Andrews and MM crossed paths in London. It was the occasion of the Royal Command Film Performance for *The Battle of the River Plate*, a British film set in World War II. Marilyn and Andrews, among a host of other celebrities, were formally presented to Queen Elizabeth II (Riese & Hitchens 456; *www.imdb.com*).

ANN-MARGRET   Award-winning actress, singer and dancer. Ann-Margret and MM never met, but on one occasion they came very close. Ann-Margret was part of a singing group appearing in Reno, Nevada, when she visited the set of *The Misfits* (1961), which was destined to be Marilyn's last completed film. It seems that Marilyn noticed the pretty young blonde but did not speak with her. Years later, Ann-Margret declined the "Marilyn" role in Arthur Miller's *After the Fall*. At various times Ann-Margret used Marilyn's stand-in and two of her hairstylists. In a magazine article Ann-Margret said of Marilyn: "She was a very healthy girl when she came on the scene, physically and mentally. Years went by, people picked on her. She was terribly abused, for no reason. She became sick—and posthumously they gave her acclaim" (*Life* 8/71). In the 1975 film *Tommy*, based on The Who's rock opera,

Ann-Margret takes her mute son to a chapel to be cured by the image of Marilyn Monroe. In 2001, Ann-Margret was in *Blonde*, a television mini-series about MM. She played Marilyn's grandmother, Della Monroe (Riese & Hitchens 14–15; Victor 14; *www.imdb.com*).

EVE ARDEN   Wisecracking comic actress, who achieved her greatest success in television with *Our Miss Brooks* (1952–1956) and in the movies, *Mildred Pierce* (1945) and *Grease* (1978). Arden's film and television career lasted from 1929 to 1987. In 1952, Eve Arden was one of the co-stars of the Fox film *We're Not Married*. MM was also in the cast as a beauty pageant contestant who cannot compete in the Mrs. America pageant because her marriage is not technically valid (Riese & Hitchens 17; *www.imdb.com*).

HAROLD ARLEN   Award-winning composer of popular music. In September 1955, in order to dampen press interest in her relationship with Arthur Miller, Marilyn made a point of being seen with Arlen, even though he was married and 21 years her senior, at the El Morocco, a chic Manhattan nightclub frequented by socialites, entertainers and politicians (Morgan 153). One evening, when they were dancing together, Arlen said to Marilyn, "People are staring at us." With a straight face she replied, "They must know who you are" (Jablonski 262).

DESI ARNAZ   Cuban bandleader and actor who founded the Desilu Studio and starred as Ricky Ricardo opposite his wife, Lucille Ball, in television's *I Love Lucy* (1951–1955). MM was enough of a fan of *I Love Lucy* that on one occasion she was in the studio audience. For a few months, in 1954, Marilyn leased a house on North Palm Drive[6] in Beverly Hills, around the corner from Desi and Lucy. On the November 8, 1954, episode of *I Love Lucy* entitled, "Ricky's Movie Offer," Ball impersonated Marilyn (Brady 205; Riese & Hitchens 36; Shevey 260; *www.youns.com/lucy*).

BEA ARTHUR   Comic-actress best known for her television-sitcom roles in the 1970s *Maude* and the 1980s *The Golden Girls*. In 1955

and 1956, Arthur attended acting classes at the Actors Studio in New York. Marilyn Monroe was among her classmates (Adams 254).

PEGGY ASHCROFT Distinguished British stage and film actress. Ashcroft met MM on July 26, 1956, the same year she was appointed Dame Commander of the Order of the British Empire. The place was playwright Terence Rattigan's country house, near London. The occasion was a ball hosted by Rattigan, Sir Laurence Olivier and his wife, Vivien Leigh, in honor of Marilyn and her husband, Arthur Miller. Marilyn was in England to film Rattigan's *The Prince and the Showgirl* with Olivier (Gottfried 2003, 300).

GENE AUTRY Actor known as "The Singing Cowboy." Gene Autry made some 93 movies, 635 recordings, and starred in several television series. In 1948, MM was an unknown contract player at Columbia Pictures. She made a grade–B musical, *Ladies of the Chorus*, and then her six-month contract was allowed to lapse. The next year, however, Marilyn made another little-known appearance in a Columbia movie. She can be seen in a photograph in a Gene Autry western, *Riders of the Whistling Pines* (1949). Autry, of course, serenades the pretty girl in the photo[7] (Riese & Hitchens 445; Victor 47; *www.imdb.com*).

RICHARD AVEDON Acclaimed American fashion and fine art photographer. For the December 22, 1958, issue of *Life* magazine, MM had a delightful time posing before Avedon's camera. The images are extraordinarily accurate impersonations by Marilyn of Lillian Russell (a statuesque singer and entertainer from the turn of the 20th century), Clara Bow (the "It" girl of the 1920s), Theda Bara (the "Vamp" of the silent screen), Marlene Dietrich (glamorous German-American actress), and Jean Harlow (blonde bombshell of the 1930s.) Marilyn's husband, Arthur Miller, contributed a two-page article and observed that the photographs were "a kind of history of our mass fantasy, so far as seductresses are concerned."

Avedon said of Marilyn: "She gave more to the still camera than any actress—any woman—I've ever photographed" (Riese &

Hitchens 27). "She understood photography, and she understood what makes a great photograph—not the technique, but the content ... she was more comfortable in front of a camera than away from it ... she was completely creative ... she was very, very involved with the meaning of what she was doing, in an effort to make it more, to get the most out of it" (McCann 76). Of her notorious tardiness, Avedon said, "If she was scheduled for a sitting at 9:00 A.M., I simply put her down in my book for 7:00 P.M.—and went ahead planning the rest of my day" (Riese & Hitchens 262).

Marilyn spoke nostalgically of her photo sessions with Avedon to French actress, Simone Signoret, who wrote:

> Listening to her you'd believe the only satisfaction as an actress she had ever felt was during these disguises, when she suddenly turned into Marlene, Garbo, and Harlow. She talked about these photography sessions the way other actors talk about their films.
>
> She seemed to have no other happy professional memories. None of those moments of uproarious giggles among pals, none of those practical jokes, none of those noisy hugs and kisses after a scene when everyone knows all have acted well together. All these things were unknown to her. I couldn't get over it [Signoret 291–2].

Other sources: Churchwell 50–1; Summers 237

GEORGE AXELROD Playwright and screenwriter who contributed greatly to two of Marilyn Monroe's best films. Twentieth Century–Fox purchased the rights to Axelrod's stage play, *The Seven Year Itch*, for $500,000 and Axelrod and director Billy Wilder wrote a memorable screen adaptation. Axelrod adapted William Inge's *Bus Stop* for the screen himself. Axelrod also wrote *Will Success Spoil Rock Hunter?* (1957). In a satirical story, believed by many to be based on Marilyn's life, Jayne Mansfield played blonde sex goddess Rita Marlowe, who tries to form her own production company. The character was described as a dumb blonde whose blonde curls and shapely rear end had made her the favorite of movie audiences everywhere. Marilyn evidently thought the play was about her, too, and was not amused. After seeing the show on its opening night, her only comment to Axelrod was a terse, "I saw your play." Axelrod went on to adapt *Breakfast at Tiffany's* (1961), reportedly with Marilyn in mind for the lead, and to write *Goodbye Charlie* (filmed in 1964), which Marilyn refused to consider.

Axelrod had seen about 20 actresses portray the unnamed girl in *The Seven Year Itch*. He had seen the girl as a redhead, a blonde and a brunette and heard her deliver her lines with a British accent and in Italian, German and French. But Marilyn was the one who came closest to the girl he had imagined when he wrote the play. "Marilyn Monroe doesn't just play the Girl," said Axelrod. "She *is* the Girl. Marilyn once told me that playing the part had helped her find out who she was. Which is a pretty nice thing for a writer to hear from an actress" (Shaw & Rosten 52). He went on to say,

I am revealing no breathtaking secret when I say that Marilyn had a reputation for not being the easiest actress in the world to work with. Her eagerness and ambition cause her to tense up. She has difficulty remembering lines. She has been known to drive directors stark, raving mad. However, an interesting thing happened during the shooting of *Itch*. My favorite scene in the picture comes close to the end. It is a kind of serious and extremely difficult scene in which the Girl explains to the hero (who, to all outward appearances, is the least dashing, least glamorous, least romantic man alive) why she finds him exciting and attractive and why his wife has every reason to be jealous.

Because of its difficulty and the fact that it ends with a long speech from the Girl, it was generally assumed that the scene would need several days to get on film. Billy Wilder patiently struggled through dozens of takes for every scene except this one. Three minutes later it was all over. Marilyn had done it, letter perfect and with an emotional impact that caused the entire soundstage to burst into applause at the end, on the first take. There was no need for a second.

She told me later she was able to do the scene because she believed every word of what she was saying and because it seemed to her like the story of her own life [Shaw & Rosten 52–4].

-B-

LAUREN BACALL   A former model and the beautiful film and stage actress who married the much older Humphrey Bogart. Bacall co-starred with MM and Betty Grable in *How to Marry a Millionaire* (1953). Bacall had met Marilyn before filming and liked her. But Bacall was never close to Marilyn and was often exasperated by her unprofessional behavior. It was apparent to Bacall that Marilyn was full of fears and insecurities and only trusted her acting coach, Natasha Lytess. If Lytess shook her head, Marilyn would insist on another take no matter what director Jean Negulesco thought. Bacall found it frustrating to do 15 takes or more and be at her best in each one, knowing that Marilyn's best take would be the one used. Marilyn was said to have rehearsed her scene with her coach before she came to the set and did not react to the other actors.

In her autobiography Bacall wrote,

[Betty] Grable and I decided we'd try to make it easier for [Marilyn], make her feel she could trust us. I think she finally did. I had only a few conversations with her. She came into my dressing room one day and said that what she really wanted was to be in San Francisco with Joe DiMaggio in some spaghetti joint. They were not married then. She wanted to know about my children, my home life—was I happy? She seemed envious of that aspect of my life—wistful—hoping to have it herself one day. One day Steve [Bacall's son] came on the set and was doing somersaults on a mattress. She sat on a stool watching him and said, "How old are you." He said, "I'm four." She: "But you're so *big* for four. I would have thought you were two or three." He wasn't, and was confused (so was I, so was she), but kept turning his somersaults. There was something sad about her—wanting to reach out—afraid to trust—uncomfortable. She made no effort for others and yet she was nice. I think she did trust me and liked me as well as she could anyone whose life must have seemed to her so secure, so *solved* [Bacall 208].

Other sources: Schwarz 385–7; Shevey 235–7; Victor 24

JIM BACKUS   Actor who supplied the voice of cartoon character Mr. Magoo, and embodied Thurston Howell III on *Gilligan's Island* (1964–1966). Backus was also a serious film actor and, in 1952, was in the cast of *Don't Bother to Knock* with MM (*www.imdb.com*).

CARROLL BAKER Blonde sex symbol of the 1950s and 1960s. Baker had met MM in the Actors Studio in New York and admitted to having been jealous and insecure in her presence. Baker wrote of their first meeting: "I was already hating her for flaunting her availability at Jack [Baker's husband] when she turned to say hello to me—and presented me with that same seductive quality of 'come on'! I suddenly felt drawn to her and leaned in a bit closer than necessary to accept her outstretched hand. Her hand was lusciously warm and plump, and I found myself clinging to it that added moment. Maybe I imagined it, but I thought I smelled the fruity aroma of sex" (Baker 146). Baker's most famous role was in *Baby Doll* (1956), a part Marilyn wanted for herself. After the film was made, Marilyn held no grudge. She was generous in her compliments to Baker and the relationship between the two actresses warmed. The *Baby Doll* premiere was a benefit for the Actors Studio. Marilyn agreed to act as an usherette and pose for a publicity shot holding a huge photograph, in the form of a ticket, of Baker from the movie (Baker 175; Riese & Hitchens 32; Victor 24).

LUCILLE BALL On May 13, 1953, MM and Lucille Ball were seen at columnist Walter Winchell's 56th birthday party. In October that year their paths crossed at a benefit for the Damon Runyon Cancer Research Foundation. Broadcast on November 8, 1954, Ball impersonated Marilyn in an episode of *I Love Lucy* entitled "Ricky's Movie Offer."[8] When a Hollywood talent scout offers to audition her husband, Ricky, Lucy decides that she wants an audition, too. Noticing that the script calls for a "Marilyn Monroe type," Lucy dons a blonde wig, slinky red dress and an oversize beauty mark. Marilyn was enough of a fan of *I Love Lucy* that on one occasion she was in the studio audience. For a time, Marilyn leased a house on North Palm Drive in Beverly Hills, around the corner from Lucille Ball and her husband, Desi Arnaz (Brady 205; Riese & Hitchens 36; Shevey 260; *www.cursumperficio.net* / biography/1953; *www.youns.com/lucy*).

ANNE BANCROFT Distinguished Hollywood character actress who made her film debut in one of MM's first big pictures, 1952's *Don't Bother to Knock*. The director, Roy (Ward) Baker, came to the realization that Bancroft and Monroe were opposites. Bancroft was a technically proficient actress at 19 while Marilyn, a few years older, was completely instinctual (Shevey 195). Bancroft recalled what it was like to be in Marilyn's presence.

> It was a remarkable experience! Because it was one of those very rare times, in all my experiences in Hollywood, when I felt that give-and-take that can only happen when you are working with good actors.... I was just somebody in the lobby and I was to walk over to her and react, that's all; and there was to be a closeup of her and a closeup of me—you know, to show my reaction. Well, I moved towards her and I saw that girl—of course, she wasn't the big sex symbol she later became, and she wasn't famous, so there was nothing I had to forget or shake off. There was just the scene of one woman seeing another woman who was helpless and in pain, and she *was* helpless and in pain. It was so real, I responded. I really reacted to her. She moved me so that tears came into my eyes. Believe me, such moments happened rarely, if ever again, in the early things I was doing out there [Guiles 201–2].

TALLULAH BANKHEAD Hard-living, gravel-voiced star of stage and screen. In early August 1962, Bankhead inadvertently caused her wardrobe mistress to faint and fall to the floor after she had blurted out the news that MM had committed suicide. The wardrobe mistress had been with Marilyn for a year and a half as her personal assistant and felt close to her. Bankhead apologized for days afterward (Brian 246).

IAN BANNEN Scottish character actor and leading man who had an extensive stage career and made 104 films between 1955 and 1999. On October 12, 1956, Marilyn Monroe was in the audience for the London premiere of Arthur Miller's *A View From the Bridge* at the Comedy Theatre. After the performance, Bannen, who was in the cast, was photographed with Marilyn (*www.imdb.com*; *www.cursumperficio.net* /biography/1956).

THEDA BARA Notorious vixen of the silent screen who was known as "The Vamp," the title of her 1915 Fox feature. For the December 22, 1958, issue of *Life* magazine, MM posed as Theda Bara. Marilyn, in a black wig and scanty harem costume, convincingly cavorted on a tiger skin rug, before Richard Avedon's camera. Marilyn's husband, Arthur Miller, contributed an essay to go with the photoshoot[9] (Churchwell 50).

BRIGITTE BARDOT Sex kitten actress who was often thought of as France's answer to MM. Bardot's breakthrough film was "*And God Created Woman* (1956), which was seen by its director, Roger Vadim, as an homage to Marilyn. On October 29, 1956, MM and BB were in the same room when they were presented to Queen Elizabeth II at a royal command film performance in London. The newspapers tried to stir up a "battle of the sex symbols," but neither woman would cooperate. Bardot saw Marilyn as delicate, beautiful and charming. Marilyn was somewhat concerned that the French actress had upstaged her but she need not have worried: Marilyn got most of the press coverage. Bardot and Marilyn were considered for the title role in *Cleopatra* (1963) but lost out to Elizabeth Taylor. Bardot was also mentioned as a possible replacement for Marilyn when she left the unfinished *Something's Got to Give* in 1962. Five years later, Paramount considered Bardot for *After the Fall*, a proposal to film Arthur Miller's play based on the life of his late wife. (Brown 89, 194; Riese & Hitchens 37; Victor 27, 29; *www. imdb.com*).

JOHN BARRYMORE Film and stage actor who died when MM was only 15. Barrymore was considered the greatest actor of his generation. As far as Marilyn was concerned, John Barrymore was the perfect actor. She read Gene Fowler's biography of Barrymore, *Good Night Sweet Prince* (1944), three times and made a point of seeing Barrymore's old films whenever she could. In the summer of 1948, Marilyn and a friend toured John Barrymore's 55–room mansion. Initially, Marilyn was awed by the memory of all the famous people who had stood where she was standing but by the end of her visit she found the empty house op-

pressive and was glad to leave (Slatzer 100–6).

LIONEL BARRYMORE Character actor of stage, radio and film who was the elder brother of Ethel and John. Lionel Barrymore was in films from 1908 and made seven movies in 1926, the year MM was born. *Right Cross*, made in 1950, was one of Barrymore's last screen appearances. Playing Dusky Ladoux, in an uncredited role, was a young Marilyn Monroe (Riese & Hitchens 40; *www.imdb.com*).

RICHARD BASEHART Actor best remembered for his starring role in the 1960s television series, *Voyage to the Bottom of the Sea*. On February 8, 1952, Basehart was seated beside Marilyn Monroe at a banquet table when she received the Henrietta Award for "Best Young Box Office Personality" (*www.imdb. com*; *www.cursumperficio.net*/files/awards).

BARBARA BATES Fresh-faced actress who played the scheming Phoebe in *All About Eve* (1950), in which MM was Miss Caswell. Bates, who was also in 1951's *Let's Make It Legal*, was an almost exact contemporary of Marilyn, and her life followed a similar tragic path. Ten months older, Bates committed suicide in 1969, about 7 years after Marilyn's death (*www.imdb.com*).

ANNE BAXTER Hollywood leading lady in films of the 1940s and 1950s. Baxter was in three early films of MM's, *A Ticket to Tomahawk* (1950), *All About Eve* (1950) and "The Last Leaf" segment of *O'Henry's Full House* (1952). For her role in *All About Eve*, in which Marilyn was a supporting player, Baxter was nominated for the Best Actress Oscar. Baxter was supposed to have been in *Niagara* (1953) but dropped out, possibly because it became apparent that Marilyn would be the real star of the picture. In 1971, Baxter took over for Lauren Bacall in *Applause*, the stage musical version of *All About Eve*. Baxter's maternal grandfather was architect Frank Lloyd Wright, with whom Marilyn and her husband, Arthur Miller, discussed having a house designed (Riese & Hitchens 41; Schwarz 355; Victor 29; *www.imdb.com*).

CECIL BEATON   British costume designer, fashion and celebrity photographer. On February 22, 1956, MM posed for a set of still photographs at the Ambassador Hotel in New York. One of the photos was of Marilyn reclining on a bed of white sheets, while clutching a long-stemmed rose. The photo became one of Marilyn's personal favorites. She hung it on the wall of her New York apartment.[10] Beaton wrote of his subject: "The tornado visit of Marilyn Monroe was the greatest fun. Although one-and-a-half hours late, Marilyn was instantly forgiven for her disarming, childlike freshness, her ingenuity and irresistible mischievousness" (Vickers 300). Elsewhere, Beaton said: "She romps, she squeals with delight, she leaps on to the sofa. She puts a flower stem in her mouth, puffing on a daisy as though it were a cigarette. It is an artless, impromptu, high-spirited, infectiously gay performance. It will probably end in tears" (Buckle 393).

WARREN BEATTY   Actor, producer, director who had a well-earned reputation as a playboy. A day or two before MM died, Beatty encountered her at a party at Peter Lawford's lavish beach house in Santa Monica. Beatty remembered Marilyn saying to herself, "Thirty-six, thirty-six. It's all over" (Amburn 113). In 1990, Beatty told a journalist that he had played cards with Marilyn the night before her death (Finstad 2006, 315).

HUGH BEAUMONT   Beaumont played Ward Cleaver, the archetypal 1950s dad, in television's *Leave It to Beaver* (1957–1962). He was also a film actor. In 1951, Beaumont had a small part in one of MM's least-known films, *Hometown Story* (*www.imdb.com*).

BRENDAN BEHAN   Hard-drinking and riotous-living Irish playwright. During a visit to New York in 1960, Behan indicated that what he most wanted to see was "Marilyn Monroe, back and front" (O'Sullivan 131). Behan got his wish when he was introduced to Marilyn during the run of his play, *The Hostage*.[11] Later he sent her a polite tribute: "For Marilyn Monroe—a credit to the human race, mankind in general and womankind in particular" (Meyers 107).

HARRY BELAFONTE   Singer, actor and social activist known as "the King of Calypso." Belafonte was on the May 19, 1962 program with Marilyn Monroe the night she warbled "Happy Birthday, Mr. President" before John F. Kennedy and an audience of 17,000 in Madison Square Garden. Belafonte also attended the after-gala party along with Kennedy and Marilyn. (Leaming 1998, 408; *www.cursumperficio.net* /files/John F. Kennedy).

SAUL BELLOW   Canadian–born American novelist who won the Pulitzer Prize, the National Book Award, and the Nobel Prize for Literature. Bellow was temporarily encamped in an isolated cabin, 40 miles from Reno, Nevada, fulfilling the residency requirements for a divorce when he got a letter from his friend Arthur Miller, who was coming to town on the same mission. Miller wrote: "From time to time there will be a visitor who is very dear to me, but who is unfortunately recognizable by approximately a hundred million people, give or take three or four. She has all sorts of wigs, can affect a limp, sunglasses, bulky coats, etc., but if it is possible I want to find a place, perhaps a bungalow or something like, where there are not likely to be crowds looking in through the windows. Do you know of any such place?" The visitor was, of course, MM. Miller and Bellow had to remain in Nevada for 42 consecutive days in order to obtain their divorces (Atlas 232).

Bellow had dinner with Marilyn in Chicago when she was in that city for the premiere of *Some Like It Hot* in 1959. Bellow could not help but notice that Marilyn was surrounded by an entourage, complete with manicurist and bodyguard. The latter even left the door open when he used the bathroom. "He's not supposed to let me out of his sight," said Marilyn, as she signed the restaurant's guest book, "Proud to be the guest of the Chicago writer Saul Bellow." In a letter, Bellow wrote of Marilyn that she "seemed genuinely glad to see a familiar face. I have yet to see anything in Marilyn that isn't genuine. Surrounded by thousands she conducts herself like a philosopher" (Atlas 277).

Many years later Bellow said of Marilyn, "I always felt she had picked up some high-tension cable and couldn't release it. She couldn't rest, she found no repose in anything. She was up in the night, taking pills and talking about her costumes, her next picture, contracts and money, gossip. In the case of a beautiful and sensitive creature like that, it was a guarantee of destruction" (Cronin & Siegal 130–1).

CONSTANCE BENNETT Glamorous movie star of the 1930s and 1940s. Her penultimate film was *As Young as You Feel* in 1951. Marilyn was cast in the film as a dimwitted secretary. After seeing Marilyn walk across the set, Bennett summed her up in one sentence: "There's a broad with a future behind her" (Kellow 146).

JOAN BENNETT Hollywood film and television actress. When Marilyn Monroe was a child and still known as Norma Jeane Baker, one of her foster parents showed her a fan magazine with Joan Bennett's picture on the cover. Her guardian concluded that Norma Jeane bore a strong resemblance to the actress, especially around the eyes and the top half of the face. Bennett was born 16 years before the girl who grew up to be MM and survived her by 28 years. Norma Jeane did not think she looked like Joan Bennett but found the comparison to be interesting; supposedly it led to her thinking about acting in the movies (Gilmore 49–50; Taraborrelli 2009, 49).

JACK BENNY Legendary comedian in radio, film and television. The master of the slow burn, Benny's other trademarks were his cheapness, his terrible violin playing and his eternally claiming to be 39. MM made her television debut on his show on September 13, 1953, in a sketch entitled "The Honolulu Trip."[12] Benny wrote: "She was so charming. She said she didn't want money, but she would love to have a car, a really nice car.[13] 'Nobody has ever given me an automobile in my life,' she said, in that wistful little girl voice, so of course I was delighted to play a fatherly role and gave her a car. It was a black Cadillac convertible. She loved it and drove it until she married Arthur Miller.... She was delicious. She was superb. She read comedy lines as well as anyone in the business. She knew the secret—that hard-to-learn secret—of reading comedy lines as if they were in a drama and letting the humor speak for itself" (Benny & Benny 242–3). Benny became friendly with Marilyn and used to accompany her to a massage parlor for facials. On one memorable occasion, the result of a dare, he accompanied her to a nude beach. Benny wore a beard and Marilyn a black wig. They were unrecognized. Marilyn and Benny were seen in public together at a couple of charity events and at the May 1962 celebration of President Kennedy's birthday at Madison Square Garden (Riese & Hitchens 43; Summers 305–6; Victor 33; *www.cursumperficio.net* /files/Benny).

EDGAR BERGEN Actor and ventriloquist. On October 18, 1952, MM was a guest on Edgar Bergen's radio show. Marilyn announced over the air that she was engaged to be married to Bergen's wooden dummy, Charlie McCarthy. According to the script even Winston Churchill was upset by the announcement saying, "Never has anyone so little taken so much from so many" (Victor 33).

MILTON BERLE Comedian known as "Uncle Miltie" who achieved his greatest success in the early days of television. In his autobiography, Berle admitted that he had an affair with MM during the making of one of her early films, *Ladies of the Chorus* (1948). He was dating the star of the film, Adele Jergens, but quickly transferred his affections to another blonde, Marilyn. As Berle recounts about their initial meeting: "She actually blushed when we shook hands. It added to that special wide-eyed quality she already had. We talked for a few minutes, and I asked her if she would have dinner with me. She said yes." Berle and Marilyn began going out together to flashy nightspots. Berle enjoyed showing them to her and thought Marilyn's innocent curiosity was completely genuine. "Marilyn didn't put on phoney airs. She didn't pretend that she was used to this world. She'd just sit at the table, wide-eyed, looking everywhere. And she'd ask question after question, and she'd almost always follow it with 'Oh, I didn't know that!' or 'Oh, really?' ...Marilyn was on the climb in Hollywood, but there was nothing cheap about her. She wasn't one of the starlets around town that you put one meal into and then threw in the sack. Maybe she didn't know exactly who she was, but she knew she was worth something. She had respect for herself. Marilyn was a lady."

After their affair ended Berle encountered Marilyn at a March 30, 1955, charity event in Madison Square Garden. Berle was the ringmaster and Marilyn rode a pink elephant. At another event, when he was opening at the Flamingo in Las Vegas, Berle had the pleasant duty of escorting Elizabeth Taylor on one arm and Marilyn on the other. Berle and Marilyn saw each other in public on about four other occasions, at charity functions.

According to Berle, the last time he and Marilyn met was in 1959 when he was in Marilyn's movie, *Let's Make Love*.[14] Berle immediately noticed a change in his old flame. She was as beautiful as ever, of course, but she seemed lost in her own thoughts and was no longer the naïve innocent. Marilyn never said a word about their relationship on *Ladies of the Chorus*. Berle believed her non-reaction was genuine. "I think she actually could not remember that she and I had been together for a while eleven years before." The only conversation they had was about the cigars Berle smoked. Marilyn said that she like the aroma. Berle gave her a box of small cigars but never discovered if she smoked any of them (Berle & Frankel 265–7).

IRVING BERLIN Famous and prodigious American composer and songwriter. In 1954, MM agreed to be in *There's No Business Like Show Business*, a showcase for some of Berlin's best-loved songs. Marilyn made the picture on the promise of the lead in *The Seven Year Itch* (1955). Allegedly, Marilyn got the part in *There's No Business Like Show Business* because

Berlin saw her nude calendar on the producer's piano and said, "She's gotta be in the picture." Berlin was intrigued by her come-hither look and thought she would be perfect for his tongue-in-cheek torch song, "Heat Wave." Despite the fact that it was two o'clock in the morning, Berlin phoned Marilyn and persuaded her to sing the song to him (Bergreen 518).

On the set, Marilyn worked hard at improving her singing, working with the composer, the pianist and vocal coach Hal Schaefer. One day Berlin dropped by the set to see how the new arrangements for his songs were coming along. He was impressed by Marilyn's performance of "Heat Wave" but she became angry that her friend Schaefer was not getting any recognition. Marilyn demanded that Berlin personally tell Schaefer what a great help he was or she would walk off the picture. Berlin calmed the situation down and the movie was completed. A photo was taken of Berlin and Marilyn in which they are both smiling and looking relaxed (Shevey 265–6; Summers 149; Victor 33–4).

YOGI BERRA Major League Baseball player and manager. In 1955, Berra was in a deleted scene in *The Seven Year Itch*. In the middle of a game at Yankee Stadium, Berra says of Marilyn's character, "I don't know her name, but she's on the Dazzledent program. The one with the teeth ... on television" (Schwarz 446). In 1959, actress Angie Dickinson took her two favorite ball players, Whitey Ford and Yogi Berra, out to dinner. She said, "They thought I was at least a little bit nifty. They said they did anyway. They did, that is, until Marilyn Monroe sat down at a table about fourteen feet away. Then both of them became unraveled." According to Dickinson, Whitey went ga-ga and Yogi lost interest in his food. All he could do was mutter 'Madonne'" (Barra 265).

JOEY BISHOP Nightclub comedian who progressed to movies and television. In 1954, opening for Frank Sinatra Bishop was at the Copacabana in New York City when MM walked in. She was draped in white ermine and all eyes were immediately on her. Bishop looked at her and said, "I told you to stay in the truck." His ad-lib stopped the show (Starr 34).

MR. BLACKWELL   Mr. Blackwell was the fashion critic notorious for his "Ten Worst-dressed Women of the Year Awards." The awards were given every year from 1960 until his death in 2008. MM made the list in 1961. Mr. Blackwell said of her: "In private life, Marilyn Monroe is a road-show version of herself. She should get off the stage" (www.wiki pedia.org).

HUMPHREY BOGART   Screen legend who became famous for portraying gangsters and tough guys. Bogart had a slight acquaintance with MM through his wife, Lauren Bacall, who co-starred with her in *How to Marry a Millionaire* (1953). Bogart attended the premiere of the film, as did Marilyn, of course. He was also at the party thrown by Billy Wilder to celebrate the completion of *The Seven Year Itch* in 1955 and was photographed dancing with Marilyn. Marilyn borrowed a red chiffon gown from the studio wardrobe department for the occasion and Bogart was in chin stubble from his work on *The Desperate Hours* (Spoto 1993, 252; Summers 118).

PAT BOONE   Clean-living actor and pop singer. Cantinflas, the Mexican film star and comedian, had plans to make a movie with himself and co-stars Pat Boone and MM. As intriguing as that sounds, the project never got off the ground. In 1964, Boone co-starred in *Goodbye Charlie*, a film Marilyn had rejected (Pilcher 177).

CLARA BOW   Silent film star who outlived MM by three years. For *Life* magazine's Christmas 1958 issue, Marilyn impersonated Clara Bow—The It Girl—before fashion photographer Richard Avedon's camera.[15] Donning a red wig, Marilyn transformed herself into a wild flapper of the 1920s. Arthur Miller, Marilyn's husband, contributed an essay. He wrote, "Marilyn came onto the set ... and a record player was started. Songs of the '20s burst forth. Marilyn aimed an experimen-

tal kick at a balloon on the floor. She said she was ready. Avedon yelled, "Go!" and she pursed her mouth around her cigaret [in a Clara Bow pose], kicked a balloon, shot the fan out forward—and she made a world. I suddenly saw her dancing on a table, a hundred Scott Fitzgeralds sitting all around her cheering, Pierce-Arrow cars waiting outside, a real orchestra on the stand, the Marines in Nicaragua. We all found ourselves laughing. Her miraculous sense of sheer play had been unloosed. Suddenly she was all angles, suddenly the wig had become her own hair and the costume her own dress" (*Life*, December 22, 1958). Bow saw the picture and was flattered by it. She admired Marilyn, thought of her as her favorite actress, but was too insecure to meet her. Bow identified with Marilyn. Both had mentally unstable mothers and grandmothers, had suffered abusive childhoods, felt trapped by their sex symbol images, were usually underpaid, and had to struggle to be taken seriously. Bow wrote: "I slip my old crown of 'It' Girl not to Taylor or Bardot, but to Monroe," (Stenn 72). After Marilyn died, Bow was desolate. She said: "She was so lovely and too young to die. God bless her.... I never met Marilyn Monroe, but if I had, I would have tried very hard to help her. A sex symbol is a heavy load to carry when one is tired, hurt, and bewildered" (Stenn 278). Marilyn had wanted to film Clara Bow's life story but Bow did not want the picture made while she was still alive (Riese & Hitchens 61).

CHARLES BOYER   Elegant French actor. Joking around with her roommate, Shelley Winters, Marilyn compiled a list of men she would like to sleep with and Charles Boyer's name was included (Gottfried 2003, 228). Even though Boyer had a long career in Hollywood he found the place insufferably inbred, sanctimonious and vindictive. The controversy that arose over MM's nude calendar photos was a case in point. Boyer was enraged that Marilyn was being condemned and was in danger of losing her movie contract. "How can these people be so vicious?" was his comment (Swindell 229).

EDDIE BRACKEN Comic actor who played Willie Fisher, a worried soldier in *We're Not Married* (1952). MM was also in the film but did not share screen time with Bracken (*www.imdb.com*).

MARLON BRANDO Virile, brooding actor with an overpowering screen presence. MM and Brando never worked together, although they came close. When Marilyn failed to get the lead in *The Egyptian* (1954), Brando abandoned the film as well. Replaced by Gene Tierney and Edmund Purdom, the movie flopped. Marilyn agreed to be in *Paris Blues* (1961) if Brando was her co-star. When the film was made it was with Paul Newman and Joanne Woodward. Marilyn met Brando as early as 1952 when she visited the set of *Viva Zapata!*[16] She visited Brando again on the set of *Desiree* in 1954. A photograph exists of the two of them together, with Brando dressed as Napoleon Bonaparte. Marilyn was quoted in a popular magazine as saying: "I read recently that, before I met Joe [DiMaggio], I had a secret romance with Marlon Brando. That's not true either. I have met Marlon and I like him both as a person and as an actor. I think he is one of finest actors on the screen. I have been receiving letters from teenagers who adore Marlon, suggesting that I play in a picture with him. Maybe I'll forward these to Mr. Zanuck" (*The American Weekly* 11/23/52).

It is alleged that, in 1955, between Marilyn's divorce from Joe DiMaggio and marriage to Arthur Miller, that the two devotees of method acting did have an affair. Marilyn never admitted to that but she did say: "Personally I react to Marlon Brando. He's a favorite of mine, one of the most attractive men I've ever met." Marilyn confided to a friend that Brando was sweet and tender and that she referred to him by the code name of "Carlo." Whatever transpired between the two, Brando became one of Marilyn's most steadfast friends. She celebrated her last birthday at his house and Brando spoke with her on the telephone just a day or two before she died. After Marilyn's death, Brando refused to discuss their relationship: "I did know her, and out of that sentiment for her, I could never talk about her for publication" (Summers 195).

After Marilyn's death, about all Brando ever said was the following: "Do you remember when Marilyn Monroe died? Everybody stopped work, and you could see all that day the same expressions on their faces, the same thought: 'How can a girl with success, fame, youth, money, beauty ... how could she kill herself?' Nobody could understand it because those are the things that everybody wants, and they can't believe that life wasn't important to Marilyn Monroe, or that her life was elsewhere" (Victor 41–2).

WALTER BRENNAN Three-time Oscar winner who specialized in playing crotchety old-timers. Brennan co-starred in two films with MM: *Scudda Hoo! Scudda Hay!* (1948) and *A Ticket to Tomahawk* (1950). Marilyn had uncredited parts in both. Brennan was also in a deleted sequence of another Marilyn Monroe picture, *We're Not Married* (1952) (Riese & Hitchens 64; Victor 42; *www.imdb.com*).

BENJAMIN BRITTEN British composer, pianist and conductor. Eager to find a way to promote the Aldeburgh Festival of classical music, which he had founded, Britten wondered if he could take advantage of Marilyn Monroe's visit to England in 1956. It would be a coup if he could get Marilyn to open the garden party fundraiser. In a letter to Edith Sitwell, dated July 29, Britten wrote, "Because you say how nice & simple, & also interested in 'cultural' things, she is, I wonder whether you could help us approach Marilyn Monroe. I don't know her at all, & in fact am slightly disturbed by her friendship with the Oliviers ... so a word from you would help enormously. Could you either write to her yourself, or write me a short note ... to enclose with an invitation to her?" (Reed 468). Sitwell replied the next day: "I'd better let you know at once, so there will be no delay in getting someone else. Alas, there *isn't* a *hope* that we can get Miss Monroe. For both she and her husband told me, when they came to see me, that she is filming—or rather *will* be filming, for she hadn't, then, actually started—twelve hours a day" (Reed 469).

JOE E. BROWN   Large-mouthed comedian who played a peculiar millionaire in *Some Like It Hot* (1959). Upon learning that the object of his desire, Jack Lemmon is not a woman but a man, Brown's response, the final line in the film, is famous: "Well, nobody's perfect." Marilyn and Brown only shared a small amount of screen time in the film. However, they had a cordial relationship and were photographed together on the set (Doll 202; Rollyson 1993, 150–1; Shevey 382–3).

YUL BRYNNER   Exotic international star with a shaven head. Brynner won an Academy Award for *The King and I* (1956). A fan magazine hinted that Brynner and MM may have had an affair. Brynner, who enjoyed playing with the truth, neither confirmed nor denied the rumor. He said: "I'm flattered. All I can say is that Marilyn has good taste in her escorts. She is an attractive and sensitive woman. When she puts on her warpaint she instantly becomes a radiant thing. She can also look like an old pancake left over from a Sunday breakfast" (Robbins 94). According to Rock Brynner, Yul's son, his father did have a fling with Marilyn Monroe in 1955. Rock recalled meeting Marilyn unexpectedly when he was 9 years old and Yul brought her home. The next morning he saw Marilyn's clothes scattered about. Yul said to him, "That will be *our* secret, laddie" (Capua 55).

WILLIAM F. BUCKLEY, JR.   Author and conservative political commentator. In 1952, Buckley was living in the same apartment complex as Marilyn Monroe. He and his wife started exiting their apartment at all hours in the hope that "one of us would one day bump into our fellow-tenant Marilyn Monroe in the elevator, but we never did lay eyes on her" (Buckley 165).

LUIS BUÑUEL   Spanish film director who was long active in Mexico. During a trip to Mexico in February 1962, Marilyn Monroe visited Buñuel on the set of *The Exterminating Angel* (Rechy 34; *www.cursumperficio.net* /biography/1962).

GEORGE BURNS   Actor, comedian and singer who enjoyed an incredible 90–year career in show business. He was 30 when MM was born; by the time he died at age 100, he had outlived her by nearly 34 years. On November 6, 1954, Burns attended an exclusive dinner party at a Beverly Hills restaurant to honor Marilyn and to celebrate the completion of *The Seven Year Itch*. Burns was seated under a cardboard cutout of Marilyn in her famous skirt-blowing scene (Learning 1998, 134). Burns was quoted as saying, "If you were married to Marilyn Monroe—you'd cheat with some ugly girl" (Crawley 14).

RAYMOND BURR   Heavyset Canadian actor who found fame as television's Perry Mason. In 1949 Burr had a small part as Alphonse Zoto in a forgettable Marx Brothers comedy, *Love Happy*. MM had an even smaller part as Groucho Marx's sexy unnamed client (*www.imdb.com*).

RICHARD BURTON   Hard-drinking Welsh actor who was married to Elizabeth Taylor. In 1953, Burton took a break from filming *The Robe* to visit the set of *How to Marry a Millionaire* (Howard 164). At one point Burton was considered for the male lead in *The Prince and the Showgirl* (1957). Marilyn told her agent, Charles Feldman, that "she would love to sleep with the Prince if his name was Richard Burton" (Meyers 158).

RED BUTTONS   Actor and comedian who had a long career in theater and film. Marilyn Monroe and Red Buttons were never in the same film but they were photographed together at a charity show organized by Danny Thomas in aid of St. Jude's Children's Hospital. The event was held at the Hollywood Bowl in July 1953 (*www.cursumperficio. net* files/charity; *www.youtube.com* "Marilyn Monroe at the Hollywood Bowl with Danny Thomas").

-C-

SID CAESAR   Emmy-winning comedian, actor and writer known for his work on television's *Your Show of Shows* (1950–1954). One evening after his live televison show, Caesar was relaxing at his favorite hangout when he felt a pair of hands on his shoulders. He turned around and was stunned to discover MM standing there. Marilyn, who was not a big TV viewer, had seen Caesar do a funny television sketch and wanted to speak to him about it. Marilyn said: "I just came over to congratulate you. I never saw anything like that. When you started playing tic-tac-toe on your face, I screamed. I almost wet my pants. So I tracked you down to this restaurant." Caesar escorted Marilyn back to her table, pulled out her chair, sat with her and thanked her for her kind words (Caesar & Friedfeld 258).

JIMMY CAGNEY Academy Award-winning film star. In 1954, MM met up with Cagney at a Beverly Hills party hosted by *Look* magazine. A photograph was taken of the two screen legends in conversation. Jimmy's sister, Jeanne Cagney, was a film and television actress who appeared with Marilyn in the 1952 movie *Don't Bother to Knock* (Anonymous 132–3; Victor 85; *www.imbd.com*).

SAMMY CAHN Lyricist who wrote many songs for the movies, often with Jimmy Van Heusen. Cahn did the songs for MM in *Let's Make Love* (1960). One Monday morning, Twentieth Century–Fox's music department phoned up Cahn and Van Heusen and told them to get over to the studio right away. Marilyn was there and she was ready to work on her music. Cahn did not want to go until Marilyn's legendary tardiness was brought up. "No way [you can't come] we'll *never* be able to get her here again," he was told (Cahn 241).

MICHAEL CAIN Versatile English actor who served in the British Army in Korea. In February 1954, MM interrupted her honeymoon with Joe DiMaggio to entertain the troops in South Korea. She flew in by helicopter, lying down on the floor of the machine with two airmen sitting on her feet, to blow kisses to thousands of soldiers. Wearing a low-cut plum-shaded gown with sequins, she sang "Bye Bye Baby," "Diamonds Are a Girl's Best Friend," and "Do It Again." The lyrics of the latter were changed to "Kiss Me Again," because the original words were considered to be too suggestive. In four days Marilyn performed ten shows for more than 100,000 (mostly American) troops. Marilyn regarded her trip to Korea as one of the high points of her life saying, "I never felt like a star before in my heart. It was so wonderful to look down and see a fellow smiling at me" (Riese & Hitchens 254). The army brass, after a near riot broke out, considered the pandemonium generated by Marilyn's visit to be harmful to service morale. During her performances she would say things such as: "You fellas are always whistling at sweater girls. Well, take away their sweaters and what have you got?" (Spada & Zeno 83). Michael Cain was one of those smiling fellows who saw Marilyn perform in a makeshift outdoor theater. He recalled: "I can still see her now, blonde and angelically beautiful, the complete love goddess. Utterly unapproachable, of course. I reckon we all dreamed about her for weeks afterward" (Hall 46).

Other sources: Summers 131–2; Victor 160

LOUIS CALHERN Character actor who had a 35 year career in Hollywood. In 1950 Calhern played opposite MM in John Huston's *The Asphalt Jungle*. Although playing the ultimate sugar daddy, the standards of the time required that Calhern be referred to as Marilyn's "uncle." Marilyn's character was, of course, Calhern's mistress in the film. Marilyn said, "Nobody would have heard of me if it hadn't been for John Huston. When we started *Asphalt Jungle*, my first picture[17], I was very nervous, but John said, 'Look at Calhern ... see how he's shaking. If you're not nervous, you might as well give up'" (Goode 200). Calhern and Marilyn were also in 1952's *We're Not Married* but did not share any scenes (Shevey 156–7; Victor 47).

RORY CALHOUN Calhoun was a mostly B–grade actor in films and television. His best film was *How to Marry a Millionaire* (1953), in which he played opposite MM. Calhoun appeared in two other pictures with Marilyn: *A Ticket to Tomahawk* (1950) and *River of No Return* (1954). On *A Ticket to Tomahawk*, recalled Calhoun, Marilyn was "like a little kid the way she bubbled sometimes, but scared as hell—scared of the crew and scared because when she was left on her own she didn't know if she was doing something right or not.... Problems came up with her in the studio, and on location which was in Durango,[18] where she got sick. I swore she had stomach poisoning because of so much pain she seemed to be having. Like someone being tortured. She said she had to take a lot of penicillin but the doctor told her it wasn't wise. He was saying a person's system couldn't handle that much, but Marilyn said it was okay. She said she could take it and it'd be okay. Like a damn fool she went ahead and took all this penicillin and sure as shit she busted out in penicillin poisoning. I thought, that's god-damned *dumb*! She had rashes all over and even in her crotch which she'd talk about in case you were interested in her rashes, and she'd show you if you wanted. I didn't see too many around who weren't interested in looking at her rashes, including me" (Gilmore 105–7).

MARIA CALLAS   Greek opera diva. On May 19, 1962, Callas was one of the invited performers at a Democratic Party fundraiser in Madison Square Garden. It was also the occasion of President John F. Kennedy's 45th birthday celebration.[19] This was the event at which MM cooed her famous rendition of "Happy Birthday, Mr. President." Marilyn was usually late and this event was no exception. By the time Callas came on to sing the 'Habanero' and 'Séguedille' from *Carmen*, the audience was clearly impatient for Marilyn. Callas received suitable applause but she resented being upstaged by the blonde bombshell. As Callas took her bows, Marilyn finally stepped on stage and instantly all eyes were focused on her. After the performance, Marilyn and Callas were photographed talking amicably together. In the 1960 film *Let's Make Love* Marilyn performed a song called "Specialization" which included lyrics about Callas

and featured a Maria Callas impersonator (Bret 208; Scott 234; *www.cursumperficio.net/biography/1962*).

CANTINFLAS   Mexican film star and comedian. Cantinflas had plans to make a movie starring himself, Pat Boone and MM. As intriguing as that combination of talents sounds, it never happened (Pilcher 177).

EDDIE CANTOR   Legendary singer, songwriter, dancer, actor and comedian. Cantor and Marilyn Monroe both attended the funeral of Hollywood talent agent Johnny Hyde who had died on December 18, 1950. Despite being 31 years older, Hyde had left his wife for Marilyn and begged her to marry him. She refused, saying she loved him but was not *in love* with him. Cantor was an honorary pallbearer at the funeral, while Marilyn was glared at by the Hyde family who blamed her for Johnnie's untimely death (Rose 150–1; Victor 147–8).

TRUMAN CAPOTE   Writer known for revolutionizing the non-fiction novel with his acclaimed book, *In Cold Blood*. Director John Huston introduced Truman Capote to MM while she was filming *The Asphalt Jungle* in 1950. The author and the actress became great friends. They became so close that on one occasion, if you can believe Capote, they danced together nude in a New York hotel room (Victor 48).

Capote had introduced Marilyn to British actress Constance Collier, who became one of her early acting coaches. On April 28, 1955, Capote accompanied Marilyn to Collier's funeral. Capote described Marilyn at the funeral: "What she had imagined to wear would have been appropriate for the abbess of a nunnery in private audience with the Pope. Her hair was entirely concealed by a black chiffon scarf; her black dress was loose and long and looked somehow borrowed; black silk stockings dulled the blond sheen of her slender legs. An abbess, one can be certain, would not have donned the vaguely erotic black high-heeled shoes she had chosen, or the owlish black sunglasses that dramatized the vanilla-pallor of her dairy-fresh skin" (Capote 1980,

227). Marilyn said, "I hate funerals. I'm glad I won't have to go to my own. Only, I don't want a funeral—just my ashes cast on waves by one of my kids, if I ever have any" (Capote 1980, 229–30).

Marilyn was Capote's first choice for the role of Holly Golightly, when his novella *Breakfast at Tiffany's* was filmed in 1961. Marilyn was so eager for the part that she prepared two scenes and presented them to Capote. In Capote's estimation Marilyn was simply marvelous, but the studio overruled him and cast Audrey Hepburn. Even though Hepburn was a friend of Capote's he thought she was not right for the role.

Capote met Marilyn for the last time just a few weeks before her death, when she was working on *Something's Got to Give*. She had lost some excess weight and was looking her best. Capote detected a new level of maturity about her. "If she had lived and kept her figure," wrote Capote, "I think she would still look terrific today. The Kennedys didn't kill her, the way some people think. She committed suicide" (Clarke 269). He summed her up by saying, "Marilyn? Just a slob, really, an untidy divinity—in the sense that a banana split or cherry jubilee is untidy but divine (Capote 1973, 378).

Other sources: Inge 317; Leaming 1998, 331–2; Victor 48

FRANK CAPRA Academy Award–winning movie director who made *It Happened One Night* (1934), *Lost Horizon* (1937), *Mr. Smith Goes to Washington* (1939), *It's A Wonderful Life* (1946), and many others. A masseur of Capra's acquaintance, with a penchant for walking on the backs of clients, told Capra that he just had to meet another of his customers, a sexy young starlet. Thinking he was satisfying a promise made to the masseur's girlfriend, Capra agreed to meet her. The masseur told Capra to pay particular attention to the starlet's breasts. The girl turned out to be MM. Capra was immediately struck by her curvaceousness but never signed her for one of his films, a fact he regretted and never quite understood. At the time, Capra didn't think Marilyn had any ability to

communicate. He said, "Breasts she had. And a wiggly figure. But to me sex is class, something more than a wiggly behind.... But how could I have passed up Marilyn Monroe?" (Capra 249).

HARRY CAREY, JR. Supporting actor, who was usually seen in westerns. Carey appeared in three non-westerns with MM: *Monkey Business* (1952), *Niagara* (1953), and *Gentlemen Prefer Blondes* (1953) (*www.imdb.com*).

MACDONALD CAREY Actor who spent nearly 30 years on the television soap opera *Days of Our Lives*. It was Macdonald Carey's voice which was heard intoning the epigram which began each episode: "Like sands through the hourglass, so are the days of our lives." In 1951 Carey appeared opposite MM in *Let's Make It Legal*. What Carey remembered from that picture was an altercation Marilyn had with the director, Richard Sale. Marilyn was chronically late, usually by 90 minutes. When the ballroom scene came to be filmed Marilyn was nowhere in sight. Carey, Claudette Colbert and a room full of extras were standing around with nothing to do. When Marilyn finally put in an appearance Sale started yelling at her.[20] Marilyn threatened to phone some executive at Twentieth Century–Fox and have him fired. Sale called Marilyn's bluff, telling her she could phone anyone she wanted but that first she owed an apology to the cast and crew. Marilyn never made the telephone call but she did apologize for inconveniencing everyone. Wrote Carey, "None of us realized how quickly she would go to the top and how just as quickly meet her death. Even though we worked together, her career is something I was never part of. To most of us in the cast, she was a complete stranger, a pretty young woman who had a few lines and who knew the right people" (Carey 178).

JEANNE CARMEN 'B' movie actress, pinup girl, and trick-shot golfer. About 20 years after Marilyn's death, Carmen started talking about the supposed intimate friendship she had with Marilyn. She claimed to have been

Marilyn's roommate and her tales were full of scurrilous details. There is little evidence to support them. Carmen was a neighbor of Marilyn's in 1961. One night Marilyn complained that she was kept awake by a loud party at Carmen's house. Carmen and her guests, aware of their famous neighbor, stood below her window and shouted an invitation for her to join the party (Spoto 1993, 472, Victor 48).

HOAGY CARMICHAEL   Pianist, singer, actor, bandleader and composer of popular songs. Carmichael wrote several songs for 1953's *Gentlemen Prefer Blondes* including "Down Boy," expressly for MM. As Carmichael recalled, "We had rehearsed the song together and she loved it. I felt it was her first choice to become a song stylist and soloist like Mary Martin after her singing of 'My Heart Belongs to Daddy'" (Sudhalter 282–3). Despite Marilyn's and Carmichael's hard work, the song was cut from the finished film. Reportedly, Darryl F. Zanuck thought it was too suggestive. Two years later, the song was recycled in a Betty Grable picture, *Three for the Show*. Carmichael summarized Marilyn when he said: "I think she really liked the simple life and was not as ambitious for success as most of the big stars" (Guiles 210).

LESLIE CARON   Gamin–like French actress and dancer. Caron met MM in March 1953, when Marilyn won the *Redbook* magazine award for "Best Young Box Office Personality." At the time Marilyn was getting 25,000 fan letters per week (Spada & Zeno 66).

DIAHANN CARROLL   Glamorous African American actress and singer. In 1960 MM went to hear Carroll sing at the Mocambo in Los Angeles. Marilyn desperately wanted to have a baby, and Carroll remembered, "I was pregnant with my daughter, Suzanne. Marilyn, so sad and so beautiful, came backstage to say hello. 'May I touch your tummy?' she asked me. I was delighted, of course. I took her hand and put it on my stomach and said, 'You pat right here, sweetheart, and say a prayer and a wish, and I hope with all my heart that your

dream comes true.' She looked at me with tears in her eye, and said, 'Oh, I do, too. I do, too'" (Taraborelli 313).

The two women encountered each other once more. It was on May 19, 1962, at a small party following President John F. Kennedy's public birthday gala at Madison Square Garden. Carroll performed at the gathering and recalled: "It's certainly her beauty I remember most. As I sang, I distinctly remember being somewhat distracted by her gaze. Her tragic beauty, so vulnerable ... so lost" (Taraborrelli 2009, 437).

JOHN CARROLL   Singer and actor who bore a strong resemblance to MM's father-figure, Clark Gable. Carroll made more than fifty movies in a career which spanned nearly 40 years. His most notable films were *Flying Tigers* (1942) with John Wayne and *Go West* (1940) with the Marx Brothers. Carroll met Marilyn in 1947 at a celebrity golf tournament at which she was his starlet caddy. She was not very good as a caddy, but no one minded. Marilyn was out of work and Carroll took his lovely caddy in and even gave her a weekly allowance. Marilyn lived with Carroll and his actress-talent scout wife, Lucille Ryman, for five months. The Carrolls had a reputation for helping struggling beginners but as they were newlyweds, having Marilyn live with them was surely an unusual thing to do. Carroll and his wife were very well connected and helped Marilyn find work in the theater and in John Huston's *The Asphalt Jungle* (1950). Huston stabled his horses at the Carrolls' ranch, and giving Marilyn a part in his latest movie would cancel his outstanding debt to them.

Inevitably, the rumors started that Marilyn and Carroll were more than housemates. The truth will probably never be known but Carroll denied the allegations claiming that all he ever did was teach Marilyn to sing. However, Ryman reported an unusual conversation. Marilyn told her that she was in love with Carroll and asked her to divorce her husband so she could have him. Marilyn could not understand that a man could be kind to her and not expect something in return.

Marilyn's close relationship with Carroll and Ryman lasted until about 1949–1950 although they had occasional contact afterward. In 1952, Ryman was startled when Marilyn offered to pay the couple back for the money they had given her. Marilyn was told to keep the money and use it to help someone else (Guiles 122–5; Slatzer 259; Spoto 1993, 126–31; Victor 48, 51).

JACK CARSON Hollywood actor known for his comic wisecracking roles. On Sunday, September 14, 1952, Carson took part in the patriotic "I Am An American" event at the Hollywood Bowl.[21] Carson was photographed standing with Danny Thomas, Marilyn Monroe and the Stars and Stripes. On December 4, 1953, Carson was seen with Marilyn at a charity benefit for children (*www.cursumperficio.net*/biography/1952/1953).

HENRI CARTIER-BRESSON Cartier-Bresson was a famous French still photographer and photojournalist who was hired to take candid photographs during the making of *The Misfits* (1961), MM's last completed film. Even in the 100–degree heat of the Nevada desert, Cartier-Bresson saw Marilyn as beautiful, intelligent, amusing and natural. In his words, Marilyn was the reality of "a certain myth of what we call in France *la femme éternelle*" (Goode 101).

JOYCE CARY Irish writer whose most famous novel was *The Horse's Mouth* (1944). Cary and MM met on July 26, 1956, at playwright Terence Rattigan's country house in Berkshire, near London. The occasion was a ball hosted by Rattigan, Vivien Leigh and Sir Laurence Olivier in honor of Marilyn and her husband, Arthur Miller. Marilyn was in England to film Rattigan's *The Prince and the Showgirl*. A couple of years later Marilyn identified with the hero of Cary's novel *Mr. Johnson*, seeing a parallel with her own life—innocence being overwhelmed by cynicism (Gottfried 2003, 301).

BENNETT CERF Television personality and publisher, co-founder of Random House. On assignment for *Esquire* magazine, Cerf was scheduled to interview Marilyn Monroe. They were supposed to have lunch but Marilyn was suffering from a cold and decided to stay in bed in her hotel room. She invited him to her room if he did not mind catching her cold. Cerf took the risk and went to Marilyn's hotel room. Beside her on the bed was a weighty volume of the *Essays of Montaigne* issued by the Modern Library, of which Cerf was the publisher. Marilyn, who was always eager to improve herself, said that someone had told her that every educated girl should read Montaigne. Cerf replied that only college students even knew that Montaigne was still in print. Cerf offered to send Marilyn a dozen Modern Library books that she would find more enjoyable. To Cerf's delight, Marilyn climbed out of bed in her very short nightgown and tossed Montaigne in the trash basket. The interview with Marilyn, "The 'Altogether' Girl," appeared in the July 1953 edition of *Esquire* (Glatzer 95).

GEORGE CHAKIRIS Dancer and leading man who won the Academy Award for Best Supporting Actor for *West Side Story* (1961). Chakiris was also in two MM films: *Gentlemen Prefer Blondes* (1953) and *There's No Business Like Show Business* (1954). He was one of the dancers in Marilyn's "Diamonds are a Girl's Best Friend" number in *Gentlemen Prefer Blondes*. On that film Chakiris was impressed by Marilyn as a committed actress and as a sweet person, but he could not help but notice that her back muscles were quivering with nerves. At a cast party for *There's No Business Like Show Business* Chakiris remembered: "No one was dressed up, everyone—including Marilyn—was in casual clothes and no make-up. My dance partner, Druscilla, wanted to ask Marilyn to kiss me, but I absolutely didn't want her to do it. Druscilla went over though, and Marilyn turned 'round, looked in my direction and said, 'But I don't know him.' I thought this was very sweet and meaningful, because she knew it was inappropriate to kiss me. I wasn't disappointed because I was shy and didn't want Druscilla to do it in the first place" (Morgan 142). Chakiris concluded that Marilyn was a very gifted artist and, although she drove her co-stars to distraction with her lateness, it did not stem from any malicious intent (Morgan 127–8, 298).

JEFF CHANDLER Prematurely gray-haired leading man, usually starring in Westerns and action features. On December 2, 1954, Chandler was at a Hollywood party in honor of his close friend, Sammy Davis, Jr. Davis had just been discharged from the hospital after losing his left eye in a devastating car crash. MM was also at the party and was photographed with Chandler (Haygood 174).

RAYMOND CHANDLER The master of hard-boiled detective fiction. Chandler was delighted with the results of an opinion poll run by the London *Daily Express*. The poll set out to uncover highbrow, middlebrow and low-brow tastes in authors, movie stars and entertainers. Chandler wrote: "Marilyn Monroe and I were the only ones that made all three brows" (MacShane 236).

CAROL CHANNING Bubbly stage actress and singer whose career has revolved around *Hello, Dolly!* and *Gentlemen Prefer Blondes*. Channing was the original Lorelei Lee on Broadway, the part MM played in the movie version in 1953. Reputedly, Channing had been considered for the film role. Marilyn saw Channing in the stage version and Channing saw Marilyn in the movie, thinking it one of her best films. Anita Loos, the author of *Gentlemen Prefer Blondes*, thought that Channing's performance was the funnier of the two but that Marilyn's portrayal was more authentic (Channing 94–5; Riese & Hitchens 84).

CHARLIE CHAPLIN Chaplin, the legendary comic actor who created the Little Tramp, was one of MM's favorites. Marilyn's business partner, Milton Greene, came up with the idea of pairing her with Charlie Chaplin in a film. But when the business arrangement unraveled so did plans for the movie. Marilyn may have met Chaplin at an acting workshop conducted by Charles Laughton. On another occasion Marilyn came very close to meeting Chaplin. Chaplin's son Sydney invited her and a few others to attend a rehearsal for a play his

famous father was directing. Chaplin's style of directing was to act out all the parts (both male and female) himself. Marilyn whispered to her friend Shelley Winters, "No one on earth can do those parts as good as him" (Winters 1989, 43). But then Marilyn's obnoxious drama coach, Natasha Lytess, stood up and shouted, "Mr. Chaplin, you mustn't do that to your actors?" Chaplin thundered back, "Who invited you people to this rehearsal?" Marilyn and her friends sneaked out before the lights came on (Winters 1989, 43–4).

CHARLIE CHAPLIN, JR. The son of a famous father, Charlie Chaplin, Jr., was only a bit player in the movies. He was MM's lover in 1947 and, thereafter, one of her best friends (Summers 43–4; Victor 51; *www.imdb.com*).

SYDNEY CHAPLIN Actor son of Charlie Chaplin. MM played tennis with Sydney and, as a rank beginner, did not understand the scoring system. She burst out laughing when Sydney yelled, "Love-fifteen," and "Love-forty." Marilyn thought of these as descriptions rather than scores (Winters 1989, 37). On one occasion Marilyn was invited to a rehearsal to watch Sydney be directed in a play by his famous father. In 1947, Marilyn had an affair with Sydney's brother, Charlie Chaplin, Jr. Monroe biographer Anthony Summers makes the allegation that at least once Marilyn shared her favors with Sydney (Summers 43; Winters, 1989, 42–3).

CYD CHARISSE Beautiful actress and dancer. In 1962, Charisse was cast in *Something's Got to Give*. It was MM's final film and was never to be completed. Charisse looked sensational in her scenes with co-star Dean Martin—too sensational. Even though Charisse was five years older, Marilyn became paranoid. Viewing the rushes, Marilyn became convinced that Charisse was padding her bra and deliberately trying to duplicate her platinum-blonde hair color. "Her unconscious wants it blonde" (Shevey 64) was Marilyn's response, when asked why Charisse wanted to resemble her. In the surviving footage from the film, Charisse's hair suddenly gets darker halfway through. Many years later, Charisse shared her memories in an interview (*Los Angeles Magazine*, November 2004, 113). "Marilyn Monroe was very sweet—she just didn't have street smarts like I did. I have a nose for horse waste, but she kind of fell into a lot of that stuff along the way. I was in the film *Something's Got to Give* with Marilyn Monroe. George Cukor was the director, and Dean Martin was in it. It was so difficult, because Marilyn was so insecure. She would be upstairs with her acting coach, and we would be waiting on the stage. She'd be gone hours and hours. Then she would come down—she was charming, she was beautiful and everything was good." After the film was canceled Charisse "got a call from Marilyn, and she asked if she could get it going again, would I go on with the film? I said, 'You wanna do it? We'll do it.' Well, they never could get it going again.[22] And shortly afterwards she died."

RAY CHARLES   Legendary rhythm and blues musician. In May 1961 Marilyn Monroe went to the Crescendo nightclub in Los Angeles and met Ray Charles. She was photographed sitting beside him (*www.cursumperficio.net*/biography/1961).

PADDY CHAYEFSKY   Acclaimed playwright and screenwriter. *As Young As You Feel*, from 1951, was one of MM's earliest films and the first Chayefsky story to be filmed. Chayevsky may have met Marilyn at that time. He certainly encountered Marilyn in 1955. It was at the Actors Studio in New York, and Marilyn was now a star. Actress Carroll Baker overheard Chayefsky express a common male fantasy: "Oh, boy, would I like to fuck that!" (Baker 146). Marilyn and Chayefsky formally met in the summer of 1955 at a party at Lee Strasberg's house. Chayefsky, for once at a loss for words, said, "Gee, I thought you'd be much fuller." Marilyn, never a one to waste a provocative remark, replied in her famous breathless voice, "Where do you think I ought to be fuller?" (Considine 1994, 116). Marilyn was well versed in Chayefsky's work, having seen *Marty* shortly before meeting the author.

Through her company, Marilyn Monroe Productions, she considered acquiring the movie rights to his play *Middle of the Night*. Chayefsky spent months revising the play, specifically with Marilyn in mind. But after she married Chayefsky's arch-rival, Arthur Miller, Marilyn decided not to do the play after all. Chayefsky then turned his attention to *The Goddess*, the story of a Hollywood sex symbol's rise and fall. The script contained eerie similarities to Marilyn's actual life, but Chayefsky denied it was based on her. Indeed, he sent the finished script to Marilyn. She read it, was not put off by the biographical details, and was keen to do it. But Miller hated the story and advised her not to have anything to do with *The Goddess*. Miller even wanted Marilyn to sue Chayefsky. The film was released in 1958, while Marilyn was making *Some Like It Hot*. Reporters were advised not to mention *The Goddess*. But Marilyn, who had obviously seen the film, thought the female lead, Kim Stanley, was marvelous. When Marilyn died on August 5, 1962, more than a few observers made the connection with the self-destructive actress in *The Goddess*. Chayefsky was asked to cover the funeral for a magazine but refused, saying that he was not a journalist (Victor 53).

MICHAEL CHEKHOV   Michael Chekhov was an Oscar–nominated actor who became a drama coach. He was the nephew of the Russian playwright Anton Chekhov, and had studied at the Moscow Art Theater under Konstantin Stanislavsky. MM was introduced to Chekhov by actor Jack Palance in 1951 and began taking lessons twice a week. Marilyn considered Chekhov's book, *To the Actor: On the Technique of Acting*, to be her Bible. She said of Chekhov that he was the only person who believed in her talent and wanted to help her develop it. Besides acting, she also said that she learned psychology, history and artistic taste from him. When he died in 1955, Marilyn had her husband, Arthur Miller, read to her from *The Brothers Karamazov*. Marilyn thought that Michael Chekhov should have been world famous. She even toyed with the notion of erecting a statue in his memory in New York. In her will Marilyn left Chekhov's widow $2,500 per annum for her lifetime[23] (Schwarz 642).

One afternoon, in the midst of a scene from his uncle's famous play *The Cherry Orchard*, Chekhov suddenly stopped the action and spoke to Marilyn, asking her if she was thinking of sex. Marilyn denied that she was. "It's very strange," he said. "All through our playing of that scene I kept receiving sex vibrations from you. As if you were a woman in the grip of passion. I stopped because I thought you must be too sexually preoccupied to continue.... You are a young woman who gives off sex vibrations—no matter what you are doing or thinking. The whole world has already responded to those vibrations. They come off the movie screens when you are on them. And your studio bosses are only interested in your sex vibrations. They care nothing about you as an actress. You can make them a fortune by merely vibrating in front of the camera. I see now why they refuse to regard you as an actress. You are more valuable to them as a sex stimulant. And all they want of you is to make money out of you by photographing your erotic vibrations" (Monroe & Hecht 172–3).

Other sources: Spoto 1993, 188–90, 199–200; Victor 53.

LEO CHERNE Cherne was an economist, political commentator and public servant. During a distinguished 50–year career, he served presidents from Roosevelt to George H. W. Bush. Cherne was also an artist of note. He met Marilyn Monroe through the Kennedys and was intrigued by her beauty and seeming sexual innocence. Marilyn saw a bust Chenrne had crafted of Abraham Lincoln, one of her personal heroes, and asked Cherne if he would do one of her. Cherne photographed Marilyn in the nude at the Carlyle Hotel in New York and started working on a clay sculpture. He had finished three-quarters of the piece when Marilyn was found dead. Cherne destroyed the clay model but later regretted that he had done so (Smith 2002, 141).

MAURICE CHEVALIER Dapper French singing star and actor. In November 1958, Chevalier visited MM on the set of *Some Like It Hot*. A series of photographs exists of the two stars laughing and joking together around a piano. Marilyn is even wearing Chevalier's trademark straw hat at a rakish angle. A year prior to this, Twentieth Century–Fox wanted Marilyn to star opposite Chevalier in *Can-Can*. That film was released in 1960, with Shirley MacLaine in the part that would have been Marilyn's (Monroe & Hecht 69; Victor 106).

RANDOLPH CHURCHILL British politician who was the son of Sir Winston Churchill. On a trip to California, Churchill invited MM to meet him at a deserted beach house to discuss a business deal. Not knowing what to expect, Marilyn brought a male friend along to the meeting. Needless to say, nothing came of the meeting (Summers 47).

SARAH CHURCHILL Film actress and dancer who was the daughter of British prime minister Winston Churchill. During the 1950s, Sarah Churchill was married to photographer Antony Beauchamp and lived in Hollywood. Around the time she made *All About Eve* (1950) MM had posed for Beauchamp's camera and was invited to his home for a cocktail party. Marilyn was thrilled by the opportunity to meet the daughter of Winston Churchill, a man she greatly admired.

In her autobiography, Sarah Churchill describes her first meeting with Marilyn:

One of the most memorable events, even at that time, when she was totally unknown, was the visit of a shy little blond girl who came in, wearing, for some extraordinary reason, an enormous mackintosh. Her agent came in with her but said perhaps Antony would like to photograph her alone and he would wait outside in the car.

Antony raised a somewhat quizzical eyebrow to me, meaning, "What the dickens am I to do with this one?" ...So, up they went on to the terrace and moments later Antony flew down the stairs in a great state of excitement and said, "Fetch me a white rug quickly and I'll tell you all about it later."

The forlorn little waif, when she saw the terrace with its plants and its view over the sparkling sea, had thrown off her mac and revealed herself in a bikini that must have taken about three minutes to knit. She spread her arms toward the sky and her whole personality changed. Antony, armed with the white rug, threw it over the cane sofa and asked her to lie down on it—which she did, with a seductive and kittenish but innocent air. Having exhausted the possibilities of the terrace, they moved to the beach. Then, the session over, she replaced her mackintosh and became the waif again. She thanked him politely, thanked me, and Antony saw her to the door and her faithful agent.

He came back bursting with excitement and said, "Unquestionably, I have photographed a star-to-be" [Churchill 205].

Other sources: Monroe & Hecht 67–8.

CINDERELLA   Cinderella was the lead character in the 1950 Disney animated film of the same name. A popular legend arose that Marilyn Monroe was the physical model for Cinderella. It seems that someone within the Disney organization heard a critic say that Cinderella was too voluptuous. This was in 1954 and the reigning queen of voluptuousness was Marilyn Monroe. The fact that Marilyn was not connected to the Disney studio and was all but unknown in 1949, when the movie was in production, did not stop the rumor mongers. An actress named Helene Stanley was the actual model for Cinderella (Genge 195; *www.wikipedia.org*).

RENÉ CLAIR   Distinguished French film director known for his sophisticated light comedies. From the set of 1960's *Let's Make Love*, director George Cukor, MM and co-star Yves Montand, sent a birthday telegram to Clair. Clair had asked his friend Cukor to tell Marilyn how much he admired her (Levy 269).

FRED CLARK   Bald character actor who was almost always in supporting roles. Clark played Waldo Brewster in *How to Marry a Millionaire* (1953) opposite MM (www.imdb.com).

MONTGOMERY CLIFT   One of the greatest stage and film actors of his generation. Clift, an old friend of Arthur Miller, met MM when he went to dinner at the Millers' New York apartment. Marilyn had long admired Clift as an actor. As early as 1949 she confided

to columnist Earl Wilson that Clift was one of her favorites and that he was an actor with tremendous talent. For his part, Clift had a high opinion of Marilyn and regretted having turned down the chance to act opposite her in 1956's *Bus Stop*. When they finally did meet, Clift and Marilyn made an immediate connection. Marilyn identified with Clift's neurotic behavior and insecurities. She commented, "He's the only person I know who's in worse shape than I am" (Bosworth 330). Marilyn and Clift really got to know each other on the set of *The Misfits* (1961). Both of them suffered from crippling insomnia and addictions to pills and alcohol. Between takes they would huddle together comparing notes about how they coped with their inner demons. Clift was Marilyn's escort at the film's premiere. Frank Taylor, the producer of *The Misfits*, said of them: "Monty and Marilyn were psychic twins. They were on the same wavelength. They recognized disaster in each other's faces and giggled about it" (Bosworth 354).

After Marilyn's death, Clift said of Marilyn: "Working with her was fantastic ... like an escalator. You would meet her on one level and then she would rise higher and you would rise to that point, and then you would both go higher" (LaGuardia 215).

ROSEMARY CLOONEY   Popular singer and actress. In her autobiography, Clooney recalls a touching incident from the winter of 1955 when MM came to her house in the company of film director John Huston. Clooney and Marilyn had met once before but had barely spoken. This time, Marilyn came right over to Clooney and asked where her baby was. On being informed that Clooney's son was upstairs, she marched straight into the nursery, not even pausing to shake the snow off her hair and fur coat. Marilyn could not resist the impulse to pick up the baby and play with him. After about an hour, John Huston finally asked, "What the hell is she doing up there?" "She's playing with the baby," said Clooney (Clooney & Barthel 219).

CHARLES COBURN   Character actor of stage, screen and radio. Coburn is remembered today for his roles in the 1940s and 1950s when he started playing benevolent sugar daddy types. Coburn was in two films with MM: *Monkey Business* (1952) and *Gentlemen Prefer Blondes* (1953).[24] In *Monkey Business*, Marilyn was Coburn's dimwitted secretary. After unsuccessfully explaining the mysteries of typing to her, Coburn approvingly watches Marilyn walk away, then shrugs and says, "Anyone can type." Co-star Cary Grant recalled how Coburn "had to chase and squirt Marilyn Monroe with a siphon of soda, a moment he approached with glee. Any seeming reluctance, he later explained, was only his indecision about *where* on Marilyn's ... um ... *ample* proportions to *squirt* the soda. Miss Monroe seemed to present so many inviting parts. Everyone on the set awaited the moment with goggling eyes. You could hear a pin drop. Eventually Charles gave it a healthy squirt, and missing Miss Monroe, he hit me full in the puss" (McCarthy 498).

Marilyn's acting coach, Natasha Lytess, recounted an odd story about Marilyn and Coburn. In *Blondes*, Marilyn had a scene with Coburn in which he had to read a line of Swahili. It was gibberish, of course, and Coburn read it differently for each take. For some reason, Marilyn became obsessed and disturbed by this, reaching a level of panic where she could no longer bear looking at Coburn and had to lock herself in her dressing room. Marilyn stayed there until Lytess coaxed her out.

On August 31, 1954, Coburn was a guest on *The Name's the Same*, a television game show in which panelists guessed a celebrity's secret wish. Coburn's wish was to dance the rhumba with Marilyn, as he had in *Gentlemen Prefer Blondes*. Coburn died at the age of 84, about a year before Marilyn (Churchwell 48; Taraborrelli 2009, 292–3).

HARRY COHN Harry Cohn, the founder and president of Columbia Pictures, was the archetypal autocratic movie mogul. Gossip columnist Hedda Hopper said of him, "You had to stand in line to hate him." At his funeral Red Skelton said of the large gathering, "It

proves what they always say: Give the public what they want to see and they'll come out for it." Cohn himself said, "I don't have ulcers, I give them!" (Victor 59).

In March 1948, Cohn was persuaded to put MM on a six-month contract at $125 a week. Cohn had known Marilyn's mother, Gladys Baker, who had worked for him as a film cutter. In one of his finer moments, Cohn kept Gladys on salary even after she entered a mental institution.

During her time at Columbia, Marilyn made a low-budget musical called *Ladies of the Chorus*. She had to convince Cohn in his office that she could do her own singing. Oddly enough, the Christian Science religion might have had something to do with Marilyn getting the part. Marilyn dropped a Christian Science publication on the floor and Cohn, whose wife was a practitioner of the religion, saw it. His attitude toward Marilyn, who had grown up in the religion, immediately changed. Even so, when her six months were up, Cohn did not renew Marilyn's contract. He said that he did not think Marilyn had potential. Biographers have suggested something different: Marilyn turned down Cohn's sexual advances, refusing to spend a weekend with him on his yacht. When he saw the rushes of *Ladies of the Chorus*, Cohn reportedly turned to the producer and said, "Why'd you put that fat cow in the picture? You fucking her?" (Shevey 136). In 1953, Marilyn sent Cohn a photo from *Gentlemen Prefer Blondes* sarcastically inscribed, "To my great benefactor, Harry Cohn" (Victor 60).

Other sources: Guiles 136–9; Slatzer 224–5; Summers 59.

CLAUDETTE COLBERT Durable screen legend who won an Oscar for *It Happened One Night* (1934). In 1951, Colbert was the star of *Let's Make it Legal*, a light comedy in which MM had a small part. Marilyn was awe-stricken by Colbert and was nervous and self-conscious in her presence. Colbert did not feel threatened in the least by the beautiful and much younger blonde starlet. In fact, Colbert went out of her way to make Marilyn feel at ease. Colbert was aware of Marilyn's difficult beginnings and saw her as someone who had risen above them.

Zachary Scott, another actor in the film, remembered: "Claudette was the soul of patience with her, for she sensed the suffering and insecurity under Marilyn's poses. I remember in one scene I was dancing with Claudette while Marilyn was dancing with Macdonald Carey, and Marilyn's and my backs touched during the scene—I think the couples were supposed to bump into each other, or something, and damned if she wasn't trembling uncontrollably. I could feel all her back muscles rippling—how it doesn't show on camera stumps me, but it doesn't. I mentioned, as I recall, something about this to Claudette later, and she gave one of her wonderful little commiserating, compassionate shrugs, as if to say: poor girl, she is a keyed-up one" (Quirk 1985, 167).

NAT KING COLE   Jazz pianist, songwriter and singer famed for his smooth-as-velvet voice. On August 5, 1962, just hours after MM had been found dead in her bed from an overdose of barbiturates, there was a black-tie gala at the Ambassador Hotel in New York in honor of Nat King Cole. Toward the end of the gala, the master of ceremonies, Steve Allen, delicately brought up the subject of Marilyn by saying that people had not waited too late to demonstrate their affection for Cole. Cole was overcome with emotion.

Even though he was only 43 he felt like he was attending his own funeral. Cole told a newspaper reporter what he thought about Marilyn's passing: "It's tragic. I really don't know what to say. I was shocked when I heard the news as I left Salt Lake City to come here. She seemed so full of life when I saw her just a few weeks ago." Cole was referring to a party at Peter Lawford's house, after which he and songwriter Jimmy Van Heusen gave Marilyn a ride home. Cole did not mention that when he returned to his own house at two A.M., his wife was so angry she threw a shoe at him (Epstein 1999, 324–5).

CONSTANCE COLLIER   British stage and film actress who worked in Hollywood from 1916 to 1950. Collier was also a drama coach with an impressive array of students that included Katharine Hepburn, Audrey Hepburn, and Vivien Leigh. Prior to her death in April 1955, Collier had MM as one of her students. Marilyn attended Collier's funeral with Truman Capote. It was Capote who brought Collier and Marilyn together. Perceiving them as polar opposites, Capote thought they would make an intriguing combination. Collier initially resisted. She was elderly, her eyesight was weak and she had never seen any of Marilyn's movies. The only thing Collier knew about Marilyn was her reputation as a notorious bleached-blonde sex goddess. But Collier's opinion of Marilyn changed when she actually met her. Collier has this to say about Marilyn: "She is a beautiful child.... I don't think she's an actress at all, not in any traditional sense. What she has—this presence, this luminosity, this flickering intelligence—could never surface on the stage. It's so fragile and subtle, it can only be caught by the camera.... But anyone who thinks this girl is simply another Harlow or harlot or whatever, is *mad*.... I hope, I really pray, that she survives long enough to free the strange lovely talent that's wandering through her like a jailed spirit" (Capote 1980, 226–7).

JOAN COLLINS   British actress who achieved her greatest fame on American television in *Dynasty* (1981–1989). At a Hollywood party Collins saw an unremarkable blonde girl sitting quietly by herself. She wandered over and started a conversation. The girl "wore a white knitted silky dress, rather low-cut, and sleeveless, and no bra, which was frightfully daring in the mid-fifties. Her short blond hair was combed carelessly. She had little makeup on her averagely pretty face. It was hard to realize that this was Marilyn Monroe in the flesh! She appeared to be at the party without a date.... She seemed glad that someone was talking to her and we discussed astrology and found out that we were both born under the sign of Gemini—'the terrible twins'.... It was fascinating to talk to the world-famous Monroe—legendary sex symbol and idol of millions. She seemed a pretty but shy girl, with some complexes and a distrust of people. She left the party early, and I wondered if we would ever bump into each other on the Fox lot. But Marilyn was so insulated from the outside world at the studio that I never did see her again" (Collins 75).

After completing *The Seven Year Itch*, in 1955, Twentieth Century–Fox planned to put Marilyn in *The Girl in the Red Velvet Swing* but she refused to consider it. When the film came to be made, Joan Collins got the part that would have been Marilyn's. The film garnered generally poor reviews (Riese & Hitchens 99).

CHESTER CONKLIN   Comic actor who started out doing slapstick in Keystone Cops silents for producer Mack Sennett. Conklin had an uncredited part in 1950's *Right Cross*, a boxing drama in which MM, as Dusky Ledoux, also went uncredited (*www.imdb.com*).

HANS CONREID   Tall, thin character actor and voice actor who was usually in light comedy roles. In 1956, Conreid was in *Bus Stop* with MM. In a non-comic role he played a photographer from *Life* magazine. Conreid, who was on screen with Marilyn for less than a minute, maintained that he was tricked into doing the film by director Josh Logan's flattery (Gargiulo 202; *www.imdb.com*).

RICHARD CONTE   In a career which lasted from the 1940s to the 1970s, Richard Conte made mostly film noir gangster movies. Fresh from her success in *All About Eve* and *The Asphalt Jungle*, MM did a screen test for Twentieth Century–Fox in 1950. The movie in question was *Cold Shoulder*. In the test, Marilyn was a gangster's girlfriend and Conte, true to form, was the gangster. The picture was never made but Fox was sufficiently impressed by Marilyn to re-sign her after having dropped her earlier. It was probably just as well that Marilyn was never in *Cold Shoulder*, because she would have had to utter lines such as these from the screen test as Conte is about to hit her. "Go ahead! It won't be the first time I've

been worked over today.... I'm getting used to it" (Victor 263). Conte noticed that during the test Marilyn was intense and utterly focused (Riese & Hitchens 102; Spoto 1993, 175; *www.imdb.com*).

ELISHA COOK, JR.   Actor who seemed to have cornered the market on neurotics and cowards. As Wilmer the gunsel in *The Maltese Falcon* (1941), Cook was the definitive neurotic coward. Cook was in the cast of *Don't Bother to Knock* (1952) playing MM's uncle (*www.imdb.com*).

ALISTAIR COOKE   Urbane British journalist and commentator who spent most of his long life in the United States. A couple of days after MM's tragic death, this is what Alistair Cooke had to say about her:

In this sense, Marilyn Monroe was all of a piece. She was confused, pathologically shy, a straw on the ocean of her compulsions (to pout, to wisecrack, to love a stranger, to be six hours late or lock herself in her room). She was a sweet and humorous person increasingly terrified by the huge stereotype of herself she saw plastered all around her. The exploitation of this pneumatic, mocking, liquid-lipped goddess gave the world a simple picture of the Lorelei. She was about as much of a Lorelei as Bridget, the housemaid.

This orphan of the rootless City of the Angels at last could feel no other identity than the one she saw in the mirror: a baffled, honest girl forever haunted by the nightmare of herself, sixty feet tall and naked before a howling mob. She could never learn to acquire the lacquered shell of the prima donna or the armor of sophistication. So in the end she found the ultimate oblivion, of which her chronic latecomings and desperate retreats to her room were tokens [Cooke 136–7].

LADY DIANA COOPER, VISCOUNTESS NORWICH   English aristocrat, socialite and actress. Lady Cooper met Marilyn Monroe in 1956 at a party at playwright Terrence Rattigan's house near London. Marilyn was in England shooting *The Prince and the Showgirl* with Laurence Olivier. Lady Cooper recalled, "Marilyn Monroe charmed everyone with her pretty face and *mal pendue derriere*— *mal pendue* yet featured by having so thin a layer of material that every fold and muscle and contraction of its cleft could be studied.

She danced in ecstasy and exclusively with her husband" (Ziegler 296).

GARY COOPER On November 6, 1954, a black-tie dinner party for 80 guests was held at Romanoff's Restaurant in Beverly Hills. The occasion was officially a celebration of the completion of *The Seven Year Itch*, but it was really to welcome MM into the ranks of Hollywood's elite. Two-time Academy Award–winner Gary Cooper was one of the invited guests. He was seated at a table which had a cardboard centerpiece of Marilyn in the skirt-blowing scene from the film (Leaming 1998, 134; Shaw & Rosten 70, 72–3).

JOAN COPELAND Actress who was the younger sister of playwright, Arthur Miller. During her marriage to Miller, MM was Copeland's sister-in-law. Copeland was a member of the Actors Studio in New York and remembered Marilyn auditing some of the classes. She was not then aware of Marilyn's involvement with her brother. Copeland recognized Marilyn, of course, and thought it took courage for her to turn her back on Hollywood.

Copeland gives us a vivid description of the wedding of Marilyn to Arthur Miller on July 1, 1956:

> It was a very hot July day. Everyone was warm from waiting a lot. Then everybody took off their jackets because it was very hot and it was outside. There was a lot of sun that day. It was an excited and exciting afternoon. I remember that she was *late* for the wedding. They were driving down from Roxbury. She was late and kept everybody waiting. She arrived in jeans or something. Afterwards she came out of the bedroom dressed in beige—wearing a beautiful off-white beige veil. There was always a low-grade fever amongst all of the spectators whenever she was around which was titillating. You always felt excited when you were around her. That day she was absolutely and incredibly radiant. She was like a "bolt of moonlight" walking into the room. Although it was daytime, she was all aglow. She was some sort of vision and she always seemed to have a halo around her. You know those creatures from outer space—how the atmosphere around them shimmers? Well, that was how Marilyn looked, her whole body glowed from within. She had the

most incredible translucent kind of skin—almost alabaster in colour [Shevey 342–3].

Copeland had been puzzled, however, by Marilyn's conversion to Judaism before the wedding. The Millers had never been a religious family and it had been her own idea to convert. Copeland sensed that, because of her deprived early years, Marilyn had a desperate need to belong to something, in this case a family, a community and a religion. Ultimately, Copeland came to think that Marilyn and Arthur were mismatched.

In 1958, Copeland had a supporting role in Paddy Chayefsky's film *The Goddess*, which was loosely based on Marilyn's life (Gottfried 2003, 333; Riese & Hitchens 104; Shevey 310, 319–20).

JOSEPH COTTEN Character actor who played MM's husband in 1953's *Niagara*. At the time, Cotten remarked: "Everything that girl does is sexy. A lot of people—the ones who haven't met Marilyn—will tell you it's all publicity. That's malarkey, they've tried to give a hundred girls the same publicity build-up. It didn't take with them. This girl's really got it!" (Riese & Hitchens 106). Cotten genuinely liked Marilyn. He enjoyed working with her, responded to her sense of humor and even forgave her compulsive lateness. Cotton described his first meeting with Marilyn at a party in his hotel room in Niagara Falls, Ontario.

> "Is this where the party is?" We shook hands. She came in and bestowed a velvety sensuous "Hi!" on those assembled. Covering her feet were large terry cloth slippers, and covering the rest of her was a large white terry cloth robe, on the back of which was written, in scarlet letters, "Sherry Netherlands Hotel, New York." Somebody behind her laughed. She said, "Oh, that. I thought I had stolen this robe, until I paid my bill."
> She took orange juice and sat on the floor. One glimpse of her figure either in that bulky robe or in what she accurately described as "my little black dress," would once again prove [director William] Dieterle's theory on nature copying art to be sound. Each curve was in the right place, but like a painted illustration in *Playboy* magazine, each was conspicuously exaggerated. Socially she tried not to rock the boat. She was outgiving and charming. If you wanted to talk about yourself, she listened. She was defensively shy. If you wanted to talk about her, she blushed.

If you wanted to sing, she joined the chorus [Cotton 109–10].

Cotten went on to say: "At times she glowed with the joy of discovery and then, suddenly, her focus would move into outer space, thrusting her into a cloud of blankness. This dilution of thought, this quick snapping of concentration sometimes happened to her in the middle of acting a scene, and recovery was not always easy for her. At the time, it seemed to me that she was cursed with less than her share of confidence and more than her share of insecurity, both dark synonyms for fear" (Cotten 110).

NOËL COWARD Prolific English playwright, songwriter, actor and director. When Coward heard that his friend Laurence Olivier was about to make *The Prince and the Showgirl* (1957) with MM, he was worried that the experience "might conceivably drive him round the bend" (Payn & Sheridan 308). Coward did approve of the finished product but after attending the film's premiere, he wrote: "Marilyn Monroe looks very pretty and is charming at moments but too much emphasis on tits and bottom" (Payn & Sheridan 358).

Upon hearing of Marilyn's death, Coward confided in his diary: "Marilyn Monroe committed suicide yesterday. The usual overdose. Poor silly creature. I am convinced that what brought her to that final foolish gesture was a steady diet of intellectual pretentiousness pumped into her over the years by Arthur Miller and "The Method" She was, to begin with, a fairly normal little sexpot with exploitable curves and a certain natural talent. I am sure that all the idiocies of her last few years, always being late on the set, etc., plus over-publicity and too many theoretical discussions about acting, were the result of all this constant analysis of every line in every part she had to play, and a desperate longing to be "intellectual" without the brain to achieve it. It is a sad comment on contemporary values that a beautiful, famous and wealthy young woman of thirty-six should capriciously kill herself for want of a little self-discipline and horse-sense" (Payn & Sheridan 511).

Noël Coward and Marilyn Monroe never met but they should have, because in January 1957 they were in close proximity. Between January 3 and January 19, 1957, Marilyn and Arthur Miller were vacationing in Jamaica, not far from where Coward had a house. There is no record that Marilyn knew of Coward's presence, but he knew she was there. In a January 12, 1957 letter to Laurence Olivier, from his house in Port Maria, Jamaica, Coward wrote, "My house on Firefly Hill is paradise and all my loved ones scrabble about down in Blue Harbour. I sometimes permit them to come up for meals and sometimes, with exquisite magnanimity, I descend to their level ... and Marilyn Monroe is just along the coast, what more can one ask?" (Coward 618).

WALLY COX Slight-statured Hollywood actor who usually portrayed eggheads and nerds. Cox's greatest success came with television's *Mr. Peepers* (1952–1954). George Cukor, director of MM's unfinished *Something's Got to Give* (1962), wanted newcomer Don Knotts to play the part of a gauche shoe salesman. But Marilyn had cast approval and wanted Cox instead, for what would have been his feature-film debut. Marilyn got her way. Cox was a friend of Marilyn's, having been introduced to her in 1961 by mutual friend Marlon Brando.

On one occasion Marilyn was feeling unwell and Cox was driving her in his car. Noticing how slowly he was driving, Marilyn said to Cox, "I'm afraid you're going to be arrested for illegal parking" (Wilson 69).

On the set of *Something's Got to Give* Marilyn celebrated her 36th birthday, her last as it turned out. Soon the party relocated to fellow cast member Dean Martin's dressing room. We are then presented with the improbable image of Marilyn Monroe sitting on Wally Cox's lap: "Thirty-six, huh?" said Cox. "Do you feel thirty-six?" She nestled her head against his shoulder. "I feel thirty-six and then some. And each day on this movie makes me feel even older." Later, Marilyn continued the celebration at Marlon Brando's house, with Cox in tow (Brown & Barham 179).

BOB CRANE Actor remembered for his role as Colonel Hogan on television's *Hogan's Heroes* (1965–1971) and the fact that he was the victim of an unsolved murder. A ca. 1961 photograph exists of Marilyn Monroe with Crane in the Fox studio dressing rooms (*www.cursumperficio.net*/files/Marilyn: 60s; *www.wikipedia.net*).

BRODERICK CRAWFORD Heavyset, tough-talking character actor who achieved lasting fame from television's *Highway Patrol* (1955–1958) and its immortal sign-off, "Ten-four." On November 5, 1954, a jealous Joe DiMaggio and his then pal, Frank Sinatra, staged what came to be known as the "Wrong Door Raid." They broke into an apartment in Los Angeles expecting to catch Marilyn in the arms of a lover. Unfortunately, they broke into the wrong apartment. One source claims that they recruited burly actor Broderick Crawford, figuring that he would be better able to kick down the door (Glatzer 115).

JOAN CRAWFORD Hollywood screen legend. Joan Crawford met MM in 1947 when Marilyn was an unknown starlet. The reports vary. It was either at producer Joe Schenck's house or at St. Victor's Roman Catholic Church which Marilyn, though a Christian Scientist, was attending. Crawford thought Marilyn looked sloppy and needed some advice. She said to her, "You're very pretty my dear, but you don't know shit about clothes" (Considine 1989, 281). Crawford invited Marilyn to her home, and Marilyn was delighted to accept. A friendship blossomed and Marilyn became a frequent visitor. Crawford took Marilyn on a tour through her vast wardrobe and on one occasion told her to try things on. Marilyn, who never wore underwear, was uninhibited about stepping out of her street clothes then and there. Crawford may have made a sexual advance which was spurned. Whatever happened or did not happen, Crawford loathed Marilyn from that time on.

Crawford's hatred burst forth at the 1953 Photoplay Awards. Marilyn was given the award for Fastest Rising Star. To the accompaniment of wolf whistles and hoots, she upstaged Crawford, who was Favorite Actress, by wiggling into the room in a gold-lamé dress which was so tight she literally had to be sewn into it. Crawford went ballistic, denouncing Marilyn as a tramp and a disgrace to the movie industry in general and womanhood in particular. In an interview Crawford said, "Kids don't like her ... and don't forget the women. They're the ones who pick out the movie entertainment for the families, underneath it all they like to know all actresses are ladies" (Thomas 1978, 174). Privately, Crawford said, "There's nothing wrong with my tits but I don't go around throwing them in people's faces" (Thomas 1978, 173).

Marilyn was deeply hurt by Crawford's remarks, but wisely held her tongue. She confined her remarks to Louella Parsons's newspaper column saying: "At first all I could think of was 'Why should she select me to blast?' She's a great star, I'm just starting. The thing that hit me hardest is that it came from her. Along with Bette Davis and Katharine Hepburn, Miss Crawford was one of my favorite actresses. I've always admired her for being such a wonderful mother—for taking four children and giving them a fine home. Who better than I knows what it means to care for homeless little ones?"[25] (Thomas 1978, 175). Crawford replied that her criticism of Marilyn was the criticism she would give her own daughter. Marilyn had no further comment.

Crawford and Marilyn crossed paths once more. It was in London on October 29, 1955. The occasion was a royal command performance, during which a host of film stars was presented to Queen Elizabeth II. Crawford snarled, "The Queen is a lady, and expects to meet other ladies, but most of today's actresses can't even act politely. That night as her majesty came up the staircase, Monroe's hairdresser was still doing her hair. And the girl didn't even know how to curtsy"[26] (Considine 1989, 304).

During the making of *Some Like It Hot* (1959) Marilyn supposedly said, "When Marilyn Monroe comes into a room nobody's going to be looking at Tony Curtis playing Joan

Crawford. They're going to be looking at Marilyn Monroe" (Victor 281).

When Clark Gable died just days after completing *The Misfits* (1960) Crawford blamed Marilyn for his death. The way she saw it, the stress of being on location in the blistering Nevada desert when Marilyn was being temperamental, always late and never able to remember her lines, brought on Gable's fatal heart attack.

Crawford was openly delighted when Marilyn was fired from *Something's Got to Give* in 1962. "I was proud to be a part of this industry when Marilyn was fired. I don't think she has a friend in this town because she hasn't taken the time to make any" (Considine 1989, 330).

However, on August 5, 1962, Crawford, like millions of others, was shocked to hear that Marilyn Monroe had died. She quickly went to director George Cukor's house. Said Cukor:

> Joan came to my house that evening. She was in bad shape. She had been drinking. She was very angry. I thought at first she was angry at me. She kept saying, "Dammit, George, this shouldn't have happened! Something should have been done!" I felt she was being a hypocrite, as were many others in town. People who were nasty to Marilyn when she was alive, with good reason perhaps, were now gathered in a weeping circle. Eventually, I said to Joan, "What is this? You never liked Marilyn."
>
> Joan answered, "Yes! You're right. She was cheap, an exhibitionist. She was *never* a professional, and that irritated the hell out of people. But, for God's sake, she needed help. She had all these people on her payroll. Where the hell were they when she needed them? Why in hell did she have to die alone? [Considine 1989, 331].

Other sources: Churchwell 218–19, 235–6; Guiles 212–14; Riese & Hitchens 107–9].

BING CROSBY   Legendary crooner and Academy Award–winning actor. In 1960, Crosby had a cameo in MM's *Let's Make Love*. That same day Crosby had completed shooting *High Times* and did a cameo with Cantinflas in *Pepe*—three movies in one day, surely a record. During the weekend of March 24, 1962, Marilyn and John Kennedy shared a guest bungalow on Crosby's Palm Springs

property (Brown & Barham 71–2; Taraborrelli 2009, 409–12; Thompson 435).

BOSLEY CROWTHER   Influential film critic at the *New York Times* who was a booster of MM. After 1956's *Bus Stop* he said: "Hold onto your chairs everybody, and get set for a rattling surprise. Marilyn Monroe has finally proved herself an actress in *Bus Stop*. Fortunately for her and for the tradition of diligence leading to success, she gives a performance in this picture that marks her as a genuine acting star, not just a plushy personality and a sex symbol, as she has previously been" (*New York Times* Sept. 1, 1956).

After Marilyn died, Crowther remarked: "The Monroe personality, as established and developed over the years, was that of a gorgeous young woman, healthy, good-humored, full of warmth and eager for honest self-improvement, despite intellectual limitations and crudities. It was a highly potential personality, apt for satire as well as farce, and open, it seemed, for extension to drama and tragedy. Indeed it appeared from the appealing and poignant performance that Miss Monroe gave in *Bus Stop* ... and from some of her ... tender scenes in her last picture *Misfits* ... that she was headed for stronger creations than those earlier comedies" (Shevey 57–8).

GEORGE CUKOR   Prolific American film director. Cukor directed MM in *Let's Make Love* (1960) and *Something's Got to Give* (1962). The first is generally considered to be Marilyn's worst movie and the second was never completed. During the shooting of those films Marilyn was deeply troubled and consumed by her fears and insecurities; plagued with poor health, drug dependency and insomnia. She needed multiple takes for even the simplest scenes, she was hospitalized, was usually late and sometimes did not turn up at all. Cukor was amazingly patient with Marilyn and endeavored to shoot around her when she was not available. Cukor devised the technique of filming Marilyn delivering one or two lines of dialogue at a time and then stitching the snippets together to make a complete performance.

Of Marilyn's inner torment Cukor said: "There's been an awful lot of crap written about Marilyn Monroe, and there may be an exact psychiatric term for what was wrong with her, I don't know—but truth to tell, I think she was quite mad. The mother was mad, and poor Marilyn was mad. I know people who say, 'Hollywood broke her heart,' and all that, but I don't believe it. She was very observant and tough-minded and appealing, but she had this bad judgment about things. She adored and trusted the wrong people." Cukor also thought Marilyn was a very accomplished natural actress but had got herself bound up with a lot of pretentious nonsense and pretentious people. As he put it, "She'd done a lot of shit-ass studying" (Lambert 174).

Despite everything she put him through, Cukor liked Marilyn. He was probably a little in love with her and always ready to forgive her. He thought she was sweet, very intelligent and driven to succeed. To him, Marilyn was the reincarnation of Jean Harlow, whom he had directed in *Dinner at Eight* in 1933. He remembered one day when, as usual, Marilyn was late for work. "I was annoyed, and then I watched her run across the stage in high heels (she always wore high heels), and it was so beautiful to watch, I just enjoyed watching her running and forgave her.... But if she was a victim of any kind, she was a victim of friends" (Lambert 180).

Cukor had met Marilyn as early as 1954 at the home of actress and drama coach Constance Collier. In 1956, Marilyn had drawn up a list of approved directors and Cukor made the list. When the opportunity came to work with Cukor, Marilyn was quite excited at the prospect.

During the making of *Let's Make Love*, Cukor would stifle his frustration over Marilyn's tardiness by stuffing his mouth with bits of paper torn from the script. When Marilyn finally arrived Cukor would swallow the paper in a gulp and greet his star with delight. Marilyn's key song in the film was "My Heart Belongs to Daddy," and she had a lot of trouble with it. Marilyn associated the lyrics with her first husband, Jim Dougherty, whom she used

to call "Daddy" and her current husband, Arthur Miller, whom she called "Papa." To finish the six-minute production number Cukor had to work with her for 11 days! On working with Marilyn on *Let's Make Love*, Cukor said, "I didn't try to treat her like I was her sugar daddy or to win her with my baby-blue eyes. I just tried to create a climate in which she felt at ease and found it possible to work. She knew that I could help her deliver the goods and she trusted me" (Phillips 157, 159).

Marilyn grew even more unstable during the making of *Something's Got to Give*. When Twentieth Century–Fox discovered that after weeks of work there was hardly any usable footage of Marilyn, they fired her. Cukor had no part in her dismissal and, as always, was gallant and sympathetic toward her: "Marilyn was more or less on time when we made *Let's Make Love*. But when we were making *Something's Got to Give*, her preoccupation with her emotional difficulties made it an agony for her to come to the studio at all; and even when she did, she might get sick or fall asleep in her dressing room and fail to report to the set anyhow. I think she knew she wasn't doing a good job when she did play a scene, and she therefore became more and more terrified of facing the cameras, with the result that she would look for any excuse not to. Her behavior often seemed bullying, as if she were simply being willfully unaccommodating in keeping everyone waiting for her. But she wasn't deliberately heedless, though practically speaking I suppose it came to that. It's sad, but she infuriated just about everyone. And in the end I found that I could no longer reach her" (Phillips 159–60). Cukor believed that Marilyn was doomed to a tragic end and was not surprised when she was found dead.

E. E. CUMMINGS American poet and playwright who died at the age of 67, just twenty-nine days after Marilyn. MM and Cummings never met but Marilyn surely would have liked to. Arthur Miller recalled Marilyn's discovery of Cummings's poetry in a bookstore: "It was odd to watch her reading

Cummings to herself, moving her lips—what would she make of poetry that was so simple yet so sophisticated? ...There was apprehension in her eyes when she began to read, the look of a student afraid to be caught out, but suddenly she laughed in a thoroughly unaffected way at the small surprising turn in the poem.... The naive wonder in her face that she could so easily respond to a stylized work sent a filament of connection out between us.... How pleased with her fresh reaction Cummings would have been" (Miller 1987, 306).

TONY CURTIS Curtis starred opposite MM in 1959's *Some Like It Hot*, one of the greatest screen comedies. Marilyn thought Curtis was handsome and was initially excited about working with him. The two knew each other before the film came to be made. They were seen in public on February 8, 1952, when Marilyn was voted "Best Young Box Office" personality; on January 7, 1955; at a press conference and party announcing the formation of Marilyn Monroe Productions; and four days later, at a trendy nightclub where Sammy Davis, Jr., was performing. Although some reports claim that the two had a one-night stand in 1949 or 1950, their relationship on the set of *Some Like It Hot* quickly became one of mutual hatred. Marilyn was fabulous on screen but getting a performance out of her was torture for everyone else, especially Curtis. Curtis was driven to distraction by Marilyn's rampant unprofessionalism. He complained that she was arrogant and vindictive. Curtis, in full drag, had to stand around for hours waiting for his co-star to show up. When she did show up, she could not remember her lines. In one scene all Marilyn had to do was say, "Where's that bourbon?" It took 65 takes to get it right! Take after take, Marilyn grew steadily better, while Curtis began to wilt. When Curtis learned that Marilyn's best takes were always the ones used, he blew his stack. Curtis famously said of her, "Kissing Marilyn was like kissing Hitler." When she heard about his remark Marilyn said, "Well, I think that's his problem. If I have to do intimate love scenes with somebody who really has that feeling to-

ward me, then my fantasy has to come into play—in other words, out with him, in with my fantasy. He was never there" (Rollyson 1993, 206; *www.cursumperficio.net*/biography/1955).

-D-

ARLENE DAHL Glamorous movie actress of the 1950s. On October 29, 1956, Arlene Dahl's and MM's lives intersected in London. It was the occasion of the Royal Command Film Performance for *The Battle of the River Plate*. Marilyn and Dahl, among other celebrities, were presented to Queen Elizabeth II. They met again in February 1962 at a New York dinner party in honor of President John F. Kennedy. Dahl noticed that when Marilyn walked in "everything stopped, everyone stopped. It was magical, really. I've never seen anyone stop a room like that.... People just wanted to stand near her, smell her fragrance, breathe the same air as she" (Taraborrelli 2009, 406; *www.imdb.com*).

DAN DAILEY American dancer and movie actor. Dailey was the star of *You Were Meant for Me* (1948), in which MM was an uncredited extra. He was also in *A Ticket to Tomahawk* (1950), in which Marilyn had a bit part as Clara, a dance-hall girl. Marilyn's big scene occurred when she and the other girls had a song-and-dance number with Dailey. By 1954 Marilyn was co-starring with Dailey in *There's No Business Like Show Business*. They did not share too much screen time in that film but were photographed chatting on the set (Riese & Hitchens 113; *www.imdb.com*).

BILL DANA Comedian famous for his dimwitted José Jiménez character. Dana was at Madison Square Garden on May 19, 1962, as part of President John F. Kennedy's birthday party and fundraiser for the Democratic National Committee. The star of the evening was MM and, true to form, she was late. Dana suggested to the master of ceremonies, Peter Lawford, that when she finally arrived he should introduce her as "the late Marilyn Monroe." Lawford followed Dana's advice (Spoto 1993, 520).

DOROTHY DANDRIDGE Acclaimed African-American actress and singer. As early as 1948, at the Actors Lab in Los Angeles and at exercise classes, Dandridge struck up a friendship with the then unknown MM. The friendship endured as the two actresses would meet and discuss their careers and hopes for the future. Dandridge had a small white rug in front of her fireplace. It was on this that Marilyn liked to stretch out, all the while bemoaning her relationships. Dandridge was one of the first to hear the news of Marilyn's nude calendar shots. She reassured Marilyn that the so-called scandal would not harm her career. Dandridge wanted to play the role of Cherie in the film version of *Bus Stop* (1956) but Marilyn got the part. Dandridge was devastated when her friend died (Bogle 178–180).

BOBBY DARIN Popular actor and singer who died at the age of 37. Darin was listed on the program at the May 19, 1962 Madison Square Garden birthday salute to President John F. Kennedy. Darin witnessed Marilyn sing "Happy Birthday, Mr. President" before 17,000 people, each of whom shelled out $100 for a ticket (*www.cursumperficio.net*/files/ Madison Square Garden).

MARION DAVIES Hollywood actress whose claim to fame was that she was the mistress of newspaper tycoon William Randolph Hearst. On May 26, 1961, MM had an operation at Cedars of Lebanon Hospital in Los Angeles. While Marilyn recovered in the hospital's VIP wing, Marion Davies was in the same ward dying of cancer. Upon learning of Marilyn's admission to the hospital, Davies told columnist Hedda Hopper, "We blondes seem to be falling apart." Davies died about four months later, at the age of 64 (Guiles 429–30).

BETTE DAVIS Two-time Academy Award winning screen legend who appeared opposite starlet MM in 1950's *All About Eve*. Davis was such an intimidating presence that Marilyn would cry and vomit after shooting a scene with her. The situation was not helped when Davis, within Marilyn's hearing, snarled: "That little blonde slut can't act her way out of a paper bag! She thinks if she wiggles her ass and coos away, she can carry her scene—well, she can't" (Quirk 1990, 336). Davis went out of her way to make cutting remarks to Marilyn, including "I know and you know and everyone knows that kitten voice of yours is goddamned lousy and it's lousy because you never trained it as a real actress does—a shame you never had stage training!" (Quirk 1990, 337).

Years later Davis commented on Marilyn in *All About Eve*. "A *mess*. Poor thing. Nobody imagined she would become a star. A nervous breakdown—*that* seemed inevitable.... I did *like* her. Of course, I didn't give her much thought. Again, anyone could have played Miss Dumb Blonde.... I really didn't think she belonged in film, and certainly she would have been out of her depth on stage. But a nice girl." Davis also said, "Did you know that Marilyn Monroe used to dye her pubic hair? ...My god! It's a wonder she didn't die sooner—from poisoning of the vulva!" (Hadleigh 212).

SAMMY DAVIS, JR. Dynamic singer, entertainer and actor who described himself as a "one-eyed Jewish Negro" (Victor 69). Davis knew MM but never worked with her. It has been alleged that sometime, between 1954–1955 they had an affair. Davis said, "To me, Marilyn was one of the sweetest creatures that ever lived" (Davis & Boyar 90–1). He denied that they were anything more than good friends. Said Marilyn about Davis: "On stage he makes me think of Cary Grant" (Haygood 171). In 1954, Davis was in a devastating automobile crash which resulted in the loss of his left eye. Making his first public appearance after his release from hospital, Davis went to see Mel Tormé perform. With him was Marilyn. A few days later Davis went to a Hollywood party in his honor and Marilyn was there as well. Marilyn saw Davis perform in Las Vegas and, near the end of her life, Davis reputedly acted as a beard for President Kennedy, escorting her to various functions. Davis, along with other stars, was turned away from Marilyn's funeral. Davis said: "Still she hangs like a bat in the heads of the men who met her, and none of us will forget her" (Victor 69). Years later, Davis recalled Marilyn telling him that she was in an orphanage as a child and had suffered so much from nightmares that she put gravel in her bed to keep herself awake. Davis came to the conclusion that saving Marilyn was an impossible task.

DORIS DAY   Highly successful singer and actress whose output of antiseptic film comedies in the 1950s and 1960s earned her the sobriquet of "The Professional Virgin." Day met MM in 1955 at the celebration following the completion of *The Seven Year Itch*. That same year, Day began plans to adapt *The Sleeping Prince* and have it filmed in England. But in 1956, Marilyn beat Day to the punch when she held a press conference to announce that she and Sir Laurence Olivier were about to film the same story in England as *The Prince and the Showgirl*. In 1962, after Marilyn had been fired from *Something's Got to Give*, Doris Day was one of a half-dozen actresses considered to replace her. Day was wary of replacing Marilyn and declined the offer. However, in 1963, after Marilyn had died, *Something's Got to Give* was retooled as a Doris Day vehicle, *Move Over Darling* (Braun 161–2 ; Riese & Hitchens 118–19; Victor 71).

OLIVIA DE HAVILLAND   Screen actress who was awarded two Academy Awards. When she was an unknown bit player, MM found herself at a star-studded Hollywood party at the home of a Hollywood agent. Feeling somewhat self-conscious, Marilyn was thrilled to spot one of her favorite actresses standing nearby, Olivia de Havilland. (Monroe & Hecht 56).

JAMES DEAN   Moody film actor who died young and posthumously attained superstar status. Dean was an occasional visitor to Lee Strasberg's Actors Studio in New York, as was MM. Even so, there is no record that the two ever met there. Marilyn and Dean should have met on March 9, 1955, at a benefit for the Actors Studio. Marilyn, volunteering as an usherette, handed out programs at the advance screening of Dean's film, *East of Eden*. James Dean chose not to attend the event. Marilyn and Dean did meet in Hollywood in 1954 at a screening of Marlon Brando's *On the Waterfront*. They did not care for each other. In Dean's opinion Marilyn was a self-obsessed movie star, personifying everything he hated about Hollywood. Marilyn thought Dean was a pretty boy, a punk and an intellectual lightweight. On the way home from the screening Marilyn was in a car with Shelley Winters. Winters recalled: "Jimmy [on his motorcycle] came roaring down the mountain. He started the deadly game of circling us. I was so angry, I was ready to run him over. I kept honking at him and he kept putting his brakes on right in front of me. He was laughing and enjoying the game.... When we got to the Chateau Marmont, I quickly drove to the underground garage. Jimmy followed. Marilyn was rigid with fear, and I was ready to punch him out" (Winters 1989, 48).

GENERAL WILLIAM F. DEAN   A major general in the United States Army, Medal of Honor winner and war hero. General Dean was the highest ranking American officer captured by the enemy during the Korean War. After three years of imprisonment in North Korea, he returned stateside in October 1953. On December 13 of that year General Dean was the guest of honor at a party at Bob Hope's house. Marilyn was one of the other guests and was photographed laughing and talking with the general (*www.wikipedia.org* ; *www.cursumperficio.net* / files / DiMaggio).

GLORIA DEHAVEN   About ten months older than Marilyn Monroe, Gloria DeHaven was an MGM contract player who had an extensive career in film and television. Marilyn was a presenter at the 1951 Academy Awards, but just before she was to step on stage she noticed a small tear in her dress. She panicked, declaring that she could not possibly go on. As the dress was quickly repaired, DeHaven was one of those backstage who helped Marilyn overcome her stage fright and make the Oscar presentation (Bilman 77, Victor 2).

REGINALD DENNY   Denny was a dapper English stage, film and televison actor in Hollywood who had an unusual side career—he manufactured radio-controlled model airplanes. At his factory in the San Fernando Valley he manufactured thousands of drones for the United States Army and Navy to be used for target practice by gun crews. One of Denny's factory employees who worked as a parachute inspector and dope painter was Norma Jeane Doughterty. Norma Jeane had started at the factory as a fresh-faced 17-year-old in April 1944 and earned $20 a week. Denny gave his permission for an army photographer, Corporal David Conover, sent by his friend Captain Ronald Reagan, C.O. of the 1st Motion Picture Unit, to visit the plant and shoot morale-building pictures of women doing war work. Denny took Conover into the main assembly room and told him to choose anyone he wanted. Corporal Conover selected Norma Jeane, who was only too happy to get a tight sweater from her locker and pose for the camera. The pictures were sensational and widely distributed. Norma Jeane then started doing print ads, modeling and walk-ons in movies. A few years after that first photo shoot the young model changed her name to Marilyn Monroe. Years later, Marilyn explained to a reporter what she did at Denny's factory.

> I had a job inspecting parachutes—not the kind of parachutes a life depends on,[27] the little parachutes they use to float down the targets after the gunners are through with them. That was before I worked in the "dope" room, the hardest work I've ever done. The fuselage and various parts of the ship were made of cloth at that time—they use metal now—and we used to paint the cloth with stiffening preparation. It wasn't sprayed on; it was worked in with brushes, and it was very tiring and difficult. We used a quick-drying preparation—a type of lacquer, I guess, but heavier—the smell was overpowering, very hard to take for eight hours a day. It was actually a 12-hour day for the other workers, but I only did eight because I was underage. After the cloth dried, we sanded it down to glossy smoothness [Riese & Hitchens 418; Victor 244].

Other sources: Conover 4; Guiles 84–6.

JOHN DEREK   Actor, director and photographer best remembered for his marriages to Ursula Andress, Linda Evans and Bo Derek. A photo ca.1950 exists of Marilyn Monroe and John Derek posing with other up-and-coming young stars. Derek was two months younger than Marilyn and survived her by 36 years (Anderson 41).

VITTORIO DESICA   Italian actor and film director. In 1955, MM submitted to Twentieth Century–Fox a list of 16 approved directors with whom she would be willing to work. Even though DeSica made the list, he and Marilyn were never destined to collaborate (Riese & Hitchens 128; Victor 81).

BRAD DEXTER   Hollywood supporting actor who usually played tough guys. Because of that, he had a very peculiar relationship with MM. Dexter was in only one movie with Marilyn, 1950's *The Asphalt Jungle*. When the movie wrapped, Dexter and Marilyn went their separate ways. Four years later, Dexter answered the telephone and was surprised to hear Marilyn's voice. She was having trouble with her marriage to Joe DiMaggio and thought that Dexter, being a man's man, might be able to get through to her husband. Marilyn invited Dexter to have dinner with her and Joe. Before DiMaggio came home Marilyn told Dexter: "Joe has isolated me; he doesn't want me to associate with anybody in the movie industry. He has a terrible insecurity. He has estranged me even from my actress friends, and I don't know who to turn to. I thought maybe you could be a bridge between us. You're a tough guy, you play poker, and you like sports, and I thought you and Joe could become friends. Then when we're together, you and I could talk about what we did at the studio all day" (Summers 136–7) Dexter left before dinner. He got nowhere with DiMaggio, who was stiff and hostile. A few nights later, in a bizarre turn of events, DiMaggio apologized for his behavior and asked Dexter to conduct a similar mission on *his* behalf. Marilyn was hiding from DiMaggio in her dressing room at Twentieth Century–Fox. Joe wanted Dexter to smuggle him into the studio under a blanket. Dexter suggested that he could phone Marilyn on DiMaggio's behalf. He did so but again got nowhere. Even more strangely, when she was having marital difficulties with Arthur Miller, Marilyn again turned to Dexter as a marriage counselor. Dexter met with Miller, but was unable to make any progress.

It is possible that Marilyn and Dexter met as early as 1946 on the set of the Roy Rogers western, *Heldorado*. The film was being shot in Las Vegas and Marilyn was in town waiting out a divorce from her first husband. Marilyn met Rogers, who invited her to join the cast and crew for dinner. Dexter had a small, uncredited part in the picture (Summers 145–6, 258; *www.imdb.com*).

JAMES DICKEY   American poet and novelist who shot to fame when his novel *Deliverance* was filmed in 1972. In London, ten years earlier, Dickey saw a newspaper headline announcing MM's death and suddenly remembered a couplet from Alexander Pope's *Epistle II: To a Lady*:

> Who purchase pain with all that joy can give
> And die of nothing but a rage to live.

Later Dickey remarked that the couplet was "the perfect expression of Marilyn Monroe's meaning, her existence and her death, and the pleasure oriented, excessive and sterile culture that created her and destroyed her" (Hart 282–3).

ANGIE DICKINSON   Glamorous Hollywood actress. In 1959, Dickinson and two male friends—baseball players Yogi Berra and Whitey Ford—went out to dinner. At first, Dickinson was the center of attention but then Marilyn Monroe came in and sat at a table 14 feet away. Instantly, Dickinson was forgotten as the two men went gaga over Marilyn (Barra 265).

MARLENE DIETRICH   Glamorous German singer and actress who became one of Hollywood's biggest stars. For *Life* magazine's Christmas 1958 issue, MM impersonated Marlene Dietrich before fashion photographer Richard Avedon's camera. Marilyn uncannily reproduced Dietrich's famous top-hatted pose

as the sexy, seductive vamp from 1930's *The Blue Angel*.[28] Marlene Dietrich had met Marilyn in 1955 at a press conference which announced the formation of Marilyn Monroe Productions. When she finished *The Prince and the Showgirl* in 1956, Twentieth Century–Fox wanted Marilyn to do a remake of *The Blue Angel*. Marilyn rejected the idea. When the film came to be made in 1959 without Marilyn, it earned indifferent reviews. According to Dietrich: "Marilyn Monroe was an authentic 'sex symbol,' because not only was she 'sexy' by nature but she also liked being one—and she showed it" (Dietrich 106). After viewing some photographs of Dietrich taken by Eve Arnold, Marilyn approached the photographer and said, "If you could do that well with Marlene, can you imagine what you can do with me?" (Arnold 1976, 56).

JOE DIMAGGIO   Legendary professional baseball player who, in 1954, was married to MM for precisely 286 days. Thereafter, DiMaggio became Marilyn's most devoted friend and support. Marilyn knew next to nothing about baseball (apart from once serving as a bat girl with her roommate Shelley Winters at a celebrity charity event); the closest she had ever come to a game before meeting Joe DiMaggio was a publicity shot she had done with Chicago White Sox players Gus Zernial and Joe Dobson. In the photograph Marilyn, fetchingly clad in high heels, white shorts and a form-fitting top, is preparing to take a swing with a bat. DiMaggio saw the picture in a newspaper and was instantly smitten. He knew Zernial and Dobbs and asked them who the blonde was. When Joe discovered that his old drinking buddy David March actually knew the enticing pinup model, DiMaggio began pestering him to arrange a date.

March approached Marilyn on Joe's behalf and at first she was reluctant. Marilyn may have been the only person in the country who did not know who Joe DiMaggio was. She said, "I don't like men in loud clothes, with checked suits and big muscles and pink ties. I get nervous" (Cramer 321). Eventually Marilyn relented. She agreed to meet Joe on a blind date at the Villa Nova Restaurant in Hollywood on the evening of March 15, 1952. For the sake of propriety it was to be a double date. March was also at the restaurant with actress Peggy Rabe. The generally accepted version of how the date went was that, despite her arriving two hours late, Joe and Marilyn hit it off immediately. During the date Marilyn noticed a curious thing: the men in the restaurant were paying more attention to Joe than they were to her.

The next day, March phoned Marilyn to find out what she thought of DiMaggio. She said, "I found myself staring at a reserved gentleman in a gray suit, with a gray tie and sprinkle of gray in his hair. There were a few blue polka dots on his tie. If I hadn't been told he was some sort of ball player, I would have guessed he was either a steel magnate or a congressman. He said, 'I'm glad to meet you,' and then fell silent for the whole rest of the evening.... I addressed only one remark to him. 'There's a blue polka dot exactly in the middle of your tie knot,' I said. 'Did it take you long to fix it like that?'" (Cramer 321). After dinner, DiMaggio asked Marilyn to drive him back to the Knickerbocker Hotel where he was staying. They ended up driving around for half the night. Marilyn agreed to go out with Joe the next night, and the night after that. Soon they became inseparable.

On March 17, Marilyn saw her first complete baseball game. Up until then she was not sure if Joe played baseball or football. It was the only time Marilyn was to see Joe play. The game was a benefit for the Kiwanis Club for Children and Marilyn was given the honor of tossing the first pitch. Joe hit a single and a home run. A month after they had met, Marilyn was admitted to a hospital with acute appendicitis. Joe was in New York and inundated her with telegrams and phone calls. Joe almost filled Marilyn's room with roses; Marilyn had told him that roses were her favorite flowers and jokingly said that when the time came she wanted fresh roses placed on her grave every week, just as William Powell had done for her idol, Jean Harlow.

Marilyn and Joe quickly became the hottest couple in Hollywood. DiMaggio, who hated the movie business, even went so far as to visit Marilyn on the set of *Monkey Business* (1952) on the final day of shooting. Subsequently, Marilyn began to make frequent weekend visits to New York, where Joe worked as a sports broadcaster, and she met his close-knit Italian family in San Francisco. But the couple had problems and these arose almost immediately. Despite his own celebrity, DiMaggio was essentially a shy man. He found it very difficult to deal with the frenzied adulation which surrounded Marilyn's every step. Also, shy as he was, DiMaggio had grown accustomed to being the center of attention himself. Joe did not approve of Marilyn's plunging necklines and for a while she attempted to tone down her wardrobe. One thing Marilyn would not do, however, was to part with her drama coach, Natasha Lytess. Lytess was always hovering around Marilyn and Joe loathed the sight of her.

Joe became involved in Marilyn's career. He urged her to fight the studio for better pictures and a higher salary. Marilyn came to rely on Joe's strength, as she would for the rest of her days. She playfully called him "Slugger" and "Giuseppe."

DiMaggio did not accompany Marilyn to many Hollywood events, but in August 1953, he traveled to the Canadian Rockies to visit her on the set of *The River of No Return*. It was declared to be a fishing trip but Joe wanted to lend Marilyn his support. Marilyn had injured her ankle and was having difficulties with the autocratic director, Otto Preminger.

On January 14, 1954, Marilyn Monroe and Joe DiMaggio were married in a brief ceremony in San Francisco. Joe wore the same polka-dot tie he had worn on their first date. The wedding ring which Joe gave to Marilyn was a platinum band with 39 diamonds.[29] After only a few weeks of marriage the couple went to Japan where Marilyn, known to the Japanese press as "Honorable Buttocks-swinging Madam" (Cranmer 356), received a tumultuous welcome. Marilyn accepted an invitation from the U.S. Army to go to Korea and entertain the troops. Joe did not want her to go but Marilyn went anyway. The result was a four-day, ten-show tour which she considered to be one of the highlights of her life. When Marilyn rejoined her husband, she was exuberant from hearing thousands of soldiers shouting her name. "Joe," she said, "you've never heard such cheering." "Yes I have," was all Joe said in reply (Kashner 335).

It has been speculated that the famous skirt-billowing scene from *The Seven Year Itch* was what finished the brief marriage. Joe was enraged by the leering crowd of 1,500 spectators, mostly men, who gathered in the middle of the night at the corner of Lexington Avenue and 52nd Street in New York to cheer and applaud when his wife's skirt was blown over her ears as she stood over a subway grating. Joe was heard to growl, "What the hell is going on here?" (Riese & Hitchens 127). That night, in the privacy of their hotel room, Joe may have hit her. Immediately after, Marilyn returned alone to Los Angeles and filed for divorce on the grounds of Joe's coldness and indifference. The divorce became final on October 27.

Although no longer married to her, Joe was so consumed by jealousy at the suspicion that Marilyn was seeing other men that he put private detectives on her tail. This resulted in the notorious "Wrong Door Raid" of November 5, 1954. DiMaggio, his pal Frank Sinatra and two private eyes planned to catch Marilyn in the arms of another man, voice coach Hal Schaefer. Without warning, the four men broke down the door of an apartment at 8122 Waring Boulevard in Hollywood. Unfortunately, it was the wrong apartment. Marilyn was in the apartment next door visiting an actress friend. Some biographers say that Schaefer was present, others not. Whether Marilyn was having an affair with Schaefer remains a matter of speculation. The resident of the wrong apartment was understandably angry and thousands of dollars had to change hands in an out-of-court settlement. It took two years before the embarrassing details became public knowledge. When it did Joe arranged to be out of the country.

On June 1, 1955, Marilyn's 29th birthday,

Joe escorted her to the premiere of *The Seven Year Itch*. It was the only time Joe was with Marilyn at a Hollywood event, and considering the effect the making of the movie may have had on their private lives, it seems an unusual choice. Following the premiere, Joe took Marilyn to a surprise birthday party at his favorite hangout. For whatever reason, they had a fight and the reconciliation failed. A year later, Marilyn was married to playwright Arthur Miller.

In 1960–61, with her marriage to Miller on the rocks, Marilyn and Joe had a reconciliation of sorts. They were seen around in public and Joe took her to Florida. Marilyn referred to him as "Mr. D." or "my ex-ex." Joe sent her a pair of his pajamas so she would be warm in bed. When Marilyn was admitted to the hospital for gynecological surgery and was mistakenly admitted to a psychiatric ward, it was Joe who came to her rescue.

When Marilyn was found dead on August 5, 1962, it was a heartbroken Joe DiMaggio who took charge of the funeral arrangements. He saw to it that it did not become a Hollywood media circus. He pointedly banned Marilyn's Hollywood associates, the people Joe blamed for what had happened to her. Joe broke down at the funeral. Honoring her wish, he arranged for fresh roses to be placed at Marilyn's crypt twice a week. Joe DiMaggio never remarried and never publicly discussed his relationship with Marilyn (Riese & Hitchens 122–7; Spoto 1993, 206–7, 260–95, 594–6; Summers 87–158; Victor 76–81).

ISAK DINESEN   Danish writer who settled on a coffee plantation in Kenya for many years and wrote about her experiences in a famous book, *Out of Africa*. Dinesen died at the age of 77, outliving Marilyn by 32 days. In 1959, Dinesen was visiting novelist Carson McCullers in New York, when she expressed an interest in meeting MM. McCullers was a friend of Marilyn's from the time they lived in the same apartment building. She also had a slight acquaintance with Marilyn's husband, Arthur Miller. McCullers arranged a luncheon at her apartment on February 5. The Millers collected

Dinesen in their car. Thanks to Marilyn they were, of course, late. Marilyn looked radiant in a black sheath dress, with fur collar and plunging neckline. The guests dined on oysters, white grapes, champagne, and a soufflé, the only things Dinesen ate, other than asparagus. Marilyn told a funny story about a disaster she had while cooking pasta; when the food was not ready on time, she tried to hurry things along with the aid of a hair dryer. McCullers put a record on the phonograph and Marilyn and the elderly Dinesen danced a few steps together (Carr 478–80). Marilyn made a strong impression on Dinesen, who confided to a friend: "It is not that she is pretty, although of course she is almost incredibly pretty—but that she radiates at the same time unbounded vitality and a kind of unbelievable innocence. I have met the same in a lion cub that my native servants in Africa brought me. I would not keep her" (Thurman 468).

WALT DISNEY   Innovative and influential animator, screenwriter, film producer and entrepreneur. Disney claimed in a newspaper article that Tinker Bell, the mischievous blonde fairy in *Peter Pan* (1953), with her curvaceous figure and pouting expression, was inspired by MM. In fact, another actress was used as the model for Tinker Bell, but an urban legend was created. In September 1959 Russian premier Nikita Khrushchev was on a state visit to the United States. One of the places he was taken to was the Twentieth Century–Fox commissary. Disney and Marilyn were both in attendance (Watts 330; Winters 1989, 271–2).

DIANA DORS   A blonde bombshell actress from Britain who was dubbed the "English Marilyn Monroe." When *The Asphalt Jungle* (1950) was shown in England a reviewer said, "How much like our Diana Dors she is." At a press conference in England in July 1956, during the making of *The Prince and the Showgirl*, Marilyn refused to be drawn into a spat after a reporter asked, "Has not the name of Diana Dors become a bit tedious for you?" Marilyn replied: "No, I've been looking forward to meeting her. There's a place for everyone, and

there's enough of the two of us for everybody" (Wilson 84; *www.imdb.com*).

FYODOR DOSTOYEVSKY   Nineteenth-century Russian novelist who had some passing connection to MM. A smart-alec reporter asked Marilyn if she wanted to play *The Brothers Karamazov*, probably expecting her to not know what he was talking about. Marilyn did know because she had read Dostoyevsky. She replied, "I don't want to play the brothers. I want to play Grushenka. She's a girl" (Taraborrelli 2009, 261). Grushenka is the heroine of Dostoyevsky's tale of sordid murder and love. Marilyn was ridiculed by the press corps and the Hollywood establishment for her presumption. One director said that he would be delighted to have Marilyn for "The Brothers Karamazov Meet Abbott and Costello." At an Oscar ceremony, Bob Hope joked, "Is Marilyn Monroe here?" Thelma Ritter, who was to act with Marilyn in *The Misfits*, replied, "Yes, she just walked in with the Brothers Karamazov" (Shevey 298). When Marilyn said of Grushenka that she was sexy, she was further ridiculed. Director Billy Wilder supported Marilyn: "People who haven't read the book don't know that Grushenka is a sexpot.... They think this is a long hair, very thick, very literary book.... There is nothing long hair about Grushenka. Marilyn knows what she is doing, too. She would be a Grushenka to end all Grushenkas" (Shevey 287). Even so, Wilder advised Marilyn not to play the part because everyone was making a joke of it. Marilyn should just stick with the character she had already created for herself and if she did so she would be a successful actress at 80, like Mae West. In 1958 an indifferent version of *The Brothers Karamazov* was made without Marilyn. Maria Schell played Grushenka. Publicist John Springer commented: "Do you remember the press reaction when Marilyn said she would like to play Grushenka in *The Brothers Karamazov*? Everybody howled! But what a perfect idea! She would have been the perfect Grushenka. I love Maria Schell. But Marilyn would have turned in a performance which was classic.

People laughed at her. This idiot thinks she can play Dostoyevsky. She wasn't such an idiot. She knew! If anybody had paid attention to her, and cast her as Grushenka, that might have been one of the great movies of all time" (Shevey 299). Columnist Sheilah Graham seconded that opinion: "Marilyn would have been superb as Dostoyevsky's sensual, confused heroine. She was born for the part, and a Maria Schell with her assured smile was completely wrong" (Graham 1969, 146).

KIRK DOUGLAS Leading man in numerous Hollywood movies. Douglas remembered the first time he met MM. It was at the home of producer Sam Spiegel: "The only woman in the room, she sat quietly in a chair watching Sam play gin rummy with friends and hoping that he'd get her a job in the movies. I felt sorry for her. I tried to talk with her, but it wasn't much of a conversation" (Douglas 87). In June 1961, there was a celebrity party at the Sands Hotel in Las Vegas for the seventh wedding anniversary of Kirk and Ann Douglas. One of the guests was Marilyn, who proceeded to make a spectacle of herself. Frank Sinatra got up to sing and Marilyn, who was drunk, began swaying and pounding on the stage floor. In response to a gesture from Sinatra, Marilyn was escorted from the room (Fisher 1981, 103).

PAUL DOUGLAS Stocky character actor who was in two movies with MM in 1952: *Clash by Night* and *We're Not Married*. This was the time when the news came out that Marilyn had posed nude for a calendar. All the publicity was coming Marilyn's way and Douglas did not like it one bit. He was heard to say: "Why the hell don't these goddamn photographers ever take any pictures of us? It's only that goddamn blonde bitch?" (Riese & Hitchens 93). On the set of *Clash by Night*, Douglas gave Marilyn a withering stare and she was probably correct when she concluded that he hated her on sight. But when Marilyn was given star billing, Douglas blew his stack: "I will never give my permission, never! Who is she? A newcomer! She'll never make it to the top grade" (Shevey 177–8). Marilyn thought Douglas was a fine actor but that

he had been unpleasant to her. She said that even though he was known as a nice guy she would never work with him again (Guiles 189–90).

MARIE DRESSLER Academy Award–winning Canadian actress who died when MM was seven years old. Dressler was a rare female role model for Marilyn who said, "I'm looking forward to eventually becoming a marvelous—excuse the word marvelous—character actress. Like Marie Dressler..." (*Redbook* August 1962)

PATTY DUKE Academy Award–winning actress who was also successful in television. In 1958, when she was only 12, Duke was in *The Goddess*, a thinly camouflaged attack on the cult of MM, written by Paddy Chayefsky. Duke portrayed the Marilyn–inspired character as a child; Kim Stanley played the character as an adult (Riese & Hitchens 137; *www.imdb.com*).

JIMMY DURANTE Singer, actor and comedian known for his big nose and comic butchering of the English language. Durante encountered Marilyn Monroe near the beginning and near the end of her career. He and Marilyn attended the funeral of Hollywood talent agent Johnny Hyde who had died on December 18, 1950. The much older Hyde had become besotted by Marilyn, going so far as to leave his wife and begging the starlet to marry him. Marilyn refused, saying she loved Hyde but that she was not *in love* with him. While Durante acted as an honorary pall-bearer, Marilyn's presence at the funeral was definitely not welcomed by Hyde's relatives. On May 19, 1962, Durante was on the same program as Marilyn at the birthday salute to President Kennedy at Madison Square Garden. Some 17,000 people were in attendance and everyone, even Marilyn and Durante, paid $100 for a ticket (Rose 150–1; Victor 147–8; *www.cursumperficio.net*/files/Madison Square Garden).

ELEANORA DUSE Known for her naturalistic and individual style, Duse was an Italian tragedienne who died two years before MM was born. Marilyn had read about Duse, identified with her and thought of her as one of her few female role models. For many years Marilyn kept a picture of Eleanora Duse by her bed. For the April 7, 1952, issue of *Life* magazine noted photographer Philippe Halsman decided to take a photo of Marilyn with Duse's picture. "He wrote, "There was a record player in the bookshelf. Marilyn, in a transparent negligee, leaned against it, listening with breathless dreaminess to a record. Her *derriere* was pointing toward Duse's immortal face. To me it was not sacrilege. It was my ironic commentary on the shift in values in our civilization" (Doll 81).

Other Source: (Riese & Hitchens 137; Victor 90).

-E-

CLINT EASTWOOD   American actor who transformed himself from the star of the Italian spaghetti westerns, *Fistful of Dollars* (1964) and *For a Few Dollars More* (1966), into a serious actor and Academy Award–winning film director. Eastwood's one-time girlfriend Sondra Locke claimed that he devised his distinctive manner of speaking by studying MM. Locke has written that Eastwood told her that "he had developed his way of whispering in his performance during the 'Dollar' films. He said he'd noticed Marilyn Monroe's breathy whisper and he thought it was very sexy. And since it had worked so well for her, he decided he'd do a male version of it himself" (Frayling 199).

ABBA EBAN   Israeli diplomat and politician who, from 1966 to 1974, served as his country's foreign minister. On May 12, 1956, to commemorate Israel's eighth independence day, there was a soccer match at Yankee Stadium in New York between the American and Israeli national teams. At the time, Eban was Israel's ambassador to the United States and the United Nations. MM was present at this event. To the delight of the crowd, Marilyn, Senator John F. Kennedy[30] and Eban were driven around the stadium in an open car.

Marilyn, wearing open-toed shoes, kicked the opening ball with such force that she sprained two toes. Even so, she gamely stayed to watch the match and award the trophy to the winners. Eban remembered: "Miss Monroe seemed to make a stronger physical impression on most of the audience than did Kennedy or I, but we could claim to have a somewhat broader conceptual range" (Eban 200).

MARY BAKER EDDY   Founder of the Christian Science religion and author of *Science and Health, With Key to the Scripture*. MM was raised a Christian Scientist. Years later she said: "I've read Mrs. Eddy and tried to put some of her ideas into my life, but it doesn't work for me" (Morgan 30).

Other sources: Spoto 1993, 58–60; Victor 54–5.

BARBARA EDEN   Actress best known for her starring role in television's *I Dream of Jeannie* (1965–1970). In 1957 Eden was in another series, *How to Marry a Millionaire*. Eden played the part MM had in the 1953 film. Eden was introduced to Marilyn on April 10, 1962, on the sound stage where Marilyn was working on *Something's Got to Give*. After Marilyn died, Eden employed her stand-in, Evelyn Moriarty (Eden & Leigh 92–3; Riese & Hitchens 138–39).

RALPH EDWARDS   Radio and television game show host and producer. Edwards was best known for creating the game shows *Truth or Consequences* (1950–1988) and *This is Your Life* (1953–1960). On March 17, 1952, Edwards and MM were photographed together at Gilmore Field in Hollywood at a charity event for children called The Hollywood Entertainers Baseball Game "Out of This World Series." Edwards is manning the microphone as Marilyn tosses out the first pitch. Edwards was nearly 13 years older than Marilyn and outlived her by 43 years (Victor 287).

ALBERT EINSTEIN   German-Jewish physicist whose name is forever linked to the formula $E=MC^2$ and the theory of relativity.

With her roommate, Shelley Winters, MM jokingly prepared a list of the men she would like to sleep with. Albert Einstein's name was on the list. "Marilyn," Winters said, "there's no way you can sleep with Albert Einstein. He's the most famous scientist of the century. Besides, he's an old man." "That has nothing to do with it," Marilyn replied. "I hear he's very healthy" (Winters 1980, 308). In 1955, when Marilyn was living in a luxurious suite at the Waldorf-Astoria Hotel in New York, visitors noticed a couple of pictures of Einstein mounted on a bulletin board.

Among Marilyn's treasured possessions was a photograph of Einstein that had a handwritten inscription: "To Marilyn, with respect and love and thanks, Albert Einstein" (Summers 74). Marilyn kept the photo in a silver frame propped up on the lid of her white baby grand piano. The picture had been given to Marilyn by acting colleague Eli Wallach as a joke after Marilyn had given him a volume of Einstein's letters. Wallach, as Marilyn knew, had written the inscription himself. In a 1985 movie, *Insignificance*, based on a stage play, Marilyn Monroe and Albert Einstein do meet (Riese & Hitchens 139; Victor 92).

Alfred Eisenstaedt　Photographer and photojournalist who took one of the most famous photographs of World War II that of a sailor kissing a nurse in Times Square, New York on August 14, 1945, V-J Day. In May 1953 Eisenstaedt did a photoshoot with Marilyn Monroe for *Life* magazine. The simple pictures of Marilyn barefoot, in a black top and white toreador pants were taken in her apartment and on her patio in Los Angeles.[31]

Eisenstaedt thought his subject was childlike and exceptionally beautiful. He remembered that "she was a bit flustered, and perhaps I was too. Somehow, I mixed up the markings on my two cameras. One was loaded with color and the other with black-and-white" (Eisenstaedt & Goldsmith 101).

Anita Ekberg　Statuesque Swedish actress who is best known for her role in *La Dolce Vita* (1960). After winning the Miss Sweden pageant, Ekberg was given a modeling contract in California. Early in her career the teenage MM and Ekberg posed around the same Palm Springs swimming pool in their bathing suits. On October 29, 1956, Ekberg and Marilyn's paths crossed again. It was at a Royal Command Film Performance in London, where the actresses (among other celebrities) were presented to Queen Elizabeth II.

In 1957, Ian Fleming wrote *From Russia With Love*, a thriller featuring master spy James Bond, Agent 007. Bond is in Istanbul, on a mission to assassinate a villain, whose hideout is reached by a trapdoor through a billboard of MM's giant face, advertising the Turkish-dubbed version of her 1953 film, *Niagara*. By the time the movie version of *From Russia With Love* came out in 1963, Marilyn had died. The producers of the film had another movie they wanted to promote—*Call Me Bwana*, a forgettable comedy starring Bob Hope and Anita Ekberg. Therefore, in *From Russia With Love* (the movie), Bond's quarry crawls through Anita Ekberg's mouth, not Marilyn's (Rubin 65–6; *www.imdb.com*).

Jack Elam　Evil–looking character actor who was usually seen as a villain in Westerns or used as comic relief. Elam had a small part in an early MM vehicle, a Western entitled *A Ticket to Tomahawk* (1950). Neither Elam nor Marilyn was important enough at that time to be credited (*www.imdb.com*).

T. S. Eliot　American poet, dramatist and literary critic who lived in England for most of his life. Decades after Marilyn Monroe's death an examination of her personal effects revealed correspondence between the actress and the poet. The letters included fragments of poetry written in pencil and were signed "All my love, T. S. Eliot." The provenance of the poetry is questionable but the signature is thought to be genuine. However, it is claimed that the verse was written by Marilyn's friend Norman Rosten who signed Eliot's name as a joke (Banner 235; Kashner 325).

Queen Elizabeth II　On October 29, 1956, MM, among a bevy of other celebrities, was presented to Queen Elizabeth II at a Royal Command Film Performance in London for the premiere of *The Battle of the River Plate*. Marilyn was in England to make a movie with Sir Laurence Olivier, *The Prince and the Showgirl*. Prior to the meeting, Marilyn had been told by a friend's mother to still her nerves by looking her Majesty straight in the eye and thinking that she was just as pretty as the queen. Marilyn was 41 days younger than Queen Elizabeth. The queen had asked playwright Terence Rattigan what the American actress was like. Rattigan had said that Marilyn was a living contradiction, a shy exhibitionist, a Garbo who liked to be photographed. As is the custom, when she met the queen, Marilyn curtsied. The Queen complimented Marilyn on her proper curtsy. Marilyn replied that is was not difficult to do because she had learned to curtsy for the movie she was making. The queen then remarked, "How do you like your home at Windsor? ...You are neighbors of mine." Marilyn and husband, Arthur Miller, were living near Windsor Great Park, close to where the queen lived. Marilyn did not realize this but quickly replied, "We love it and as we have a permit my husband and I go for bicycle rides and walks in the Great Park" (Shevey 352–3).

HOWARD ENGEL   Canadian writer and television producer who wrote a series of bestselling detective novels which were set in the Niagara Falls region.[32] Engel was the uncredited "Man at the Bus Station" in *Niagara*, filmed on location in Niagara Falls, Ontario. Engel was waiting to board a bus as Marilyn walks out of the building (*www.imdb.com*).

DALE EVANS   Actress who was usually associated with cowboy star Roy Rogers. Evans may have met MM in 1946. As an unknown 19-year-old starlet, Marilyn was in Las Vegas waiting out a divorce from her first husband. Evans and Rogers, who were not yet married, were in town making the Western *Heldorado*. Rogers met Marilyn and invited her to join the cast and crew for dinner at a local hotel (Guiles 98; *www.imdb.com*).

DAME EDITH EVANS   Distinguished British stage actress who also made films.

Evans visited the set of *The Prince and the Showgirl* (1957) and told MM: "When I saw you on the set, I thought you weren't even working. Then I saw the rushes in the projection room, and the scenes are all yours" (Churchwell 69).

TOM EWELL   Character actor known for his excellent timing. Ewell starred in the Broadway production of *The Seven Year Itch*, turning in more than 750 performances as the rumpled middle-aged man tempted to the point of distraction by "The Girl" upstairs. In 1955, Ewell co-starred with MM in the film version of the George Axelrod play. The scene where Ewell stares appreciatively at Marilyn as she stands over a subway grate, her skirt billowing over her hips, is one of the most famous in cinema history. At the completion of the film there was a star-studded wrap party which doubled as Marilyn's coming-out party.

Ewell recalled that Marilyn was late for her own party. She drove herself, but ran out of gas. Marilyn did not own any evening wear and had to raid the studio's wardrobe department for a suitable dress and fur coat. As Ewell recalled, "She was told she could ask anyone she wished to the party, but confided to me: 'Golly, I don't know many people. I wonder whom I could ask. I know Betty Grable. We worked on a picture together. Maybe she'd bring Harry James. And I know Lauren Bacall. She was in *How to Marry a Millionaire* too. She and Humphrey Bogart might come.' Yet, when she came into that room filled with.... Hollywood's finest—including the Jameses and the Bogarts[33]—she outshone everyone in it" (Shevey 292). Ewell also said that Marilyn was wonderful to work with and that Marilyn "had that odd spark that's more than beauty or brains. Although she is personally shy and reserved, she can turn on her personality so that you forget anyone else is present" (Mobilio 53–4).

-F-

DOUGLAS FAIRBANKS, JR.   American cinema star who spent much of his time in

Britain. Fairbanks met MM on July 26, 1956, at playwright Terence Rattigan's country house near London. The occasion was an after-theater ball hosted by Rattigan, Vivien Leigh and Sir Laurence Olivier in honor of Marilyn and her husband, Arthur Miller. Marilyn was in England to film Rattigan's *The Prince and the Showgirl* with Olivier (Gottfried 2003, 300–1; Shevey 347).

WILLIAM FAULKNER Nobel Prize-winning novelist from Mississippi. In 1960 or '61, Faulkner saw a photograph of MM in a newspaper in which she was smiling and conversing with Eleanor Roosevelt, of all people.[34] Speaking of Marilyn, Faulkner said, "She's something of the new age, wiggling even when she's standing still" (Blotner 683). Marilyn had been offered a lead role in the film adaptation of Faulkner's *The Sound and the Fury* but turned it down in favor of *Some Like It Hot*. Faulkner died 20 days before Marilyn (Victor 108).

MIGUEL FERRER Award–winning American actor who was the son of Rosemary Clooney and José Ferrer. When Miguel Ferrer was an infant in his crib, Marilyn Monroe visited his mother at home. All Marilyn wanted to do was go straight into the nursery and play with baby Miguel (Clooney & Barthel 219).

W. C. FIELDS, JR. W. Claude Fields, Jr., the son of the irascible film comedian, was MM's attorney for the years 1954 and 1955. During that period Marilyn was hauled into court for driving without a valid license. She was fined $55 and warned that she wouldn't win an Oscar that way (Riese & Hitchens 157; Slatzer 230; Victor 51).

EDDIE FISHER Actor and singer who is chiefly remembered for being one of Elizabeth Taylor's husbands. Fisher knew MM near the end of her life and the portrait he paints of her is not flattering. He claimed to have never been attracted to her, saying, "As physically beautiful as she was, the drinking and the pills made her ugly." In June 1961, in Las Vegas, Fisher saw Marilyn at her worst. The occasion was the seventh-anniversary party for Kirk Douglas and his wife, Ann. Frank Sinatra was performing on stage. Fisher, Elizabeth Taylor and Dean Martin were in the audience. "But," as Fisher writes, "all eyes were on Marilyn as she swayed back and forth to the music and pounded her hands on the stage, her breasts falling out of her low-cut dress. She was so beautiful—and so drunk. She came to the party later that evening, but Sinatra made no secret of his displeasure at her behavior and she vanished almost immediately."

Fisher appeared in two films which featured Marilyn. In 1950 he was a stage manager in *All About Eve*. Although he received a screen credit, his scene ended up on the cutting-room floor. Fisher appeared as himself in the 1959 documentary, *Premier Khrushchev in the U.S.A.* (Fisher 1981, 103; *www.imdb.com*).

ELLA FITZGERALD Legendary jazz singer. In March 1954, when MM first went to hear Ella Fitzgerald at a club, she was already a devoted fan. Howard Hawks, Marilyn's director in *Gentlemen Prefer Blondes* (1953), had given her a copy of *Ella Sings Gershwin*, upon which to model her singing style. Even though the Mocambo had never featured an African-American performer, Marilyn pressured the owner to book Fitzgerald. That booking at the Mocambo, a classy West Hollywood nightspot, was an important stepping stone in Fitzgerald's career. Marilyn ensured that the audience was sprinkled with stars including Judy Garland and Frank Sinatra.[35] Fitzgerald later said: "It was because of her that I played the Mocambo. She personally called the owner ... and told him she wanted me booked immediately, and if he would do it, she would take a front table every night. She told him—and it was true, due to Marilyn's superstar status—that the press would go wild. The owner said yes, and Marilyn was there, front table, every night. The press went overboard.... After that, I never had to play a small jazz club again. She was an unusual woman—a little ahead of her time. And she didn't know it" (*Ms*, August 1972).

On May 19, 1962, Fitzgerald performed at the birthday gala for John F. Kennedy at which Marilyn sang her famous, "Happy Birthday, Mr. President." Three months later,

Fitzgerald and most other celebrities were turned away from Marilyn's funeral. Fitzgerald kept a framed photograph of Marilyn Monroe on her living-room wall (Brown & Barham 142; Krohn 89; Nicholson 149; Spoto 1993, 298).

IAN FLEMING   English writer who created James Bond, agent 007. MM was a voracious reader but her tastes did not usually run to spy thrillers. She never met Ian Fleming but she did own a copy of *From Russia with Love* (published in 1957) and must have been aware of her part in the book's plot development. Chapter nineteen of *From Russia with Love* is entitled, "The Mouth of Marilyn Monroe." In the back streets of Istanbul, Turkey, James Bond and Kerim Bey are on a mission to assassinate a villain by the name of Krilencu. The entrance to Krilencu's hideout is a trapdoor through a billboard advertising the Turkish-dubbed version of Marilyn's 1953 film, *Niagara*.

Examining the infrared lens of a sniper scope, Bond "raised the tube to his right eye. He focused it on the patch of black shadow opposite. Slowly the black dissolved into grey. The outline of a huge woman's face and some lettering appeared. Now Bond could read the lettering. It said: 'NIYAGARA MARILYN MONROE VE JOSEPH COTTEN'.... Bond inched the glass down the vast pile of Marilyn Monroe's hair and the cliff of forehead, and down the two feet of nose to the cavernous nostrils. A faint square showed in the poster. It ran from below the nose into the great alluring curve of the lips. It was about three feet deep. From it, there would be a longish drop to the ground." A few moments later Bond saw that "out of the mouth of the huge, shadowed poster, between the great violet lips, half-open in ecstasy, the dark shape of a man emerged and hung down like a worm from the mouth of a corpse."

The movie version of *From Russia with Love* was released in 1963, and Marilyn had died before it went into production. The producers of the movie, Albert R. Broccoli and Harry Saltzman, had another film they wanted

to promote—*Call Me Bwana*, a forgettable comedy starring Bob Hope and Anita Ekberg. Therefore, in *From Russia with Love* (the movie), Krilencu crawls through Anita Ekberg's mouth, not Marilyn's (Rubin 65–6).

ERROL FLYNN   Hollywood action star who became equally famous for his scandalous escapades off-screen. According to Truman Capote, when MM was just starting out as a model she went to a Hollywood party that Errol Flynn attended. Marilyn witnessed Flynn play *You Are My Sunshine* on the piano with a certain part of his anatomy. When she was a child, Marilyn had been taken to see Errol Flynn in *The Prince and the Pauper* (1937) at least three times (Capote 1980, 231–2; Spoto 1993, 53–4; *www.cursumperficio.net*).

HENRY FONDA   Screen legend whose career spanned 45 years. In 1958, Fonda moved his family to Malibu Beach for the summer. Nearby neighbors were Lee and Paula Strasberg, MM's acting mentors. The Fondas and the Strasbergs would get together on the beach for barbeques and Marilyn would sometimes attend. The Strasbergs were getting Marilyn prepared for *Some Like It Hot*. Of Marilyn and her relationship with the Strasbergs, Fonda remembered how "that girl wouldn't move an inch without asking them. Monroe was a fragile little thing in person. We all saw each other, we weren't close, but we saw each other" (Fonda & Teichmann 284).

Fonda was on hand for the May 19, 1962, gala for John F. Kennedy, during which Marilyn sang her famous, "Happy Birthday, Mr. President." Her first meeting with Fonda was when she was an unknown starlet and posed for a picture with him at the Fox Studio Club annual golf tournament in July 1947.

JANE FONDA   Film actress and activist, daughter of Henry Fonda. As a young adult in 1958, Fonda lived with her parents a few houses away from Lee and Paula Strasberg, MM's acting coaches. Fonda accompanied the Strasbergs' daughter, Susan, to visit Paula on the set of *Some Like It Hot*. Fonda watched the filming of an early scene in the picture in which Marilyn is in a railway sleeping car with Tony Curtis and Jack Lemmon, both of whom were in drag. Fonda recalled: "An eternity of held breath elapsed before a voice yelled, '*Cut!*' Suddenly people sprang into action, moving out of the darkness, doing their precise, union prescribed tasks inside that circle of light. Then into the darkness stepped Marilyn Monroe, bringing the light with her, shimmering, in her hair and on her skin. She walked with Paula toward where Susan and I were standing while someone draped a pink chenille bathrobe over her shoulders to cover her revealing nightgown. Her body seemed to precede her, and it was hard to keep my eyes from camping out there. But when I looked up at her face, I saw a scared, wide-eyed child. I was dizzy. It was hard to believe she was right there in front of me, all golden iridescence, saying hello in that breathy, little-girl voice. There was a vulnerability that radiated from her and allowed me to love her right there and feel glad that she had someone wide and soft, like Paula, to mama her. She was very sweet to Susan and me, but I could tell she wanted Paula's undivided attention, to give her what she needed so that she could go back and do the scene one more time. I wondered how it could be that she seemed so frightened when she was probably the most famous woman in the world" (Fonda 115).

Later, Fonda took classes at Lee Strasberg's Actors Studio in New York where she encountered Marilyn again. Twice a week for a month Fonda sat directly behind Strasberg's most famous student. Marilyn, who wore no makeup, was quiet and earnest as she sat near the back of the room, clad in a head scarf and ordinary trench coat. Fonda never witnessed Marilyn present a scene. She had been told that the prospect made Marilyn so nervous that she would get sick to her stomach. Following her out of the studio, Fonda noticed Marilyn hail a cab while being completely unrecognized. Fonda wondered how Marilyn could handle the rapid shift between extreme adulation at one moment and anonymity the next.

Near the end of Marilyn's life, Fonda ran into her at a Hollywood party. Fonda said that she was eager for the time "when all the superficial beauty is gone and I can begin to play character parts and rely on acting alone." Marilyn replied, "Oh no, I can't imagine surviving that way. I don't think it will be possible for me" (Brown & Barham 174).

MARGOT FONTEYN   Acclaimed British ballet dancer. Fonteyn was introduced to MM on July 26, 1956, at playwright Terence Rattigan's house near London. The event was a ball given in honor of Marilyn and her husband, Arthur Miller. Fonteyn wrote: "She was astoundingly beautiful, without the trace of a line or wrinkle on her beguiling face. What fascinated me most was her evident inability to remain motionless. Whereas people normally move their arms and head in conversation, these gestures in Marilyn Monroe were reflected throughout her body, producing a delicately undulating effect like the movement of an almost calm sea. It seemed clear to me that it was something of which she was not conscious; it was as natural as breathing, and in no way an affected 'wriggle,' as some writers have suggested. Her beauty was so fresh and her personality so compounded of the childlike and the vulnerable that, although her early death was a tragedy, I can't help thinking it fitting that she never had to contend with the erosions that time brings to the rest of us." Although Fonteyn's husband was a Panamanian diplomat, she was unable to get Marilyn to visit the embassy (Fonteyn 163).

GLENN FORD   Canadian–born Hollywood dramatic actor who was about ten years older than Marilyn Monroe. Ford was a pallbearer at the funeral of Johnny Hyde, who had died on December 18, 1950. Hyde was one of the top talent agents in Hollywood and had taken starlet Marilyn under his wing. Marilyn was also at the funeral, but Hyde's family was none too pleased about it. When he spotted Marilyn, Hyde's nephew was overheard saying, "There's the bitch who killed my uncle" (Rose 150–1). On March 8, 1960, Glenn Ford presented Marilyn with the Golden Globe Award for "Best Actress of 1959" at the Cocoanut

Grove in Los Angeles (*www.cursumperficio. net*/biography/1960).

JOHN FORD   Four-time Academy Award–winning film director. As her career blossomed, MM prepared a list of 16 directors with whom she would be willing to work. John Ford made the list, but he and Marilyn never worked together (Riese & Hitchens 128).

TENNESSEE ERNIE FORD   Country-and-Western recording star and television host. The title song for the movie, *River of No Return* (1954), was sung by Ford, as a voice-over, at the opening and at the end. Marilyn sang it in the film (De la Hoz 154).

CONNIE FRANCIS   Pop singer known for her 1957 hit, "Who's Sorry Now?" Francis was a friend of MM's. and tried to cheer her up near the end of her life (Guiles 428; Riese & Hitchens 165).

WILLIAM FRAWLEY   Gruff character actor remembered for playing Fred Mertz on *I Love Lucy* (1951–1960). Frawley is featured in an alternate story of how MM met her second husband, baseball legend Joe DiMaggio. In this version, it was the spring of 1952 and Marilyn was having lunch with her agent at the Brown Derby restaurant. At another table was DiMaggio and Bill Frawley. DiMaggio noticed Marilyn but was too shy to approach her. Frawley came over to Marilyn's table to say that Joe would like to meet her. Joe and Marilyn said hello and shook hands, and that was all. Joe obtained Marilyn's telephone number but it is not known if he phoned for a date. After Frawley and DiMaggio had left, Marilyn turned to her agent and asked who this Joe D. was" (Engleberg 240; Taraborrelli 2009, 184–5).

ANNA FREUD   A psychoanalyst in her own right, Anna Freud was the daughter of one of MM's heroes, Sigmund Freud. The stress of working on *The Prince and the Showgirl* was so great that Marilyn became even more reliant on sleeping pills. In London she had several sessions with Anna Freud. On Freud's recommendation, Marilyn started see-ing a new psychoanalyst when she returned to New York (Morgan 201, 263; Victor 110).

SIGMUND FREUD   Famous Viennese psychoanalyst. MM was devoted to the writings of Dr. Freud and was known to have read his *Psychology of Everyday Life* and *The Life and Work of Sigmund Freud*, complete in three volumes. For most of her adult life she was on a journey of self-discovery and she was convinced that she could only arrive at her destination with the help of psychoanalysis. Don Murray, Marilyn's co-star in *Bus Stop* (1956), recalls her discussing Freud and phallic symbols with him. "At the age of thirty," said Murray, "she was going through what we did at eighteen: reading Freud and so on. I remember that about her. She was Freudian-obsessed" (Shevey 333). Near the end of her life Marilyn was considered for a John Huston picture about the life of Sigmund Freud. On seeing a photograph of Freud Marilyn said that he looked like a man who had died disappointed (Leaming 1998, 311; Spoto 1993, 448; Victor 110).

-G-

CLARK GABLE   Legendary film star dubbed "the King" of Hollywood. As a young girl, Norma Jeane Baker had kept a publicity photograph of Clark Gable and had fantasized that he was her real father. In 1950's *All About Eve*, Marilyn's character, Miss Caswell, says "There's something a girl could make sacrifices for. Sable!" Another character asks, "Did she say 'sable' or 'Gable?'" Miss Caswell replies eagerly, "Either one." It was a thrill for Marilyn to finally meet Gable. That happened in 1954, at a party to celebrate the completion of *The Seven Year Itch*. Marilyn and Gable danced together twice and, as all actors do, they discussed making a picture together. Marilyn even asked Gable for his autograph, saying that she had wanted it since she was twelve years old. Six years later they did work together. *The Misfits* was to be the last film either of them completed. Gable was intrigued by the script for *The Misfits* and his part in it as an aging cowboy reduced to trapping wild mustangs for the dog food trade. But he had reservations about working with Marilyn. Even though Marilyn's screen persona reminded him of his late wife, Carole Lombard, Gable was worried that Marilyn would be neurotic and self-indulgent—which, indeed, she was. Also, Marilyn was devoted to Lee Strasberg's 'Method' acting which Gable despised.

Marilyn was characteristically two hours late for her first scene with Gable. She was so nervous about working with the King that she had gobbled Nembutal the night before. She had to be roused by black coffee and Benzedrine. Upon seeing Gable, Marilyn became so sick that she had to race to the honey wagon to vomit. After her entourage put her back together, Marilyn apologized to Gable, who put his arms around her and said, "You're not late honey" (Wayne 494). He then took her by the hand and led her to a secluded corner for a private chat. Whatever Gable said to her, Marilyn was soon relaxed and laughing. The feared explosion never occurred and, from then on, Gable and Marilyn had a good working relationship—that is, when she showed up. Gable found the endless delays very frustrating but, for the most part, kept his feelings to himself. With Marilyn, Gable was always soothing and reassuring. He would give her friendly pats on the behind and get a smile out of her by calling her "Chubby" or "Fatso" (Wayne 501). Marilyn said to a reporter, "Mr. Gable likes me. Ask him if I'm the temperamental person I'm pictured" (Tornabene 378). Gable even ran interference for Marilyn with the press, offering to meet with them himself until Marilyn could pull herself together. One day he saw Marilyn being made up for a magazine photo shoot and refused to allow it to go ahead. After a hard day's work it was just too much to expect. The photo session was rescheduled.

The Misfits was shot under blistering conditions in the Nevada desert. Two weeks after filming was completed, Clark Gable died of a massive heart attack. Marilyn was devastated and, believing that Gable's widow Kay blamed her for his death, went into seclusion. In Feb-

ruary 1961 she admitted to a friend that she had considered suicide by jumping from her 13th-floor apartment window. There were people on the street who shouted to Marilyn that she was a murderer.[36] Kay Gable did not have to mention Marilyn by name when she said, "It wasn't the physical exertion that did it. It was the horrible tension, that eternal waiting, waiting, waiting. He waited around forever, for everybody. He'd get so angry waiting that he'd just go ahead and do anything to keep occupied. That's why he did those awful horse scenes where they dragged him behind a truck. He had a stand-in and a stunt man, but he did them himself. I told him he was crazy, but he wouldn't listen" (Wayne 506–7). Marilyn felt even worse because Gable and his wife were expecting a baby. Marilyn was not invited to Gable's funeral but was pleased that she was invited to the christening ceremony for the baby boy Clark Gable never lived to see (Harris 2002, 335–9; Riese & Hitchens 168–9; Tornabene 376–87; Victor 114–15).

ZSA ZSA GABOR   Glamorous Hungarian-American actress and personality. Gabor was no fan of MM, in fact she could not stand the sight of her. Both of them arrived on the Hollywood scene at about the same time, but Marilyn attracted much more attention. When she was a relatively unknown starlet, Marilyn was invited to a party at which Gabor and her then-husband, actor George Sanders, were also present. According to Marilyn, Gabor threw a jealous fit and threatened to leave. Marilyn maintained that Gabor planted spies on the set of *All About Eve* (1950) to keep her away from Sanders. On Gabor's orders, Sanders was not to lunch with Marilyn at the studio commissary and was to confine his communication with her to a chaste "Good morning" and "Good evening." Reportedly, Marilyn managed to have an affair with Sanders anyway. *We're Not Married* (1952) was the only movie to feature both Zsa Zsa Gabor and Marilyn Monroe, although never in the same scene. This is what Gabor had to say about Marilyn: "[She] was a very dull girl. She thought that if a man who takes her out for dinner doesn't sleep with her that night—something's wrong with her. When George was making *All about Eve* in San Francisco, we had a suite and next to us Marilyn Monroe had a room. George made a thing out of it and said, 'Let's see how many men are going to go into her room tonight!' I'd seen about *four*. That's a terrible thing to say about somebody who the whole country admires" (Riese & Hitchens 170, q. *Playboy Video* Magazine). Marilyn described Zsa Zsa as "A blonde with a funny accent" and "one of those blondes who put on ten years if you take a close look at them" (Monroe & Hecht 68, 69).

Other sources: Guiles 159; Shevey 147

GRETA GARBO Enigmatic Swedish film actress who retired at age 36, the same age at which MM died. The two screen legends never met but they were often compared, and in her final years Marilyn began to identify with Garbo. It is noteworthy that Marilyn chose Eugene O'Neill's *Anna Christie* to make her debut before the members of the prestigious Actors Studio in February 1956. Garbo had made her talking film debut in *Anna Christie* in 1930. Truman Capote reported that Garbo wanted to make *The Picture of Dorian Gray*, with herself in the title role and Marilyn as one of the girls Dorian Gray seduces. One of Marilyn's favorite hairstylists, Sydney Guilaroff, once worked exclusively for Garbo. Joshua Logan, the director of *Bus Stop*, thought Marilyn was an unusual combination of Greta Garbo and Charlie Chaplin "because to me she had the beauty of Garbo and this comic, pathetic thing that I had only really seen in perfection before from Chaplin" (Shevey 335–6). Marilyn once said that she had never met Greta Garbo but would give anything to do so. She hated to miss any of Garbo's movies on television (Capote 1980, 226–7; Riese & Hitchens 170–1).

AVA GARDNER In July 1956 MM, and Sir Laurence Olivier held a press conference in a London hotel to announce their intention to make a film called *The Prince and the Showgirl*. Such was the hoopla that Ava Gardner, one of Hollywood's biggest stars, was able to walk through the hotel lobby completely unnoticed (Shevey 351).

JOHN GARFIELD Brooding Hollywood leading man of the 1930s and 1940s. Garfield starred in *We Were Strangers*, a 1949 melodrama set in Cuba. Both Garfield and director John Huston wanted to give newcomer MM a screen test for the movie. Unfortunately, the producer heard about this and would not allow it, unless Garfield and Huston paid for it themselves. This they were unwilling to do, and Marilyn was not in the picture (Beaver 34; Huston 286; *www.imdb.com*).

JUDY GARLAND MM was a huge Judy Garland fan and was fond of playing her records when she was relaxing at home. A particular favorite was Garland's rendition of "Who Cares?" Just three months before her death, Marilyn attended a live recording session that Garland did in Manhattan. For her part, Garland identified with Marilyn, not the least because they shared a dependence on barbiturates. The two women had known each other from Marilyn's earliest days in Hollywood, and Marilyn's death sent Garland into a deep depression. For weeks afterward she scarcely left home. Garland told an interviewer from *Ladies Home Journal*:

> I knew Marilyn and loved her dearly. She asked me for help. Me! I didn't know what to tell her. One night at a party at Clifton Webb's house, Marilyn followed me from room to room. "I don't want to get too far away from you," she said, "I'm scared." I told her, "We're all scared. I'm scared too."
>
> I don't think Marilyn really meant to harm herself. It was partly because she had too many pills available, then was deserted by her friends. You shouldn't be told you're completely irresponsible and be left alone with too much medication. It's too easy to forget. You take a couple of sleeping pills and you wake up in twenty minutes and forget you've taken them. So you take a couple more, and the next thing you know you've taken too many.

At Marilyn's funeral on August 8, 1962, Garland's classic recording of "Over the Rainbow" was played (Edwards 1974, 199–203; Riese & Hitchens 171–2; Schechter 242; Shipman 421; Victor 117).

DAVE GARROWAY   Leading radio and television host and interviewer. Garroway had the pleasure of interviewing Marilyn Monroe on television early in 1954 and on the radio on December 18, 1956. From the 1956 interview:

DG: [I] wonder if I'm scared of you. Are most men scared of you? I'm not sure whether I should be frightened of you or not.
MM: No, nobody's scared of me.
DG: I don't know. I bet a lot of guys are scared of you, though, because you're such an institution, really you are, you're kind of a national possession. Do you feel that you belong to the nation as a whole?
MM: I don't know quite what you mean by that. I live here.
DG: (Laughing) That'll do it very nicely. I hear that you moved into New York to live. Is this so?
MM: Yes, this will be my home from now on, that is, until I retire, and when I retire, I'm going to retire to Brooklyn [Hart 52].

MITZI GAYNOR   Singer, dancer and actress best known for her starring role in the film version of *South Pacific* (1958). Gaynor co-starred with MM in two films: *We're Not Married* (1952) and *There's No Business Like Show Business* (1954). In 1960, on the set of *The Misfits*, an extra asked Marilyn if she was really Marilyn Monroe. Marilyn put on Estelle Winwood's wig and jokingly replied that no, she was Mitzi Gaynor. Marilyn and Gaynor did not get along and Marilyn believed, that Gaynor had mocked her on the set of *There's No Business Like Show Business*.

Marilyn's chronic lateness on that film tested everyone's patience, especially that of co-star Ethel Merman. Gaynor said that she "found a way to keep Ethel cool. Whenever Marilyn wouldn't come out of her dressing room, I gave Ethel a wink, hinting that something naughty was going on in there. Of course that wasn't true, but if Ethel thought maybe some hanky-panky was going on, she could enjoy the situation" (Thomas 1985, 132–3). Despite such antics, Gaynor wanted to attend Marilyn's funeral, but she was turned away (Shevey 56, 266;).

BEN GAZZARA   Respected film, stage and television actor. The first time Gazzara met MM was in New York after a run-through of a play he was in. As he recalled, "The time she came backstage, she wore no makeup, her hair was windblown, she was girlish and very pretty, and she was ecstatic about what she'd seen." During her association with the Actors Studio in New York City, Gazzara had a casual acquaintance with Marilyn. One day he sat beside her in class. "Even though she wore no makeup Marilyn looked terrific. Everyone seemed to like her too, including me. I think we all respected the fact that the best-known woman in America wanted to learn more about her craft." After watching a scene that was not too good Marilyn turned to Gazzara and asked if he would like to work on the scene with her. Gazzara wrote: "As exciting as that would be, I didn't think it was such a good idea, so I told her I wasn't up to working at the studio just then. She looked at me sternly and said, 'What's the matter, don't you want to grow?' A perfect straight line if there ever was one! I had no easy punchline to come back with" (Gazzara 89–90).

SAM GIANCANA   Notorious Chicago mobster. If you believe the conspiracy theories, then Giancana was with MM at the Cal-Neva Lodge in Lake Tahoe on the last weekend of her life. Giancana supposedly knew about Marilyn's relationship with the Kennedy brothers and planned to use that knowledge to his own advantage. A couple of mob heavies were said to have administered (via suppository) a fatal dose of barbiturates to Marilyn in order to frame Robert Kennedy who had been with her a few hours earlier (Schwarz 605–6; Victor 120).

JOHN GIELGUD   Acclaimed English stage actor who also made films. Gielgud and MM crossed paths on July 26, 1956, at a ball at playwright Terence Rattigan's country house near London. The event was hosted by Rattigan, Sir Laurence Olivier and Vivien Leigh in honor of Marilyn and her husband, Arthur Miller. Marilyn was in England to film Rattigan's *The Prince and the Showgirl* with Olivier. Gielgud observed: "Marilyn wore an Edwardian dress—she had, I think, worn it to wear in the tests for the film—and she held court in a tent in the garden, where everyone queued up to shake her hand. As I was speaking to her, a rather formidable-looking lady in black suddenly appeared at Marilyn's side and introduced herself as Louella Parsons. Arthur Miller kept a discreet distance. I had no opportunity of talking further with Marilyn, but remembered how graceful she looked, dancing with Terry Rattigan as I took my departure" (Morgan 196). For a time Marilyn considered doing a version of Somerset Maugham's *Rain* opposite Gielgud (Gottfried 2003, 301; Shevey 347–8).

HEMIONE GINGOLD Sharp-tongued English actress with much Hollywood and theatrical experience. One evening during the December 1953–June 1954 run of *John Murray Anderson's Almanac* on Broadway, MM saw the show and enjoyed it enough to go backstage and congratulate Gingold (Gingold 132).

LILLIAN GISH Silent film star who continued her long career into the talkies. On what would have been Marilyn Monroe's 57th birthday, June 1, 1983, Lillian Gish was in New York City to cut a ribbon opening Marilyn Monroe Hall, a garden with 20 flowering cherry trees and a thousand pink-and-white begonias. In her remarks, Gish shared her memories of Marilyn. "I couldn't help thinking how many telephone calls were made for today's effort, and how much Marilyn Monroe would have appreciated this attention. This event is a far cry from those Hollywood premieres she attended. What relief this would have been. She never owned much and here is a piece of New York covered with flowers.... She was such a skillful comedienne in *Some Like It Hot* [1959] but such a tragic person. Now that she's gone, they call her a legend. She paid a terrible price to earn the title legend. Sad" (Oderman 332–3).

JACKIE GLEASON Movie and televison comedian who will always be remembered as the blustering bus driver Ralph Kramden on *The Honeymooners* (1955–1956). In 1956, Glea-

son held his 40th birthday party at Toots Shor's, his favorite New York hangout. Among the guests were MM and Joe DiMaggio. Some of the more exuberant males attempted to hoist Marilyn onto a wooden trestle table. The attempt was not too successful and the screen goddess had to flee to the ladies' room to have a splinter removed from her rear end. With the aid of a straight pin sterilized in the flame of a cigarette lighter, relief was soon forthcoming. Gleason's co-star from *The Honeymooners*, Audrey Meadows wrote, "When we told Jackie, he reported that his carnation pin was carefully honed for just such emergencies, and we should please keep him in mind for the next surgical procedure. Especially if Marilyn was afflicted again" (Meadows 123).

On another occasion, borrowing two men, Marilyn took them to the lake in Central Park for some vigorous rowing. Meadows recalled:

> While she wore sunglasses and a black wig as a disguise, she insisted one of the guys don a flowing blond wig. Marilyn was to be the rowboat's one-man crew, and the boy-girl passengers sat in the back as ballast. Up the lake, down the lake, around the lake they toured as Marilyn heaved and stretched strong arms to encourage surprised muscles and tendons to make firm the Monroe chest.
> When Jackie was told about this singular water sport, I steeled myself for a superbawdy response. But the very picture of this endeavor to maintain and enhance two of the great wonders of the modern world had stunned him into a state approaching awe.
> "If she'll let me ride in her rowboat," he said in a solemn prayer, "I'll buy her a battleship." And he added, "I'll even wear the wig" [Meadows 124].

SAMUEL GOLDWYN Autocratic Hollywood movie mogul. On the evening of November 6, 1954, Goldwyn was a guest at an exclusive dinner party to commemorate the completion of *The Seven Year Itch* and to welcome MM into the ranks of Hollywood's elite. At Goldwyn's table was a cardboard centerpiece of Marilyn's soon-to-be famous skirt-blowing scene. Marilyn said of the evening that she felt like Cinderella. That same year, Marilyn approached Goldwyn about getting a part in the film version of *Guys and Dolls*. But it was not to be (Summers 158, 194).

BENNY GOODMAN   Jazz musician and bandleader who was known as "The King of Swing." In 1948, when Columbia did not renew starlet MM's contract, she auditioned as a singer with the Benny Goodman band. Goodman complimented Marilyn on her singing but did not invite her to join his band (Riese & Hitchens, 182; Victor 124).

LOU GOSSETT, JR.   Respected dramatic actor who was about ten years younger than Marilyn Monroe. In 1955–1956, Gossett took classes at the Actors Studio in New York City. At that time, Marilyn was auditing some of the classes. One afternoon, as part of a class presentation, Marilyn phoned Gossett and asked him if he wanted to do a love scene with her from Tennessee Williams's *The Rose Tattoo*. Surprisingly, Gossett turned down the opportunity. He felt he was so star struck he would not be able to utter a single line. As Gossett remembered of his famous classmate: " She would walk into class with Arthur Miller's shirts tied at her waist, her feet in flip-flops, the sweet musky smell of Lifebuoy soap wafting after her. Her hair, pulled back with a rubber band, was always a little wet, as if she'd just stepped out of a shower. If she'd stayed with Arthur Miller she would easily have won five Academy Awards." Decades later, Gossett claimed that he was still aroused by the whiff of Lifebuoy soap (Gossett 76).

BETTY GRABLE   On July 19, 1946, MM did her first screen test. It was for a Betty Grable movie, *Mother Wore Tights*. Marilyn did not get a part in the film but, on the strength of the test, she did get her first six-month contract with Twentieth Century–Fox. Marilyn's first screen role was also in a Betty Grable vehicle, *The Shocking Miss Pilgrim* (1947). Although the movie is not usually included in the Marilyn Monroe filmography, she had a tiny uncredited part as a switchboard operator. Her performance, however, ended up on the cutting-room floor.

Known as "The Girl With the Million Dollar Legs," Grable was the queen of the Fox lot when Marilyn exploded on the scene. Surprisingly, the two blondes did not meet until they co-starred in 1953's *How to Marry a Millionaire*. Grable's contract gave her top billing, but all the publicity revolved around Marilyn. Grable could see that she was being eclipsed by the new blonde but was very gracious about it. She even accepted that Marilyn had been cast as Lorelei, the part she had wanted for herself. Grable told Marilyn, "Honey, I've had mine—go get yours." The press tried to build up a "Battle of the Blondes," but it never happened. The two got on famously. Grable told a newsman, "Go easy on Marilyn. She's a good kid. She's the biggest thing that's happened in this town in years. She'll make it to the top" (McGee 211).

Grable and Marilyn were so friendly that Grable gave her a pedicure and often invited Marilyn to her house for dinner. "We used to cook up a couple of steaks, drink some champagne, and have a load of laughs. Marilyn was easy to get along with. She was a much wittier person than she was ever given credit for, and it used to make me so angry when I read some of the stories put out about her. She was a hard-working actress determined to consolidate her success, and she was determined to succeed in drama. Already she had proved what a fine comedienne she was" (McGee 222–3).

Shortly after the premiere of *How to Marry a Millionaire*, Grable and Marilyn went to a birthday party for columnist Walter Winchell. Grable recalled:

> The funniest incident of all was when it came to the buffet. Marilyn and I both had chicken drumsticks with a side salad. And the only way to enjoy drumsticks is to eat them with your fingers. Marilyn and I were seated at the same table with a couple of crusty old matrons. When Marilyn had finished eating she casually dipped her gloved fingers into the fingerbowl of water, swished them around a couple of times and then proceeded to dry them on her napkin. She had kept her gloves on while eating as she knew she would have problems trying to get them off.
> One of the old dears raised an eyebrow at Marilyn's table manners. Marilyn and I exchanged glances. I was dying to laugh. Like a scene out of

one of her films, Marilyn shrugged innocently at the old ladies, then turned to me and winked. We both dissolved with laughter. It was very rude of us, and I am sure the ladies thought we were bombed. But it was a great night, and I hadn't had so many laughs in ages [McGee 224–5].

When Grable's daughter was hospitalized after a riding accident, Marilyn was the only one to call. Grable appreciated Marilyn's concern and never forgot it. Grable did like to tease Marilyn, however. When Marilyn phoned, saying in that famous whispery voice, "Hello, Betty? This is Marilyn." Grable always responded with, "Marilyn who?" Marilyn never realized that she was being kidded (Shevey 236).

For her part, Marilyn admired Grable, studied her films and modeled herself after her. More than one observer commented that they could see Grable in Marilyn's early film performances. After Grable left the Fox lot, Marilyn inherited her dressing room. Newspaper reporters wanted Marilyn to pose by the door while Grable's name was still on it. Out of respect for her friend, Marilyn refused (Riese & Hitchens 184–6; Victor 124–6).

BILL GRAHAM Rock-and-roll impresario of the 1960s and 1970s who operated the famous Fillmore West and Fillmore East historic music venues in San Francisco. Earlier in his life, Graham was an aspiring actor who attended classes at the Actors Studio in New York. Graham remembered MM auditing a class he was taking. He nearly passed out when the famous screen goddess approached him after class and asked him if he would practice a scene with her. "Well, give me your phone number," she said, "and I'll call you." Graham sat by the phone and she did call, saying, "Bill? This is Marilyn. You know. Marilyn from *class*" (Graham 108).

BILLY GRAHAM Television evangelist. Billy Graham was asleep in a Seattle hotel when he woke suddenly, full of foreboding for Marilyn Monroe. Graham was moved to pray for her soul and had his assistants try and telephone her. But it was to no avail. Marilyn's people said she was too busy to speak to Gra-

ham. They said that Marilyn "would meet with the Reverend Graham—*sometime*. Not now, maybe two weeks from now" (Jeremiah 167). Two weeks later was August 5, 1962, and Marilyn Monroe was dead.

In her autobiography, actress Debbie Reynolds corroborates Graham's story. Graham wanted her to intervene with MM. Reynolds, only a slight acquaintance of Marilyn's and heavily pregnant at the time, got hairdresser Sidney Guilaroff (who was much closer to Marilyn) to speak to her. But it was too late. A few days later Marilyn was dead. Graham felt guilt-ridden that Marilyn had not been saved in time. About two weeks later, at Debbie Reynolds's home, Graham spoke to a gathering of about 40 Hollywood celebrities. With Marilyn's passing still in everyone's thoughts, Graham felt that there were many in Hollywood who were in danger (Reynolds & Columbia, 1988).

SHEILAH GRAHAM Hollywood gossip columnist. In 1948 or 1949 Graham met MM in the Café de Paris at Twentieth Century–Fox.

I watched Marilyn pause at the entrance of the café. She was accompanied by a young man (she always made her entrances with a man, even if he was just the office boy, to indicate her popularity with men). In one hand she held a big book. The free hand furtively creased the skirt of her thin beige suit between her buttocks, to emphasize them. The jacket was cut in a deep U so that you could see the rising mounds of her breasts. Every part of her shook as she walked. I thought she was tarty, pretty, eager to answer questions. I asked her what the book was about. It was *The Basic Writings of Freud*. She didn't look like an intellectual and I asked her, "Are you really reading it?" "Oh, yes," she breathed, and opened her blue eyes to the widest extent. She had a beautiful brow. It had not always been so beautiful. I knew her agents in those early days.... They had suggested she remove the frizzy hair around her hairline before signing at Columbia for *Ladies of the Chorus*. Her hair was naturally curly, baby soft, and hard to manage. A new hairline was drawn for her at Columbia and the excess fuzz removed with hot wax, later by electrolysis."

Marilyn's new wide brow transformed her from being merely attractive into a beauty. But she always had a problem with her hair. She had resisted dying it blonde. Her hair broke under the continual assaults of peroxide. What a pity she was too soon for the wig era. Always concerned with how she looked, Marilyn washed and set her hair every day. Her greatest treasure was her beauty-parlor-size hair dryer. She lugged it to every city she visited in the United States.

There was fine, downy, blonde hair all over her face, which, although covered with make-up, gave a luminous quality to her skin on the screen. She would spend hours experimenting with make-up—putting it on, taking it off. She was never really sure she was beautiful, and she thought her nose was unattractive, a piece too long. Photographers learned to take her full face. When she was powerful, she killed every "still" showing her in profile. On the photographs she liked, she placed a star. Instinctively she knew where to turn when she saw a camera. Her eyelashes, half an inch long, were completely white and had to be dyed constantly. Her fingers were tiny and ineffectual. Her fingernails, often dirty, were chewed to the quick [Graham 1969, 136].

In 1963, Graham called upon the Motion Picture Academy to give MM a posthumous Oscar. They never did (Graham 1965, 103–5; Riese & Hitchens 186; Victor 125).

FARLEY GRANGER   Hollywood film actor who appeared in 1952's *O'Henry's Full House*. MM was also in the picture, but she and Granger did not share any screen time (Granger & Calhoun 131).

STEWART GRANGER   Handsome British actor who became a leading man in Hollywood films. Granger was acquainted with MM from Hollywood parties and describes the effect she had: "But the real catch at all these parties was a newcomer called Marilyn Monroe. Amazing the effect this zany beauty made on her entrance, which was invariably late. I was always amused by the silence that came over the room and the looks of envy on the faces of the other famous beauties." Granger had first met Marilyn on a visit to MGM in 1950. "I had seen a forlorn figure coming towards me. I couldn't take my eyes off her, or to be more exact, off the swaying behind as it passed. No behind ever swayed like Marilyn's."

Granger learned that after playing a small

part in John Huston's *The Asphalt Jungle* in 1950, MGM dropped Marilyn. One of the studio's female dramatic coaches concluded that Marilyn had no talent and should be fired. Granger speculated that it was because Marilyn had too much sex appeal and some "stupid cow" was envious. Granger thought Marilyn had integrity and was an "incredible young lady" (Granger 281–2).

CARY GRANT   Cary Grant probably saved MM's film career. Grant did one movie with Marilyn, a fountain-of-youth comedy called *Monkey Business*, released in 1952. Although Marilyn was merely a supporting player she lit up the screen. Unfortunately, due to her personal problems, she disrupted the filming. It was at this time that the news broke of how she had posed for a nude calendar. As if that was not enough, she was hospitalized with appendicitis. The director, Howard Hawks, was ready to fire Marilyn but Grant, who had suffered a bout of illness himself on a Hawks picture, talked him out of it. If Marilyn had been dismissed at this stage in her career, she would most likely never have worked again.

Grant gave his impressions of Marilyn in an interview: "I found her a very interesting child. I was able to have several chats with her on the set and I thought her most attractive, very shy and very eager to learn her job. We discussed books and I mentioned a few she might want to read" (Harris 1987, 159). Grant also said, "I had no idea she would become a big star. If she had something different from any other actresses, it wasn't apparent at the time. She seemed very shy and quiet. There was something sad about her." He recalled that Marilyn seemed embarrassed when studio workers whistled at her (McCarthy 499).

When Joe DiMaggio visited the set, a publicity photo was taken of Joe, Marilyn, and Cary. However, when the picture was published, Grant, at Joe's insistence, had been cropped out. Marilyn's final film, the uncompleted *Something's Got to Give*, was to be a remake of a successful Cary Grant and Irene Dunne vehicle from 1940, *My Favorite Wife* (Eliot 280–1; Truscott 157–8).

BUDDY GRECO   Singer and pianist who was two months younger than MM. Marilyn spent the last weekend of her life, July 28–29, 1962, at the Cal-Neva Lodge in Lake Tahoe, where she stayed with Frank Sinatra and Peter Lawford. Greco was performing at the lodge that weekend and a photograph exists of him and Marilyn, both smiling broadly as they share a friendly embrace (Morgan 280).

MERV GRIFFIN   Former singer and actor who went on to become a television talk show host and media mogul. In 1955, Griffin was subletting Marlon Brando's New York apartment. Before moving out he decided to find a new tenant. At 9:00 one morning there was a loud knock on the door. Griffin describes what happened next:

> When I opened the door and saw who was standing there I thought I was hallucinating. She was wearing a gray raincoat but there was no mistaking the face. I just stood and stared and tried to wake myself.
>
> "I'm Marilyn Monroe," she said.
>
> For all I know it might have been five minutes before I answered her. "What d'ya want?" I ad-libbed.
>
> "Can I see the apartment?"
>
> "You're here to look at the apartment?"
>
> "It is Marlon Brando's isn't it?"
>
> "Yes."
>
> "Then I'm at the right place."
>
> Jay Kantor [a talent agent] popped his head into the doorway and started laughing so hard he started Marilyn and me laughing too.
>
> I put some water on for coffee, and got myself dressed while Marilyn and Jay poked around the apartment. She was, indeed, looking for an apartment because she was planning to spend some time in town working with Lee Strasberg. Brando was her idol, and this visit was a pilgrimage. She was like a child in a toy shop as she wandered through the apartment, peeking into closets and touching the furniture. When she reached the locked storage closet, she asked me about it.
>
> "Marlon left some things in there. He asked me to keep it locked."
>
> She gave me a pleading look that weakened my knees. "Can't I just have a look?"
>
> "I promised him..."
>
> Then she walked over to the piano, ran her hand over the keys and asked if it was mine or Marlon's.
>
> "It's his."
>
> "Really? Will you play something for me?"
>
> "Sure, if you'll sing."
>
> "We'll all sing."
>
> And we did, the three of us, for over an hour, running through all my sheet music of show tunes.
>
> Marilyn left, and she never sublet the apartment, but I'm sure that wasn't her purpose from the start. I went back to bed and decided I wouldn't even *bother* telling my friends that Marilyn had come to visit [Griffin & Barsocchini 209–10].

Griffin had an unusual theory as to why Marilyn became a star: "Many of the great Hollywood stars—Joan Crawford, Bette Davis, even Marilyn Monroe—had outsize heads," he wrote. "For some reason the camera compensates for the disparity by making their features stand out, thus causing them to appear more attractive on-screen" (Griffin & Bender 102).

ANDY GRIFFITH   Actor who starred in *The Andy Griffith Show* (1960–1968) and *Matlock* (1986–1995). Griffith was born the same day as MM—June 1, 1926. Marilyn was born in Los Angeles, California, and Griffith on the other side of the country in Mount Airy, North Carolina. Andy Griffith's name came up as a possible Bo Decker to appear opposite Marilyn in *Bus Stop* (1956). Don Murray was given the part (De la Hoz 198; *www.wikipedia.org*).

CHARLES GRODIN   As a young actor, Grodin perfected his craft at Lee Strasberg's prestigious Actors Studio in New York. During 1955–1956, Marilyn Monroe audited some of the classes. Grodin remembered how "one day I turned my head to glance at a blonde with no makeup sitting against the wall and thought how much she looked like, and realized she was, Marilyn Monroe. After class I watched as she walked down the street alone. People's mouths dropped open as they recognized her. She had a very powerful, magnetic beauty, even without makeup" (Grodin 70).

ANDREI GROMYKO   Career Russian politician and diplomat. In September 1959, Nikita Khrushchev, leader of the Soviet Union, was on a state visit to the United States. When he came to Twentieth Century–Fox Studio in

Hollywood for a luncheon, Gromyko, his minister of foreign affairs, was with him. MM sat about 15 feet away from the Russians. Gromyko wrote:

> After the official part of the reception was over and the guests were leaving, I was passing her table when she suddenly turned to me: "Mr. Gromyko, how are you?" Although we'd never met before, she spoke as if we were old friends.
>
> Mostly out of courtesy, I replied: "Hello, I'm just fine. And how about you? I've seen a lot of your films."
>
> She held out her hand and said something, but I missed her words, and the crush of people was already pushing me into the next room. But at least I could tell my children I had actually talked with Marilyn Monroe.

Three years later, when Marilyn died, Gromyko was skeptical that it was a suicide: "Always the happy, radiant Marilyn, and now suicide—and only thirty-six years old. Drugs were mentioned, but the stories made no sense."

In his memoirs, Gromyko does not actually claim that Marilyn was the victim of a conspiracy but he does point out her relationships with the Kennedy brothers, the F.B.I.'s files on her, and Marilyn's association with people of leftist views, especially her husband, Arthur Miller (Gromyko 67–8).

ALEC GUINNESS Versatile Oscar-winning British actor who reportedly hated being Obi-Wan Kenobi in *Star Wars* (1977), *The Empire Strikes Back* (1980), and *Return of the Jedi* (1983). Guinness met MM on two occasions. The first meeting was on July 26, 1956, at playwright Terence Rattigan's country house near London. The event was a ball given in honor of Marilyn and her husband, Arthur Miller. Guinness said of her: "She's a bit dippy but there's no doubt she has charm and appeal and personality" (Read 345). The second meeting occurred at comedian Ernie Kovacs's home in Hollywood, at a party for Marilyn and poet Carl Sandburg. According to Guinness: "Poet and superstar sat opposite each other at a small table, gazing at each other open-mouthed; that is, Marilyn's lips were parted and her eyes adoring and Sandburg never closed his mouth to cease talking" (Guinness 1986, 287). Toward the end of his life, Guinness expressed a desire to never again see any reproductions of the portrait which Andy Warhol had made of Marilyn (Gottfired 2003, 300; Guinness 1997, 3).

-H-

BUDDY HACKETT Cherubic comedian and actor. On August 21, 1960, Buddy Hackett was on *What's My Line?*, a television game show on which panelists attempted to guess the occupations of ordinary people and the identities of celebrities. Hackett signed in as Marilyn Monroe. Whether or not Marilyn was tuned in that evening will never be known (*www.wikipedia.org* ; *www.imdb.com*).

JEAN HAGEN Actress who excelled at comic roles. Hagen's most famous screen appearance was in *Singin' In the Rain* (1952), in which she played a silent film star who could not adjust to the talkies. In 1950, Hagen had a non-comedy role in a MM picture, the gritty film-noir drama *The Asphalt Jungle*. When she met people who did not realize she was in the film, Hagen would say, "There were only two girl roles, and I obviously wasn't Marilyn Monroe" (Hagen & Wagner 83). The two actresses did not share any screen time but they posed together for publicity stills (*www.cursumperficio.net*/biography/1950).

ALAN HALE, JR. Burly light comedy actor who was the Skipper on television's *Gilligan's Island* (1964–1967). Hale was in one of MM's least-known films, 1951's *Hometown Story*. He played a newspaper reporter and shared a couple of scenes with Marilyn, who played the office secretary (*www.imdb.com*).

OLIVER HARDY Tubby, perpetually exasperated, half of the Laurel and Hardy comedy duo. When Marilyn, (who was still known as Norma Jeanne) resided at the Los Angeles Orphans Home, one of the matrons was a relative of Oliver Hardy. Hardy was generous with donations of furniture, toys and books for the orphanage (Morgan 25).

JEAN HARLOW Wisecracking platinum-blonde screen goddess of the 1930s, who died young. For the December 22, 1958, issue of *Life* magazine, MM posed as her childhood idol, Jean Harlow. Marilyn perfectly captured Harlow's femme fatale image before fashion photographer Richard Avedon's camera. Of her idol's importance to her, Marilyn said: "Since I was a child, I had nothing to do. I was poor. I used to look at movie magazines and cut the pictures out of Jean Harlow and Clark Gable. That's what I wanted to be some day—a Jean Harlow and to act with Clark Gable" (Shevey 114).

In conversation, Marilyn claimed to have once seen Jean Harlow. When she was about nine years old, in 1935, Marilyn's mother took her to Grauman's Chinese Theater to watch a Hollywood movie premiere. Marilyn remembered seeing her idol, Jean Harlow, alight from a limousine in a lovely white gown. Harlow released three films in 1935: *Reckless* with William Powell (whom Marilyn came to know during the making of *How to Marry a Millionaire*); *China Seas* with Clark Gable (with whom Marilyn was paired in her final movie, *The Misfits*, 26 years later); and *Riffraff*, featuring a very young Mickey Rooney (with whom Marilyn made *The Fireball* in 1950).

Marilyn expressed an interest in portraying Harlow on the screen, but it never happened. A script was written for Marilyn but Arthur Miller convinced her not to do it, as it would not conform to her "new image." In 1965, *Harlow* was filmed with Caroll Baker in the role that would have been Marilyn's. The picture opened to universally bad reviews. About a month before she died, Marilyn and Hollywood columnist Sidney Skolsky visited Jean Harlow's mother, "Mamma" Jean Bello, to ask her permission to make the film. Reportedly, "Mamma" Jean said, upon seeing Marilyn, that her baby had come back to life.

Marilyn used hairdressers who had worked with Jean Harlow, including the one who had invented "hot platinum" for her. Har-low's third husband was Harold Rosson, a cinematographer who worked with Marilyn on *The Asphalt Jungle* (1950). Rosson received an Academy Award nomination for his work on the film. In 1954, Marilyn lived on the same street Harlow had lived, North Palm Drive in Beverly Hills. Marilyn lived at No. 508. Nearly 20 years earlier, Harlow had lived at No. 512. Anita Loos, who wrote three movies for Harlow, also wrote *Gentlemen Prefer Blondes* which starred Marilyn in 1953. Loos knew both actresses and said, "There was so much Harlow in Marilyn, it couldn't have been by chance" (Guiles 42).

Other sources: Brown & Barham 13,20; Summers 97; Victor 136

AVERELL HARRIMAN Harriman was a politician, businessman and diplomat who served in various posts under presidents Truman, Kennedy and Johnson. A photograph exists of Marilyn Monroe with Milton Berle, Jerry Lewis, Dean Martin, and Averell Harriman. It was taken on March 17, 1955, at the Friars Club, while Harriman was serving as governor of New York (Martin & Smith 98; *www.cursumperficio.net* / Biography / 1955).

REX HARRISON Urbane, Academy Award–winning British stage and film actor. After seeing Harrison play Professor Higgins in *My Fair Lady* on Broadway, MM went backstage to congratulate the star. Harrison remembered how Marilyn did "wondrous things while looking at herself in two mirrors simultaneously" (Wapshott 183).

HUNTINGTON HARTFORD Between October 12 and November 2, 1947, MM was the second lead in a stage play, a comedy entitled *Glamour Preferred*. The play was at the Bliss-Hayden Miniature Theater in Beverly Hills, and it was Marilyn's debut in legitimate theater. Huntington Hartford was the heir to the Great Atlantic & Pacific Tea Company millions and would become one of the world's richest men. Hartford saw the play one evening and was so taken with Marilyn that he went backstage to ask her for a date. It is not certain whether or not she accepted. Although he was

15 years her senior, Hartford survived Marilyn by nearly 46 years (Guiles 121).

HENRY HATHAWAY   Director of such films as *Lives of a Bengal Lancer* (1935), *Call Northside 777* (1948), *The Desert Fox* (1951), and *True Grit* (1969). Hathaway probably met Marilyn Monroe at a New Year's Eve party, December 31, 1948, at producer Sam Spiegel's house in Beverley Hills. Hathaway wanted to make *Of Human Bondage* with Marilyn Monroe and James Dean, but Darryl F. Zanuck was not interested.[37] He said, "You want to put Monroe in such a movie? In a comedy this girl can make us four million dollars" (Hickey & Smith 133). Hathaway directed MM in *Niagara*, a non-comedy film which made her a star. Despite their mutual success, Hathaway was not on Marilyn's list of approved directors. Hathaway had a reputation as a gruff misogynist, but he adored Marilyn. While making *Niagara*, Hathaway said of her, "She's the best natural actress I've directed. And I go back. I worked with ... Jean Harlow.... And she's got the greatest natural talent" (Riese & Hitchens 203, Hathaway to Sidney Skolsky, July 16, 1952). Hathaway went on to say how Marilyn was "marvelous to work with, very easy to direct and terrifically ambitious to do better. And *bright*, really bright. She may not have had an education, but she was just naturally bright. But always being trampled on by bums. I don't think anyone ever treated her on her own level. To most men she was something that they were a little bit ashamed of—even Joe DiMaggio" (Spoto 1993, 222). One day on the soundstage Hathaway encountered Marilyn in despair. She had created the Marilyn Monroe character and now she could not escape it. She was constantly striving to improve herself and do different things but feared that all she could manage was an imitation of herself. After her death, Hathaway thought there was no need for an inquest. He blamed Marilyn's death on the studio executives.

Hathaway asked Marilyn to wear her own clothes in *Niagara*, but this caused a problem because she hardly owned any. Hathaway did not believe her until he visited her apartment and saw that she was telling the truth. Marilyn's closet was nearly empty. Marilyn does wear her own black suit in the bell-pealing scene when she is murdered (Shevey 211–13; Taraborrelli 2009, 337–8; *www.cursumperficio.net*/biography/1948).

JUNE HAVER   Popular blonde film actress of the 1940s and 1950s. Haver was nine days younger than MM but outlived her by nearly 43 years. Haver was the star of *Scudda Hoo! Scudda Hay!* (1948), which is usually considered to be MM's first screen appearance. Marilyn's part was cut to insignificance because the studio thought it would be too confusing to have two blondes in the same film.[38] In 1951, Haver co-starred with Marilyn in a comedy called *Love Nest*.

Some 15 years later, Haver remembered Marilyn on the set: "She was so young and pretty, so shy and nervous on that picture, but I remember the scene where she was supposed to be sunning in the back yard of the apartment house we all lived in. When Marilyn walked on the set in her bathing suit and walked to the beach chair, the whole crew gasped, gaped and seemed to turn to stone. They just stopped work and stared; Marilyn had that electric something—and mind you, movie crews are quite used to seeing us in brief costumes. They've worked on so many musicals and beach sequences. But they just gasped and gaped at Marilyn as though they were stunned. In all my years at the studio, I'd never seen that happen before. Sure, the crew gives you the kidding wolf-whistle routine, but this was sheer shock" (*Coronet* 1 / 1966).

HOWARD HAWKS   Movie director who made such classics as *Scarface* (1932), *Bringing Up Baby* (1938), *His Girl Friday* (1940), *To Have and Have Not* (1944), *The Big Sleep* (1946), and *Red River* (1948). Hawks also directed two MM pictures, *Monkey Business* (1952) and *Gentlemen Prefer Blondes* (1953).

Hawks had met Marilyn in Palm Springs in 1948. At the time he thought she was stupid and vulgar, with little potential. However, four years later, Hawks cast Marilyn as Miss

Laurel, Charles Coburn's incompetent secretary in *Monkey Business*. Hawks thought Marilyn had a certain overdeveloped quality which could be funny. Hawks had this to say about Marilyn:

> Marilyn Monroe was the most frightened little girl who had no confidence in her ability. She was afraid to come on the screen. Very strange girl.... But when she got out in front of the camera, the camera liked her, suddenly she was a great sex symbol. I was lucky to work with her early, before she became frightened. Cary [Grant] was a lot of help with her in *Monkey Business*. She seemed to listen to him. But I had an easy time compared to other directors who worked with her. The more important she became the more frightened she became [Truscott 157–8].

Marilyn was not feeling her best during the making of the picture and even though she had relatively few scenes, the other cast members were often forced to work around her. She had her appendix removed as soon as her work on the film was completed.

By the time of *Gentlemen Prefer Blondes* Marilyn had become more of a handful. Co-star Jane Russell was often the go-between for Marilyn and Hawks. Hawks remembered, "It wasn't easy, that film, but it wasn't difficult because I had Jane there.... I'd hear them talking, Marilyn would whisper, 'What did he tell me?' Jane wouldn't say, 'He's told you six times already,' she'd just tell her again" (McCarthy 506).

Then there was the problem of Natasha Lytess, Marilyn's acting coach, whom she brought to the set with her. If Lytess was not satisfied, even if Hawks was, Marilyn would demand additional takes. Hawks ordered Lytess off the set but then Marilyn would not come out of her dressing room. Lytess came back. Hawks learned to go through the motions and shoot extra takes without film in the camera. When studio head Darryl F. Zanuck asked how the production could be speeded up, an exasperated Hawks replied that he had "three wonderful ideas: replace Marilyn, rewrite the script to make it shorter, and get a new director" (McCarthy 506). In 1955, when Marilyn drew up a list of approved directors, Howard Hawks was not included

(Leaming 1998, 16, 68–71; McBride 20–1; Victor 138).

STERLING HAYDEN   Rugged Hollywood leading man remembered for his role as General Jack D. Ripper in *Dr. Strangelove or: How I Learned to Stop Worrying and Love the Bomb* (1964). Hayden was the star of *The Asphalt Jungle*, a breakthrough movie for MM. Hayden saw that Marilyn was very frightened on set and, although he played no scenes with her, did what he could to calm her nerves. Marilyn and Hayden were posed together in publicity stills for the picture (Doll 76; Guiles 154–5; Riese & Hitchens 205; *www.imdb.com* ; *www.cursumperficio.net* /biography/1950).

GABBY HAYES   Crotchety, bewhiskered old-timer and sidekick in countless Westerns. As improbable as it sounds, Gabby Hayes and MM were once in the same room at the same time. It was 1954 at the Copacabana nightclub. Hayes and Marilyn had gone—separately—to see Frank Sinatra and his opening act, Joey Bishop. Offscreen, Hayes was an elegant man-about-town. Even more improbably, Gabby and Marilyn may have met once before. In May 1946, the 19-year-old starlet was in Las Vegas waiting out her divorce from her first husband. She ran into Roy Rogers who was in town shooting a Western called *Heldorado*. Rogers invited Marilyn to join the cast and crew for dinner. Gabby Hayes was one of the supporting actors in the film (Starr 34).

SUSAN HAYWARD   Oscar–winning Hollywood leading lady, who had a 35-year career in films. When *Photoplay* held its annual awards party on February 9, 1953, all eyes were on Susan Hayward, magnificently gowned and beautiful. But the flash bulbs started popping in another direction the moment MM arrived, late as usual. Marilyn was in a skin-tight gold-lamé gown which conveniently burst apart at the seams. Innocently protesting her embarrassment, Marilyn had her dress sewn up in view of everyone. Marilyn had been voted "Fastest Rising Star of 1952." Hayward received an award of her own but never got everyone's attention back and quietly left the party. Overnight, Hayward had been dethroned by Marilyn as queen of the Twentieth Century–Fox lot. Hayward continued to work but from that time on her movies were mostly second-rate. Hayward did not direct her resentment toward Marilyn but to studio boss Darryl F. Zanuck, who became increasingly indifferent to her performances. Even so, on November 6, 1954, Hayward was one of the "A" list guests in attendance for the wrap party following the completion of *The Seven Year Itch* (Linet 1981, 132–3, 141; Shevey 116, 291).

RITA HAYWORTH   Known as "The Love Goddess," Rita Hayworth was one of Hollywood's biggest stars. Nearly eight years older than MM, she survived her by almost a quarter of a century. Early in 1958, as she was preparing to marry her fifth and final husband, Hayworth said, "Marilyn Monroe and Jayne Mansfield can have all the headlines. I've had enough! From now on the only headlines I want are on my acting" (Morella & Epstein 1983, 251).

EDITH HEAD   The premier Hollywood costume designer. Head won eight Academy Awards, including one for her work on *All About Eve* (1950), which featured MM in a small but important role. Head thought that Marilyn was "entirely too voluptuous," but that she had a perfect nose. The two knew each other socially and every time they met the conversation would turn to clothes. Head was surprised how knowledgeable Marilyn was about fabric and fit. Marilyn always wanted to make her legs look better. Marilyn's legs were far from chubby but they were not perfect, and she always strived for perfection. Head suggested that shaded hosiery would make her legs look longer and more attractive. Head wanted to design for Marilyn but she never got the call. She worked every Hollywood contact she had but to no avail. Marilyn was always friendly to Head but she continued to use other designers. Head was quoted as saying: "I never thought she looked especially comfortable in what she wore, and she once told a reporter that she didn't feel comfortable in clothes. Naturally the press made a big production of the sexual

angle of the remark, but I think she really meant it seriously. Every designer who worked with her cinched her and harnessed her. Marilyn was a free spirit who should have been dressed in such a way that she would be able to forget about her clothes. When a woman is sexy, she knows it and she doesn't need clothes that constantly remind her. Marilyn should have been a star in the late 1960s—she could have been devastating as a sensual flower child. I hated the hippie look, but Marilyn would have loved it" (Head & Calistro 106).

BEN HECHT   Academy Award–winning screenwriter responsible for *Wuthering Heights* (1939), *Spellbound* (1945) and *Notorious* (1946). In 1952 Hecht co-wrote *Monkey Business*, which featured MM.

In 1954, just after Marilyn's marriage to Joe DiMaggio, Hecht spent five days with her in San Francisco. He was hired to ghostwrite her autobiography. Hecht listened as Marilyn spun the version of her life that she wanted him to hear—the unwanted little orphan girl who made good. Hecht was sometimes skeptical about what Marilyn was saying. "When I say lying, I mean she isn't telling the truth. I don't think so much that she is trying to deceive me as that she is a fantasizer. [Hecht interpreted Marilyn's] odd little physical body language, to react when she was going into something fictional or when she was leveling" (Summers 12–13). For her part, Marilyn, as quoted by Arthur Miller, said, "I never intended to make all that much about being an orphan. It's just that Ben Hecht was hired to write this story about me, and he said, 'Okay, sit down and try to think up something interesting about yourself.' Well, I was boring, and I thought maybe I'd tell him about them putting me in the orphanage, and he said that was great and wrote it, and that became the main thing suddenly" (Miller 1987, 370). Two months later, Hecht had banged out a 160–page manuscript for Doubleday. Hecht's widow recalled Marilyn's reaction to the finished product. "Marilyn laughed and cried and expressed herself 'thrilled.' She said she never imagined so wonderful a story could be written about her and that Benny had captured every phase of her life" (Summers 12).

Joe DiMaggio was somewhat less thrilled and objected to the book being published. Marilyn then also refused to agree to its publication. The book project languished but without his knowledge, Hecht's agent sold the manuscript for $50,000 to an English tabloid, *The Empire News*. Marilyn's story was serialized in England between May 9 and August 1, 1954. Hecht angrily telegraphed his agent: "Your sale of the copy is a violation of the arrangement I made with Miss Monroe on which I phoned you and telegraphed you a dozen times. The first knowledge I had of the sale of this copy was a telephone call from Miss Monroe's lawyer. I denied to him that such a sale had been made because I couldn't imagine it being done without my knowledge or consent. I also denied to Miss Louella Parsons [who revealed the story in her newspaper column] that the copy in the English papers was mine. I am making all these statements because your action has put me personally into the sort of hole I have never been in before" (MacAdams 269).

Hecht never saw any of the money and Marilyn threatened to sue him for misquotation. Eventually the Marilyn Monroe autobiography was simply dropped and forgotten. It was forgotten until 1974 when, with some alterations, it was published by Stein and Day as *My Story*, with Marilyn Monroe listed as the sole author. The book was reissued in 2007 (Featherling 179–80; Monroe & Hecht; Summers 12–14).

EILEEN HECKART   Award–winning stage and screen actress who became a familiar face on television. In 1956, Heckart played opposite MM in *Bus Stop*. She was the only member of the cast whom Marilyn befriended. Heckart had just appeared in a stage production of *A View from the Bridge*, a play by Marilyn's future husband, Arthur Miller. Marilyn told Heckart about her "secret" romance with Miller, and Heckart pretended that it was not already common knowledge. Heckart's two young sons were often on the set and Marilyn would grab

an orange and a grapefruit and play catch with them. Marilyn said that playing catch with Heckart's children was the best part of her day and besides, Vitamin C was important for growing boys. As Heckart's son wrote:

> Whenever anyone said, "Eileen, what was it like working with Marilyn?" she would give two very different responses. The first was dismissive. With a wave of her hand, she'd say, "My God, she was so undisciplined. She was a star, not an actress!" She'd speak of a woman who was moody, making people wait for hours on end, and with the potential to be extremely vindictive to anyone who had crossed her on her way to stardom. Then there was the other response. Mama would get a wistful faraway look in her eye. In a soft material voice, she'd say, "What a sad, lonely young lady. She was adored by millions, but never believed that she was loved." ...When she spoke of Marilyn tears would stream down her face [Yankee 80–1].

Other sources: Glatzer 133; Guiles 316; Victor 42–3

HUGH HEFNER   Founder and publisher of *Playboy* magazine. On May 27, 1949, MM was just another out-of-work Hollywood starlet. At an earlier date, photographer Tom Kelley had asked Marilyn to pose nude, but she had refused. But now she phoned Kelley to see if his offer was still good. It was. A total of 24 nude shots were taken, two of which were used on pinup calendars. Marilyn, who signed the release form as "Mona Monroe," was paid $50, which she used to pay her rent and enjoy a quiet dinner—of which she recalled enjoying every mouthful. She saw no other money from the photos, which went on to generate millions.

The pictures were not used until the following year, by which time Marilyn's film career had begun to take off. Kelley sold the photos for $500 to the Baumgarth Company which distributed girlie calendars to garages, tool shops and the like. Eight million calendars were printed. Marilyn gave a copy of the calendar to her husband, Joe DiMaggio. In February 1952, a wire service reporter learned that the girl on the "Golden Dreams" calendar was none other than the fast-rising star Marilyn Monroe. Twentieth Century–Fox went into a panic and advised Marilyn to deny the story. Marilyn, who thought she had done nothing wrong, did the exact opposite. She admitted everything. She made the right decision. Marilyn and the film she had just made, *Clash by Night*, and the film she was currently making, *Don't Bother to Knock*, received enormous free publicity.

Hefner read in *Advertising Age* that nude pictures of Marilyn Monroe, the hottest new actress in Hollywood, were owned by a calendar company in suburban Chicago, the city in which he lived. Without waiting for an appointment, Hefner raced over to Baumgarth and offered to buy the rights to publish Marilyn's pictures in a men's magazine he was about to launch. Baumgarth sold the images to Hefner. Included was a nude study which had never been used, the sexiest one, in Hefner's considered opinion. The photograph depicted Marilyn stretched out on a red-velvet sheet with her mouth open and her eyes partly closed, peeking out from behind an upraised arm. Asked what she had on during the photo shoot, Marilyn had quipped, "The radio."[39]

Hefner's magazine was to be called *Stag Party*. In a letter to newsstand wholesalers, Hefner wrote, "But here's the really BIG news! The first issue of STAG PARTY will include the famous calendar pictures of Marilyn Monroe—in *full colour*! In fact—every issue of STAG PARTY will have a beautiful full-page, male-pleasing nude study—in full natural colour!" (Miller 1984, 37). By the time the magazine came out in December 1953, it had been retitled *Playboy*. Marilyn, who also appeared on the cover, became *Playboy's* first "Playmate of the Month" or "Sweetheart of the Month," as the feature was originally known. In order to see herself in the magazine Marilyn had to buy a copy on the newsstand.

In 1962, Hefner paid $25,000, a record price, for a series of nude pictures of Marilyn from *Something's Got to Give*. Marilyn also agreed to do a cover shot for *Playboy*. After Marilyn died in August 1962, Hefner waited a decent amount of time, January 1964, before publishing a 14-page tribute to Marilyn. Over the years, photos and features about Marilyn have appeared many times in the magazine.

Hefner purchased the crypt next to Marilyn's for his final resting place (Miller 1984, 37–9; Riese & Hitchens 395–6; Shevey 149–50; Talese 79–81).

LILLIAN HELLMAN American playwright. Hellman found the marriage of fellow playwright, Arthur Miller, to MM to be fascinating. After a telephone conversation with Miller, Hellman was convulsed with laughter. A friend asked Hellman what was so funny. Hellman replied: "I was talking with Arthur Miller and he said to me, 'I've got to get off the phone now. Marilyn just put breakfast on the table.' The picture tickles the hell out of me!"[40] When Hellman learned that Miller and Monroe had gotten divorced, she groused, "Well, that's that—I always knew he married *her* for money" (Martinson 308). After Marilyn's death, Hellman savaged Miller's thinly disguised portrait of her, *After the Fall*. She said, "So you put on stage your ex-wife who is dead from suicide and you dress her up so nobody can mistake her. Her name is Marilyn Monroe, food at any box office, so you cash in on her, and cash in on yourself, which is maybe even worse" (Bryer 59).

ERNEST HEMINGWAY Arguably the most famous American novelist of the Twentieth Century. MM is known to have read *The Snows of Kilimanjaro* and *The Old Man and the Sea* and, even though Hemingway appeared on her list of desirable men, she never really cared for his novels. As an animal lover who could not stand to see an animal hurt or killed, Marilyn could not relate to Hemingway's glorification of the manly pursuits of hunting and bullfighting. Upon hearing of Hemingway's death from a self-inflicted gunshot wound, Marilyn said of suicide, "I don't believe it's a sin or a crime ... although it doesn't get you anywhere" (Rollyson 1993, 186). When asked if the repeated mention of Joe DiMaggio would date his novel *The Old Man and the Sea*, Hemingway said, "Joe DiMaggio is not as dated as Marilyn Monroe. What I was trying to do was present a true picture of a fisherman, and down here the fishermen are crazy about baseball" (Bruccoli 1986, 100). After Marilyn's death it was discovered that she owned copies of Hemingway's *Farewell to Arms* and *The Sun Also Rises* (*www.cursumperficio.net*/files/Marilyn:stuff).

AUDREY HEPBURN   Elegant Hollywood star and philanthropist. One of Hepburn's most famous roles came in 1961 with Holly Golightly in *Breakfast at Tiffany's*. George Axelrod, who had written *The Seven Year Itch* and *Bus Stop* for MM, wrote a screenplay based on *Breakfast at Tiffany's*, a novella by Truman Capote. Axelrod tailored the script for Marilyn, but she turned it down. The film's producer reported that "within forty-eight hours, we were told by Monroe's dramatic adviser, Paula Strasberg, that she would not have her play a lady of the evening" (Harris 1994, 171).

WOODY HERMAN   Jazz clarinetist and big-band leader. In 1948, a date took Marilyn to the Palladium dance hall in Hollywood to see Woody Herman. As usual, Marilyn created a sensation. Herman was staring at Marilyn so hard he nearly fell off the stage (Morgan 75).

CHARLTON HESTON   Imposing film actor who, despite a long and varied career, is remembered for his biblical and medieval epics. Heston knew MM socially but never worked with her. He declined an offer to appear opposite Marilyn in *Let's Make Love* (1960).

Heston once observed:

She was perhaps the last of the stars created, then grossly abused, by the studio system. After Garbo, there's probably never been a woman the camera loved more than Marilyn, not only for her stunning sexual beauty, but for the oddly innocent carnality she projected.

By this time, though, the years when Fox made millions while making her the world's favorite sex goddess had ravaged her ... from the inside out. She still looked marvelous, but whatever demons of anxiety lurked in her head had all but crippled her professionally.... Like many very beautiful actresses, she was deeply insecure about her acting; she was convinced her survival as a star depended on looking perfect in every setup. She'd become almost impossible to coax out of her dressing room onto the set. There were horror stories from the *Misfits* shoot of her keeping Clark Gable (something of an icon himself) waiting literally all day for her to appear at the cameras. At dinner with the Wylers, Laurence Olivier told me acting with and directing her in *The Prince and the Showgirl* had been the worst experience of his career.

When Heston set his hand and shoeprints in cement at Grauman's Chinese Theater he noticed that he had an enviable position. "There I was, right on top of Marilyn Monroe and Jane Russell. How many men can say that?" (Heston 217–18).

DARRYL HICKMAN   A former child star, Hickman was a movie and television actor who became a television executive. Marilyn had a small part as a waitress in *Dangerous Years* with Hickman. The film, completed in 1947, was the second movie in which MM appeared but the first to be released. Hickman said that Marilyn was "very attractive but standoffish without acting like she meant to be that way.... It was like you'd say, hey, she's got some scene going and it's nothing to do with a movie. Not to say she wasn't sweet, but kind of goofy, you know? She seemed to spook easily and get upset over something going wrong that didn't mean anything" (Gilmore 93).

TOMMY HILFIGER   In 1999, when many of MM's personal effects were sold at Christie's Auction House, fashion designer Tommy Hilfiger purchased the three pairs of blue jeans she had worn in *River of No Return* (1954). The auction price was $42,550. Marilyn was one of the first women to wear blue jeans on screen (De la Hoz 158).

HIROHITO   Hirohito became emperor of Japan in December 1926, when MM was six months old. He reigned until 1989, 27 years after Marilyn's death. Marilyn received a valuable gift from Emperor Hirohito. It was a single-string necklace of natural pearls with a diamond clasp. The occasion was Marilyn and Joe DiMaggio's 1954 honeymoon visit to Japan. Marilyn wore the pearls the day she divorced Joe. On Christmas 1957, Marilyn re-gifted the pearls to her acting coach, Paula Strasberg, who had admired them (*www.cur-sumperficio.net* /biography/1954).

ALFRED HITCHCOCK   Rotund British movie director who was known as "The Master of Suspense." In 1955, MM drew up a list of approved directors and Hitchcock's name was on it. For his part, Hitchcock said that there were only three genuine female stars in Hollywood: Elizabeth Taylor, Ingrid Bergman and Marilyn Monroe. Despite their mutual admiration, Hitchcock and Marilyn never worked together (Riese & Hitchens 208; Victor 139).

JOHN HODIAK   Actor who became a major movie star when he appeared opposite Tallulah Bankhead in *Lifeboat* (1944). In 1953, MM lived in a first-floor apartment on Doheny Drive in Beverly Hills. Her upstairs neighbor, with whom she was on friendly terms, was Hodiak. In 1961, Marilyn briefly moved back to the same apartment. Hodiak had died of a heart attack at the age of 41 in 1955 (Gilmore 20–1).

JIMMY HOFFA   Notorious crime figure and leader of the International Brotherhood of Teamsters. Some of MM's more sensation-alist biographers have claimed that Hoffa had bugged her house and obtained incriminating audio tapes of the actress with the Kennedys. A further claim is made that Hoffa planned to use the tapes for blackmail (Summers 510; Victor 139).

WILLIAM HOLDEN   Dependable Hollywood actor. On November 6, 1954, Holden was one of 80 invited guests at a swanky dinner party in honor of MM and the completion of *The Seven Year Itch*. Holden sat at a table which was decorated with a cardboard cutout of Marilyn's famous skirt-blowing scene from the film. Six years later, Holden turned down the opportunity to be Marilyn's co-star in *Let's Make Love* (Shevey 291; Victor 168).

BILLIE HOLIDAY   Soulful performer who is regarded as one of the greatest jazz singers who ever lived. MM went to a New York

nightclub to hear Billie Holiday. After being told that a copy of her famous nude calendar was hanging on the wall in the club's office, Marilyn wanted to see it. Holiday, who was using the office as a dressing room, assumed that Marilyn had come backstage to speak to her. Learning otherwise, she yanked the calendar off the wall, crumpled it, threw it in Marilyn's face and called her a dirty name. Marilyn was stunned by this reaction and left the club, even though the manager implored her to stay for the show (Riese & Hitchens 209–10; Summers 113).

JUDY HOLLIDAY   Actress who won an Oscar for *Born Yesterday* (1950). Reportedly, MM did a screen test for the role in 1948 when she was briefly under contract to Columbia. Studio head Harry Cohn refused to look at it. Holliday got the part which would make her a star and Marilyn was dropped by Columbia. Prior to her first ever screen test in 1946, Marilyn was asked to read a few lines of dialogue from *Winged Victory* (1944), which Holliday had spoken in the film.

In April 1958, *Life* did a feature on the parts well-know actresses would most like to play. Holliday's New York apartment was chosen as the location. Holliday and Monroe had met on the street a couple of years earlier. Monroe had seen Holliday do an impression of her on television and liked it. The two went to Holliday's apartment for tea and an afternoon of conversation. Holliday was less happy during the *Life* photoshoot when she saw Marilyn change her clothes in full view of her young son (Holtzman 245–6; Riese & Hitchens 210; Spoto 1993, 110).

CELESTE HOLM   Elegant film actress who was nominated for an Oscar for her performance in *All About Eve*, in which MM had a supporting role.

Holm on Marilyn: "I never thought of Marilyn as being an actress. Even in the films she did later on. I mean—even a puppy dog will act cute and silly, if you give it enough encouragement. I confess I saw nothing special about her Betty Boop quality. I thought she was quite sweet and terribly dumb and my natural reaction was: 'Whose girl is that?' ...She was scared to death because she was playing in a pretty big league" (Shevey 164).

OSKAR HOMOLKA   International screen actor who, with his indefinable foreign accent, played screen heavies, often for comic effect. In 1955, Homolka played Dr. Brubaker in *The Seven Year Itch* (*www.imdb.com*).

J. EDGAR HOOVER   For 49 years the autocratic J. Edgar Hoover was director of the Federal Bureau of Investigation. Hoover kept a copy of MM's famous nude calendar in the basement recreation room of his home. But that did not deter him from directing the bureau to amass a thick file on Marilyn's activities and associations,[41] including those with John and Robert Kennedy. Hoover had also been involved in the blacklisting of Marilyn's leftist husband, Arthur Miller. At a dinner party in February 1962, Marilyn asked Robert Kennedy, who was attorney general, if he was going to fire Hoover. Kennedy replied that he would like to but did not feel he was in a strong enough position to do so. Some biographers have made far-fetched claims that Hoover had wiretapped Marilyn's home and was involved in a coverup of the circumstances surrounding her death. A photograph exists of Hoover shaking hands with Marilyn, both of them smiling broadly. The picture was snapped on April 26, 1955, at a function at the Waldorf Astoria Hotel (Gentry 493–4; Theoharis & Cox 336–8; Victor 142; *www.cursumperficio.net* /biography/1955).

BOB HOPE   Wisecracking comedy legend. On December 4, 1953, Marilyn was with Bob Hope at a charity event for children in Los Angeles. She was photographed between Hope and Jack Benny. Just two weeks later, with Joe DiMaggio in tow, Marilyn attended a party at Hope's home. Hope wanted MM for his 1955 USO tour of Alaska and Korea. Hope personally called Milton and Amy Greene's house in Connecticut, where Marilyn was staying, but was incorrectly told that no one knew where she was. Amy Greene said: "Tell me Mr. Hope, is Miss Monroe lost?"

(Riese & Hitchens 217; Summers 167; *www. cursumperficio.net* /biography/1953).

DENNIS HOPPER   Actor and filmmaker who cultivated the reputation of a rebel and an outsider. Hopper was at a party in the Hollywood Hills at which MM met drug guru Timothy Leary (Summers 377).

HEDDA HOPPER   Much-feared Hollywood gossip columnist. On July 29, 1946, Hopper gave the 20-year-old MM her first mention in a newspaper column. She suggested that Howard Hughes, then in a hospital recovering from an air crash, saw Marilyn's picture on a magazine cover and was interested in her. Hopper was generally supportive of Marilyn in her early career. In 1952, Hopper wrote, "Blowtorch Blondes are Hollywood's specialty, and Marilyn Monroe, who has zoomed to stardom after a three-year stretch as a cheesecake queen, is easily the most delectable dish of the day" (Victor 142).

But later on, Hopper became less friendly. It was Hopper, in fact, who broke the news of Marilyn's affair with Yves Montand. When Marilyn wanted to make a statement or reply to critics, she began using Hopper's arch-rival, Louella Parsons. At one public event, Hopper and Parsons literally engaged in a tug-of-war with Marilyn, to see who could get an exclusive photograph with her. After Marilyn's death, Hopper wrote of her: "We built her up to the skies, we loved her, but we left her lonely and afraid when she needed us most" (Riese & Hitchens 217).

LENA HORNE   Glamorous African-American singer and actress. Horne and Marilyn compared notes about their public images and did not like what they found. All too often the public thought they were frivolous. Marilyn agreed with Horne when she said, "It would be nice if we could be strong enough in ourselves as women and weren't just there to make the male audience want to go to bed with us" (Gavin 247). A year after Marilyn Monroe's death Horne commented: "I felt very sad about it. I knew her casually. I always found her very shy and I felt that sometimes shy and sensitive people must find it very hard in this business—this is a rough racket, particularly if you are a woman.... I think that possibly she found herself in a business she couldn't cope with. She probably would have been a good school teacher. That she wanted this business is something else. I presume she wanted it, and I just think it made her too nervous and she took too many pills" (*Ebony* May 1963, 67).

ROCK HUDSON Rugged Hollywood heartthrob. In 1955, director Joshua Logan and MM were initially interested in casting Rock Hudson as the male lead in *Bus Stop*. But then Marilyn began to reconsider. She was worried that he was too good-looking and might overshadow her. Hudson had agreed to take the part, but by the time Marilyn had conquered her insecurities and also agreed to be in the film, Hudson had other commitments. In 1960, Marilyn wanted Hudson for *Let's Make Love*, but that fell through as well. Rock and Marilyn were photographed together at the 1962 Golden Globe Awards. In 1963, Hudson provided the narration for a documentary entitled *Marilyn*. It was a compilation of clips from Marilyn's Twentieth Century–Fox films (Gilliatt 34; Shevey 327; Victor 146).

HOWARD HUGHES Eccentric tycoon, movie mogul and collector of beautiful actresses. Jane Greer was a young unknown when she modeled the first Women's Army Corps uniform on the cover of *Life* magazine's issue of June 8, 1942. Hughes saw the cover, became obsessed with the 19-year-old Greer and gave her a start in movies. Four years later, almost the same thing happened again with another 19-year-old, but this time it was with MM.

Hughes, recovering from an airplane accident, saw Marilyn on the cover of *Laff* magazine and just had to meet her. Hughes and Marilyn went on a few dates, but not ordinary dates. Hughes's idea of a date included a limousine, a private plane and a jaunt to Palm Springs. They may have had a brief affair. Hughes gave Marilyn a jeweled pin; later, Marilyn was surprised to discover that it was only worth $500. Marilyn's drama coach,

Natasha Lytess, recalled her coming home at dawn with her face rubbed raw. "Mr. Hughes doesn't like to shave," was Marilyn's straightforward explanation (Brown & Broeske 203).

Marilyn never got a movie contract from Hughes but she did get some valuable publicity—her first mention in a newspaper column. On July 29, 1946 (five days after her name was changed to Marilyn Monroe) Hedda Hopper wrote, "Howard Hughes is on the mend. Picking up a magazine, he was attracted by the cover girl and promptly instructed an aide to sign her for pictures. She is Norma Jean [sic] Dougherty." Emmeline Snively, head of the Blue Book Model Agency for which Marilyn worked early in her career, claimed to have invented the story and to have leaked it to Hopper and arch-rival Louella Parsons (McCann 43; Riese & Hitchens 224; Shevey 139–40; Summers 109; Victor 146).

LANGSTON HUGHES African-American poet, novelist and playwright. In the autumn of 1955, he met MM at the reading of a play. In his column in the *Chicago Defender*, Hughes had jokingly professed a passion for the actress. In person he found Marilyn "awfully pretty and awfully nice too, seemingly" (Rampersad 249).

HUBERT HUMPHREY The 38th vice-president of the United States and a senator from Minnesota. A friend of President Kennedy, Senator George Smathers, claimed that he, the president, Hubert Humphrey and a few others took Marilyn Monroe on a boat ride down the Potomac River when she showed up unexpectedly in Washington, D.C. (Taraborrelli 2009, 393–4).

TAB HUNTER Movie actor and teen idol. After the release of *Clash by Night* (1952) Tab Hunter and Marilyn crossed paths at a function at the Beverly Hills Hotel. Hunter told Marilyn how much he liked her in the film and that "no one wears a pair of Levis like you." Marilyn Monroe was one of the first female movie stars to be seen in blue jeans (*www.marilynmonroecollection.com*).

JOHN HUSTON   John Huston directed MM in her first major movie, *The Asphalt Jungle* (1950) and her last, *The Misfits* (1961). Huston was aware of Marilyn at least a year before *The Asphalt Jungle* when he wanted to test her for *We Were Strangers* (1949). However, the studio did not want to spend the money on it and Marilyn was not tested for the movie. Huston recalled his earliest memories of Marilyn: "She used to come to the set and watch the shooting.... There was some talk of Columbia giving her a screen test. She was a very pretty girl, young and appealing, but so are thousands of girls in Hollywood. Such talk often leads to the casting couch rather than the studio floor, and I suspected someone was setting her up. Something about Marilyn elicited my protectiveness, so to forestall any hanky panky, I expressed my readiness to do a test in color, with John Garfield playing opposite her. It would not by any means be a cheap test to make. I didn't see Marilyn around after that. She just disappeared and I forgot about her" (Huston 286).

In *The Asphalt Jungle*, Marilyn was up for the part of a corrupt lawyer's mistress. When he met her, Huston immediately recognized her as the girl he had saved from the casting couch. For the screen test Marilyn had memorized a scene that would have her stretched out on a couch. Unfortunately, there was no couch in Huston's office. Marilyn said to the director,

> "I'd like—to—read the first scene on the floor."
> "Sure, dear, anyway it feels right to you."
> Kicking off her shoes, she got down on the carpet and acted out the scene. Then, before he could say anything, she asked if she could do the scene again. He nodded. After the second run-through she got up and nervously waited his reaction.
> "You didn't have to do it twice honey. You had the part on the first reading" [Madsen 1978, 98].

Marilyn was forever grateful to Huston for giving her the opportunity and she considered her work in the picture to be among the best things she ever did. Marilyn later described her first impression of Huston: "Mr. Huston was an exciting-looking man. He was tall, long-faced, and his hair was mussed. He interrupted everybody with outbursts of laughter as if he were drunk. But he wasn't drunk. He was just happy for some mysterious reason, and he was also a genius—the first I'd ever met" (Riese & Hitchens 225).

Marilyn's second Huston picture, *The Misfits*, was written by her husband, Arthur Miller. It was originally a novelette about contemporary cowboys rounding up wild horses for the dog food industry. When Miller rewrote it as a screenplay, he added the part of Roslyn, specifically with Marilyn in mind. With a budget of $4 million, *The Misfits* was one of the most expensive black-and-white movies ever made. Shooting began near Reno, Nevada, in July 1960. Unusually, it was filmed in sequence. Problems arose with Marilyn almost immediately. She was wracked with fears and insecurities, was often indisposed, would only work a few hours a day and not in the mornings. She needed drugs to go to sleep and drugs to wake up, while her marriage to Arthur Miller was falling apart. At one point, production was suspended for two weeks when she was admitted to a Los Angeles hospital. Somehow the film was completed and it was one of Marilyn's most compelling performances. During the making of *The Misfits*, Huston figured Marilyn was taking 20 Nembutal sleeping pills a day and washing them down with vodka and champagne. "Marilyn would come to the set and she'd be in her dressing room, and sometimes we'd wait the whole morning," Huston noted. "Occasionally she'd be practically *non compos mentis*. I remember saying to Miller, 'If she goes on at the rate she's going she'll be in an institution in two or three years, or dead. Anyone who allows her to take narcotics ought to be shot'" (Summers 260).

Huston summed up Marilyn when he wrote: "People say Hollywood broke her heart but that is rubbish—she was observant and tough-minded and appealing but she adored all the wrong people and she was recklessly willful.... You couldn't get at her. She was tremendously pretentious (she'd done a lot of shit-arced studying in New York) but she acted as if she never understood why she was funny and that was precisely what made her so funny.... In certain ways she was very shrewd.... If she was a victim, it was only of her own friends" (Morley & Leon 104).

Other sources: Churchwell 264–8; Grobel 522; Kaminsky 70–1, 129–37; Pratley 126–31; Shevey 157–64; Summers 260–4; Victor 146–7

BETTY HUTTON   Popular film comedienne and singer of the 1940s and 1950s. In 1950, MM went to a party at the Beverly Hills Hilton hotel hosted by Hutton. Marilyn had caught the eye of Johnny Hyde, Hutton's agent, who had escorted her to the party (Riese & Hitchens 227; Guiles 144).

WILFRID HYDE-WHITE   Dignified British stage and screen actor who was usually cast in light comedy roles. Hyde-White was in *Let's Make Love* (1960) with MM, sharing some screen time with her (*www.imdb.com*).

-I-

WILLIAM INGE   Acclaimed playwright who wrote *Come Back, Little Sheba, Picnic* and *The Dark at the Top of the Stairs*. In 1956, MM starred in the film version of Inge's play *Bus Stop*. Inge took part in publicity for the film and in the process met Marilyn. The playwright and the actress developed an instant rapport. Inge could see that Marilyn was an intelligent young woman who was frustrated by her image as a sex symbol. For her part, Marilyn sensed that Inge's interest in her was based on genuine concern. The press attempted to link them romantically but it was not true; Marilyn and Inge became friends and nothing more.

At dinner one evening Inge said:

"I must have labored on *Bus Stop* for over a year, only to watch it being changed from day to day during the shooting. Then I realized the script is merely a skeleton for the director." With a courteous ironic smile toward Marilyn, he added, "And maybe for the actress who loves to add a line or two in her speech."

Marilyn laughed. "You writers are always complaining. Why can't we help out characters with

our own insights, you know, to help what's on the page?"

"Because dear lady," Bill replied gently. "Actors aren't writers, and get paid only to act" [Voss 164].

CHRISTOPHER ISHERWOOD   British writer who spent most of his adult life in Southern California. In a diary entry for May 18, 1960, Isherwood complains how meeting Marilyn Monroe led to an interruption of his writing. "Sunday, we went to the Selznicks' and I got drunk and hugged Marilyn Monroe a lot, and then banged my fist on the piano, saying, 'That's how I feel.' In the morning, my wrist was so sore I had to stop typing." Isherwood liked to tell that story to his students (Isherwood 856).

-J-

ANNE JACKSON   MM was a good friend of Eli Wallace and his actress wife, Anne Jackson. Marilyn even babysat their children. Jackson, being only three months younger than Marilyn, was almost her exact contemporary. She was perfecting her craft at the Actors Studio in New York at the same time Marilyn was attending classes. When rumors arose that Marilyn was romantically involved with Wallach, assurances were given to Jackson that her husband was only a decoy for Marilyn's actual boyfriend, Arthur Miller (Morgan 151; Victor 319).

SAM JAFFE   Eccentric-looking character actor who had a long and distinguished career in films and television, especially remembered as Dr. Zorba in the *Ben Casey* series. In 1950, Jaffe played a criminal mastermind in a MM movie, the gritty, film-noir drama, *The Asphalt Jungle*. Jaffe's performance earned him an Oscar nomination for best supporting actor. Jaffe and Marilyn did not share any scenes in the movie but they posed together for publicity stills. (Anonymous 39; Doll 74; *www.imdb. com*)

ZIZI JEANMAIRE   French ballet dancer who had a brief career in Hollywood musical films. On November 6, 1954, Jeanmaire was one of the invited guests at Romanoff's restaurant in Hollywood, where a party had been organized to honor MM and her new film, *The Seven Year Itch*. On Jeanmaire's table was a centerpiece of Marilyn in the skirt-blowing scene from the movie. Jeanmaire was appearing on Broadway in *The Girl in Pink Tights*, the film version of which Marilyn had refused to do (Shaw & Rosten 76).

ADELE JERGENS   Film actress of the 1940s and 1950s who was mostly in "B" films. Despite the fact that Jergens was only nine years older than MM, she played her mother in *Ladies of the Chorus* (1948). Jergens noticed how eager Marilyn was to make a good impression and have her lines perfect when the cameras rolled. More than 40 years later, Jergens remembered how Marilyn "told me very tearfully she had lost her mother, and that, just like the chorus girls of the story, she knew what social ostracism was like. Marilyn was the sort of girl you instinctively wanted to protect, even though she obviously had brains and probably didn't need much protection" (Spoto 1993, 141).

GEORGE JESSEL   Actor and singer who earned the nickname of 'Toastmaster General' for his frequent duties as the master of ceremonies at public events. Jessel, who was in his 50s when MM was a young starlet, was eager to pursue a relationship with her. But Marilyn was not interested. According to columnist Earl Wilson, "George said that he held out to [Marilyn] the lure of fine clothes and good contacts if she would—and she wouldn't" (Shevey 119). During August 1948, Marilyn attended a Hollywood play with Jessel, who had produced it. Sometime in 1952 or 1953 she posed for photos with Jessel, clad in white shorts and top, with a Shriner's fez (*www.cursumperficio.net* /files/Marilyn: 50s).

ELTON JOHN   Pop-music superstar. In 1997, Elton John sang a revised version of "Candle in the Wind" (lyrics by Bernie Taupin), at the funeral of Diana, Princess of Wales. The song was originally a tribute to

MM and had appeared on John's 1973 album, *Goodbye Yellow Brick Road*. For years the song had served as the finale at Elton John's concerts, prompting audiences to hold aloft burning matches and cigarette lighters. "When I think of Marilyn," said John, "I just think of pain. I can't ever imagine her being that happy" (Norman 246).

NUNNALLY JOHNSON   Film scriptwriter, producer and director. Johnson was nominated for the Academy Award for best screenplay for *The Grapes of Wrath* (1940) and by the Directors' Guild of America for the Best Director award for *The Man in the Gray Flannel Suit* (1956). In 1952 Johnson was an uncredited writer of *O'Henry's Full House* and writer and producer of *We're Not Married*, both of which featured Marilyn Monroe.

Johnson's most memorable association with Marilyn was through *How to Marry a Millionaire* (1953), which he wrote and produced. Johnson recognized that Marilyn had star power, but privately he was not one of her fans. In a letter he wrote, "Miss Monroe is generally something of a zombie. Talking to her is like talking to somebody underwater. She's very honest and ambitious and either studying her lines or her face during all her working hours, and there is nothing whatever to be said against her, but she's not material for a warm friendship" (Johnson & Leventhal 106). Working closely with her on the set of the film Johnson said, "Marilyn made me lose all sympathy for actresses. In most of her takes she was either fluffing lines or freezing. She didn't bother to learn her lines. I don't think she could act her way out of a paper script. She had no charm, delicacy or taste. She's just an arrogant little tail switcher who's learned to throw sex in your face" (Shevey 62). After Marilyn had ruined dozens of takes and wasted an entire day over a short scene requiring her to answer a telephone while having breakfast in bed, the director, Jean Negulesco, was in despair. Johnson came up to Marilyn, who had a bemused expression on her face, and tenderly took her hand. He said, "We'll do it in the morning, honey. Don't worry about it." When Marilyn replied "Don't worry about what?" Johnson dropped her hand in astonishment (Kanin 321).

Despite harboring a low opinion of her, Johnson wrote a light comedy, *How to Be Very, Very Popular* (1955), expressly for Marilyn. Johnson could see that Marilyn had a magical screen presence but he could not explain it. "Marilyn's a phenomenon of nature, like Niagara Falls or the Grand Canyon. You can't talk to it. It can't talk to you. All you can do is stand back and be awed by it" (Zolotow 191). *How to Be Very, Very Popular*, which Johnson also produced and directed, was not helped when Marilyn refused to do it. She wanted more substantial roles. With Sheree North in the part that would have been Marilyn's, the film flopped. In 1962, Johnson was called in to rewrite the screenplay of *Something's Got to Give*, Marilyn's final and unfinished picture. Marilyn was not someone you could spring script changes on, and Johnson could see that she had become completely unhinged at the notion of having to master fresh dialogue (Guiles 441–2).

VAN JOHNSON   Film and television actor remembered for his red hair and boy-next-door roles. On June 22, 1954, Johnson was a guest on the ABC television game show, *The Name's the Same*. The aim of the show was for panelists to guess a celebrity guest's secret wish. Johnson's secret wish was for MM to sit on his lap. If Marilyn ever saw the program, she never mentioned it to anyone (*www.wikipedia.org*; *www.imdb.com*).

CAROLYN JONES   Leading lady, who achieved stardom as Morticia on *The Addams Family* (1964–1965). Jones was in the cast of *The Seven Year Itch* (1955) (*www.imdb.com*).

JENNIFER JONES   Academy Award-and Golden Globe–winning actress who starred in *The Song of Bernadette* (1943), *Madame Bovary* (1949), and *Beat the Devil* (1953), among many other films. When she was an unknown bit player, MM encountered Jones at a party given by a Hollywood agent. Years later, Jones was at a party in the Hollywood Hills, at which

time Marilyn met drug guru Timothy Leary. At least once, Marilyn was also a dinner guest at the home of Jones and her producer-husband, David O. Selznick. In May 1954, Marilyn's photographer / business partner, Milton Greene, found the costume Jennifer Jones had worn in *The Song of Bernadette*—tight black jacket, long green skirt, stockings, and black wooden clogs—in the Fox wardrobe department. Marilyn put on the costume, wandered into the back lot and posed before Greene's camera for a series of photographs in the French village built for *What Price Glory* (1952) (Monroe & Hecht 56; Shevey 120; Summers 377; *www.cursumperficio.net* /biography/1954).

SPIKE JONES   Band leader of the 1940s and 1950s known for his crazy sound effects and wild spoofs. On March 17, 1952, Marilyn Monroe saw Joe DiMaggio play baseball for the first time. It was a benefit game for the Kiwanas Club for Children. Spike Jones and Marilyn were photographed together at this event. Laughing and smiling, they appear to be about to draw the winning entry for a door prize (*www.cursumperficio.net* /Files/S/Sports).

VICTOR JORY   Canadian screen actor who usually played evil villains. In 1954, Jory went to the Copacabana nightclub to see Frank Sinatra and his opening act, Joey Bishop. While he was there, MM walked in by herself, swathed in white ermine. Of course, all eyes turned her way (Starr 34; *www.imdb.com*).

JAMES JOYCE   Irish literary figure who was one of the most influential writers of the 20th century. MM was painfully aware of her deprived background and lack of education. She often turned to books for self-improvement. A photograph exists of Marilyn deeply immersed in James Joyce's *Ulysses*. Some 30 years after the fact, the photographer, Eve Arnold, recalled the circumstances surrounding the picture. "We worked on a beach on Long Island. She was visiting Norman Rosten, the poet. As far as I remember ... I asked her what she was reading when I went to pick her up (I was trying to get an idea of how she spent her time).

She said she kept *Ulysses* in her car and had been reading it for a long time. She said she loved the sound of it and would read it aloud to herself to try to make sense of it—but she found it hard going. She couldn't read it consecutively. When we stopped at a local playground to photograph she got out the book and started to read while I loaded the film. So, of course, I photographed her. It was always a collaborative effort of photographer and subject where she was concerned—but almost more her input" (Brown 174). Marilyn finished the book and thought Joyce was "a very interesting writer." Commenting on the character Molly Bloom, Marilyn said, "She certainly has sex on her mind a lot. I think it's amazing that a writer like Mr. Joyce can get into a woman's mind" (Slatzer 268). In a private acting class, Marilyn delivered a powerful and sensual rendition of Molly's soliloquy.

-K-

GARSON KANIN Writer and director of films and plays. MM and Kanin were acquainted but never worked together. On one occasion, Marilyn confided to Kanin that her late manager, Johnny Hyde, was the only person upon whom she could ever rely. As she explained, "Look I had plenty of friends and acquaintances—you know what I mean, acquaintances? But not one of them, not one of those big shots, ever did a damn thing for me, not one, except Johnny. Because he believed in me" (Kanin 318). Hyde wanted to make a movie of Kanin's hit Broadway play *Born Yesterday* starring Marilyn, but nothing came of it. When the film was made in 1950, it starred Judy Holliday. Marilyn and Kanin attended Hyde's funeral on December 18, 1950. Kanin directed and co-wrote *My Favorite Wife* (1939), the film upon which Marilyn's uncompleted *Something's Got to Give* was based. In 1979, Kanin wrote a novel, *Moviola*, which fictionalized Marilyn's life story. It became a made-for-television movie the following year (Brown & Barham 59; Rose 150; Summers 66).

DANNY KAYE Actor and singer who became one of the world's most beloved comedians. In August 1950, Marilyn Monroe attended a party at Danny Kaye's home in honor of Vivien Leigh, who had come to Hollywood to make *A Streetcar Named Desire*. In December of that year, Kaye was a pallbearer at the funeral of Johnny Hyde, a top Hollywood talent agent. Marilyn Monroe was Hyde's protégée and her reception at the funeral was the opposite of Kaye's. Marilyn was swathed in black and was sobbing. The Hyde family blamed her for Johnnie's untimely death and were not pleased to see her there. Although they never worked on a movie, Kaye and Marilyn Monroe were photographed together at the Hollywood Bowl in July 1953. The occasion was a charity show for the benefit of St. Jude's Children's Hospital, organized by Danny Thomas (Rose 150–1; Victor 147–8; *www.youtube.com* "Marilyn Monroe at the Hollywood Bowl with Danny Thomas"; *www.cursumperficio.net* /biography/ 1950/ 1953).

ELIA KAZAN Award-winning stage film director and co-founder of the Actors Studio. Kazan directed *Gentleman's Agreement* (1947), *A Streetcar Named Desire* (1951), *Viva Zapata* (1952), *On the Waterfront* (1954), *East of Eden* (1955), and *Splendor in the Grass* (1961).

Kazan met MM in August 1950 at a party at Danny Kaye's house in honor of Vivien Leigh who was starring in Kazan's current film, *A Streetcar Named Desire*. The married Kazan and Marilyn then had a brief affair and afterward remained on friendly terms. At a business meeting, as a joke, Kazan tried to pass off the luscious Marilyn, severely dressed as a secretary, as his personal assistant. Kazan and Arthur Miller had been close friends, and he was the one, in fact, who introduced Marilyn to her future husband in 1951. The two men parted company over Kazan's decision to name names before the House Un-American Activities Committee. It is ironic that the two reconciled over Marilyn's dead body. It was Kazan who directed Miller's play, *After the Fall*, Miller's thinly disguised story of Marilyn.

Kazan summed up Marilyn this way: "A simple, eager young woman, a decent-hearted girl whom Hollywood brought down, legs parted" (Considine 1994, 115).

Other sources: Gottfried, 2003, 172–4; Kazan 406–9; Schickel 227–8; Victor 154–5; *www.cursumperficio.net*/biography/1950

BUSTER KEATON   Legendary comic actor and film maker. During the production of *The Buster Keaton Story* in 1956, a newspaper reporter interviewed Keaton on the all-important subject of breasts. Asked to name the most beautiful sweater girls of all time, Keaton selected mostly forgotten names from the silent era. When pressed for his opinion of more contemporary bosoms, all Keaton would say about MM was that she was "all right" (Meade 1995, 275).

HOWARD KEEL   Actor and singer who starred in many classic movie musicals. When Marilyn was still known as Norma Jeane, she developed a crush on the 20-year-old man who lived in a boarding house across the street from her. The young man, who is believed to have been Howard Keel, took Norma Jeane to a movie. She wanted to be sophisticated but was by her own acknowledgment, stupid, gawky and giggly. In the late 1940s, as Marilyn Monroe, she actually dated Keel (Morgan 32).

EMMETT KELLY   Circus performer who created the famous sad-faced clown, Weary Willie, basing him on Depression–era hobos. Near the end of her life MM took a friend's young daughter to the Ringling Bros. Circus for a joint-birthday celebration. They were both born on June 1 and Joe DiMaggio had provided the tickets. Years later the girl, Edie Shaw, vividly recalled the evening:

> Marilyn and I had two center seats up front. We were munching away at popcorn and cotton candy. Emmet [sic] Kelly the famous clown was doing his broomstick routine. He suddenly noticed this beautiful blonde, not me, chewing at the candy. He swept his light to her section and completed his act.... A little later a group of circus hands came down the aisle to Marilyn's seat. Their spokesman said, "Excuse me, miss, but aren't you Marilyn Monroe?" She smiled at them

and said, "No, I wish I was, she's so beautiful." The spokesman said, "We have a bet, three of us said you were and the other three said you weren't." She replied, "I'm sorry if you lost, but thank you for thinking I'm pretty like Marilyn" [Shaw & Rosten 155].

GENE KELLY   Dancer, choreographer, actor and director who starred in *On the Town* (1949), *An American in Paris* (1951) and *Singin' in the Rain* (1952). MM knew Kelly and attended parties at his home. The day Marilyn died, Kelly was scheduled to meet with her to discuss an upcoming film project, *What a Way to Go*, a big-budget musical comedy. Kelly had a cameo in *Let's Make Love* (1960) (Brown & Barham 307; Victor 155–6).

GRACE KELLY   "A" list Hollywood actress who starred in *High Noon* (1952), *Rear Window* (1954), *To Catch a Thief* (1955), and *High Society* (1956). Kelly retired from movies in 1956 to marry Prince Rainier of Monaco. Upon her engagement, MM sent Kelly a message congratulating her for finding a way out of the movie business. Oddly enough, the two superstars never met, although they came close on several occasions. Once they were on the same airplane flying from New York to Los Angeles. Marilyn was sleeping up front in the first-class compartment, while Kelly was reading a book in economy class. In New York, when Kelly and Rainier were making their first public appearance at a gala ball, Marilyn was a block away at Madison Square Garden. Marilyn, dressed like a showgirl, was riding a pink elephant at a charity event. For a time, Marilyn and Princess Grace shared the same publicist, Rupert Allan. He even phoned Marilyn from the royal palace in Monaco. Kelly attended the premiere of *The Seven Year Itch* at the crowded Loew's State Theater in New York on June 1, 1955 (Brown & Barham 235, 276; Riese & Hitchens 245; Victor 156).

EDWARD KENNEDY   Younger brother of John and Robert Kennedy. After the assassination of his brothers Edward had a long career in the United States Senate. Actress Cloris Leachman remembered being at a party at Peter Lawford's house in 1961 or 1962 at which both Marilyn Monroe and Edward Kennedy were present[42] (Leachman 81, 83).

ETHEL KENNEDY   Wife of the attorney-general of the United States, Robert F. Kennedy, and sister-in-law of President John F. Kennedy. Ethel Kennedy had jokingly said that she wanted Marilyn Monroe to play her when her husband's book, *The Enemy Within*, was filmed by Twentieth Century–Fox.[43] It is unlikely that this was a source of conversation when Ethel and Marilyn met on February 1, 1962. The occasion was a star-studded party at actor Peter Lawford's 27-room Santa Monica beach house. Ethel and her husband, who were about to embark on a lengthy Asian trip, were the guests of honor. Ethel watched as Marilyn quizzed Bobby about what the attorney-general does and gave him a lesson on the latest dance craze, the Twist. The only other time the two women met was on May 19 of that same year. It was at Madison Square Garden in the company of thousands of spectators. Marilyn sang a sexy "Happy Birthday, Mr. President" at a Democratic Party fundraiser. The next month, Ethel sent Marilyn an invitation to visit her and her husband at their home in Virginia. Marilyn replied with a note saying that she would be unable to attend (Oppenheimer 232–43; Spoto 1993, 486–93; Taraborrelli 2000, 398–402, 459–61).

JACQUELINE KENNEDY   The first lady, wife of John F. Kennedy, 35th president of the United States. President Kennedy was a womanizer and Jackie was well aware of his proclivities. She had a suspicion that her husband had a relationship with Marilyn Monroe and did not like it. Marilyn and Jacqueline Kennedy never met and, undoubtedly, would not have wanted to. On May 19, 1962, Marilyn sang her erotic rendition of "Happy Birthday, Mr. President" at a Madison Square Garden political fundraiser. Clad in a dress so tight she had to be sewn into it, Marilyn's performance that evening was seen by many as an insult to the dignity of the first lady. Mrs. Kennedy had no intention of watching such a vulgar display and pointedly did not attend the event, even though it doubled as a birthday celebration for her husband. She made no secret of her plans to attend a horse show in Virginia. Marilyn felt no ill will or envy toward Jacqueline Kennedy; she knew that her relationship with the president could only be fleeting. Reportedly, Jackie gave her husband an ultimatum—break off all contact with the Hollywood bombshell or face a divorce and political ruin. The president did as Jackie wished. Privately, Jackie said that life wasn't long enough for her to worry about Marilyn Monroe. Publicly, after Marilyn died, she said "Marilyn will be remembered eternally"[44] (Spoto 1993, 486–93; Taraborrelli 2000, 417–18, 435–9).

JOHN FITZGERALD KENNEDY   The 35th president of the United States. An ocean of ink has been spilled over the supposed love affair between JFK and MM. Most of that ink has been wasted on the rankest sort of tabloid rubbish. The president and the movie star met on precisely four occasions and were intimate on one of them. There were a few telephone calls as well. Neither participant had any expectation of an enduring relationship. Allegations of earlier meetings and a long-term affair have no substantiation. Kennedy was a philanderer and Marilyn was just another conquest. The president, for Marilyn, was an attractive man made all the more attractive by his power and position. Marilyn was thrilled that she, a one-time resident of an orphanage, could catch the fancy of the most powerful man in the world. When he was hospitalized for a back problem, before he ever met Marilyn, Kennedy tacked a pin-up of Marilyn in tight sweater and shorts over his bed. He hung the picture, to his wife's annoyance, upside-down so that Marilyn's legs were in the air.

Their first meeting was on October 2, 1961, at actor Peter Lawford's lavish Santa Monica beach house. Lawford's wife, Pat, was JFK's sister, and the evening was a dinner party in honor of the president. Knowing that his brother-in-law liked the company of pretty women, Lawford made sure other glamorous actresses—Angie Dickinson, Kim Novak, and Janet Leigh—would also be present.

The second meeting was in February 1962, when Marilyn was an invited guest at another presidential dinner party. This one was at the home of a Manhattan socialite.

The third time they were together was on the weekend of March 24, 1962, when Marilyn and Kennedy shared a bedroom in Bing Crosby's Palm Springs home. Kennedy was suffering from a sore back and Marilyn telephoned her masseur, Ralph Roberts, for advice. Roberts was startled when the familiar Boston-accented voice came on the line to thank him for his help.

The final meeting was as public as it could be. It was on May 19, 1962, at a Madison Square Garden fundraising gala for the Democratic Party and birthday celebration[45] for the president. This was the occasion when Marilyn, clad in a dress so tight she had to be sewn into it,[46] minced up to the podium and warbled her famous or perhaps infamous, rendition of "Happy Birthday, Mr. President." After the sexy song the president came on stage and said "Thank You. I can now retire from politics after having 'Happy Birthday' sung to me in such a sweet, wholesome way." Afterwards, Marilyn, Kennedy, and a host of others, attended a party at the home of a movie executive (Guiles 433–4, 444–6; Spoto 1993, 486–93).

JOSEPH P. KENNEDY   Businessman, political figure and father of President John F. Kennedy, Attorney General Robert F. Kennedy and Senator Edward Kennedy. In December 1961, the elder Kennedy suffered a devastating stroke. Evidently, Marilyn sent the Kennedy patriarch a get-well note. His daughter, Jean Kennedy Smith, replied, thanking Marilyn for the note, saying that her father enjoyed it. Joe Kennedy died in 1969, at the age of 81 (Victor 279).

ROBERT F. KENNEDY   Attorney-General of the United States and brother of President John F. Kennedy. Robert Kennedy's relationship with Marilyn Monroe has been subject to outrageous allegations. There is no reliable evidence that Bobby Kennedy had a sexual relationship with Marilyn, had anything to do with her death, or was implicated in a coverup. The actress and the attorney-general did know each other, however. They met four times and exchanged a few telephone calls during the last ten months of her life.

The first meeting was during a dinner party on October 2, 1961, at the beach house of his brother-in-law, actor Peter Lawford. President Kennedy was the guest of honor. Marilyn drank too much champagne during the evening.

The second meeting, also at Lawford's house, was on February 1, 1962. Bobby was the guest of honor this time, and Marilyn was careful to remain sober. Marilyn was interested in the civil-rights struggle and she did not want to miss the opportunity to discuss the subject with the attorney-general. She went so far as to ask him questions she had jotted down with lipstick. Marilyn was impressed with Kennedy, finding him smart, mature and possessing a great sense of humor. But romantically, she was drawn to his brother, the president.

The third meeting was on May 19, 1962, at Madison Square Garden. It was the evening when Marilyn sang her famous "Happy Birthday, Mr. President" at a Democratic Party fundraiser and birthday gala for President Kennedy.

In June, Marilyn received an invitation from Robert Kennedy and his wife, Ethel, to visit their home in Virginia for a dinner for Peter Lawford. Marilyn wired her regrets, wittily linking her troubles with Twentieth Century–Fox with the "freedom riders' fighting for civil rights.

> Dear Attorney General and Mrs. Kennedy:
>   I would have been delighted to have accepted your invitation honoring Pat and Peter Lawford. Unfortunately, I am involved in a freedom ride protesting the loss of the minority rights belonging to the few remaining earthbound stars. After all, all we demanded was our right to twinkle.
>   Marilyn Monroe [Spoto 533]

The last meeting between Robert Kennedy and Marilyn Monroe was on June 27, 1962, again at the Lawford home. Lawford and Kennedy picked Marilyn up at her new home, were given a tour, and then drove her to the party. At the end of the evening, Kennedy's driver took Marilyn home.

The Ambassador Hotel in Los Angeles was where the 19-year-old Marilyn Monroe, then Norma Jeane Dougherty, began her modeling career in 1945. Tragically, it was also where Robert Kennedy was assassinated in 1968. (Thomas 2000, 191–4; Guiles 449–54, 457–8; Spoto 1993, 486–93).

JACK KEROUAC   American novelist of French-Canadian background who became the icon of the Beat Generation. In 1960, Kerouac briefly considered becoming an actor. He was introduced to Lee Strasberg at the Actors Studio in New York, but quickly lost interest in the acting profession when he discovered they did not serve drinks at the studio. The only reason Kerouac hung around was that he hoped to meet some celebrities. Upon learning that MM was in the building, Kerouac declared, "I want to fuck her!" (Nicosia 620). After being introduced to Marilyn, all Kerouac said to her was, "I like your legs." Marilyn stormed off in a huff. Later, in a bar, Kerouac started gushing over meeting Marilyn but finished by calling her a "trash broad" (Dittman 103). After Marilyn's death, a copy of Kerouac's *On the Road* was discovered among her personal effects (*www.cursumperficio.net* /files/Marilyn stuff).

EVELYN KEYES   Film actress who played Scarlett O'Hara's sister in *Gone With the Wind* (1939) and Tom Ewell's vacationing wife in *The Seven Year Itch* (1955). Along with MM, Keyes was invited to the latter film's star-studded wrap party which was held on November 6, 1954. Keyes and Marilyn had been acquainted since January 1951, when they both attended another Hollywood party. On that occasion Marilyn was on the arm of Arthur Miller, the man who would become her third husband five years later. Keyes was one of the first to notice their budding relationship. Upon meeting Marilyn for the first time Keyes thought she was just "one more little blonde with the preferred size tits and a funny walk" (Schwarz 275).

Other Source: Gottfried 2003, 174–5

NIKITA KHRUSHCHEV   Crude, blunt-talking leader of the Soviet Union after the death of Joseph Stalin. In September 1959, Khrushchev was on a state visit to the United States when he came to the Twentieth Century–Fox Studio in Hollywood. MM, as well as Elizabeth Taylor, Debbie Reynolds, Frank Sinatra, Gary Cooper, and Kirk Douglas, were invited to a luncheon for Khrushchev at the studio's Café de Paris. Marilyn was asked to wear something tight and sexy and she did not disappoint. Marilyn spent five hours beautifying herself and, uncharacteristically, arrived early. The Russian leader stopped to speak with her and, having been coached by the Russian–speaking Natalie Wood, Marilyn greeted the Russian leader in his own language. Marilyn observed, "Khrushchev looked at me like a man looks at a woman." Marilyn, who offered greetings on behalf of her husband, Arthur Miller, was repelled by Khrushchev because he was "fat and ugly and had warts on his face and growled." Marilyn also said: "I could tell Khrushchev liked me. He smiled more when he was introduced to me than for anyone else at the whole banquet. He squeezed my hand so long and hard I thought he would break it. I guess it was better than having to kiss him, though" (Taubman 430).

Two months before Khrushchev's visit, the American National Exhibition had opened in Moscow. Among the wonders on display was an exhibit on American movies. None of Marilyn's films had been seen in the Soviet Union, but about 40,000 people a day saw a close-up of Marilyn from *Some Like It Hot* (1959). The Russian leader had seen the exhibit and may have remembered Marilyn's face from it. Khrushchev once observed that America could be summed up by three things—Coca Cola, baseball and Marilyn Monroe (Guiles 383–6; Riese & Hitchens 249–50; Summers 244; Victor 159).

DOROTHY KILGALLEN   Syndicated newspaper columnist and panelist on the television game show *What's My Line?* (1950–1967). Kilgallen and MM were photographed together a few times, but were not close. Kilgallen had a house in Amagansett, Long Island, when Marilyn and Arthur Miller lived there. She saw them walking along the beach and wondered what the couple, from such different backgrounds, would have talked about.

After *Gentlemen Prefer Blondes* was released in 1953 Kilgallen persuaded studio head, Darryl F. Zanuck, to testify in her column that Marilyn had done her own singing in the film. Kilgallen replied to Zanuck.

> Of course I DO take your word for it, notarized or otherwise, but you can understand my skepticism, can't you? It just floors me that a girl who can sing as well as Marilyn does on the *Gentlemen Prefer Blondes* soundtrack (okay, it's not Dinah Shore, but it's a competent professional job) just happened to pick up the talent recently. I would have thought that a girl who looked like Marilyn, and could sing like that—or even considerably worse—would have bought herself an $18 black satin dress with a low-cut V neckline and snagged a job as a singer in a grade B nightclub when things got tough for her. I listen to a great many singers in all kinds of cafes in the course of a year, and I guarantee you most of them warble a lot worse than Marilyn and don't come anywhere near her in the appearance department. My question is, if she could sing that well, why did she have to pose in the nude for calendar pictures to get eating money? [Riese & Hitchens 250].

For her part, Marilyn thought Kilgallen was a drunk who hated her and who had written some bitchy stuff about her.

On Marilyn's last day alive, August 4, 1962, she was the subject of Kilgallen's column, which hinted at a relationship with a Kennedy. With unconscious irony she wrote: "Marilyn Monroe's health must be improving. She's been attending select Hollywood parties and has become the talk of the town again. In California, they're circulating a photograph of her that certainly isn't as bare as her famous calendar, but is very interesting.... And she's cooking in the sex-appeal department, too; she's proved vastly alluring to a handsome gentleman who is a bigger name than Joe DiMaggio in his heyday. So don't write off Marilyn as finished" (Israel 327).

Kilgallen then prerecorded a radio show to be broadcast a few days later. It was full of gossip about Marilyn. When she learned the tragic news of Marilyn's death, Kilgallen was stunned. She considered her death to be an accidental suicide. Three days after Marilyn's death Kilgallen wrote:

> The death of a tortured creature running from the black shapes of a nightmare into the path of an onrushing locomotive. I think she took a few pills to help her get over whatever her last problem was, and sleepily thought, "Oh, THAT feels better," and took a few more to make sure she wouldn't wake up until morning came along to make the day safe for her.... This is a story I have known I was going to be writing about in the not too distant future. When I first heard Marilyn was dead I said, "Oh, no—it can't be true" which is what almost everyone else said, but as the voice filled in the details I found myself thinking, of course. Of course. This is the way it would have to be.... Nude ... the pill bottle ... the record player. And alone.
>
> Among the things the friends kept asking is, "I wonder why she didn't leave a note?" ...Her life was a suicide note, written for everybody to read, but nobody would believe the message.
>
> Sleep well, sweet girl. You have left more of a legacy than most, if all you ever left was a handful of photographs of one of the loveliest women who ever walked the earth [Israel 328–9].

Marilyn died with a telephone receiver in her hand. Kilgallen believed that Robert Kennedy had been on the line but, of course, she could never write that or prove it (Capote 1980, 232; Israel 327–9; Riese & Hitchens 250; Victor 159).

EARTHA KITT   African-American actress and singer known for her sultry purr, whether playing Catwoman on TV's *Batman* or crooning "Santa, Baby." Kitt was a guest at the New York premiere of *The Prince and the Showgirl* on June 13, 1957, when she and Marilyn Monroe were photographed in earnest conversation. Kitt was about seven months younger than Marilyn and survived her by 46 years (*www.wikipedia.net* ; *www.cursumperficio.net* /Files/T/The Prince and the Showgirl).

HILDEGARD KNEF   German actress, singer and writer. Knef met Marilyn one morning at Twentieth Century–Fox. Marilyn was only half awake and not at her best. Even so, she was carrying a copy of Rainer Maria Rilke's letters and was keen to discuss German literature. Knef remembered "the sleepy-looking girl, with the transparent plastic shower cap over her white-blonde hair and a thick layer of cream on her pale face, sits down beside me. She digs around in a faded beach bag and takes out a sandwich, a pillbox, a book. She smiles at my reflection in the mirror. 'Hi, my name's Marilyn Monroe, what's yours?'"

Knef thought Marilyn was "a child with short legs and a fat bottom, scuffing over to the makeup room in old sandals." But a mere 90 minutes later, Knef was amazed at the transformation in her new friend.

Only the eyes are still recognizable. She seems to have grown with the makeup, the legs seem longer, the body more willowy, the face glows as if lit by candles [Later, at an awards ceremony] Now she's wearing a red dress that's too tight for her; I've seen it before in the Fox wardrobe—although it's too tight, it looks like one of Mum's old ones dug out of the wardrobe. Eyes half-closed, mouth half-open, hands trembling a little. One glass too many, a child's first go at the punch. The photographers hold their cameras up high, flash into her cleavage. She leans and stretches, turns and smiles, is willing, offers herself to the lenses. Someone bends forward and whispers into her ear. "No, please," she says, "I can't." The trembling hand knocks over a glass. Finally she stands up, the people snigger, the tight skirt presses her knees together, she trips to the microphone. The walk is absurd and she's got miles to go; they stare at the dress, wait for it to burst and liberate the bosom, the belly, the bottom. The master of ceremonies roars: "Marilyn Monroe!" She steadies herself on the mike stand, closes her eyes, leaves a long pause in which one hears her amplified breathing—short, panting, obscene. "Hi," she whispers and starts the trip back [Knef, 254–5].

DON KNOTTS Comic actor known for his portrayal of Deputy Barney Fife on television's *The Andy Griffith Show* (1960–1968). Don Knotts was set to play the part of a nerdy shoe salesman in MM's unfinished film, *Something's Got to Give*, but the star had other ideas. Marilyn was a friend of Wally Cox and she wanted him for the role. Marilyn had cast approval and overturned the decision of the director, George Cukor (Brown & Barham 163; Riese & Hitchens 106–7).

WILLEM DE KOONING Durch–born American abstract painter. In 1954, the year

MM made *The Seven Year Itch*, de Kooning painted a picture of Marilyn as a peach-skinned blonde. De Kooning had seen Marilyn in *Gentlemen Prefer Blondes* (1953) and kept a copy of her nude calendar in his studio. When asked why he painted her, de Kooning answered:

"I don't know. I was painting a picture, and one day—there she was."
"Subconscious desire?"
"Subconscious, hell!" he laughed [Gaugh 49].

Marilyn made no comment about de Kooning's painting, but husband Arthur Miller was offended by it. During 1956 and 1957, the artist lived near Marilyn and Miller on Long Island.

MICHAEL KORDA British novelist and publisher. During the making of *The Prince and the Showgirl* in England, Korda struck up a friendship with Milton Greene, MM's business partner and the producer of the film. No one really wanted Greene on the set, so he had plenty of free time. Korda took to coming over to Greene's rented London house and playing chess with him. Korda remembered that "occasionally, Marilyn wandered through the house, dazed and distracted, with a shopping list of complaints for Milton" (Korda 219–20).

ERNIE KOVACS Zany and innovative television comedian who also made a few movies. Kovacs hosted a party in his Hollywood home for MM and poet Carl Sandburg. British actor Alec Guinness was also a guest at the party and reported what he saw:

Poet and superstar sat opposite each other at a small table, gazing at each other open-mouthed; that is, Monroe's lips were parted and her eyes adoring and Sandburg never closed his mouth to stop talking.
"Don't disturb them," Ernie said. "They are either on another planet or playing footsy under the table. You never can tell with poets and broads."
"But he's in a wheelchair," I protested.
"Maybe they like it that way. Give him a push and take his place."

On his television show, Kovacs featured his wife, Edie Adams, doing comic impersonations of Marilyn (Guinness 1986, 286–7).

-L-

ALAN LADD   Pint-sized Hollywood tough guy. Ladd and MM won the Photoplay Gold Medal Awards as the most popular performers of 1953, he for *Shane*, she for *How to Marry a Millionaire*. The ceremony was held on March 9, 1954. Although Ladd and Marilyn were seated in close proximity and were photographed together, they had little to say to each other. Marilyn, in a clinging white dress which left nothing to the imagination, upstaged Ladd and everyone else present (Linet 1979, 20).

HEDY LAMARR   Beautiful Hollywood leading lady from Central Europe. Errol Flynn was known for his wild parties and Hedy Lamarr attended a few of them. She reports that one of Flynn's favorite stunts was organizing a "greyhound" race on his spacious lawn. Six men with numbers on their backs chased a topless girl who was the "rabbit." Lamarr claimed that Marilyn Monroe was once the "rabbit." For being a good sport Marilyn got a fur coat and the fastest racer got a kiss and a photo of himself with Marilyn (McNulty 312).

MARTIN LANDAU   Film, stage and television actor. Landau knew MM casually from the Actors Studio in New York. Landau was one of the first to witness the intensifying relationship between Marilyn and playwright Arthur Miller. After a class at the Actors Studio, Landau, with Ben Gazzara and Elia Kazan, escorted Marilyn to the window table at a Times Square restaurant. Landau noticed that Marilyn's attention seemed to be somewhere else. Following her gaze, Landau glanced at the building across the street which housed the office of the theatrical producer working on Miller's *A View From the Bridge*. High up in the building, framed in a window, was Miller himself. "He stood there for the longest time, with his foot on the windowsill, looking down at her," said Landau. "I was the only one who noticed, and nothing was said. Only later did I put it all together" (Considine, 1994, 118).

FRITZ LANG   German director who made *Metropolis* (1926) and *M* (1931) before moving to Hollywood to escape the Nazis. In 1952, Lang cast MM in a working-class film noir drama, *Clash by Night*, in which she earned excellent reviews. Years later, Lang said:

> But it was not easy to work with Marilyn Monroe; this was practically her first big picture. She was a very peculiar mixture of shyness and uncertainty and—I wouldn't say "star allure"— but, let me say, she knew exactly her impact on men. And that's all. Now, just at that time, the famous calendar story came up. I didn't mind— what a woman does with herself is nobody's business—but the thing was, because of her shyness, she was scared as hell to come to the studio—she was always late. I don't know why she couldn't remember her lines, but I can very well understand all the directors who worked with her getting angry, because she was certainly responsible for slowing down the work. But she was very responsive. One very bad thing: she asked me would I mind if her female coach was there during shooting in the studio; I said, "No, under one condition—that you don't let her coach you at home." Because when an actress has learned her lines and thinks she has caught the feeling of the part, got under the skin of the character, it's very hard to *change* it. At the beginning I had trouble—until I found out that behind the camera, unseen by me, this female coach was standing and gesturing with her hands. I said to Marilyn, "Look—either/or..." and told her the coach could not come on the set any more [Bogdanovich 81].

On another occasion Lang said of Marilyn, "Such a beautiful child, so misguided. I liked her very much, but in the film, Stanwyck was the real star, and she never complained about the number of retakes Monroe required" (Grant 75).

WALTER LANG   Film director who had a 35-year career in Hollywood. On July 19, 1946, at Twentieth Century–Fox, Lang directed MM in her first screen test, one hundred feet of silent color film. The test was shot at six in the evening after Lang had finished work on the Betty Grable movie *Mother Wore Tights*. He sat on a stool near the camera and spoke to Marilyn to elicit various reactions and expressions from her. On the strength of the test she got her first studio contract.

Lang also directed Marilyn in *There's No*

Business Like Show Business in 1954. Lang did not like Marilyn, thinking she slept her way to the top and did not deserve stardom. In his opinion she was only in *There's No Business Like Show Business* because the studio wanted her name on the marquee. Marilyn had become the hottest thing in Hollywood. Lang thought that Marilyn did a good job in the film but that she never fit in with the rest of the cast. In his opinion she was always lost in her own world and worried about her lack of experience when compared to the seasoned professionals with whom she was working. Lang was frustrated by Marilyn's utter inability to arrive on time. In his view, she gave no thought to who she might be inconveniencing and how much money she was costing the producers. Marilyn complained that she was anemic, suffering from bronchitis and that she was on medication. According to Lang, "It was a *terrible* experience. There were days—*days* spent shooting around Marilyn because she couldn't make an appearance. Everyone was furious—fit to be tied. She wouldn't listen to me and I was directing the goddamn picture" (Gilmore 151).

The Shocking Miss Pilgrim, a Betty Grable vehicle from 1946, is not a movie that is usually included in Marilyn's filmography, but Lang recalled watching her getting coached to play a two-minute walk-on, and he was not impressed: "Monroe had a bit part as a switchboard operator. Visiting the set one day, [I] heard a woman's voice repeating the word 'Hullo' over and over in various inflections. It was Marilyn, aided by her voice coach, practicing for her big moment. But when it came she'd completely forgotten what to say" (Shevey 111).

Other sources: Guiles 101–2; Shevey 102–3; Victor 163; *www.imdb.com*

HOPE LANGE   Blonde actress who appeared opposite MM in *Bus Stop* (1956). Marilyn, who was not happy at the idea of having two blondes on the same movie, insisted that Lange's hair be dyed a darker shade than her own. Reportedly, Lange had to do her close-ups with a male stand-in because Marilyn was

unwilling to participate (Riese & Hitchens 259; Summers 207; Victor 163; *www.imdb. com*).

MARIO LANZA   Handsome opera singer who became popular in Hollywood musicals. MM met Lanza a few times at the home of a mutual friend, photographer Andre DeDines (DeDines 115).

LASSIE   Lassie was a collie dog who played the title role in a series of heartwarming movies and in various television series. Tommy Rettig, the child actor who appeared opposite MM in *River of No Return* (1954), was the dog's best friend in the *Lassie* televison series (1954–1957). Marilyn met Lassie in late 1952 at a party at bandleader Ray Anthony's house. The star-studded party was to launch a song written in Marilyn's honor. Marilyn was quoted, "Dogs never bite me. Just humans" (Victor 13, 350).

CHARLES LAUGHTON   Portly British character actor who starred in *The Private Life of Henry VIII* (1933), *Mutiny on the Bounty* (1935) and *The Hunchback of Notre Dame* (1939). Laughton died at age 63, four months after Marilyn. In 1952, Laughton had a scene with MM in *O'Henry's Full House*. Laughton thought Marilyn played her role of a street-walker without preconception or artifice. Marilyn once described Laughton as "the sexiest man she'd ever seen" (Winters 1980, 235). Playing opposite Laughton, Marilyn said that initially she felt overawed. But Laughton soon put her at ease by treating her as an equal. Courtesy of her roommate, Shelley Winters, Marilyn had already met Laughton and had attended some of his acting workshops as an observer. Winters recalled, "I took Marilyn with me a couple of times to Laughton's group, which I was attending religiously. Her whispery voice would become completely inaudible, and she seemed to shrivel up. After the second time I realized it was such agony for her that I resolved not to invite her again unless she asked me and I really felt she could handle it" (Winters 1980, 309).

Other Source: Callow 216

PETER LAWFORD   "B" grade English actor who had a career in Hollywood. Lawford's claim to fame was his marrying into the Kennedy family. His wife, Pat, was the sister of President John F. Kennedy and Attorney-General Robert F. Kennedy. Marilyn Monroe and Lawford met in the spring of 1951 at an agent's office. They dated a few times but there were no sparks. Lawford thought Marilyn was breathtakingly beautiful, but he could not abide her dreadful housekeeping. They remained casual friends for most of the 1950s but by the end of the decade the relationship deepened, with Marilyn becoming a close friend of Peter and Pat Lawford. Lawford became well known for throwing celebrity-studded parties at his 27-room Santa Monica beach house. Marilyn frequently attended the parties. It was at Lawford's home that she met JFK and RFK.

It was Lawford who invited Marilyn to top the bill by singing "Happy Birthday, Mr. President" to JFK at a Democratic Party fundraiser and presidential birthday party at Madison Square Garden on May 19, 1962. Marilyn became nervous about performing before a live audience and started drinking. As usual, she was late. Lawford made Marilyn's tardiness into a joke. He introduced her by saying: "Mr. President, on the occasion of your birthday, this lovely lady is not only pulchritudinous but punctual. Mr. President—Marilyn Monroe!" The audience roared its approval but Marilyn did not appear. Lawford shrugged his shoulders, walked offstage and several other acts came out. Then Lawford returned and said how Marilyn was "a woman about whom it may truly be said—she needs no introduction." There was a drum roll and a pause but still no Marilyn. Lawford continued: "Because Mr. President, in the history of show business, perhaps there has been no one female who has meant so much ... who has done more ... Mr. President, the *late* Marilyn Monroe!" (Guiles 444–5). The audience cheered as this time Marilyn *did* appear. Visibly tipsy, she minced out on the stage in a sequined gown so tight she had been sewn into it, and launched into her now-famous birthday song. Little did anyone realize but less than three months later, she would really be the *late* Marilyn Monroe.

About 7:00 P.M. on Marilyn's last day alive, August 4, 1962, Lawford telephoned her to invite her to one of his parties. Marilyn declined but phoned back about an hour later. Her speech sounded slurred and she seemed disturbed, but Lawford did not take any action. Thereafter, Lawford blamed himself for her death and bitterly regretted that he had not done anything to save her. Wild allegations have been made that Lawford covered up Marilyn's death to protect the Kennedy brothers. There is no hard evidence that any of this is true. Although Lawford and his wife wanted to attend Marilyn's funeral, her ex-husband Joe DiMaggio banned all of her Hollywood friends (Guiles 444–61; Taraborrelli 2009, 395–491).

CLORIS LEACHMAN   Stage, film and television actress who is 32 days older than Marilyn Monroe. Leachman met Marilyn at a party at Peter Lawford's house in 1961 or 1962. Marilyn and Robert Kennedy were dancing and everyone else was discretely trying to eavesdrop. The two dancers ignored the other guests at the party. Leachman writes, "When you met Marilyn she was even more gorgeous, more voluptuous—her eyes, her mouth, her body—in person than she appeared in her pictures. But I saw her as part of a classic Hollywood pattern: a beautiful young girl comes to town, her exquisite face and body wow the industry, and she becomes a star. But inside, she's still the ordinary person she's been since she grew up. She had no training in being a star, has no knowledge of how to meet the assaults and pressures that come with this new status" (Leachman 81).

DAVID LEAN   Academy Award–winning British film director and producer. Lean and Marilyn were never to work together, even though he was on her list of approved directors (Victor 81).

TIMOTHY LEARY   Psychologist, counterculture icon and advocate of psychedelic drug use and research. When MM met Leary on

May 15, 1962, he was a lecturer in psychology at Harvard University. Marilyn was in a fragile emotional state and under constant psychiatric care. The meeting came at the end of a Hollywood party which Marilyn attended expressly to meet Leary. Leary was exhausted and had gone to one of the bedrooms. Marilyn came in to the party and, not seeing Leary, she went into the bedroom, woke him up and asked him to introduce her to LSD. Leary explained that LSD was not something to be played with and should only be used with caution. No LSD was taken that night. Indeed, it was Marilyn who gave drugs to Leary. As she was quoted as saying: "You go around turning people on. I've got just the magic pills for you. Something of my own, called 'Randymandys.'[47] They turn off your mind and turn on your body" (Brown & Barham 120–1). Leary washed one of the cough-drop-shaped burnt-orange pills down with a couple of swigs from a bottle of Dom Pérignon Marilyn had brought with her. Ten minutes later, Leary felt "like a balloon filled with honey" (Brown & Barham 121), and fell into a deep sleep.

The next day Leary and Marilyn met for lunch at a restaurant on Hollywood Boulevard. Leary found Marilyn "wobbly" and "full of contradictions. Funny and playful, but very shrewd. We talked about drugs, and I told Marilyn about a project I was setting up in Mexico that summer. She wanted to come on down and join us. But she also wanted to try LSD then and there" (Summers 378). The reports are contradictory, but that night Leary may have given Marilyn a small dose of LSD. Marilyn said to Leary that she had experimented with just about everything—at least once. In any case, they went to Venice Beach and walked in the surf after dark. Three days later, Marilyn was in Madison Square Garden singing "Happy Birthday, Mr. President," to President John F. Kennedy.

BERNARD LEE Distinguished British actor who found fame as M in the first 11 James Bond movies. In 1956, Lee was one of the stars of a British war film *The Battle of the River Plate*. It was because of that film that Lee met Marilyn Monroe. On October 29, there was a Royal Command Film Performance of *The Battle of the River Plate* in London. Marilyn, who was in England making *The Prince and the Showgirl* with Sir Laurence Olivier, was one of those invited to the event. She stood three places away from Lee in the receiving line to meet Queen Elizabeth II (Calhoun & DeWalt 511; *www.imdb.com*).

PEGGY LEE Jazz singer known for her cool style. Peggy Lee was on the bill at Madison Square Garden the night MM sang her famous rendition of "Happy Birthday, Mr. President." Marilyn went on stage before Lee, who wrote about the evening in her autobiography. "She walked out onto the stage as the lights went up full. The whole audience gasped, and I thought it was just Marilyn's charisma. I turned to look and I gasped too. She had nothing on under a sheer gown, and no wonder the audience gasped, and I'm sure J.F.K. did too. She looked stark naked. Well, I guess she was, except for a little chiffon. There was a whole lot of shouting going on from the press and the photographers. It's a good thing 'Happy Birthday,' is such a short song" (Lee 1989, 224). Lee had been told that she was Kennedy's favorite singer. But coming on stage after Marilyn, Lee thought that "somehow I don't think it mattered" (Lee 1989, 225). Lee's ex-husband, Brad Dexter, had worked with Marilyn in *The Asphalt Jungle* (1950) (Brown & Barham 142, 146).

JANET LEIGH Actress who played the stabbing victim in the famous shower scene from Alfred Hitchcock's *Psycho* (1960). Leigh was married to MM's co-star in *Some Like It Hot*, Tony Curtis. During visits to the set, Leigh observed Marilyn's behavior during the making of the movie: "Marilyn was tortured by insecurity. This exquisite creature, so talented, so vulnerable, labored just to come on the set. She was there at the studio, but was hard put to muster the courage to appear. It was not malicious game playing or status tactics but just plain terror that forced her to retreat. This was very trying, especially for the boys. They would report for makeup and wardrobe, and then wait. And wait. The more intolerable their position, the more intolerant their attitude. Of course they were sympathetic to her plight; it was an unfortunate situation. But, oh boy, when she *did* make it, when Billy [Wilder] *did* get it out of her, the screen sizzled. What a high price to pay!" (Leigh 1984, 245–6). Leigh had met Marilyn four years before, in January 1955. It was at a press conference and after-party announcing the creation of Marilyn Monroe Productions (*www.cursumperficio.net* /biography/1955).

VIVIEN LEIGH   British actress who won Oscars for portraying southern belles in *Gone With the Wind* (1939) and *A Streetcar Named Desire* (1951).

In August 1950, when she was just another contract player, MM briefly met Vivien Leigh and her husband, Sir Laurence Olivier, at a Hollywood function. It was a party at Danny Kaye's house in honor of Leigh, who was making *A Streetcar Named Desire*. When next they met it was in London on July 14, 1956, by which time Marilyn was a superstar. Marilyn had come to England to film *The Prince and the Showgirl* with Olivier, who was to be her co-star and director. Compounded by the fact that both women were in poor health, Leigh and Marilyn developed little warmth for each other. Leigh, who had originated Marilyn's film role on stage, did not express any bitterness. Privately, however, she thought Marilyn was vulgar and obtuse. Marilyn felt awkward and uncomfortable around the sophisticated Lady Olivier and resented Sir Laurence's expectation that she play her film role exactly as Leigh had done it in the theater. Leigh grew fond of telling a story she had heard about Marilyn visiting Arthur Miller's house. After being repeatedly served matzo balls Marilyn innocently asked, "Isn't there any other part of the matzo we can eat?" (Walker 1988, 306). Leigh, who had just announced that at age 42 she was pregnant, was confident she had upstaged her younger Hollywood rival. She was asked if Marilyn was going to be the child's godparent. Leigh gave a diplomatic reply. She said that the idea was

interesting but that godparents had already been selected. Leigh's happiness was short lived as she suffered a miscarriage a month later (Edwards 1977, 421–5; Shevey 324, 347, 355, 358; *www.cursumperficio.net* /biography/1950).

MARGARET LEIGHTON   Respected British stage and film actress. Leighton was introduced to MM on July 26, 1956, at an after-theatre ball at playwright Terence Rattigan's house in Berkshire, near London. It was the social event of the year, a party in honor of Marilyn and her husband, Arthur Miller. Marilyn was in England to film Rattigan's *The Prince and the Showgirl* with Olivier (Gottfried 2003, 301).

JACK LEMMON   Academy Award-winning actor who starred in *Mister Roberts* (1955), *The Apartment* (1960), *The Days of Wine and Roses* (1962), *The Odd Couple* (1968) and many more films. In 1959 Lemmon appeared in drag opposite Tony Curtis and MM in *Some Like It Hot*. Before work on the film commenced, Lemmon met Marilyn at a party. As he recalled: "True to form, Marilyn arrived two hours after everybody else. She was with her then husband Arthur Miller. She came over to me and grabbed me and kissed me and she couldn't have made me feel more wonderful. She was so sweet and charming, and she started reeling off different parts that I'd played and what she liked and didn't like about each. I was stunned. She had me right in the palm of her hand" (Wagner 303).

Unlike co-star Tony Curtis, Lemmon got along with Marilyn, although he found her baffling, completely unpredictable and was often frustrated by her pathological tardiness and need to do the simplest of scenes over and over again. Lemmon never felt that he really understood Marilyn.

> As for Marilyn, she was a good light comedienne, unique. She wasn't that enormously talented, but her gift was knowing how to use the special kind of talent she possessed to great advantage.
>
> I found that I couldn't really get to know what was inside her, despite a good working relationship. She would put up a glass window, and never let anyone in.
>
> Anyone looking at her in retrospect could see

that she was never really happy, never really fulfilled, never able to live with being M-A-R-I-L-Y-N M-O-N-R-O-E [Baltake 97–8].

Lemmon observed that Marilyn had an uncanny sense of what was right for her and if things were not exactly right she would suddenly stop and not wait for the director to shout "Cut." Lemon noted, "Marilyn would drive everybody crazy just psyching herself up for a performance. Even after everything was set and the cameras were rolling, Marilyn would be flapping her wings and screwing her head around like a chicken on a block. She must have wasted $250,000 worth of film doing that" (Shevey 378).

Lemmon recounted an exception to Marilyn's usual filming style: "Funnily enough that whole upper berth bed scene was done on the first take, it totally shocked me. It was the first take straight through, Billy Wilder said 'print' and she said 'I loved it too' and I thought 'what happened,' I was ready to go all day. It was lucky I got my words right because I had learned to pace myself with Marilyn. The day before we had gone 37 takes and she had exactly two lines to do, but the next morning we did the whole upper berth scene, before he goes down to get the booze, in one, she had it in the first take so you never knew" (Victor 166).

At one point Marilyn took a liking to Lemmon's flapper dress, requiring a new gown to be designed for him. She thought the picture would have been better if it had ended with her going off with Lemmon rather than Tony Curtis (Freedland 60–1; Widener 170).

OSCAR LEVANT   Pianist, composer, actor, wit and notorious hypochondriac. Levant met Marilyn Monroe in the makeup department of Twentieth Century–Fox. When Levant heard of Marilyn's decision to divorce baseball legend Joe DiMaggio, he quipped: "I guess no one can expect to excel at more than one national pastime." Marilyn's conversion to Judaism almost cost Levant his television talk show when he said, "Now that Marilyn Monroe is kosher, Arthur Miller can eat her." Levant denied he had done anything improper, saying he "hadn't meant it *that* way" (Levant 194).

JERRY LEWIS   Zany comedian and film-maker who was long paired with crooner Dean Martin. Lewis met MM at the 1952 Photoplay magazine awards. Marilyn caused a sensation when she arrived in a gold lamé gown which was so tight she had to be sewn into it. Lewis expressed his approval by leaping on a table on all fours, pawing and hooting. After that, the whole room erupted into catcalls and laughter. Over the next several years Lewis and Martin saw Marilyn a few times and on a couple of occasions took her out to dinner. Lewis appreciated Marilyn's sense of humor but detected an underlying sense of sadness. Lewis summed up Marilyn when he wrote: "She was kind, she was good, she was beautiful, and the press took shots at her she didn't deserve. They got on her case from day one—a textbook example of celebrity-bashing" (Lewis & Kaplan 222).

ABRAHAM LINCOLN   MM had an enduring fascination with Abraham Lincoln, the 16th president of the United States (1861–1865). Wherever she lived, a framed print of Lincoln and the Gettysburg Address were prominently displayed. This is how Marilyn thought of Lincoln: "My father is Abraham Lincoln—I mean, I think of Lincoln as my father. He was wise and kind and good. He is my ideal, Lincoln. I love him" (Riese & Hitchens 273). Marilyn even struck up a friendship with poet Carl Sandburg, who was Lincoln's most celebrated biographer. At the beginning of her romance with Arthur Miller, Miller wrote to Marilyn suggesting that if she wanted someone to admire, Abraham Lincoln would be a good choice. Of course Marilyn was already a huge admirer of Lincoln. The idolatry had started in junior-high school when her essay on President Lincoln had been judged the best in the class. One of the reasons she married Miller was because of his supposed resemblance to Abraham Lincoln. On the set of *Bus Stop*, Marilyn remarked to director Joshua Logan how much Miller looked like Abraham Lincoln. On another occasion, Marilyn showed Miller's daughter by his first marriage a shiny new penny and joked that her daddy was on the coin.

In 1955, Marilyn went to tiny Bement, Illinois, at the behest of the National Arts Foundation, to open an art show and commemorate the centenary of the town. Bement was the place where, in 1858, Lincoln met with Stephen A. Douglas, to work out the details of the famous Lincoln-Douglas Debates on slavery. Marilyn made a short speech about Lincoln, which she wrote herself. Sadly, there does not seem to be any record of what she said, apart from referring to "our late beloved president," which made it sound as if President Eisenhower had just died. Throughout her visit to Bement, Marilyn carried the coffee-table edition of Carl Sandburg's *Abraham Lincoln* (Arnold 1976; 89–93 Gottfried 2003, 181; Riese & Hitchens 273; Summers 41, 87; Victor 171).

VIVECA LINDFORS   Swedish-American film and theater actress. In 1954, Lindfors met MM at Lee Strasberg's Actors Studio in New York. Of Marilyn, Lindfors wrote:

> Marilyn had an extraordinary perception. She was one of Lee's pet pupils and almost on her way to tearing down the images of the sex symbol. Had she only had the courage to stick through this vulnerable period of adjustment, letting down her defenses, unavoidable when you open yourself up to the kind of work Lee and the Method demanded, she would have become a great actress. I understood, for eventually I had to go for help myself. Marilyn did, too. But the analysis wasn't enough for her. The screams within her were too filled with pain, or fury, or both. She gave up. A tragedy for us all.
> The night her death was announced and headlines splashed all over the front pages, I was performing *Brecht on Brecht* at the Theatre De Lys. Sitting on my stool with Brecht's oversized face behind me, I was filled with Marilyn. She was in me and around me and I wanted to share it with the audience. "In memory of Marilyn Monroe," I announced before the section "Hollywood Elegies," Brecht's brilliant poems: "I fled from the tigers. I fed the fleas. What got me at last, mediocrities." It was deadly quiet in the house. Truth happened that instant [Lindfors 215].

ANATOLE LITVAK   Academy Award–nominated film director who made such movies as *All This and Heaven Too* (1940), *The Snake Pit* (1948) and *Anastasia* (1956). Litvak

and Marilyn Monroe most likely became acquainted at a New Year's Eve party in 1948 at producer Sam Spiegel's home in Beverly Hills. They never worked together (*www.wikipedia.net*; *www.cursumperficio.net* /biography/1948).

HAROLD LLOYD   Bespectacled silent film comedian who became famous for his death-defying stunts. After he retired from the movies, Lloyd pursued his hobby of photography. During 1952 and 1953, Lloyd had several photo sessions with MM. Lloyd had done a series of three-dimensional color photographs and wanted to use Marilyn as a subject. On his first session, Lloyd was obliged to share Marilyn with another photographer, Phillipe Halsman, who was shooting her for a *Life* magazine cover (April 7, 1952). Marilyn was conducting two photo sessions simultaneously! Lloyd took his stereopticon equipment to the tiny apartment Marilyn was living in at the time. While Lloyd perched on a chair with his camera (the only spot he could find), Marilyn posed while wedged between a dresser and the bathroom. The door had to be left open to counter the heat from the photo lamps[48] (Arnold 1987, 30–1; Victor 171).

HENRY CABOT LODGE, JR.   United States senator and diplomat. In September 1959, the Russian premier, Nikita Khrushchev, on a state visit to the United States, came to Los Angeles for a tour of the Fox Studio. As U.S. ambassador to the United Nations, Lodge was given the responsibility of escorting Khrushchev. Among the bevy of Hollywood stars in close proximity, Lodge could not help but notice Marilyn Monroe (Lodge 163).

JOSHUA LOGAN   Director and playwright, known for such plays and musicals as *Annie Get Your Gun*, *South Pacific*, and *Picnic*. Logan was the director of one of MM's best films, 1956's *Bus Stop*. Marilyn was memorable as Cherie, the down-at-the-heels saloon singer. At first, Logan did not want Marilyn for the role, thinking that she was not a very good actress. But he soon changed his mind, coming to see Marilyn as nothing less than the greatest artist he ever worked with. Unlike many other directors, Logan got on well with Marilyn, partly because he, like her, was a disciple of the Method school of acting. Logan first met Marilyn at the Connecticut home of her business partner, Milton Greene. Marilyn was hours late for the party and, when she finally put in an appearance, she seemed slightly disheveled. At that moment, Logan knew that Marilyn was the perfect image of Cherie. Logan had been warned that Marilyn was difficult to handle and made a promise to himself to never raise his voice to her or grow upset at her chronic lateness and inability to remember dialogue. Logan generally kept his promise but was sorely tried by his temperamental star. The closest Logan came to losing his cool was in Phoenix on an exterior shot. After waiting three hours for Marilyn, Logan could stand no more. He marched into her trailer and wordlessly grabbed her by the wrist and dragged her before the camera to get the shot before the sun set. Logan observed that Marilyn was "on" whenever the camera was. When the camera was off, Marilyn crashed and had to work herself up again for the next take. Logan developed the technique of leaving the camera rolling so as to be ready to catch Marilyn at her best, whenever those magical moments occurred. It was an expensive way to film but probably saved days of lost production time. After multiple takes, Logan would compile snippets of film and edit them into a seamless whole. The result was one of Marilyn's most acclaimed performances. Despite all the aggravation, Logan remained on Marilyn's side. Even the tantrum she threw when she saw the finished film did not alter the director's opinion of her. Marilyn thought her best work had been cut out, and she blamed Logan.

After her death, Logan said of Marilyn: "I had no idea she had this incandescent talent. She made directing worthwhile. She had such fascinating things happen to her face and skin and hair and body as she read lines, that she was—it's a cliché, but she was inspiring. She got me all hot and bothered just with her acting. Sexually it went way beyond that, *ca va sans dire*. She was gorgeous to look at, to get close to, to smell, and feel—that, with her tal-

ent too. I was a goner for her. I still am" (Summers 202).

Other sources: Riese & Hitchens 275–6; Shevey 320–7; Victor 171–2

LINDSAY LOHAN Actress, model and singer who was born 24 years after MM's death. Six weeks before she died, Marilyn spent three days posing for the camera of Bert Stern. It was to be Marilyn's final photo session and has come to be known as "The Last Sitting." For the February 18, 2008, issue of *New York* magazine Stern recreated the famous portrait session using Lindsay Lohan as his model. In 2006 Lohan graced the cover of *Vanity Fair*. She wore a white bathing suit in imitation of a young Marilyn Monroe.

GINA LOLLOBRIGIDA Known as the Italian Marilyn Monroe, Gina Lollobrigida met the real Marilyn Monroe in New York on September 15, 1954. The meeting took place at the Trans Lux Theater on the very evening that Marilyn shot the most famous scene of her career, the billowing dress scene in *The Seven Year Itch*. Lollobrigida was wearing a white pleated dress similar to the one Marilyn was about to make famous. Newspaper columnist Earl Wilson and his wife were nearby having dinner with Lollobrigida, who was in New York promoting a new film. Wilson was wondering where they were next going to go with Lollobrigida until his wife suggested that they take her over to meet Marilyn. Lollobrigida had to be convinced that this would be a good publicity move. For her part, Marilyn did not care one way or another. Director Billy Wilder was all for the meeting and said, "Have Gina slip in the side door and wish Marilyn luck" (Wilson 1984, 79). The two bombshells met on the stairway going down to the ladies room, smiled and exchanged pleasantries. Marilyn was heard to remark, "I have been called the Gina Lollobrigida of American films" (Wilson 1984, 80). Lollobrigida was then ushered out and she did not witness Marilyn's big scene. The two met again at a party in honor of the Italian actress. Both Marilyn and Lollobrigida were considered for *Cleopatra* (1962), but the role went to Elizabeth Taylor. Many years later, Lollobrigida made a bronze sculpture entitled "My Friend Marilyn Monroe" (Brown & Barham 89; Evans 2004, 162–3; Victor 172).

THE LONE RANGER   As a child, MM was a fan of *The Lone Ranger* on radio. Recalling those days, Marilyn said, "I'd listen to The Lone Ranger, and get terribly excited. Not at the horses and chases and the guns but ... the drama. The wondering of how it would be for each person in the situation" (*Ms* vol. 1 1972, 37). It is possible that Marilyn met Clayton Moore, the 'B' actor who played *The Lone Ranger* on television. It was 1946, and Marilyn, an unknown starlet, was in Las Vegas waiting for a divorce from her first husband. Moore had an uncredited part in a Roy Rogers western called *Heldorado*, which was shooting in the city. Marilyn met Rogers, who invited her to join the cast and crew for dinner (*www. imdb.com*).

ANITA LOOS   Writer whose novel was turned into the successful play and movie musical, *Gentlemen Prefer Blondes* (1953). MM's role in the film turned her into a superstar. Loos had no part in the casting of the film but felt that Marilyn was an inspired choice. Loos thought Carol Channing was funnier as Lorelei in the stage version but that Marilyn's film performance was more authentic. When Marilyn died, there was a typewritten note in her home from a representative of Loos offering her the starring role in a new Anita Loos musical (Carey 1988, 231; Riese & Hitchens 278; Victor 172).

JACK LORD   Actor remembered as the star of the original version of television's *Hawaii Five-O* (1968–1980). Early in 1956, Marilyn Monroe and Jack Lord were photographed walking through the streets of New York City (*www.cursumperficio.net* /files/M/Marilyn: 50s).

SOPHIA LOREN   Voluptuous Italian actress whose dark good looks made her almost an anti–MM. In 1967, Loren's husband, producer Carlo Ponti, wanted to star Loren in the film version of *After the Fall*, Arthur Miller's thinly disguised biography of Marilyn. Miller, sensitive to the charge that he had exploited the memory of his dead wife, wanted Loren as well; if only to prove to the world that his play was not about Marilyn. The picture never went into production.

Upon hearing of Marilyn's death, Loren, thinking of her own experiences, commented:

> We both rose from the same place ... and she is like a sister to me. And of course I feel like I could've [saved Marilyn] if I tried. But it's a full-time job to save someone like that. Maybe if I'd met her I could have.... I would've written her things, poems, plays. Sure I could have saved her ... just to take her to lunch every once in a while. I've known women like that who are still around. Not that I saved them, but they just needed some friends, some encouragement, and no one ever called her. She was a marvelous actress with a lively personality. Her life cannot have been very happy, but she always succeeded in appearing happy and serene [Riese & Hitchens 278].

Other sources: Victor 172; Zec 203

CLARE BOOTHE LUCE   Playwright, diplomat, socialite and U.S. congresswoman. Luce visited the set of *Something's Got to Give* in May 1962 and was disturbed by her encounter with Marilyn Monroe. "Her despair," wrote Luce "was akin to that of a painter who discovers that he is going blind or of a pianist whose hands are becoming arthritic" (Brown & Barham 174).

CAROL LYNLEY   In January 1962, actress Carol Lynley accompanied her agent-husband, Michael Selsman, to a meeting with MM. When they drove up to Marilyn's Los Angeles apartment, Selsman did not want to leave Lynley alone as she was nine months pregnant. Marilyn was obviously having a bad day. The sight of a younger blonde actress who was about to do what she was never able to—have a child—did not put Marilyn in a better mood. She invited Selsman in to help her select negatives from a photo shoot but callously made Lynley, whom she already knew, wait in the car for three hours (Taraborrelli 2009 381–2).

-M-

CHARLIE MCCARTHY   Wooden figure associated with actor, radio personality and ventriloquist Edgar Bergen. On October 18, 1952, MM was a guest on the Edgar Bergen-Charlie McCarthy radio show. Marilyn took the opportunity to announce her engagement to the lucky Charlie McCarthy (Spada & Zeno 61; Victor 33).

KEVIN MCCARTHY   Distinguished character actor who accepted a small part opposite MM in *The Misfits* (1961). As the husband Marilyn's character was divorcing, McCarthy only spoke 27 words. (As compensation McCarthy was given a prominent title credit.) The scene, shot on the steps of the courthouse in Reno, Nevada, required police to keep onlookers at bay. It was McCarthy's only experience of working with Marilyn. He said: "Marilyn had the difficult scene, the blast-off for the picture. She had considerable anxiety but, like a wild child, she uses it" (Goode 43). McCarthy had been nominated for an Oscar in the category of Best Supporting Actor for his work in *Death of a Salesman* (1951), based on the play by Marilyn's actual husband, Arthur Miller.

McCarthy had first encountered Marilyn in New York in 1955 at the Actors Studio. They were seated together watching a scene and at first McCarthy did not recognize her. Marilyn wore no makeup and was casually dressed in baggy sweater and jeans. McCarthy recalled, "This tousled piece of humanity was sitting on my right, looking like nothing. Then, fifteen minutes later, after I'd interrupted the scene with some fairly rude comments, I looked again. I realized that a breathing, palpitating Marilyn Monroe had developed out of that nothing.... I remember looking and thinking, 'My God, it's her'—she'd just come to life" (Summers 175). Visiting Marilyn and Arthur Miller at their apartment, McCarthy noticed Marilyn "in high heels, without stockings, wobbling about in a short black dress. She had gashes in her legs because she'd made a mess of shaving them. She had a

strange manner—sweet, poignant, a little distrait" (Summers 229).

In 1983, McCarthy narrated a television documentary on Marilyn entitled *In Search of a Dream*. In 2002, he participated in a documentary about the making of *The Misfits*.

CARSON MCCULLERS   American novelist who wrote about Southern misfits and outcasts in *The Heart is a Lonely Hunter* and *Reflections in a Golden Eye*. In 1959, the famous Danish writer Isak Dinesen was visiting McCullers in New York and expressed a desire to meet MM. McCullers knew Marilyn from the time they both lived in the same apartment building and she had a slight acquaintance with Marilyn's husband Arthur Miller. She arranged a luncheon at her apartment on February 5. The guests dined on oysters, white grapes, champagne and a soufflé, the only things the Danish writer ate, apart from asparagus. Marilyn told a funny story about a disaster she had while cooking for her in-laws and then briefly danced with the elderly Dinesen when McCullers put a record on the phonograph (Carr 478–81; Thurman 467–9).

RODDY MCDOWALL   British child actor who became successful in Hollywood as an adult. It was probably in 1948 or 1949 when McDowall and MM met. McDowall needed to improve his dancing and Marilyn was brought in to assist. She was not there to teach McDowall any steps, merely to pace him. McDowall and Marilyn danced together for weeks during which time she scarcely spoke. He was told that Marilyn did not like men because they were always making unwanted sexual advances. Early in 1949 they were photographed together at a party. Later they crossed paths in Chicago, where (so McDowall claimed) they played strip poker to pass the time. They were to meet again in New York. Long after Marilyn's death, McDowall said that he admired her professionally and personally (Strasberg 1992, 155–6; *www.cursumperficio.net* /biography/1949).

DARREN MCGAVIN   Actor who appeared in many film and television roles during a 50-year career. Beginning in 1955, Marilyn Monroe attended acting classes at the prestigious Actors Studio in New York. Among her classmates was the young actor Darren McGavin (Adams 254).

FRANK MCHUGH   Versatile character actor who usually portrayed the hero's sidekick or provided comic relief. In 1954, McHugh was Eddie Dugan, MM's agent, in *There's No Business Like Show Business* (*www.imdb.com*).

JOHN MCGIVER   Comic actor who usually looked worried and harried. In 1962, McGiver was cast as the Judge in *Something's Got to Give* (*www.imdb.com*).

SIOBHAN MCKENNA   Distinguished Irish actress of stage and screen. On August 15, 1957, MM and her husband, playwright Arthur Miller, came to Harvard University to see McKenna as Lady Macbeth. They stayed to congratulate McKenna after her performance.

SHIRLEY MACLAINE   Academy Award–winning actress, dancer and writer. Twentieth Century–Fox threatened to replace MM with Shirley MacLaine in the ill-fated *Something's Got to Give* in 1962. After Marilyn's death, MacLaine took over several projects which had been earmarked for her. In 1963, MacLaine earned an Oscar nomination for her performance in *Irma La Douce*, a film Billy Wilder had offered to Marilyn in 1960. In 1964, MacLaine was the star of *What a Way to Go*, which Marilyn had planned to make after *Something's Got to Give* (Brown & Barham 143, 194–5, 228; Riese & Hitchens 292; Victor 178; *www.imdb. com*).

ALISTAIR MACLEAN   Popular Scottish novelist who specialized in thrillers and adventure yarns. *The Guns of Navarone, Ice Station Zebra, Where Eight Bells Toll, Where Eagles Dare*, and *Puppet on a Chain* are just a few of MacLean's titles. MacLean lived in California for a few years and rented MM's former home at 882 North Doheny Drive in Beverly Hills. Marilyn had rented the house on two occasions, once in 1953–1954 and once in 1961–1962 (Webster 178).

ED MCMAHON   Television personality who spent 30 years as Johnny Carson's straight man and announcer on *The Tonight Show*. McMahon had been a Marine Corps fighter pilot during World War II and was called back to duty during the Korean War. It was 1953, and MM was shooting *How to Marry a Millionaire*. Marilyn had no idea who McMahon was but agreed to meet him in her trailer when she was told that he was a television star from Philadelphia who was about to go to Korea.

McMahon writes:

> It was just the two of us in her trailer, just Marilyn Monroe and Ed McMahon. We spent a half hour together. Marilyn Monroe in person was as beautiful as she was in the fantasies of every American male. She was dressed casually in a pair of slacks and a loose blouse, but she was radiant. She was also sweet. I don't remember what we spoke about, but as I prepared to leave, she said, "It's so nice to meet you. Now I'll know somebody when I go to Korea.[49] How can I find you when I get there?"
>
> The Marine Corps would know where I was stationed, I replied, then said, "I've got to ask you a favor. If I could have a picture of you I could show it to the guys in the squadron, I'd be the hero of heroes. They'd go wacko!" Actually, looking back, "wacko" was probably a poor word choice.
>
> "I've got a better idea," she said. "Why don't we take a picture? Let me just fix my hair and I'll be right out."
>
> I waited outside for her. When she finally came out, she was dressed in a gorgeous fur coat. She kind of snuggled in next to me and, as the photographer got ready to take our picture, whispered to me, "You know, Ed. I don't have anything on under this" [McMahon & Fisher 64].

AIMEE SEMPLE MCPHERSON   Charismatic and controversial Canadian evangelist who founded the International Church of the Foursquare Gospel in Los Angeles and inspired a mass following. On December 6, 1926, six-month-old Norma Jeane's grandmother and foster mother brought her to be baptized by Sister Aimee Semple McPherson in the evangelist's giant Angelus Temple in Hawthone, California (Doll 15; Victor 185).

GORDON MACRAE   Actor and singer who starred in the film versions of *Oklahoma!* (1955) and *Carousel* (1956). Gordon MacRae was a friend of MM's husband, Joe DiMaggio. Learning that the Gordon and his wife, Sheila, and Marilyn were booked on the same transcontinental flight to New York, DiMaggio asked them to keep an eye out for Marilyn. They did so, but Gordon found Marilyn's infamous disregard for time extremely annoying. After waiting for what seemed like hours for her to come out of the airplane lavatory, where she was fixing her face, and again at lunch, MacRae was heard to grumble, "She's such a jerk." MacRae never worked with Marilyn except on one occasion when he agreed to use her offstage voice in the nightclub act he did with his wife. Gordon was not very happy with Marilyn's soft little whispery voice. He complained, "Geez, I could hardly hear her" (MacRae & Jeffers 110).

SHEILA MACRAE
Actress and singer. Sheila MacRae met MM at an acting class conducted by Michael Chekhov late in 1951. MacRae remembered Marilyn from those days as "a pretty, curly-haired girl in a polo coat. She was very intense." MacRae continued to run into Marilyn at acting classes and Hollywood events. She never worked with Marilyn other than on one evening, when Marilyn agreed to lend her offstage voice to the nightclub act that Sheila did with her husband, Gordon. MacRae thought Marilyn was far more intelligent and talented than many people gave her credit for being (MacRae & Jeffers 108).

ANNA MAGNANI
Earthy Italian actress. On May 13, 1959, MM was presented with the prestigious David di Donatello statuette. The equivalent of an Oscar in Italy, it was given to Marilyn as Best Actress in a Foreign Film for her work in *The Prince and the Showgirl* (1957). The honor, one of the few she would ever receive for acting, was presented to her at a reception at the Italian Cultural Institute in New York. Anna Magnani was on hand to embrace Marilyn and congratulate her. On December 2, 1955, Marilyn had attended the postpremiere party for *The Rose Tattoo*, for which Magnani won an Oscar. It was probably then that the two actresses met for the first time. (Guiles 380; *www.cursumperficio.net* /biography/1959).

NORMAN MAILER
Norman Mailer was a controversial figure who became one of the major American writers of the 20th century. Mailer never met MM, but he desperately wanted to. In the fall of 1956, he moved to rural Connecticut, not five miles from the town of Roxbury, where Marilyn and Arthur Miller lived in a farmhouse. Mailer spent several years waiting by the telephone "for the call to visit, which of course never came" (McCann 163). The only time Marilyn did invite her celebrated neighbor to a party was on an occasion when she knew that he would be unable to attend. Miller and Mailer were already acquainted but did not much like each other. Undoubtedly, Marilyn was influenced by her husband's poor opinion of Mailer. She was known to have read *The Deer Park* and *The Naked and the Dead* but was decidedly reluctant to meet the author himself. Marilyn said of Mailer: "He is too impressed by power, in my opinion" (Riese & Hitchens 295); she also said, "One writer is enough for me."

After she was dead, Mailer skillfully blended fact and fiction to publish *Marilyn*, a novel-biography of the actress. Based on the work of an earlier biographer, the project started out as a 25,000-word introduction to a photographic collection. But gradually Mailer's text took over, reaching nearly 100,000 words. Miller hated the book and thought Marilyn would have as well. Mailer spun theories about Marilyn's involvement with the Kennedy brothers and, to his way of thinking, her unexplained death. Mailer developed something close to an obsession with Marilyn Monroe. In 1980 he published an "imaginary diary" of Marilyn entitled, *Of Women and Their Elegance*. Six years later he cast his own daughter in a play about Marilyn, *Strawhead*.

Writing about himself in the third person, Mailer said, "The secret ambition after all, had been to steal Marilyn; in all his vanity he thought no one was so well suited to bring out the best in her as himself, a conceit which fifty million other men may also have held" (Riese & Hitchens 295).

Other sources: Mailer; Mills 395–410; Victor 180

MIRIAM MAKEBA South-African singer and civil-rights activist. Makeba was listed on the program[50] with Harry Belafonte at the May 19, 1962, birthday salute to President John F. Kennedy at Madison Square Garden. That was the night Marilyn Monroe sang "Happy Birthday Mr. President." (*www.cursumperficio.net* /files/Madison Square Garden).

JOSEPH L. MANKIEWICZ Academy Award–winning writer and director. Mankiewicz was responsible for *All About Eve* (1950), a film which featured MM in a small part as Miss Caswell "a graduate of the Copacabana school of acting." Mankiewicz auditioned Marilyn before he had even finished the script. She won him over because she had worked well for John Huston in *The Asphalt Jungle*, and that "there was a breathlessness and sort of glued-on innocence about her that I found appealing" (Mankiewicz & Carey 76–7). Mankiewicz found Marilyn to be a strange loner who needed as many as 25 takes to get the simplest scene right. But the effort he took with her was worth it in the end. As he explained, "Marilyn was the most frightened little girl. And yet scared as she was, she had this strange effect when she was photographed ... in fact, the camera loved her" (Victor 180). Mankiewicz seemed to think of Marilyn as a real-life Miss Caswell. Before she came to him, Marilyn had been under contract to Fox but her duties had little to do with acting, or so he declared: "For the most part she auditioned a great deal, late in the afternoons, in executive offices. She also functioned agreeably as a companion for corporative elder statesmen visiting from the east, and on hostess committees for sales conventions. Occasionally, she was squeezed into old Betty Grable costumes and used as a dress extra for unimportant bits in some films" (Mankiewicz & Carey 75).

Marilyn thought Mankiewicz was intelligent and sensitive as a director and was happy to work with him. One day Mankiewicz observed Marilyn reading the autobiography of left-wing journalist Lincoln Steffens. He took her aside and warned her to be careful. It would not do her career any good to get a reputation as a political radical. In 1954, Marilyn lobbied to get the part of Adelaide in *Guys and Dolls*, but director Mankiewicz decided on Vivian Blaine who had originated with the role on Broadway.

As hard as it sounds, Mankiewicz thought that Marilyn had probably died at the right time. He said, "Imagine Marilyn alive today—very fat, boozing it up. I think she'd have been a pitiful, dreadful mess and nobody would be able to remember what they do remember" (Riese & Hitchens 297).

Other sources: Monroe & Hecht 118–23; Victor 180–1

JAYNE MANSFIELD A blonde bombshell of the 1950s who was never able to outshine MM. Mansfield said: "Marilyn and I are entirely different. We've really never been in competition. I admire Marilyn and she's told me she admires me" (Riese & Hitchens 297). On December 2, 1955, the two actresses were at a dinner after a benefit showing of *The Rose Tattoo* for the Actors Studio. Marilyn and Jayne were photographed together. Jeanne Carmen, an actress friend of Marilyn, claimed to have given Marilyn and Mansfield a joint golf lesson. She said, "They were so bad. They showed up in high heels and I had to drop those in the golf cart.... They were resting the clubs in their crotch and having a fun time. I was a little more serious about golf. I decided this was not going to work out" (Engleberg & Schneider 279). On a 1956 television show Mansfield imitated Marilyn. She was seen in a bubble bath reading *The Brothers Karamazov*. Marilyn had recently announced that she would love to make a movie of the Dostovevsky novel. Mansfield also sang "Heat Wave," which Marilyn had sung in *There's No Business Like Show Business* (1954). Upon learning of Marilyn's death in 1962, Mansfield commented: "They probably expect me to do that someday, but they don't know me well enough to know it couldn't happen" (Reise & Hitchens 298; Victor 181).

Mansfield was successful on Broadway and in film with *Will Success Spoil Rock Hunter?* (1957), a George Axelrod story which features a MM-like movie star involved with a famous athlete. Mansfield and Monroe both had places of Mr. Blackwell's Ten Worst–dressed Women of the Year Awards for 1961.

On November 26, 1963, Jayne Mansfield was the guest on *The Jack Benny Show* in a skit entitled, "Jack Takes a Boat from Hawaii." It was a repeat of a September 1953 skit which featured Marilyn. In this version Mansfield did Marilyn's role. It was probably not in the best taste as Marilyn had died only the year before (Faris 17, 125).

JEAN MARAIS French actor and film director. On April 11, 1957, Marais and Marilyn Monroe were together at the New York Waldorf Astoria Hotel to commemorate the 200th birthday of the Marquis de Lafayette, a French general who fought in the American Revolutionary War (*www.cursumperficio.net* /biograqphy/1957).

FREDRIC MARCH Academy Award–winning screen and stage actor. When Norma Jeane was seven or eight, one of the only periods when she lived with her mother, there was a lacquered white Franklin baby grand piano in their house. The piano was battered, but it meant a great deal to Norma Jeane. The instrument had once belonged to Fredric March, and she remembered her mother picking out a few simple tunes on it. Norma Jeane herself learned to play a few classical pieces. The piano was sold for $235 when her mother was institutionalized and Norma Jeane was placed into an orphanage. In 1951, Marilyn found the piano at an auction, had it refurbished and installed in her apartment. The piano, almost the only surviving object from her childhood, was with her from then on. In October 1999, at an auction of Marilyn's personal effects, the piano was purchased by singer Mariah Carey for $662,500! In the spring of 1961, Marilyn was set to act opposite March in a television adaptation of W. Somerset Maugham's *Rain*.

But the deal fell through when NBC refused Marilyn's demand that her acting coach, Lee Strasberg, be the director (McDonough 212; Monroe & Hecht 1–9; Summers 227; Victor 182).

PRINCESS MARGARET Younger sister of Queen Elizabeth II. On October 29, 1956, MM met the queen and her sister at the Royal Command Film Performance for *The Battle of the River Plate*. Marilyn and Princess Margaret briefly discussed cycling and the possibility of the princess seeing a performance of Arthur Miller's *A View From the Bridge*. Shortly afterward the princess did attend a performance of the play (Morgan 204–5; Victor 92–3).

CATHERINE MARSHALL Author of bestselling religious and inspirational books. Marshall was not the type of person one would expect to meet Marilyn Monroe, but she did. On a trip to Hollywood to discuss getting her book *A Man Called Peter* filmed, she saw MM up close. As she recalled, "One day Queen Frederica and King Paul of Greece came to see Twentieth Century–Fox studio. That morning I watched Marilyn Monroe and Debra Paget jockey—female fashion—for top position in the receiving line" (Marshall 241).

DEAN MARTIN Singer and actor who was initially paired with comedian Jerry Lewis. In 1962, Dean Martin was to be MM's last leading man in the ill-fated *Something's Got to Give*. When Marilyn was fired from the film, Martin announced that he was walking out as well. He said, "I have the greatest respect for Miss Lee Remick and her talent and for all the other actresses who were considered for the role, but I signed to do the picture with Marilyn Monroe, and I will do it with no one else" (Tosches 343–4). Martin claimed that he had not wanted to do the picture at all until Marilyn asked him to. Marilyn appreciated Martin's gallantry in supporting her. Suits and countersuits were filed but they were all dropped after Marilyn's death. Martin was certain that Marilyn's death was an accident. She had visited his house just a few days before and was in good spirits. They had discussed plans to restart the movie.

Martin had first met Marilyn at the 1952 *Photoplay* magazine awards and had immediately liked her. Over the next few years Martin and his partner, Jerry Lewis, often ran into Marilyn and on a couple of occasions took her out to dinner (Lewis & Kaplan 222; Riese & Hitchens 313; Tosches 335–57; Victor 184).

DEAN PAUL MARTIN   Son of crooner and actor Dean Martin, who was 'Dino' in the pop group Dino, Desi & Billy. During the making of *Something's Got to Give*, MM visited co-star Dean Martin's home. Marilyn wore a scarf around her head and dark sunglasses, never removing either. Ten-year-old Dino and his sister were in the living room listening to music and entertained their famous visitor by dancing an impromptu twist. Around the same time, Dean Marin, Sr., gave Dodgers baseball tickets to Marilyn. She decided to take Dean Paul and her friend, actor Wally Cox. Marilyn pulled up in a black limo and off they went to the stadium (Martin & Smith 97–9).

STROTHER MARTIN   Character actor who was often a grizzled cowboy in westerns. Probably his most famous screen moment occurred in *Cool Hand Luke* (1967) when he uttered, "What we have here is a failure to communicate." In 1950, in what was only his second movie role, Martin had a small part as a suspect in a police lineup in *The Asphalt Jungle* (*www.imdb.com*).

TONY MARTIN   Big-band singer and film actor. In 1952, Martin had a voice cameo in *Clash by Night*. Martin can be heard singing "I Hear a Rhapsody" (*www.imdb.com*).

AL MARTINO   Italian-American pop crooner of the 1950s, '60s and '70s who also did some film acting. In September 1952, Marilyn Monroe was seen out and about in New York City with Al Martino (*www.cursumperficio.net* /biography/1952).

LEE MARVIN   Tough-guy character actor. One of Marvin's first film roles was as a soldier in the 1952 MM film, *We're Not Married*. Marvin's part was uncredited and he did not appear in a scene with Marilyn (*www.imdb.com*).

CHICO MARX   Eldest of the zany Marx Brothers. In 1949, Marilyn Monroe had a tiny part in a Marx Brothers movies called *Love Happy*. Marilyn posed with the brothers for a series of publicity stills. She can be seen draped over Chico Marx's piano (*www.cursumper ficio.net* /files/L/Love Happy).

GROUCHO MARX   Screen and television comedian who is remembered for his work with his brothers Harpo, Chico and Zeppo. In 1949, Groucho was casting a bit part for *Love Happy*. What Groucho was looking for was, in his words, a "young lady who can walk by me in such a manner as to arouse my elderly libido and cause smoke to issue from my ears" (Monroe & Hecht 99). MM walked into the audition room and said, matter of factly, that if the Marx Brothers were looking for a sexy blonde then they had found her. According to Marilyn, "There were three girls there and Groucho had us each walk away from him. I was the only one he asked to do it twice. Then he whispered in my ear, 'You have the prettiest ass in the business.' I'm sure he meant it in the nicest way" (Schwarz 140).

Groucho knew he had found the girl he wanted, declaring that Marilyn was "Mae West, Theda Bara and Bo Peep all rolled into one" (Monroe & Hecht 100). Groucho was sufficiently impressed by Marilyn to add a couple of lines of dialogue for her in the script, giving her four, in all. Years later, Groucho ungallantly confided to an interviewer: "Boy, did I want to fuck her. She wore this dress with bare tits. The scene I did with her took only about four days to shoot. I think she may only have gotten a couple of hundred dollars for the part. She was goddamn beautiful. I couldn't keep my eyes off her. I may have tried to lay her once but I didn't get anywhere with her. I don't think any of the boys did.... She was the most beautiful girl I ever saw in my life. And she later turned out to be a great comedian in some picture Billy Wilder directed" (Shevey 142–3).

Marilyn was paid $500 for her work in *Love Happy* plus $300 for a still photo session. She was then sent on a cross-country publicity tour, given a wardrobe allowance and a salary of $100 per week. Marilyn went to Detroit, Chicago, Cleveland, Milwaukee and New York. The clothes she bought were too warm for New York, and she returned to Los Angeles after a month.

Marilyn did not think too much of her performance in *Love Happy*, a film which is generally regarded as the Marx Brothers' worst. She said, "No acting, just sex again. I had to wiggle across a room. I practiced jiggling my backside for a week. Groucho loved it" (Riese & Hitchens 314).

In 1962, Groucho was approached about doing a cameo in *Something's Got to Give*, Marilyn's aborted final movie. A few days after Groucho's death in 1977, his son, Arthur, found a letter from Groucho saying that he wanted to spend eternity lying beside the remains of Marilyn Monroe at the Westwood Cemetery.

Other sources: Arce 399; Mitchell 166

HARPO MARX The silent member of the Marx Brothers. Harpo was present when MM auditioned for a small role in *Love Happy* (1950). Marilyn thought Harpo and his brother Groucho smiled at her as if she was a piece of French pastry. All Marilyn had to do was walk up and down and display her assets. Harpo grinned, honked the horn on the end of his cane, stuck his fingers in his mouth and emitted a loud whistle. Harpo even spoke, advising the starlet, "Don't do any walking in unpoliced areas" (Monroe & Hecht 100). Marilyn got the part. Harpo and a laughing Marilyn Monroe were photographed together on the set of the movie (Summers 61–2; *www.cursumperficio.net*/files/Love Happy).

JAMES MASON British stage and film actor whose distinctive voice earned him roles as menacing villains and urbane leading men. Mason met MM during the filming of *Bigger Than Life* in 1956, when, despite a strict no visitors policy, she was invited to the set for drinks on the final day of shooting. Marilyn, who was completing *Bus Stop* on an adjacent stage, was a friend of director Nicolas Ray.

Mason recalled:

She came over to our stage before we had shot our very last scene. I was lying in the hospital bed, beside which a doctor was standing. A nurse entered and offered the doctor a selection of instruments on a tray. That was it, just one of those connecting shots. When it was done, Nick said,

"Hey, I've got an idea. Wouldn't it be funny if we took a shot of Marilyn carrying the tray instead of the nurse?"

A number of the boys laughed their approval.

"It will be a terrific laugh at the rushes," said one of them. Another said,

"They'll think our rushes got mixed up with *Bus Stop* rushes. Ha, ha, ha."

"Okay," said Nick, "turn them over..."

Action.

A child would have understood what we were up to, but not Marilyn. Instant panic took over.

"Oh Nick," she said, "tell me what you want me to do! I can't do it, Nick! Tell me!"

"Cut," said Nick.

He hugged Marilyn and comforted her and then said that he did not think it was such a funny idea after all, so let's not do it. "Come on, Marilyn, what do you want to drink?" [Mason 287–8].

MARCELLO MASTROIANNI Italian movie actor who was often paired with Sophia Loren. Mastroianni recorded that one of his saddest moments came in 1962 when, shortly before leaving for a visit to the United States, he heard about the death of Marilyn Monroe. As he later said, "One of my greatest unfulfilled dreams was to work with her. I even had a film in mind that we could do together. It was going to be about Marilyn coming to Rome to shoot some colossal epic and meeting this two-bit actor who was scheduled to play a Roman soldier in the film. I was going to call it *Quo Vadis, Marilyn?* There was a time that I spent hours dreaming about her and the film. Of course, I was too embarrassed to mention it to anybody else, let alone write to her and suggest it as a project. What a woman she was! She had so much sweetness about her: maternal and yet provocative. You felt that she needed protection. She was, or so it seemed to me, everything that a woman needs to be for a man" (Dewey 134).

Mastroianni never met Marilyn but thought: "Maybe I liked her more than any woman ... but it was obvious that she couldn't make it alone. This made me want to protect her, to possess this small blond cloud.... She was the last of a species" (Dewey 164). After completing *Marriage Italian-Style* in 1964, Mastroianni toyed with the notion of starring in Arthur Miller's thinly disguised portrayal of his late wife, *After the Fall*, on the Italian stage.

WALTER MATTHAU Rumpled-looking actor who is remembered as Oscar Madison, the ultimate slob, in *The Odd Couple* (1968). Matthau was the original choice to play opposite MM in *The Seven Year Itch*, but Darryl F. Zanuck, head of Twentieth Century–Fox, wanted Tom Ewell. Marilyn met Matthau in 1956 on the set of *Bigger Than Life* when she came for a visit. Marilyn had been filming *Bus Stop* on an adjacent stage. Matthau said: "I never worked with Marilyn Monroe, but if she'd lived, I think she would have been all right. She would have been President of the United States" (Riese & Hitchens 343).

Other Source: Hunter 34, 64–5

VICTOR MATURE Brawny Hollywood leading man who was often seen in beefcake roles. On October 29, 1956, Mature stood next to MM in the receiving line at a Royal Command Film Performance in London. The occasion was the premiere of *The Battle of the River Plate*, a British film about a naval battle in World War II. Marilyn, Mature and other film luminaries were introduced to Queen Elizabeth II.

British actor, Anthony Quayle recalls what happened:

> Just ahead of her in the alphabetical line was Victor Mature, enormous and broad-shouldered. He had not said a word to her as we slowly shuffled towards the opening in the curtain. Just as he was about to have his name called and walk out onto the stage, she turned to him and said, "Oh, Victor. Tell me, Victor. What do I do? I don't know what to do. Tell me."
>
> He turned his head very slightly toward her and said, "Fall on your ass, baby," and walked though the curtains to a big round of applause. Next moment she followed him, dithered to the right, to the left, and brought the house down [Quayle 337–8].

W. SOMERSET MAUGHAM British playwright, novelist and short-story writer who was immensely popular in his day. In 1961, MM had plans to do a television adaptation of one of Maugham's most famous short stories, *Rain*. Maugham thought Marilyn would be "splendid" in the role of Sadie Thompson. He sent her a letter dated January 31, 1961, thanking her for a birthday greeting she had sent and expressed his pleasure that she would be in the TV production and wished her good luck. Unfortunately, the film was never made as NBC objected to Marilyn's insistence that her acting mentor, Lee Strasberg, be the director. Although he was 54 years older than Marilyn, Maugham survived her by three years (Banner 186; Guiles 426; Kashner 331; Victor 107).

LOIS MAXWELL Canadian actress who found fame as Miss Moneypenny in 14 James Bond movies. In 1949, Maxwell was one of eight starlets who posed for a *Life* magazine photo spread which appeared in the October 10 issue under the title, "Eight Girls Try Out Mixed Emotions." One of the other starlets was MM. The cover of the magazine featured J. Robert Oppenheimer, "No. 1 Thinker on Atomic Energy" (*www.imdb.com*).

ELAINE MAY Elaine May is a film director, screenwriter and actress but is best remembered for her comedy routines with partner Mike Nichols. May and Nichols were on the program, May 19, 1962, the night Marilyn Monroe sang her famous rendition of "Happy Birthday, Mr. President" for John F. Kennedy at Madison Square Garden (*www.cursumperficio.net* /file/M/Madison Square Garden).

LOUIS B. MAYER Canadian-raised Hollywood movie mogul. On at least one occasion Marilyn Monroe and Louis B. Mayer were at the same place at the same time. It was at the funeral of talent agent Johnny Hyde, who had died on December 18, 1950 (Rose 150; Victor 147–8).

VIRGINIA MAYO Hollywood leading lady of the 1940s and 1950s. Mayo did not know MM but had a connection with her nonetheless. One of Mayo's best friends was a Los Angeles police officer named James Dougherty. Dougherty was Marilyn's little-known first husband. Norma Jeane Baker was only 16 years old when she married Dougherty in 1942. The marriage ended in divorce in 1946 (Mayo 72, 131, 233).

MIKE MAZURKI Craggy wrestler-turned-movie tough guy and hoodlum. Mazurki was in 1959's *Some Like It Hot.* Mazurki played Spats Colombo's henchman (*www.imdb.com*).

AUDREY MEADOWS The long-suffering wife of bus driver Ralph Kramden (Jackie Gleason) on *The Honeymooners.* Meadows knew MM socially and observed, with amusement, the effect Marilyn had on men and women:

> Marilyn possessed the magical gift of transforming all men into Irish setters who, upon seeing her, frolicked about for no sensible reason, pawed the floor, and smiled many teeth. They fawned in such an absurd manner that you were sure they wanted to be scratched behind the ears. Their tongues didn't exactly loll from gaping mouths, but they came close as they fixated on her every aspirated word.
> Despite the fact that a Monroe entrance had the effect of transforming every other woman in the place into a soft boy, we women liked her too. She was the ultimate Homecoming Queen, sensuously bathing in the tidal waves of affection, nay, idolatry, while not trying to put her brand on any of the mouth breathers who had come to do her homage. Marilyn Monroe was a sterling silver star, whose real acting ability was often obscured by her physical attributes. She knew she was a star, and we knew, and she played the role from first loge to last balcony. It was a drama lesson just to watch her shine [Meadows 121–2].

In 1956, Jackie Gleason had his 40th birthday party at his favorite New York bar. Meadows, Marilyn, and Joe DiMaggio, among others, attended. Some of the more exuberant males attempted to hoist Marilyn onto a wooden trestle table. The attempt was not too successful as it gave Marilyn an embarrassing problem which required her to retreat to the ladies' room.

Marilyn swept in wearing that molded-to-the-body black dress with spaghetti shoulder straps, and she looked most fetching, but she had a problem.

In that wispy little girl voice, she exhaled, "Ladies, I wonder if you could help me. I seem to have gotten a splinter in my ass."

Proving her point, she upped her skirt, and I will give testimony that she certainly did have a splinter in her ass [Meadows 123].

With the aid of a straight pin sterilized by Meadows's cigarette lighter, relief was soon forthcoming.

Meadows knew Marilyn fairly well as they shared the same dressmaker in New York.

> The dressmaker would always be very late for my appointment if he had a prior one with Marilyn. Thirty minutes, forty, an hour he'd be perched in an anteroom of her apartment awaiting the Monroe presence. She was not just tardy. She was unreachable until her personal clock struck.
> What was more important to her? She had moved her bed over to the window. She would be lying on it munching ripe, red apples while observing the chaos of Manhattan traffic from her private perch as a form of entertainment.
> The designer was hesitant to complain, but I was not. I told her, in spirited tones, that when she kept him waiting she was keeping me waiting. She was apologetic in her kittenish way, and promised to be good in that breathy child's voice, so we switched to grown-up girl talk about gossip, movies, men, and other vital concerns [Meadows 123–4].

ETHEL MERMAN Brassy singer with a booming voice. Merman co-starred with MM in a tribute to Irving Berlin, *There's No Business Like Show Business* (1954). Marilyn did not really want to make the movie and only agreed because she was promised *The Seven Year Itch.* At the time, she was having trouble with her marriage to Joe DiMaggio and would often arrive on the set hours late or not at all. Merman was intensely irritated by Marilyn's antics, considering them unprofessional. Nor was Merman pleased when she realized that most of the publicity material featured Marilyn. But she was enough of a realist to admit, "Hell, *she's* the one we need to sell the picture" (Thomas 131). But as Marilyn's unreliableness grew worse, Merman's patience wore out. Fellow cast member Mitzi Gaynor knew the only way to keep Merman cool was to suggest that Marilyn was up to "hanky-panky" in her dressing room, a situation she knew Merman would enjoy (Bergreen 518).

JAMES A. MICHENER   Prolific writer who specialized in lengthy works of historical fiction. Michener claimed to understand the Joe DiMaggio-Marilyn Monroe relationship. Being press favorites, he reasoned, it was logical that they would get together. But the Monroe-Arthur Miller connection left Michener perplexed. Michener recalled that the first time he met Marilyn was "when she was dating Truman Capote and they were dancing at the El Morocco. She was barefoot so that she wouldn't tower over him. And she was just radiant. But her makeup was so heavy that I never really saw her, just what she was presenting. She had an enormous can and was not my ideal of beauty at all. She certainly was no Audrey Hepburn. But when she turned that face on, My God, it was something. Just like a sunbeam" (Grobel & Michener 153).

ARTHUR MILLER   One of the most celebrated American playwrights of his day, Arthur Miller was the author of *Death of a Salesman, The Crucible* and *A View From the Bridge*, among others. Miller and MM met in January 1951 on the set of *As Young as You Feel*. The two were introduced by Elia Kazan, who was having an affair with Marilyn at the time. The following day Kazan, Miller and Marilyn (tricked out with eyeglasses and steno pad as Kazan's secretary) went to see studio mogul Harry Cohn about a screenplay Miller had written. Later that week Marilyn and Miller met at a party thrown by agent Charles Feldman. Marilyn and Miller felt an immediate spark but, although they kept in contact, it would be four years before they acted upon their feelings. In the interval Marilyn married and divorced Joe DiMaggio. Only two months after marrying DiMaggio Marilyn startled a columnist friend, Sidney Skolsky, when she told him that she was going to marry Arthur Miller. The romance between Marilyn and Miller really started early in 1955, when she

moved to New York. When their budding relationship began to get noticed they admitted to being good friends but nothing more. In early 1956, when Marilyn returned to Hollywood to work on *Bus Stop*, Miller phoned her daily and made some clandestine visits. At the time he was residing in Reno, Nevada, a legal requirement for obtaining a divorce from his first wife. Without consulting Marilyn, Miller publicly announced their intention to marry on June 11, 1956. Miller was then under investigation by the House Un-American Activities Committee as a possible Communist fellow traveler. Marilyn, risking her own career, flew to Washington to be at Miller's side and pledge her support. The couple actually married twice. The first time was a civil ceremony on June 29, 1956: two days later they were married by a rabbi in a Jewish ceremony. Marilyn had formally converted to Judaism, even though Miller was not very religious and had not asked her to do so.[51] The press headline was "Egghead Weds Hourglass." Smart Alecs said of Marilyn that "she had married her college education" (Arnold 1987, 21).

The newlyweds took a working honeymoon in England where Marilyn began filming *The Prince and the Showgirl* with Sir Laurence Olivier. Miller wanted to attend the British premiere of his play *A View From the Bridge*. Trouble in their relationship emerged almost immediately. Marilyn came across Miller's diary in which he admitted to being disappointed in his wife and worried about the negative effect she was having on his creative output. Miller's fears were well-founded. His work began to take second place to the job of supporting Marilyn with her many professional and personal problems. When the movie was completed, they returned to America, dividing their time between a New York apartment and a farmhouse in Roxbury, Connecticut.

Part of the difficulty in their relationship was that Marilyn desperately wanted to have a baby but was unable to do so. In the summer of 1957 she had a dangerous pregnancy which had to be terminated. During the making of *Some Like It Hot* (1959), Marilyn became pregnant again but suffered a miscarriage. She was devastated and made a suicide attempt from which Miller rescued her.

Marilyn and her husband began to grow steadily apart. By the time she was working on *Let's Make Love* (1960), the two were leading almost separate lives. Marilyn embarked on a torrid affair with co-star Yves Montand while Miller was away in Ireland working with director John Huston on the screenplay for *The Misfits* (1961). The filming of *The Misfits,* in the heat of the Nevada desert, was an emotional nightmare. By the end of it Marilyn and Miller were living in separate hotel rooms, riding in separate cars to and from the set and were not on speaking terms. On November 11, 1960, their divorce was announced. The end of the marriage took effect on January 20, 1961. Marilyn chose that date because it was the day of President John F. Kennedy's inauguration. Marilyn was correct in assuming that the press would have more important things to dwell upon than the state of her personal life.

A scant 17 months later, Marilyn was dead from a drug overdose. Miller was wracked with guilt that perhaps their divorce had hastened her death. To allay those feelings Miller penned *After the Fall* (1964), a play about a doomed Marilynesque character named Maggie. Miller was soundly criticized for laying bare the soul of his dead ex-wife in so public a manner. Miller denied he had done any such thing. Miller married again, fathered children and survived Marilyn by 43 years. He seldom spoke about his life with Marilyn.

In the theatre scene in *All About Eve* (1950), one of Marilyn's important early films, Bette Davis mentions playwright Arthur Miller (Gottfried 2003 171–340; Miller 1987, 378–87, 412–36, 462–85; Riese & Hitchens 324–8; Victor 190–6).

MARILYN MILLER Marilyn Miller (1898–1936), Mary Pickford's sister-in-law, was a beautiful star of the *Ziegfeld Follies*. In 1946, Twentieth Century–Fox casting director Ben Lyon decided that fresh-faced starlet Norma Jeane Dougherty needed a different name. Carole Lind was tried but soon rejected.

Lyon recalled: "I finally said to her, 'I know who you are. You're Marilyn!' I told her that once there was a lovely actress named Marilyn Miller and that she reminded me of her. 'But what about the last name?' Marilyn said, 'My grandmother's name was Monroe and I'd like to keep that.' I said, 'Great! That's got a nice flow, and two M's should be lucky.' That's how she got her name" (Summers 37–8). Many years before, Lyon had been engaged to Miller. Marilyn, with her blonde hair and blue-green eyes, brought back memories of his former love.

Marilyn also recalled the origin of her new name: "There was a meeting. Mr. Zanuck said I should have a different name. He said Norma Jeane Dougherty would be too long on a marquee. Mr. Lyon began putting down names, asking my opinion. I told him my mother's maiden name was Monroe. He liked that. Then I said, 'How about *Norma Jeane Monroe*?' Mr. Zanuck said he thought that was still too long. He felt I was a mixture of Jean Harlow and Marilyn Miller. I said, 'How about *Jeane Monroe*?' That wasn't good either. Then Mr. Lyon came up with *Marilyn Monroe*. Mr. Zanuck liked it. I wish now I would have held out for Jeane Monroe, though, because it was difficult for me to get used to a whole different name. And, as you know, I had a hell of a time learning how to spell Marilyn" (Slatzer 263–4). Of course, when Marilyn Monroe married Arthur Miller she became Marilyn Miller herself (Riese & Hitchens 329–30; Victor 197).

JOHN MILLS Versatile British character actor on stage and screen. Mills and MM were introduced on July 26, 1956, at a ball at playwright Terence Rattigan's home in Berkshire, near London. The event was hosted by Rattigan in honor of Marilyn and her husband, Arthur Miller. Marilyn was in England to film Rattigan's *The Prince and the Showgirl* with Sir Laurence Olivier (Shevey 347–8).

VINCENTE MINNELLI The father of the modern musical, Minnelli was an award-winning stage and film director. In 1964, he directed *Goodbye Charlie*, the story of a man who dies and is reincarnated as a beautiful blonde woman. Minnelli recalled: "I hadn't seen the stage version with Lauren Bacall, but it had been criticized for some of Betty's masculine antics. She smoked cigars and swatted women on the rump, among other things. The approach, as I saw it, should have been more feminine, and Monroe could well project the vulnerability of the reincarnated, the prey of every predatory male. The original Charlie had been the most predatory of all." The film role of Charlie was reserved for MM by Minnelli. But even though Minnelli was one of her approved directors and the writer was George Axelrod, who wrote *The Seven Year Itch* (1955) and *Bus Stop* (1956), Marilyn turned it down. About a year before her death she told gossip columnist Hedda Hopper: "Fox wanted me for *Goodbye Charlie*, but as far as I'm concerned, it's goodbye *Goodbye Charlie*" (Minnelli & Arce 353).

CAMERON MITCHELL   Actor who was the star of television's *High Chaparral* (1967–1971). In December 1949, Mitchell and MM were on their way to the Fox commissary, when they ran into playwright Arthur Miller. Mitchell knew Miller, having been in the Broadway run of his *Death of a Salesman*, the year before. Mitchell had the honor of introducing Marilyn to Miller.[52] Mitchell acted opposite Marilyn in *How to Marry a Millionaire* in 1953.[53]

Mitchell recalled the early MM: "Then, as you know her, you find out she's no goddamn gold-plated birdbrain. She's a serious dame. At the time I first met her, she was on a big psychiatry kick. She was studying Freud, Menninger, that kind of thing" (Riese & Hitchens 335).

Other sources: Summers 77; *www.imdb. com*

ROBERT MITCHUM   In 1954, Robert Mitchum co-starred with MM in Otto Preminger's *The River of No Return*. It was not Mitchum's and Marilyn's first meeting, however. Mitchum had met Marilyn about ten years earlier when she was still Norma Jeanne Dougherty and he was an unknown factory worker. It was at the end of World War II and

Mitchum was working at the Lockheed Aircraft plant in Burbank, California, alongside Marilyn's first husband, Jim Dougherty. Mitchum recalled Dougherty showing him a revealing photograph of his beautiful teenaged wife. Sometimes Dougherty would bring sandwiches, tuna salad or bologna, which Norma Jeanne had packed, and he shared them with Mitchum who never brought a lunch to work. Mitchum also remembered how he accompanied Marilyn and her husband to a dance hall to hear the Tommy Dorsey Orchestra and its young singer, Frank Sinatra. Years later, however, Dougherty denied that any of this happened.

The River of No Return was not a happy set, although the co-stars got on well together. Mitchum never made any sexual advances to Marilyn and acted like an older brother. Under the advice of her acting coach, Natasha Lytess, Marilyn would enunciate every syllable of every word to an absurd degree—that was until Mitchum playfully slapped her on the rump and said, "Stop the nonsense! Let's play it like human beings" (Server 249). Mitchum interrupted a love scene with Marilyn by saying, "How can I take aim when she's undulating that way?" (Marill 33). Everyone laughed, including Marilyn. Mitchum thought Marilyn was sweet and funny but also sad and confused. Her chronic lateness and neurotic mannerisms never seemed to bother him. For her part, Marilyn thought Mitchum was one of the most fascinating men she had ever met.

Mitchum was offered the Clark Gable part in Marilyn's last completed picture, *The Misfits* (1961), but declined. He regretted not accepting the part because he believed that, if he had, Gable would not have died and Marilyn probably would not have either. As Mitchum said about Marilyn: "She would have been up and out like *that*, on time, all the time, if I'd been there. She trusted me. Anything I told her, she believed and she'd do it" (Grobel 522).

Years later, Mitchum claimed that on the night in 1962 when Marilyn was scheduled to perform her famous "Happy Birthday, Mr. President" before John F. Kennedy, she was in such a state of nervousness that she fled Madison Square Garden to the safety of his nearby hotel room. Mitchum then convinced Marilyn to return, in the company of secret service agents, and give her performance. Just days later, when Marilyn was fired from *Something's Got to Give* and her co-star Dean Martin quit, Mitchum was offered Martin's part but he refused to consider it (Eells 1984, 49–50, 166–70; Server 52–4, 248–53; Victor 201).

JAMES MONROE Fifth president of the United States (1817–1825). MM was born as Norma Jeane Mortenson, but her mother's maiden name was Monroe. Through that connection Marilyn could claim a descent from President Monroe. Of course, when Marilyn established Marilyn Monroe Productions, Inc., she was entitled to call herself President Monroe (Riese & Hitchens 337; Shevey 55).

RICARDO MONTALBAN Suave Mexican actor who became a big star with television's *Fantasy Island* (1978–1984). In 1950, Montalban was one of the stars of *Right Cross*, a boxing drama in which MM had a small uncredited part. Montalban had a brief scene with Marilyn. On June 1, 1955, Marilyn's 29th birthday, Montalban attended the premiere of *The Seven Year Itch* at Loew's State Theater in Times Square, New York, and the reception afterward (*www.imdb.com*; *www.cursumperficio.net* /biography/1955).

YVES MONTAND French singer and actor. Montand was a big star in Europe but relatively unknown in America. He had met MM's husband, Arthur Miller, when he starred in the French version of *The Crucible*, but apart from her reputation for lateness, Montand did not really know very much about Marilyn. He had never even seen *The Seven Year Itch* or *Bus Stop*.

In 1959, Montand had a one-man show on Broadway. Marilyn saw the show twice and thought the urbane Frenchman would be an excellent choice as the co-star in her upcoming film, *Let's Make Love* (1960). This was after the likes of Cary Grant, Charlton Heston,

Rock Hudson and Gregory Peck turned down the picture. When Montand accepted the role, his English was so limited that he had to learn his dialogue phonetically. Some observers were struck by a physical resemblance between Montand and Marilyn's ex-husband, Joe DiMaggio.

During the filming of *Let's Make Love*, Montand and his actress wife, Simone Signoret, and Marilyn and Miller occupied adjacent bungalows at the Beverly Hills Hotel. They became a tight foursome until both Signoret and Miller were called away. Left on their own, Marilyn and Montand embarked upon a torrid affair. Marilyn took the relationship seriously but, to Montand, it was merely an enjoyable dalliance. Marilyn's feelings were hurt when she read Montand's statement in Hedda Hopper's newspaper column: "She has been so kind to me, but she is a simple girl without any guile. Perhaps I was too tender and thought that she was as sophisticated as some of the other ladies I have known.... Had Marilyn been sophisticated, none of this ever would have happened.... Perhaps she had a schoolgirl crush. If she did, I'm sorry. But nothing will break up my marriage" (Riese & Hitchens 348). Montand later denied using the words "schoolgirl crush," saying that he did not understand what they meant. On June 30, 1960, Montand returned to France and met Marilyn at Idlewild Airport in New York. There, in the back of a limousine, they said their goodbyes and drank champagne. Although Marilyn sent Montand a gift on his next birthday and cabled him that she was coming to Paris, they never met again.

Let's Make Love was a commercial and critical flop and Montand did not score a Hollywood breakthrough. He returned to his wife and resumed his position in France as a major movie and recording star (Guiles 398–401; Montand, Hamon & Rotman 297–333; Summers 247–51; Victor 204).

ALVY MOORE Light comic actor remembered by fans of television's *Green Acres* (1965–1971) as the loopy county agricultural agent, Mr. Kimball. Moore had an uncredited part in a Marilyn Monroe film, *Gentlemen Prefer Blondes* (1953)[54] (*www.imdb.com*).

CLAYTON MOORE *see* LONE RANGER

ZERO MOSTEL   Award–wining film and stage actor who starred in the stage version of *Fiddler On the Roof, A Funny Thing Happened On the Way to the Forum* (1966) and *The Producers* (1968). Mostel was one of MM's actor friends. Early in her career Marilyn jokingly drew up a list of her "Most Wanted" men. Zero Mostel's name was there alongside the likes of Ernest Hemingway and Albert Einstein. During 1955, when Marilyn lived in a fancy suite at the Waldorf-Astoria Hotel in New York, visitors noticed a sketch of Marilyn executed by Mostel, which she hung on a wall (Victor 14, 318).

ARTHUR MURRAY   Famous dance instructor who founded the chain of dance studios which bear his name. After seeing MM perform her "Heat Wave" number in *There's No Business Like Show Business* (1954), Murray was inspired to create a dance called "The Marilyn Monroe Mambo" (Riese & Hitchens 307; Victor 68).

DON MURRAY   Don Murray was plucked from the relative obscurity of the theater to star opposite MM in *Bus Stop* (1956). Murray received an Oscar nomination while Marilyn was ignored. Murray and Marilyn did not get along during the making of the film. She did not want him in the role and did not take the trouble to hide her feelings. Murray was inexperienced, three years younger than she was, as good looking as she was, and carrying on a romance with Hope Lange, who was also in the film.

Murray recalled, "When she thought I'd ruined a scene of hers, she continued the action as rehearsed, taking her costume and hitting me across the face with it. Some of the sequins scratched the corner of my eye and she ran off. But she wasn't deliberately mean" (Victor 208).

Marilyn pointedly refused to apologize for that incident.

During the filming Murray gave his impression of Marilyn to a newspaper reporter, opinions which could not have pleased his co-star. "Here she is, one of the country's most important personalities. Suddenly she discovers that, well, something is missing. So right now she is going through what most of us experience in our teens, trying to get inside her own personality through philosophy and psychology" (Victor 208).

As an example of this we have the record of a fluffed scene from the movie. In the scene Murray was supposed to say, "No wonder you're so pale and white." Instead he said, "No wonder, you're so pale and scaly." Marilyn seized on this and said:

> "Don, do you realize what you just did? You made a Freudian slip. You see you were in the proper mood because it's a sexual scene and you said 'scaly' which means you were thinking of a snake. A snake is a phallic symbol. Do you know what a phallic symbol is?"
>
> "Know what it is?" replied Murray angrily, "I've got one" [Shevey 333].

Other Source: Riese & Hitchens 357–8

EDWARD R. MURROW   Famous journalist who turned to television, interviewing celebrities in their homes. On April 8, 1955, MM was the guest on Murray's televison show, *Person to Person*. At the time, Marilyn was a guest of her business partner, Milton Greene, and his wife, Amy. Marilyn was at the Greenes' home in Westport, Connecticut. TV transmission was by line-of-sight in those days and two weeks had been spent erecting a 200–foot antenna to allow Murrow to have a live feed from his studio in New York City to Marilyn in Connecticut. Marilyn had spent five hours beautifying herself for the broadcast and was very nervous about appearing on live television before millions of viewers. She got a grip on herself when one of the production crew told her, "Just look at the camera, dear. It's just you and the camera—just you two" (Victor 209).

Marilyn came across as shy, tentative and vulnerable, although she was probably more artful than she seemed. She subtly made her case against Twentieth Century–Fox for meatier film roles and better directors. After it was over, Marilyn thought the interview was dismal and that Amy Greene had come off better than she had.[55] (Persico 35–6; Shevey 304–5).

-N-

VLADIMIR   NABOKOV Russian-American novelist whose most famous novel was the controversial *Lolita*. In 1960, Nabokov met MM at a Hollywood party and she took quite a liking to him. But when the writer was invited to Marilyn's birthday party, Mrs. Nabokov answered the telephone saying: "Indeed not. He is working very hard. He doesn't need distractions like that." Upon being asked his opinion of sex symbols Marilyn Monroe and Jayne Mansfield, Nabokov said: "Miss Monroe is one of the greatest comedy actresses of our time. She is simply superb. Miss Mansfield I've never seen" (Shevey 397).

J. CARROL NAISH   Character actor who usually played ethnic roles. Naish played Uncle Vince in a 1952 MM movie, *Clash by Night* (Victor 57; *www.imdb.com*).

JEAN NEGULESCO   Romanian film director in Hollywood who made *Three Coins in the Fountain* (1954) and *Daddy Long Legs* (1955). Negulesco probably met Marilyn at a New Year's Eve party on December 31, 1948, at producer Sam Spiegel's house in Beverly Hills. In 1953, Negulesco directed MM in *How to Marry a Millionaire*. Unlike most of her directors, Marilyn got on well with Negulesco. He made a drawing of Marilyn and recommended books for her to read, which they later discussed. Negulesco said of Marilyn: "She represents to men something we all want in our unfulfilled dreams. She's the girl you'd like to double-cross your wife with" (Negulesco 215).

Negulesco approached Marilyn on the set of *Gentlemen Prefer Blondes* and presented her with the script for *How to Marry a Millionaire*. Marilyn was not sure if she should do the picture and not sure if she understood the character she was to play. A short time later she marched, unannounced, into Negulesco's office seeking clarification.

Marilyn's voice quiet, childlike, out of breath: "Mr. Feldman [her agent] asked me to see you."

"Charlie is a good and generous friend." (I made this into a compliment to her. No reaction.)

"Mr. Feldman said you'll explain to me."

"Explain?"

"My part."

(Now I knew there was some trouble.)

"Have you read the script, Miss Monroe?"

"Yes."

"And?"

"I don't know..."

"Miss Monroe, you read the script. It is a brilliant script by Nunnally Johnson. Your part is right for you. Shall I tell you what it is about?"

She took off her glasses and said in a loud voice, "I know what it is all about, but—" (Silence.)

"But what?"

(Still loud): "Who *are* we?"

(Wow. That's a good one. So answer the lady. Be clever)

"Miss Monroe, you are three beautiful girls, Loco, Schatze, and Pola, wishing to marry millionaires. And the kind of girls you are, the contents of your icebox explains: hot dogs, orchids, and champagne. Does that answer your question?"

It didn't. She started to put her dark glasses back on but didn't. Finally she looked at me—not her uncertain sidelong look, but straight at me. And again she found her voice: "What is the *motivation* of my character?"

Now it was all clear. Her Russian coach, Natasha Lytess, had put her up to this. So this called for my most know-how voice: "The motivation, Miss Monroe? You're blind as a bat without glasses. That is your motivation."

Her eyes came out from under her drooping lids. The puzzled child had resolved the "if": "That's all?"

"Yes, Marilyn. That's all."

She put back her dark glasses and left—satisfied [Negulesco 217–8].

When work on the film commenced, Marilyn followed her own internal clock, ignoring schedules and call times. Sometimes Marilyn became so immersed in her character that if Negulesco said "Hello," or "Good morning," she would blurt out a line of dialogue in response. It was apparent to Negulesco that Marilyn was terrified of appearing before the camera. "But once she faced it, an extraordinary unseen love affair took place between her and the lenses. A love affair nobody around her was aware of—director, cameraman, soundman. It was a language of looks, a forbidden intimacy. Only when the film was put together did this love affair become apparent to us. The lenses were the audience" (Negulesco 219).

In later years Negulesco was called in to work with Marilyn on retakes and additional scenes for movies made by other directors. In 1962, when *Something's Got to Give* was restarted, the original director, George Cukor, was fired, and Marilyn asked for Negulesco to take over. Negulesco accepted the job, but Marilyn died before any new footage could be shot (Negulesco 215–27; Summers 117–18; Victor 212; *www.cursumperficio.net* /biography/1948).

PAUL NEWMAN   Durable Hollywood leading man. Shortly before her death, MM had agreed to play the lead in *What a Way to Go!*, with co-star Paul Newman. When the film was made in 1964, Newman played opposite Shirley MacLaine. Italian producer Carlo Ponti wanted to star his wife, Sophia Loren, and Paul Newman in Arthur Miller's thinly disguised biography of Marilyn, *After the Fall*. It never happened (Brown & Barham 293).

JULIE NEWMAR   Actress, dancer and singer made famous by her Catwoman role in the 1960s television series *Batman*. Commencing in 1955, MM took twice-weekly classes at the famous Actors Studio in New York. Among her classmates was Julie Newmar. Of the Studio's artistic director, Lee Strasberg, Newmar recalled, "He loved Marilyn but many actresses felt that same feeling from him. I always felt he favored me, too" (Adams 258).

MIKE NICHOLS   Mike Nichols is a film director and producer who is also remembered for his comedy routines with partner Elaine May. Nichols and May were part of the program on May 19, 1962, when Marilyn Monroe sang "Happy Birthday, Mr. President" before 17,000 people (and President John F. Kennedy) at Madison Square Garden (*www.cursumperficio.net* /file/M/Madison Square Garden).

DAVID NIVEN   Versatile British actor who became a smooth Hollywood leading man. In 1948, when MM was an unknown starlet, David Niven had a one-night stand with her. In a deleted paragraph from his autobiography, *The Moon's a Balloon*, Niven did not have nice things to say about Marilyn. He thought she was ungrateful, unprofessional and exhibited "bad temper, hysterics, thoughtlessness and dedicated love of self. When she was at the top, she thought nothing of keeping huge casts waiting for hours till she was ready to work. 'Go fuck yourself!' she screamed at a quivering young assistant director who had been dispatched to enquire when her presence could be expected on the set." Niven concluded that Marilyn was "not beautiful unless her mouth was slightly open" (Lord 356).

MARNI NIXON   Legendary voice double who recorded the singing for such top stars as Natalie Wood, Audrey Hepburn and Deborah Kerr. In *Gentlemen Prefer Blondes* (1953) Marilyn Monroe almost lost her signature tune, "Diamonds Are a Girl's Best Friends." Twentieth Century–Fox originally wanted Nixon to record the song. But Marilyn proved that she could sing, and in the finished film does her own rendition of the song, apart from one half of one line. The lyric, "These rocks don't lose their shape" is sung by Nixon (Glatzer 92).

RICHARD NIXON   The 37th president of the United States (1968–1974). Marilyn was happy that Nixon lost the 1960 election to John F. Kennedy. For that election Marilyn jokingly coined a campaign slogan—"Nix on Nixon" (Kashner 335). She considered Nixon to have been a Red-baiter of the type who had persecuted her husband, Arthur Miller. In 1962, the City News Service Editors of Los Angeles rated Nixon's failure to get elected governor of California as the year's second-biggest story. The number-one story was Marilyn Monroe's death (Riese & Hitchens 373).

TOMMY NOONAN   Comedian, film actor, screenwriter and producer who is best remembered for his role as Gus Esmond, Marilyn Monroe's rich but nerdy and bespectacled suitor in *Gentlemen Prefer Blondes* (1953). Marilyn's feelings were hurt when she heard Noonan say that kissing her in the movie was "like being sucked into a vacuum." She replied, "How can people be so cruel? Nobody can be so cruel and not pay for it one day" (Summers 110).

KIM NOVAK   A former department store model and beauty queen—Miss Deepfreeze of 1952—Kim Novak was groomed to be Columbia's answer to MM. Studio head Harry Cohn put it bluntly when he said that he wanted a young girl who could become another Monroe. The first thing Cohn had to do was change her name from Marilyn Novak to Kim Novak. The public's association of the name "Marilyn" with Monroe was just too strong. Novak had a successful career starring in *Picnic* (1955), *The Man With the Golden Arm* (1955), *Pal Joey* (1957), *Vertigo* (1958), and *Bell Book and Candle* (1958), but she never achieved Marilyn's level of superstardom. Novak was offered the lead in *Something's Got to Give*, when Marilyn was fired from the picture in 1962, reportedly at a higher salary. But Novak sympathized with Marilyn and refused to even consider the offer. The two actresses knew each other socially but never worked together. In April 1961, at a dinner party at actor Peter Lawford's home, Novak was seated with Marilyn and Robert Kennedy (Brown & Barham 194–5, 226; Guiles 431; Riese & Hitchens 375–6; Victor 218; *www. imdb.com*).

-O-

MERLE OBERON   Academy Award–nominated British actress known for her exotic looks. In 1954, MM took time out from her own work on *There's No Business Like Show Business* to visit Oberon on the set of *Désirée*. A photograph was snapped of a smiling Marilyn and Merle with director Henry Koster (Anonymous 98; *www.cursumperficio.net /files/*There's No Business Like Show Business).

HUGH O'BRIAN   Hollywood leading man remembered for his television series *The Life and Legend of Wyatt Earp* (1955–1961). In 1954, O'Brian was in *There's No Business Like Show Business* with MM although they shared no scenes (Victor 304; *www.imdb.com*).

PAT O'BRIEN   Hollywood veteran who was in *The Front Page* (1931), *Angels With Dirty Faces* (1938) and many more movies. In 1959, O'Brien had a supporting role as a police detective in *Some Like It Hot*. In 1950, O'Brien had been in one of Marilyn's lesser known pictures, *The Fireball*.[56] During the shooting of *Some Like It Hot*, co-star George Raft remembered how he and O'Brien were director Billy Wilder's "utility infielders." Whenever Marilyn did not show up for work, be it for physical or psychological reasons, he and O'Brien were called upon to do a scene that was to occur later in the shooting schedule (Yablonsky 217; *www.imdb.com*).

SEAN O'CASEY   One of the most important Irish dramatists of the 20th century. After Marilyn's death, O'Casey said what was on everyone's mind: "Who killed Marilyn Monroe—that's a question?" He went on to say that her death "was a tragedy that affected me very much. I hate the idea of Hollywood in which she had to survive. She said she wanted to meet me when she was over here, and I wish I had. I would have liked to have talked with her.... I never knew she had such a hard upbringing—all those foster homes, never a real one" (Weatherby 215–6). O'Casey was 82 when Marilyn died, and he survived her by two years. Marilyn was known to have read O'Casey's autobiography. In 1956, when accompanying her husband, Arthur Miller, to the Royal Court production of *The Crucible*, Marilyn did indeed remark that the person in England she most wanted to meet was Sean O'Casey (Murray 369).

ARTHUR O'CONNELL   Film actor with lengthy Broadway credentials. O'Connell usually played characters who were mildly bewildered. In 1956, he played the mildly bewildered Virgil in *Bus Stop* (Riese & Hitchens 379; *www.imdb.com*).

DONALD O'CONNOR   Singer, dancer and actor best known for his "Make 'Em

Laugh" number in *Singin' in the Rain* (1952). Two years later O'Connor was MM's love interest in *There's No Business Like Show Business.* Marilyn did not want to play opposite O'Connor because, in her opinion, he was three inches too short for her and, despite being a year older, looked too young. "Don't make me Donald O'Connor's girl," she complained, "I could eat him for breakfast" (Shevey 267). Marilyn was overruled and promised the lead in *The Seven Year Itch* (1955) in compensation. Her instincts were correct. Marilyn's screen presence overpowered O'Connor, and the pairing did not seem convincing. O'Connor said of Marilyn: "I thought she was going to throw her weight around. She's subtle. She's an ingenious actress" (Riese & Hitchens 379).

CLIFFORD ODETS Playwright and scriptwriter who met Marilyn in June 1947 after the reading of a play. Joking with her roommate, a young Marilyn drew up a list of ideal lovers, and Odets was one of the names. Odets' play of jealousy and tragedy, *Clash by Night*, was filmed in 1952 with MM in a small but important role. Odets attended Marilyn's 33rd birthday party. He stayed until 4:30 A.M., reading palms. Summing up Marilyn, Odets said of her that she was "spontaneous, tender and original ... a coquette playing somewhat for your affection and esteem" (Considine 1994, 115).

Other sources: Mendelsohn 106; Shevey 398; Victor 224

JOHN O'HARA Author of *Appointment in Samarra*, *Butterfield 8* and *Pal Joey*. In a letter dated December 9, 1961, O'Hara commented on George Cukor, who was then directing Marilyn in *Something's Got to Give*: "I shouldn't think Cukor would have much difficulty with MM. I've met him only briefly once or twice, with no memorable conversation, but I'll bet he had more trouble with Kate Hepburn and Norma Shearer than he had with Garbo. And with Arthur Miller (who I think is a prime horse's ass) out of the way, MM should be more tractable." O'Hara was spectacularly wrong in his prediction. Marilyn was so unre-liable that she was fired and the film was never completed (Bruccoli 1978, 380).

MAUREEN O'HARA Red-haired Irish-American movie actress. During her brief marriage to Joe DiMaggio in 1954, MM asked her friend Maureen O'Hara to play a prank on Joe for his 40th birthday.

O'Hara describes the scene: "Apparently, Joe was a fan of mine and always teased Marilyn about how attracted to me he was. She was sick and tired of hearing her husband talk about me and I don't blame her. She asked me if I would mind being wrapped in a big box with a ribbon tied in a bow around it, to be her gift to Joe on his birthday. The huge box would be on a large table, and right before he opened it, she was going to say, 'Now, Joe, after I give you this, I don't ever want to hear about Maureen O'Hara again.' Then as he pulled the bow and ribbon off, I was supposed to pop out of the box while the crowd shouted, 'Surprise!'" O'Hara was keen to play her part, but Marilyn and DiMaggio separated before she got the opportunity (O'Hara & Nicolette 215–6).

SIR LAURENCE OLIVIER Olivier was considered by many to be the finest dramatic actor of his generation. It was nothing short of a sensation when Olivier and MM jointly announced that they were going to make *The Prince and the Showgirl* in England. Marilyn's own production company, Marilyn Monroe Productions, Inc. had purchased the screen rights to Terence Rattigan's play *The Sleeping Prince*, and retitled it. Marilyn would bring to the screen the role which Olivier's wife, Vivien Leigh, had created on stage. Olivier had agreed to co-star in the film as well as produce and direct. Marilyn was technically Olivier's boss, but things did not work out that way in practice.

The press conference announcing the film was held at the Plaza Hotel in New York on February 9, 1956. True to form, Marilyn kept Rattigan, Olivier and 200 restless reporters cooling their heels until she could make a suitably grand entrance. At last, clad in a slinky black gown, Marilyn swept down a marble staircase on Olivier's arm. Marilyn and Olivier expertly fielded questions until, right on cue, one of the spaghetti straps holding up Marilyn's dress broke. Flash bulbs popped and safety pins were quickly produced. All eyes were on Marilyn and the upstaged Olivier was reduced to holding a microphone for her. Marilyn had planned the whole thing, of course.

Olivier had expected to fall "most shatteringly" (Holden 301) in love with Marilyn, but something close to the opposite is what happened. He quickly concluded that she had a schizoid personality; at one moment adorable, witty and fun; the next moment rude, vindictive and selfish. Marilyn's insecurities, always close to the surface, were brought out by Olivier. She was in awe of him, even terrified, and thought that he did not respect her as an artist. She came to believe that he only wanted her to be in the film because of her commercial value.

The newly married Marilyn and her husband, Arthur Miller, arrived in London on July 14. Olivier and Vivien Leigh were all smiles as they welcomed the Millers to England. A press conference ensued, in which Marilyn was deluged with impertinent questions. It was the beginning of a media frenzy. Her every move in Britain, real or not, was lavishly reported.

It is an understatement to say that Marilyn and Olivier did not get along. Marilyn had been studying the Method style of acting which emphasizes psychological motivation. Olivier, a technical actor, considered the Method to be pretentious nonsense. Olivier strongly resented the on-set presence of Marilyn's personal exponent of the Method, her acting coach Paula Strasberg. It was Olivier's considered opinion that Strasberg was a nuisance and a fraud. Olivier was driven to distraction by Marilyn's constant unprofessionalism and lateness. He made a superhuman effort to be patient but finally he exploded, shouting at Marilyn: "Why can't you get here on time for fuck's sake?" Marilyn replied, "Oh, do you have that word in England too?" (Holden 308). Another time an exasperated Oliver said to Marilyn, "Act sexy." She coldly replied, "Larry, I don't have to act sexy. I *am* sexy" (Holden

308). Behind his back, Marilyn started referring to Sir Laurence as "Mr. Sir."

Olivier spent four excruciating months filming *The Prince and the Showgirl*. He tried being encouraging and supportive with his co-star and he tried being stern and authoritative, but nothing worked. Olivier described the experience as being the worst in his professional life. He threw up his hands at one point and said, "Shit, let's just get on with it and get it over with" (Kiernan 258).

The finished film was not a commercial success, but the two stars (considering their personality clashes) gave surprisingly good performances, especially Marilyn. By comparison, Oliver's performance suffered. After scores of takes of a single scene, Olivier's energy would begin to flag, but Marilyn would grow steadily better. When Marilyn finally nailed the scene she was splendid. Naturally, that would be the take which would be used because there was no guarantee when she would next show up for work. Looking back, Olivier said, "I was as good as could be," and then generously added, "Marilyn was quite wonderful, the best of all" (Olivier 213).

Olivier had briefly met Marilyn in Los Angeles in August 1950, when he was introduced to her by Shelley Winters. It was a party at Danny Kaye's home in honor of Olivier's wife, Vivien Leigh, who had come to Hollywood to make *A Streetcar Named Desire*. At the time Olivier thought Marilyn was a "cute little girl" (Winters 1989, 295), and he graciously kissed her hand. Olivier did not even remember Marilyn when they came together to make *The Prince and the Showgirl*. He said, "I wished I had remembered meeting Marilyn that night so long ago but she looked so different in London, I didn't realize it was the same girl" (Winters 1989, 296). Marilyn, if she remembered, never referred to their first meeting at all.

In January 1958, after the completion of *The Prince and the Showgirl*, Olivier was appearing on stage in New York and decided to drop by the Actors Studio. Marilyn was there that day. Whether or not Olivier spotted Marilyn, he did not acknowledge her. Marilyn definitely did recognize Olivier and took care to avoid having to speak to him, going so far as to hide in the lavatory (Hirsch 1979, 114–15; Holden 301–13; Olivier 205–13; Riese & Hitchens 381–2; Spoto 1992, 273, 316–17, 322–4, 338; Victor 226–8; Winters 1989, 212–13; *www.cursumperficio.net* /biography/1950).

ARISTOTLE ONASSIS   Greek shipping tycoon who married Jacqueline Kennedy. In 1955, MM was the subject of a bizarre scheme which, had it succeeded, would have turned her into Her Serene Highness Princess Marilyn of Monaco! Onassis had heavily invested in Monaco and concluded that the tiny principality needed a facelift. He thought, who better to bring some glamor to Monaco than a beautiful Hollywood actress? It was time for the prince, Rainier, to marry and through intermediaries, Onassis approached Marilyn. It did not seem to bother Onassis that Marilyn was not Catholic and was twice divorced. Marilyn found the idea appealing but did not really take it seriously. She admitted that she did not know where Monaco was and jokingly referred to Rainier as "Reindeer." Marilyn was involved with playwright Arthur Miller at the time, and Rainier went on to wed another Hollywood star, Grace Kelly (Lacey 218–9, 236–7; Riese & Hitchens 382; Robyns 135–6; Summers 193).

EUGENE O'NEILL   Nobel- and Pulitzer Prize–winning playwright who wrote *Anna Christie* in 1922. In February 1956, two years after O'Neill had died, MM electrified the New York theatre community when, opposite Maureen Stapleton, she performed the saloon scene from *Anna Christie* before the members of the Actors Studio. One of the lucky few who got a ticket to this memorable one-nighter was publicist John Springer: "The day that Marilyn did her scene with Maureen Stapleton at the Actors Studio you couldn't get close to it. Everyone was there. Most of the great stars of the Actors Studio were there to see Marilyn do *Anna Christie* with Maureen Stapleton. I was there, and it was a night I'll never forget. How was she? She was marvelous. It was Mar-

ilyn's own thing—Marilyn playing this beat-down old streetwalker. She walks into this bar and chats to this older hooker. It was a joke that Marilyn was going to do a scene from *Anna Christie*. But it was no joke. It was really an extraordinary moment in the theatre. She would have been marvelous in the theatre" (Shevey 312).

Marilyn was very nervous before she went on stage. She said: "I couldn't feel anything. I couldn't remember one line. All I wanted to do was lie down and die. I was in these impossible circumstances and I suddenly thought to myself, 'Good God, what am I doing here?' Then I just had to go out and do it" (Victor 14). Marilyn was overwrought and in tears when she finished, even though she received an honor which was almost unheard of in the Actors Studio—applause.

-P-

JACK PAAR   Actor and pioneering television talk show host. Paar was one of many in the Hollywood community who underestimated MM. Paar acted opposite Marilyn in *Love Nest*, a forgettable comedy from 1951.

Wrote Paar:

> I was to play the part of the sexy boyfriend opposite a new young starlet. She was a handful and very difficult to know because her status at the studio with executives had little to do with her ability as an actress. She was always late and never knew her lines, yet everyone was very careful in their relationship with her.
>
> Since she was the object of constant sexual remarks behind her back and to her face, I felt some sympathy for her. It must be a bore, I would think, being constantly propositioned. To this constant barrage of priapic offers, she would reply in that strange, funny, whispering voice, "Promises, promises."...
>
> She was never without a book on the set with the title turned out for all to see. I recall quite vividly that it was a book by Marcel Proust, a rather exotic French author much in vogue among the intellectually pretentious of the time. I found her "act" interesting, but must admit I was quite surprised that this sad, shy, arrogant loner became a star. She was, of course, Marilyn Monroe. The

secret was—and I am not certain whether it was planned or luck—that what Marilyn later dazzled the world with was something that "happened" only on the screen. On the set she was just another Hollywood starlet, not as attractive as many and not as likeable as most. Marilyn was like a caricature of a woman ... I fear that beneath the façade of Marilyn Monroe there was only a frightened waitress in a diner [Paar 85–6].

For her part, Marilyn was hurt by Paar's opinion of her. To a friend, she confided: "Jack Paar saw me with a book under my arm when we were doing a movie together. And he couldn't get over the way I was always carrying it around. He thought I was just trying to show people I was intelligent or something. But I was actually reading it" (Slatzer 267).

After *Love Nest* was completed, the studio called Paar back to pose for some publicity pictures with Marilyn.

It should have taken a few hours. Well, a few hours went by, and she didn't show—her usual "act." Then she arrived and said with that silly voice, "Oooooo, I'm late." She then went directly to the phone and talked to somebody for another twenty minutes. I have a low threshold of tolerance for unprofessional behavior and finally said for all to hear on the set, "Tell that broad to get her peroxide butt over here as I am leaving in half and hour."

She did come and we made the silly pictures, but I was cautioned by the photographer, "Come on, Jack, you'll simply have to act like you like her. The pictures we have taken are not good, and it's my job. Please help me!"

So I hugged and kissed her, bit her ear, breathed down her neck, which was really her navel, left the set, and never spoke to the poor darling again [Paar 86].

GERALDINE PAGE Academy Award–winning actress who enjoyed a 35-year career in film, television and on stage. In February 1956, Page was at the Actors Studio in New York City to witness Marilyn Monroe's memorable performance of the saloon scene from Eugene O'Neill's *Anna Christie*. Page said of Marilyn that "she could handle the heavy stuff wonderfully" (Considine 1994, 123).

DEBRA PAGET In 1951, Marilyn Monroe made her only appearance at the Academy Awards. She was invited to present the Best Achievement in Sound Oscar to Thomas Moulton, for his work on *All About Eve* (1950). In a lavender off-the-shoulder gown, borrowed from the Twentieth Century–Fox wardrobe department, Marilyn looked radiant. But moments before going on stage Marilyn detected a small rip in the dress and went into a panic, tearfully declaring that she could not go on. Debra Paget, an up-and-coming young actress, was one of those backstage who calmed Marilyn down and helped her overcome her stage fright. Meanwhile, minions from Fox fixed the dress. Marilyn presented the award but barely looked up from the podium. Paget and Marilyn met again on November 14, 1953, at Twentieth Century–Fox. They jostled for position in a receiving line to meet the visiting king and queen of Greece (Bilman 77; Marshall 241).

JACK PALANCE Gaunt Hollywood actor who was usually cast as a psychotic villain. In the fall of 1951, Palance was a New York stage actor and he introduced MM to the man who became one of her drama coaches, Michael Chekhov. Palance had himself studied acting with Chekhov, who was the nephew of the famous Russian writer Anton Chekhov. Marilyn had met Palance the year before. Palance was also a protégé of theater and film director Eli Kazan, with whom Marilyn had a brief affair (Guiles 182, 212; Riese & Hitchens 385; Victor 230; *www.imdb.com*).

JOSEPH PAPP Theatrical producer and director. Early in his career Papp spent time at the Actors Lab in Los Angeles. He remembered MM coming to class with a little dog and being so shy that she scarcely said a word. Papp also claimed to have been in a body-training class with her (Turan & Papp 35).

JERRY PARIS Amiable supporting player and successful television director. Paris was the next-door neighbor on *The Dick Van Dyke Show* (1961–1966). He had an uncredited role as a scientist in an MM film: *Monkey Business* (1952). Paris and Marilyn also knew each other socially. He drove Marilyn and Shelley Winters to the premiere of *On the Waterfront* (1954) (Winters 1989, 46; *www.imdb.com*).

DOROTHY PARKER   Wisecracking poet and writer known for her sarcastic wit. Parker admired MM's beauty and sensitivity, describing her as "adorable and fey" (Guiles 214). For about a year between early 1953 and January 1954, Marilyn lived in a modest apartment on Doheny Drive in Beverly Hills. This was just two blocks from where Parker lived and the two became friendly neighbors. In 1961, after separating from Arthur Miller, Marilyn briefly moved back to the same apartment. Toward the end of her life it was proposed that Marilyn make a film based on a Parker play, *The Good Soup*. In 1958, Dorothy Parker was elected to membership in the prestigious National Institute of Arts and Letters in New York City. Parker was drunk when she showed up for the ceremony. She was then introduced to Arthur Miller, who was given a prize for drama, but was thrilled to meet his famous wife, Marilyn Monroe (Fitzpatrick 110–11; Meade 1988, 365).

GORDON PARKS   Photographer, writer and film director remembered for making the movie *Shaft* (1971). In March 1956, during the making of *Bus Stop*, Parks had a photo session with Marilyn Monroe (*www.cursumperficio.net /files/P/photographers*).

LOUELLA PARSONS   Much-feared newspaper gossip columnist. MM, however, did not have too much to fear from Parsons. The columnist knew Marilyn from her earliest days in Hollywood and was always favorably disposed toward her. That might have had something to do with the fact that an early MM picture, *Clash by Night* (1952), was produced by Harriet Parsons, Louella's daughter. When Marilyn issued public statements or replied to critics it was often through Parsons's column or on her radio show. Parsons thought Marilyn was the most exciting movie personality of her generation (Parsons 21–37; Riese & Hitchens 397–8; Victor 230).

KING PAUL OF GREECE   On November 14, 1953, Marilyn Monroe turned up at a reception at Twentieth Century–Fox for the visiting King Paul and Queen Frederika of Greece (Marshall 241; Spoto 1993, 241; *www. cursumperficio.net /biography/1953*).

DREW PEARSON   Pearson was a muckraking journalist whose column 'Washington Merry-Go-Round' was syndicated in newspapers coast to coast. In the summer of 1954, Pearson invited a bevy of glamorous Hollywood actresses to fill-in for him while he was on vacation. Marilyn Monroe's turn came on August 30. Her column was basically a puff piece for her latest movie, *There's No Business Like Show Business*, and her upcoming *The Seven Year Itch*. The hands of the Fox publicity department were all over it but even so, Marilyn wrote honestly about her difficult beginnings and how hard she works to perfect her craft. She expresses surprise at being invited to contribute to a column which dealt with national affairs: "In brief, as Lorelei would say, what is a girl like I doing in Drew Pearson's column?"

Marilyn went on to write, "You might like to know that my pin-up days are over—well, sort of. I still want to look nice and have our servicemen and others take pleasure in my pictures, but I also want to be known as a good actress. I think *Seven Year Itch*, which I will start soon, will give me a wonderful opportunity to show how I've improved since my first small part in *Ladies of the Chorus*."[57] Marilyn (or some studio hack) went on to write, " As to the future, I just don't know. On the horizon, like a black cloud, is the frightening figure of Dior, who has decreed that girls must be flat-chested. If this comes about, I will be a dead duck and people will be speaking of Marilyn in the past tense because no matter what Dior decrees come out of Paris, I just won't qualify" (Warsaw Times-Union, August 30, 1954).

GREGORY PECK   Peck was set to co-star with MM in the 1960 comedy, *Let's Make Love*, but dropped out before principal photography was to commence. The reason given for Peck's departure was that the Monroe picture conflicted with his commitment to make *The Guns of Navarone*. Peck said, "I am genuinely sorry not to be able to work with Miss Monroe. I am mercenary enough to know that with her in a picture the chances of success are improved" (Riese & Hitchens 389).

The real reason was that Marilyn's part had been rewritten and expanded by Arthur Miller, at Peck's expense. In the original script Marilyn was in just four scenes. She began scheming right from the start to fatten her part. Peck, however, had script approval. He said: "My part began to diminish. Marilyn's part kept getting bigger and bigger and the whole thing stopped being funny" (Fishgall 216). The completed movie is generally considered to be Marilyn's worst as a major star. Peck's assessment was correct. It was not very funny. It was probably just as well that Marilyn and Peck never worked together. Peck was the model of punctuality while Marilyn boasted, "I've been on a calendar but never on time" (Haney 291).

After Marilyn's death, Peck said of her: "Monroe may have been a bit of an extreme example, but she was given the best stories to suit her talents, she was stroked and cared for and treasured and treated like a little princess, treated as a valuable, talented person. What it was that led her to drink and take pills, I don't know. I don't think anyone can put it all together, but it's too easy to say that Hollywood wrung her out and exhausted her, strained her nerves and destroyed her. I think she'd have gone to pieces even sooner without the adulation and the care she received at the hands of her directors and producers and the big studios" (Haney 294–5).

GEORGE PEPPARD Actor known for his roles in *Breakfast at Tiffany's* (1961) and in the 1980s television series *The A-Team*. Sometime after 1955, Peppard and Marilyn Monroe attended classes at the Actors Studio in New York. At one class Marilyn watched closely as Peppard presented a scene from Shakespeare (Adams 254).

ANTHONY PERKINS Actor forever associated with the role of Norman Bates in *Psycho* (1960). Perkins was invited to the premiere of *Let's Make Love* which starred Yves Montand

and MM. Perkins was not looking forward to the event as he was nursing a hangover at the time (Winecoff 201).

NEHEMIAH PERSOFF Persoff was a character actor who usually had an intimidating screen presence. He was cast as the gangster Little Bonaparte in *Some Like It Hot* (1959) (*www.imdb.com*).

JEAN PETERS Movie actress from the 1950s who retired to marry Howard Hughes. Peters met Marilyn in 1946 when, as starlets, they both attended acting classes. It was the time when Norma Jeane Doughterty was in search of a suitable professional name. Carol Lind was one possibility, but neither Marilyn nor Peters liked it. Peters argued that Meredith would be a good name for her friend.

After Norma Jeane was renamed Marilyn Monroe, Peters co-starred with her in two films: *As Young as You Feel* (1951) and *Niagara* (1953). Marilyn's part as the faithless wife plotting murder in *Niagara* had originally been written for Peters. That same year, director Samuel Fuller had selected Peters over Marilyn for the female lead in the gritty film noir *Pickup on South Street*. He thought Marilyn looked too innocent for the part. During the production of *Let's Make Love*, when Marilyn and her husband, Arthur Miller, along with co-star Yves Montand and his wife, Simone Signoret, were staying at the Beverly Hills Hotel, Peters and Howard Hughes occupied a downstairs apartment. Peters was four months younger than Marilyn and outlived her by 38 years (Riese & Hitchens 391; Schwarz 354–6; Victor 231; *www.imdb.com*).

PRINCE PHILIP Prince Philip and his spouse, Queen Elizabeth II, were introduced to MM in London on October 29, 1956. The occasion was the Royal Command Performance of *The Battle of the River Plate*, a British film about a naval victory in World War II (Miller 1987, 433).

MARY PICKFORD Canadian actress who became a star of silent films, earning the nickname of "America's Sweetheart." As a child, Marilyn Monroe and her mother had seen

Mary Pickford leave a hotel in Hollywood. In 1949, MM appeared in *Love Happy*, with the Marx Brothers. *Love Happy* was released in early 1950 by United Artists, the studio created by Charlie Chaplin, Douglas Fairbanks, D. W. Griffith and Mary Pickford. The movie was produced by Pickford and it was credited as "A Mary Pickford Presentation." Despite the fact that Marilyn was on screen for less than a minute, Pickford agreed to send her out on a cross-country promotional tour (Victor 173; Zolotow 19).

JOAN PLOWRIGHT Acclaimed British theater actress, occasionally in films and television. In 1958, Plowright was rehearsing a play in New York when she went to visit Lee Strasberg's Actors Studio. During a coffee break Strasberg introduced her "to a serious-looking young woman in a raincoat with short-ish hair which was dyed blonde but already going dark at the roots. She wore no make-up, appeared to be alone, and seemed rather nervous and shy. I had no idea who she was, until he said, 'Marilyn,' and I realized that I was meeting the sex-goddess Monroe, who had discarded her Hollywood image for New York and was studying along with other actors at the Studio. I would meet her again, briefly, in Los Angeles after she came with Strasberg to the first night of *A Taste of Honey*. There in Hollywood, she was back in full warpaint as the Monroe she had invented for the cinema, dressed in a skin-tight shimmering dress, giggling and pouting and blowing kisses to ardent admirers" (Plowright 86).

MICHAEL J. POLLARD Eccentric-looking actor who is best remembered for his role in *Bonnie and Clyde* (1967). Among the actors Marilyn did scenes with when she studied the Method at the Actors Studio was a very young Michael J. Pollard. The two of them did a scene from Truman Capote's *Breakfast at Tiffany's* (Guiles 359).

COLE PORTER Composer and songwriter for Broadway musicals. On New Year's Day, 1953, Marilyn attended the Cinemascope Party at the Cocoanut Grove of the Ambas-sador Hotel in Los Angeles. She met Cole Porter that evening and was photographed, deep in conversation, at his table (*www.cursumperficio.net* /biography/1953).

DICK POWELL Reliable Hollywood leading man who was also a singer, producer and director. MM had a small uncredited part—she had less than 20 words of dialogue—as Powell's girlfriend, Dusky Ledoux, in a nightclub scene in the 1950 boxing drama, *Right Cross*. Powell survived Marilyn by only five months, dying in January 1963. Powell had never expected the unknown starlet to become a star (Allyson 217; *www.imdb.com*).

ELEANOR POWELL Tap-dancing star of movie musicals of the 1930s and 1940s, arguably the best female dancer of them all. Powell argued that Marilyn Monroe "wasn't at all like the 'sex pot' role she portrayed on the screen. She was an extremely intelligent woman and a fine actress" (McCann 50).

WILLIAM POWELL Dapper actor known for his role as Nick Charles in six *Thin Man* films. In 1953, Powell appeared in scenes with MM in *How to Marry a Millionaire*. In December of the following year, Powell and Marilyn were photographed together at the Palm Springs Racquet Club (Francisco 226; *www.cursmperficio.net* /biography/1954).

TYRONE POWER Handsome Hollywood film star and heartthrob. Power and MM were introduced on July 26, 1956, at an after-theatre ball at playwright Terence Rattigan's house in Berkshire, near London. The event was hosted by Rattigan, Sir Laurence Olivier and Vivien Leigh in honor of Marilyn and her husband, Arthur Miller. Marilyn was in England to film Rattigan's *The Prince and the Showgirl* with Olivier. Marilyn had already listed Power as one of her favorite actors, but she never worked with him. He died four years before Marilyn did.

Between April 1955 and the end of that year, Marilyn lived in the Waldorf-Astoria Hotel in New York. She should have met Power then. Power was starring in *The Eddy Duchin Story* and was shooting some scenes in the hotel. Marilyn had expressed a desire to meet Tyrone Power, and he was expecting her to come down for a visit. Instead she had some champagne in her suite and went to sleep (Gottfried 2003, 301; Guiles 297–8).

OTTO PREMINGER Autocratic Hollywood film director. In 1953, Preminger directed Marilyn in a Western filmed in the Canadian Rockies, *The River of No Return*. From first sight[58] they heartily disliked each other. The tension on the set between star and director was so thick you could cut it with a knife. Much of it centered around Natasha Lytess, Marilyn's personal acting coach. Marilyn wanted Lytess by her side at all times and would only listen to her. This drove Preminger to distraction. He recalled: "Natasha had a theory that Marilyn should not speak in the soft, slurred voice that was so much part of the unique image she projected on the screen. She wanted her to enunciate every syllable distinctly. Marilyn didn't question Natasha's judgment. She rehearsed her lines with such grave ar-tic-yew-lay-shun that her violent lip movements made it impossible to photograph her. Natasha applauded her on her marvelous pronunciation, which inspired Marilyn to exaggerate even more" (Preminger 128).

Preminger considered Lytess to be a fake and angrily ordered her off the set. In response, Marilyn refused to work without her coach. She appealed to studio head, Darryl F. Zanuck, and Preminger was forced to knuckle under. Marilyn called Preminger "a pompous ass," and Preminger said he would not work with her again for a million dollars. Preminger also said, "Directing her was like directing Lassie. You need fourteen takes to get one of them right" (Riese & Hitchens 400).

During one scene Marilyn was obliged to stand on a river raft. Her friend Shelley Winters was visiting the set and made a startling observation: "Otto Preminger, never having been known for his patience ... was terrorizing Marilyn into total immobility.... She was terrified of not knowing her lines the next day, and she was convinced that Preminger hadn't wanted her in the picture ... and that he was

secretly planning to do away with her while she was going over some rapids in a raft, then claiming it was an accident. These difficult stunts were usually done at the end of the picture by stunt people, but for some strange reason Preminger was doing them at the beginning and *not* with the stunt people" (Winters 1980, 446).

Preminger screamed at Marilyn and implied that she was no better than a prostitute. Marilyn did not say anything. She just kept smiling, but she got her revenge. She slipped and broke her leg, or so she claimed. Doctors examined her but could find no sign of a break. Even so, Marilyn insisted on a cast and crutches. She was off work for ten days, putting the movie 28 days behind schedule. After that, Preminger was somewhat tamed. The making of *The River of No Return* was not a happy experience for anyone involved. Marilyn summarized the film as "a grade–Z cowboy movie in which the acting finished second to the scenery and the CinemaScope process" (Churchwell 65).

Other sources: Preminger 127–9; Shevey 244–52; Summers 122–3

ELVIS PRESLEY Iconic singer and actor. In December 1960 Elvis Presley watched *Let's Make Love*. The pivotal moment for Elvis came when MM performed a song entitled "Specialization," which contained lyrics about him and his manager, Colonel Tom Parker. There were even Elvis impersonators in the film. Elvis was delighted that Marilyn, the blonde bombshell, knew who he was. Although he was keen to make her acquaintance, Elvis Presley and Marilyn Monroe were never to meet. Or did they?

A recent biography of Elvis Presley claims that the two legends did, in fact, meet. It was early in the summer of 1960 and Marilyn was working on *Let's Make Love*. A couple of Elvis's friends dared him to ask Marilyn for a date. Elvis thought Marilyn was out of his league, but finally agreed. Elvis encountered Marilyn coming out of her dressing room on soundstage 23 on the Twentieth Century–Fox lot. She was clad in a bathrobe. Elvis politely introduced himself and asked Marilyn to accompany him to a party. Marilyn, with equal politeness, declined (Nash 327–8; Pierce).

DOROTHY PROVINE Bubbly blonde actress known for her television work and light comedies of the 1950s and 1960s. Provine met MM in March 1960, at the 17th Golden Globe Awards. Provine presented Marilyn with the award for Best Actress—Musical or Comedy. Marilyn won for her work on *Some Like It Hot*. She was up against Dorothy Dandridge (*Porgy and Bess*), Doris Day (*Pillow Talk*), Shirley MacLaine (*Ask Any Girl*), and Lilli Palmer (*But Not For Me*) (*www.cursumperficio.net* /biography/1960).

JULIET PROWSE South-African dancer and actress. In February 1962, Marilyn Monroe heard the unwelcome news that Frank Sinatra was engaged to Juliet Prowse. Sinatra had been involved with Marilyn and this may have been his way of breaking from her. Sinatra's engagement to a woman ten years younger than herself, famed for her beauty and long legs, hit Marilyn very hard. Prowse's engagement to Sinatra did not last long, however (Taraborrelli 2009, 380n).

TITO PUENTE Famous salsa and jazz musician who had a 50-year career as "The King of Latin Music." In his reminiscences, Puente implied that he met Marilyn Monroe at "that famous drugstore Schwab's, where they discovered Lana Turner.[59] I went there every day for breakfast. All the agents were there for lunch, I remember, because they all had their offices right there on Sunset Boulevard, Schwab's was loaded with stars then. Marilyn Monroe was there. I ate there every day" (Powell 200). Marilyn certainly frequented Schwab's in the late 1940s and into the 1950s. A good friend of hers, Sidney Skolsky, a Hollywood newspaper columnist, conducted most of his business at Schwab's lunch counter. As Skolsky never learned to drive a car, Marilyn sometimes acted as his chauffeur to and from Schwab's (Victor 276–6).

-Q-

ANTHONY QUAYLE Distinguished British stage and film actor. In 1956, when Quayle was appearing on stage in Arthur Miller's *A View from the Bridge* in London, he saw quite a bit of Miller and his glamorous wife, MM. Marilyn was in London to make *The Prince and the Showgirl* with Laurence Olivier. Quayle, in common with many, seriously underestimated Marilyn, and thought that she and her intellectual husband were an odd pairing.

Quayle wrote:

> There have been so many books written about Marilyn that I do not want to add another word to them beyond saying that she was a most enchanting, lovable, self-destructive creature. She came to our house one day partly pleased and partly disturbed at having been mobbed on a shopping expedition. She asked to be left alone for a while to put herself to rights. When she had not appeared after an hour, we sent out a search party and found that she had hidden herself away in a little loo which happened to have a slippery floor and a rug on it. She had pushed the rug up so that the door would not open, thought she was trapped there by some alien force, and had just sat down and waited to be rescued. She never thought of straightening the rug [Quayle 337].

On another occasion, hearing Marilyn make a compassionate remark about animal welfare, Quayle eyed the mink coat she was wearing and said: "And what about the poor little animals whose skins you're wearing on your back?" (Shevey 348).

Quayle and Marilyn crossed paths for the last time in London, on October 29, 1956. The occasion was a Royal Command Performance for *The Battle of the River Plate*, in which Quayle had a leading role. He later recounted how Marilyn became rattled at the prospect of meeting Queen Elizabeth II:

> Marilyn never came to the very short rehearsal in the morning intended to show us where to stand behind the giant screen and how we should walk out one by one into the audience through a gap in the curtains. So when she arrived—late as always—she had no idea where to go or what to do. At a distance she looked very pretty, but close to it was not so good. White make-up was slip-

ping off her face and her flame-red, strapless dress was falling off altogether. The designer, Bumble Dawson, had literally sewn her into it at the very last moment.

"Tony, Tony," she whispered. "Tell me what I do. I walk on the stage and turn left and curtsey. Is that right?"

"No Marilyn, dear. You walk on, you curtsey to your front and go off to your right."

"Oh, I see. Thank you. Tony, would you just shake me down into this dress a bit? I think it's coming off."

So I grabbed a handful of the top of the bodice and shook her down into it. And again she would say, "Tony, Tony. Tell me again. I'm sorry. Which did you say? Curtsey to the right, walk off to the left?"

"No, Marilyn, curtsey to the front and walk off to your right." So we went on and on all the way along the line....

Whether the dithering was to wind herself up to what she had already half decided to do or whether it was entirely natural, I have no idea. You could not tell. She was a young woman of such total contrasts and yet a seamless garment [Quayle 337–8].

ANTHONY QUINN   Mexican-American actor who was a two-time Academy Award-winner. In 1952, when Quinn was in Brownsville, Texas, working with Marlon Brando on Elia Kazan's *Viva Zapata!*, there was a visitor to the set who did nothing to impress him, as he thought of her as[60]

an empty-headed blond with a fat rear who would soon reign as the leading sex symbol of her time. Marilyn Monroe had surfaced in a handful of pictures, but had yet to make her mark, and she arrived on the scene to soak up the director's insights on acting.

Oh, Monroe was pretty enough to look at, but there were hundreds of better-looking actresses poking around Hollywood. Even after she hit the big time, with *Gentlemen Prefer Blondes*, I never could see what all the fuss was about, but what the hell did I know? All I knew was that she walked around our dusty Texas set in a slinky dress that showed the crack of her ass, apparently unaware that her clothes could not hold her. All I knew was that there seemed to be precious little going on beneath her glorious blond mane [Quinn & Paisner 211].

-R-

GEORGE RAFT   Tough guy actor, mostly of the 1930s and 1940s, who specialized in por-

traying heartless gangsters. In *Some Like It Hot* (1959), Raft was cast, of course, as gangster and killer Spats Columbo. Raft was a close friend of Marilyn's second husband, Joe DiMaggio, and knew the actress years before the movie was made. In 1952, when Raft was starring in a television series, *I Am the Law*, DiMaggio often visited the set and usually telephoned Marilyn. One day Raft said to Joe: "'I'm seeing some girl, so why don't all of us have dinner tonight?' He'd answer, 'I'd like to, but Marilyn is usually knocked out by evening and we don't go out at night'" (Yablonsky 217).

During the making of *Some Like It Hot* Marilyn's third husband, Arthur Miller, was on hand to prop her up, as she was pregnant and full of insecurities. Raft noticed that Miller would sometimes hold Marilyn's arm as he guided her on and off the set. Raft came to think of himself as one of director Billy Wilder's "utility infielders." Whenever Marilyn failed to show up on the set, be if for physical or psychological reasons, Raft was called upon to film a scene that was to occur later in the shooting schedule.

Raft wrote:

Her life as a star was hell. I can imagine what it must have been for her. Everywhere she looked, some photographer or reporter wanted to get at her. She seldom had a chance to relax or concentrate on her acting. Whenever she appeared on the set, some photographer was there trying to take a picture of her for *Look* or *Life*, while a reporter was begging for just the smallest interview. Wouldn't she please answer just *one* question?

Even at night, when a person likes to take it easy, the studio forced her to do publicity things. Here was a sex symbol who'd become a slave to her career and what the public wanted. I only talked with her a few times, but she was always friendly, someone who'd go out of her way to say hello. It was Marilyn's suggestion that the picture end with Sugar and Spats together, and going into the sunset. Billy Wilder liked the idea at first, but then decided to end the movie on a comedic note with Joe E. Brown and Jack Lemmon— maybe because Marilyn wasn't always available [Yablonsky 217].

Raft recalled the last time he ever saw Marilyn: "I was driving down Sunset, near the Beverly Hills Hotel, and had to stop for a light alongside a big, chauffeur-driven black Caddy with the shades down. All of a sudden, Marilyn, who was in the limousine, saw me. The shade went up and there she was, with her big smile, waving hello. She looked pale, but gorgeous as ever. I cried when I heard what finally happened to her" (Yablonsky 218).

PRINCE RAINIER　Prince of Monaco. MM was the subject of a crazy scheme which, had it succeeded, would have transformed the former resident of an orphanage into Her Serene Highness Princess Marilyn of Monaco! Greek shipping tycoon Aristotle Onassis, who had sunk large amounts of money into Monaco, felt that the tiny country was in desperate need of a new image. He thought, who better to bring some glamor to Monaco than Hollywood's sexiest actress? It was time for Rainier to marry and, through intermediaries, Marilyn was approached. Marilyn was amused by the idea and never took it seriously. "Is he rich? Is he handsome?" were her only questions. Marilyn jokingly referred to Rainier as "Reindeer" and admitted that she could not find Monaco on a map. When asked if she thought she could arouse the prince's interest, Marilyn gave a confident reply: "Give me two days alone with him and of course he'll want to marry me" (Lacey 219).

All of this was going on without Rainier's knowledge or approval and he was furious when he found out. He soon married a Hollywood star of his own choosing, Grace Kelly. Marilyn was involved with playwright Arthur Miller at the time and was soon to film *The Prince and the Showgirl* with Sir Laurence Olivier. Rainier and Marilyn never met, but on March 30, 1955, they came close. Rainier and Grace Kelly were making their first public appearance together at a gala in New York City. Marilyn was a block away at Madison Square Garden. Dressed as a showgirl, she was riding a pink elephant at a charity fundraising event (Robyns 135–6).

TONY RANDALL　Comic actor who was the co-star of television's *The Odd Couple* (1970–1974). In the movies, Randall usually played the hero's friend. In 1960, he played Yves Montand's friend in *Let's Make Love*, which starred MM. Randall was distressed and shocked when he saw how depressed Marilyn had become during the shooting of the picture. She would barely be able to function until the cameras started rolling, at which point the magic would return—at least until the director shouted "Cut." Randall never got to know Marilyn well but observed that in some inexpressible way the camera was in love with her, which made all the waiting around for her to appear worthwhile (Riese & Hitchens 419; Taraborrelli 2009, 319; *www.imdb.com*).

TERENCE RATTIGAN　Rattigan was one of the most important English dramatists of the 20th century. In 1955, MM wanted to change the direction of her career and prove herself as an actress. Rattigan's play, *The Sleeping Prince*, was the vehicle upon which she decided. Hearing that Rattigan had a ten-hour layover in New York on the way back to England from California, Marilyn waylaid him. She invited Rattigan to have a drink in a swanky Manhattan cocktail bar. Marilyn wanted to secure the film rights to Rattigan's play before director William Wyler got them. She also wanted Sir Laurence Olivier to be her co-star. Marilyn arrived, late as usual, wearing dark sunglasses. She was ready to draw up a contract on a napkin and sign it then and there. Although they did not actually do that, Rattigan was won over. "Gazing into those beautiful and childishly knowing eyes—she had removed her dark sunglasses—what could I reply but yes? I was sure 'Sir Larry' would leap at the chance, I said, and I would leave no stone unturned to see that he did" (Wansell 267). Rattigan also recalled how Marilyn "greeted me with that deliciously shy self-confidence that had overwhelmed so many thousands of tough and potentially hostile press men" (Wansell 267). Marilyn Monroe Productions paid Rattigan $125,000 for the film rights, and an additional $50,000 for the screenplay he wrote.

Rattigan was keen for Marilyn to star in the film which was retitled *The Prince and the Showgirl*. "As an admirer of Miss Monroe, I believe her to be ... an actress of high potentialities which have hardly yet been, and then only most grudgingly acknowledged by the critics.... I would love to see her in the part ... because I think it would be a brilliant piece of personality casting.... The chief quality which the part requires in an actress ... is 'style.' That, it seems to me, is a quality that Miss Monroe shares almost equally with Vivien [Leigh] as certainly as regards this kind of comedy" (Wansell 262).

The movie, made in England, did not live up to expectations and by its completion, Marilyn and Olivier were barely on speaking terms.

On July 24, 1956, Rattigan gave a supper-ball at Little Court, his country home near London. It was the social event of the season, with a guest list that included Tyrone Power, Louella Parsons (who had flown in from Hollywood to cover the production in her syndicated gossip column), Margot Fonteyn, Peggy Ashcroft, John Gielgud, Alec Guinness, Lady Diana Cooper and Sybil Thorndike, among other luminaries. The garden was aglow with Chinese lanterns and the buffet table was set with lobster curry. Marilyn, with husband Arthur Miller, arrived at 11 and stayed until three in the morning. Wearing a low-cut white chiffon gown (a costume rejected from the movie), Marilyn even danced the Charleston with her host, a famously bad dancer (Darlow 332–9; Leaming 1988, 257–8; Wansell 261–71).

JOHNNIE RAY   Songwriter, singer and pianist whose energetic style was a precursor of rock 'n' roll. Ray's only film role was in the 1954 MM film, *There's No Business Like Show Business* (Riese & Hitchens 420).

NICHOLAS RAY   Ray was the acclaimed director who made such films as *They Live by Night* (1949) and *Rebel Without a Cause* (1955). Ray's name appeared on MM's list of desirable men. Marilyn and the much older Ray went out on a few dates. They probably met at a party for the release of *The African Queen* on February 2, 1952 (Winters 1989, 46; *www.cursumperficio.net* /biography/1952).

NANCY REAGAN   Widow of President Ronald Reagan and first lady of the United States (1981–1989). As Nancy Davis she was a minor film actress of the 1940s and 1950s. On June 17, 1953, Nancy Reagan was photographed in conversation with Marilyn Monroe at Charles Coburn's 76th birthday party (*www.cursumperficio.net* /biography/1953).

RONALD REAGAN   Hollywood actor who became governor of California (1967–1975) and president of the United States (1981–1989). Indirectly, Reagan was responsible for the birth of MM's career. It was near the end of World War II and Reagan was a captain in an army unit that made training propaganda films. Reagan ordered a photographer to go to the Radio Plane factory in Los Angeles and take some morale-boosting photographs of pretty girls doing war work. The factory was owned by actor Reginald Denny, one of Reagan's friends. The model selected was 19-year-old spray-gun painter named Norma Jeane Dougherty. When given the opportunity, Norma Jeane was only too happy to put on a tight sweater and pose for the camera. The photos were widely distributed and led to prints ads, modeling assignments and walk-ons in movies. Norma Jeane Dougherty soon began using the name Marilyn Monroe. Reagan knew Marilyn socially after she rocketed to stardom, but never worked with her. Reagan and Marilyn were photographed together on June 17, 1953, at actor Charles Coburn's 76th birthday party. It is not certain if Reagan ever knew about his role in the birth of Marilyn Monroe's career (Conover 4–5; Summers 16; Victor 245–6; *www.cursumperficio.net* /biography/1953).

VANESSA REDGRAVE   Academy Award–winning British actress and political activist. On November 18, 1956, while still a teenager, Redgrave attended a meeting at the Royal Court Theatre in London on the theme, "What is wrong with the British theatre?" MM was sitting nearby as her husband, Arthur Miller, was one of the invited speakers. Most people were more interested in seeing Marilyn sitting demurely in the fourth row than in following the discussion (Redgrave 84).

CAROL REED   English film director who won an Academy Award for *Oliver!* (1968). Although they were not destined to work together, Reed's name was on a list of approved directors MM submitted to Twentieth Century–Fox in 1955 (Victor 81).

MAX REINHARDT   Innovative Austrian-American theatre director who had worked with MM's trusted drama coach, Natasha Lytess. On December 3, 1952, Marilyn attended an auction in Beverly Hills and for $1,335 purchased a collection of the late Max Reinhardt's production notebooks—178 annotated scripts, plays and books. Marilyn was criticized for depriving a research institution of the collection. A rare-book dealer had been bidding on behalf of the Reinhardt Collection housed at the University of Southern California's Doheny Library. Possibly at the urging of Lytess, Reinhardt's son Gottfried approached Marilyn after the sale, saying that the notebooks should be his. Marilyn was persuaded and gave them to Gottfried for the price she had paid. Reputedly, Gottfried Reinhardt then sold the manuscripts to the university library at a healthy profit.

Gottfried Reinhardt recorded his own memory of the auction sale and its aftermath: "A small voice caroled out a second before the wooden hammer was banged down. Harvard and UCLA, my only serious competitors, had gone as high as their budget allowed and had owed out before the small voice—Marilyn Monroe's—suspended the auctioneer's hammer in mid air.... So M.R. belonged to M.M. The world press whooped up stories about 'Sex Symbol Goes Intellectual.'" Gottfried Reinhardt then sent Marilyn a letter which he hoped would appeal to her better nature. "'Surely you will understand, dear Miss Monroe, that, aside from monetary expenditure, these books belong to Max Reinhardt's son and not to you.' She answered very promptly and affirmatively. Whether her better nature was genuinely touched or whether the whole thing was a publicity stunt that had served its purpose, I couldn't say. Didn't care. All that mattered was that the books were rescued.... The story has a moral. The moral is never mail a check in haste. For I was just on the point of mailing [a check] to Miss Monroe when the auctioneer telephoned me. He said he was glad I had 'bought the stuff after all' and added that it could be picked up at his place any time with a check made out to him. Monroe had not collected it or paid for it" (Reinhardt 396).

Other sources: Guiles 204; Spoto 1993, 233–4; Victor 246

LEE REMICK   Actress who was hired to replace MM when she was fired from *Something's Got to Give* in 1962. Marilyn's friend and co-star Dean Martin remained loyal to her and refused to do the picture without her. The project was shelved, but not before Remick made some harsh statements about Marilyn:

> I feel Marilyn should have been replaced. I don't believe actors should be allowed to get away with that type of behavior.
> I don't know whether to feel sorry for her or not. I feel she should have been replaced. The movie business is crumbling down around our ears because of that kind of behavior. Actors shouldn't be allowed to get away with that kind of thing.
> It's a business anyway, despite all the glamour. Other people get fired from their jobs for behaving the way she did [Riese & Hitchens 432].

Years later Remick denied that she had made those comments, maintaining that they were made up by the studio publicity department. She never believed that she was seriously considered as a replacement for Marilyn. Lee Remick hosted a television documentary tribute to Marilyn in 1987, *Remembering Marilyn* (Brown & Barham 226–7; Rivadue 9–10,17).

MICHAEL RENNIE   British film, television and stage actor best known for his role as Klaatu in the classic 1951 science-fiction film, *The Day the Earth Stood Still*. Rennie met MM on November 6, 1954, at a party for the elite of Hollywood. The evening was to commemorate the completion of *The Seven Year Itch* and to honor its star (Shaw & Rosten 77).

PIERRE-AUGUST RENOIR French impressionist painter who celebrated feminine beauty and sensuality. During a break from filming *The Prince and the Showgirl* in England, cinematographer Jack Cardiff had a private photo session with MM. Cardiff shot a series of stills with Marilyn as a Renoir girl. The pictures are considered to be some of the most beautiful ever taken of Marilyn Monroe (Riese & Hitchens 73–9; *www.cursumperficio.net* files/C/Cardiff, Jack).

TOMMY RETTIG Child actor who was in the television series *Lassie* from 1954 until 1957. In 1954, the 12-year-old Rettig was MM's co-star in *River of No Return*. Later he became Marilyn's youngest-ever date, when he escorted her to the film's premiere. During the first few days of filming Rettig had kept his distance from Marilyn because his priest had told him she was a scarlet woman. But Marilyn (and Joe DiMaggio) soon won him over, even taking him on a fishing trip. Through no fault of his own, Rettig was the cause of tension between Marilyn and the movie's tyrannical director, Otto Preminger. Marilyn's personal acting coach, Natasha Lytess, scared the boy and made him cry when she told him that he had better get acting lessons right away or his talent would dry up by the time he was 14. Preminger ordered Lytess off the set. Marilyn objected to this and went over Preminger's head to the studio's boss, Darryl F. Zanuck. Eventually, Lytess was readmitted to the set (Riese & Hitchens 434; Victor 250; *www.imdb.com*).

DEBBIE REYNOLDS Wholesome-looking actress and comedienne who starred in such films as *Singin' in the Rain* (1952), *The Affairs of Dobie Gillis* (1953), *Goodbye Charlie* (1964), and *The Singing Nun* (1966). In her autobiography, Reynolds tells a strange story of how, in early August 1962, she was approached by evangelist Billy Graham. While in prayer, Graham had a vision that Marilyn Monroe was in mortal danger and he wanted Reynolds to intervene. Reynolds, who was no more than a casual acquaintance of Marilyn's and was just days away from giving birth, was in no condition to become directly involved. She contacted Sidney Guilaroff, a Hollywood hairdresser, who was much closer to Marilyn. Guilaroff went to see Marilyn but there were too many hangers-on and he was unable to speak with her. Reynolds said to him, "Sidney, you have to go back. This is very important. This is a possible death" (Reynolds & Columbia 255). Guilaroff made another attempt the next day but still could not get through to Marilyn. Two days later it was too late; Marilyn Monroe was dead. The night of her death, Marilyn reportedly phoned Guilaroff, complaining that she was feeling depressed. Reynolds reflected that everyone used Marilyn for their own gain.

Said Reynolds: "She was a gentle, child-like girl who was always looking for that white knight on the white horse. She lived in a total dream world. And why not? What sex symbol is happy?" (Reynolds & Columbia 256).

In 1961, Marilyn had rejected *Goodbye Charlie*, even though it was based on a play by George Axelrod (who had written *The Seven Year Itch* and *Bus Stop* and was to be directed by Vincente Minnelli, one of her approved directors. Marilyn said to newspaper columnist Hedda Hopper: "Fox wanted me for *Goodbye Charlie*, but as far as I'm concerned, it's goodbye *Goodbye Charlie*." When the film came to be made in 1964, Debbie Reynolds took the part that would have been Marilyn's. Reynolds purchased the famous white dress which Marilyn wore while standing on the subway grate in *The Seven Year Itch* and for a number of years displayed it in a Las Vegas museum she operated (Riese & Hitchens 443–4; Victor 250).

TONY RICHARDSON British film and theater director and producer. On a trip to New York with Laurence Olivier, Richardson visited the Actors Studio on a day when MM was also there (Winters, 1989 242).

NELSON RIDDLE American bandleader, arranger, and composer of popular music. In May 1955, Riddle wrote pages of arrangements for *The Seven Year Itch*. It was Riddle's first experience of working with a large orchestra and writing for films (Levinson 107).

RAINER MARIA RILKE   Considered to be one of the greatest German language poets. His themes of disbelief, solitude and anxiety were sure to strike a chord with Marilyn. On the set of *All About Eve* (1950) director Joseph L. Mankiewicz was surprised to see Marilyn walking around with a book. He had thought it more likely for Marilyn to be carrying a thin snake than a book. Mankiewicz was even more flabbergasted when he discovered the book she was reading was Rilke's *Letters to a Young Poet*. "I'd have been less taken aback," he recalled, "to come upon Herr Rilke studying a Marilyn Monroe nude calendar" (Mankiewicz & Carey 78). After Mankiewicz got over his surprise, he did not belittle Marilyn. He asked her how she came to choose that particular book. She replied, "I was never told what to read, and nobody ever gave me anything to read. You know—the way there are certain books that everybody reads while they are growing up? ...So what I do is—nights when I've got nothing else to do I go to the Pickwick Bookstore on Hollywood Boulevard. And I just open books at random—or when I come to a page or a paragraph I like, I buy that book. So last night I bought this one. Is that wrong?" (McCann 44). Mankiewicz replied that not only was it not wrong it was the best way to choose books. The next day, Marilyn sent Mankiewicz a copy of the book.

THELMA RITTER   Character actress who was nominated for an Oscar six times. Ritter was in three MM features: *All About Eve* (1950), *As Young As You Feel* (1951), and *The Misfits* (1961) (Riese & Hitchens 446; *www. imdb.com*).

PHIL RIZZUTO   A shortstop with the New York Yankees who went on to have a 40-year career as a radio and television sports announcer. On weekends in June and July 1952, Marilyn would come to New York to be near her boyfriend, Joe DiMaggio, in his job as a broadcaster for the Yankees. Rizzuto, who was a friend and teammate of DiMaggio, remembered, "A lot of guys used to hang around that studio just to see her. She'd sit in the stands before the games and talk to some of the players. They were kids and just liked the idea of going home and telling their friends they knew a movie star" (Spoto 1993, 222). It was obvious to Rizzuto that Joe did not like the male attention Marilyn was getting. Upon hearing that Joe DiMaggio was going to marry Marilyn Monroe, Rizzuto joked: "I don't know if it's good for baseball, but it sure beats the hell out of rooming with Phil Rizzuto" (Stewart 112).

JASON ROBARDS   Respected actor who had a 50-year career in theatre, film and television. In the summer of 1957, Robards was at Harvard University acting the title role in Shakespeare's *Macbeth*. MM and her husband, Arthur Miller, saw the play and stayed behind to congratulate Robards.

CLIFF ROBERTSON   Academy Award–winning actor. When Marilyn Monroe began taking twice-weekly classes at New York's Actors Studio in 1955, Cliff Robertson was one of her classmates (Adams 254).

DALE ROBERTSON   Rugged actor who served as the host of television's *Death Valley Days* (1968–1972). In her starlet days, MM and Robertson were supposed to take part in a magazine photo shoot. The piece was to depict correct nightclub etiquette. But Marilyn's manager, Johnny Hyde, did not want to give the impression that Marilyn was involved with the handsome Robertson and canceled the shoot. She was involved with the much older Hyde at the time. Robertson and Marilyn did, however, get to know each other quite well. Robertson remembered: "We would go to ball games together and she was very pleasant company, but we were never boyfriend and girlfriend because we just weren't attracted to each other.... She had a rough time for a while, and her biggest enemy was herself" (Morgan 89). Robertson was in the anthology film *O'Henry's Full House* (1952), but not in the same episode as Marilyn. Robertson and Marilyn were photographed together at a charity event, 1952's Hollywood Entertainers' Baseball Game. Robertson found success in television westerns, notably *Tales of Wells Fargo* (1957–1962) and on *Dynasty* (1981) (Summers 66; *www.imdb.com*).

EDWARD G. ROBINSON   *The Stars and Stripes*, the U. S. Army's magazine, gave MM its Miss Cheesecake Award in 1951 and 1952. For the earlier ceremony, August 4, 1951, Marilyn was fetchingly attired in a white bathing suit, oversized chef's hat and frilly apron, and was photographed while cutting a huge cake. Marilyn met actor Edward G. Robinson at the event and a photograph exists of the two of them together. Marilyn is pictured serving Robinson a slice of cake (*www.cursumperficio.net* /files/awards).

EDWARD G. ROBINSON, JR.   Son of Edward G. Robinson who had bit parts in two MM pictures: *Bus Stop* (1956) and *Some Like It Hot* (1959). A close friend of Marilyn's, Robinson may have introduced her to drugs. (Summers 114–15; Victor 254; *www.imdb.com*).

ROCHESTER (Eddie Anderson) Comic actor who played Jack Benny's wisecracking valet, chauffeur and nemesis in radio, film and television. On September 13, 1953, MM made her television debut on Jack Benny's show. Rochester met her at that time and they were photographed together (Doll 138; *www.cursumperficio.net* /files/Benney).

LAURANCE S. ROCKEFELLER   Prominent venture capitalist, financier and philanthropist. On July 2, 1957, MM and Rockefeller were invited to the inauguration ceremony at the construction site of the Time-Life Building in New York. Characteristically, Marilyn was nearly two and a half hours late. By that time Rockefeller had left, grumbling: "I've never waited that long for anyone." Marilyn's excuse was that she had celebrated her first wedding anniversary the night before. "Oh, was I sick.... We celebrated with champagne, but instead of it going to my head it went to my stomach" (Morgan 211–12).

RICHARD RODGERS   Multiple award-winning composer who provided the music for more than 40 Broadway musicals. On January 7, 1955, MM hosted a cocktail party and press conference to announce the formation of Marilyn Monroe Productions. Among those in attendance was Richard Rodgers. He also attended the premiere of *The Seven Year Itch* at Loew's State Theater in Times Square, New York, on June 1, 1955. A rare photograph of Marilyn without makeup was taken at Rodgers's Connecticut home in 1953. She is shown splashing about in the swimming pool (Victor 266; *www.cursumperficio.net* /biography/1955).

AUGUSTE RODIN   French sculptor. Rodin became a favorite of MM's after she went to an exhibition of his work at New York's Metropolitan Museum of Art in 1955. She was particularly taken with a work called *The Hand of God* which depicts a curving hand holding a man and woman locked in a passionate embrace. Marilyn's friend, the poet Norman Rosten, remarked how "she stood before this vision, transfixed, finger at her lips" (Shaw & Rosten 146). In 1962, Marilyn bought a bronze copy of Rodin's piece for $1,000. She said, "Look at them both, how beautiful. He's hurting her, but he wants to love her too" (Rollyson 1993, 195). Marilyn went so far as to demand that her psychiatrist explain the meaning of the statue to her (Summers 185, 359).

GINGER ROGERS   Singer and dancer, often paired with Fred Astaire. Rogers was in two movies with MM, *We're Not Married* and *Monkey Business* (both 1952). Rogers and Marilyn shared no screen time in the first film but did so in the second. That same year, Marilyn had met Rogers when she visited the set of *Dreamboat*. Marilyn noticed that Rogers was wearing a gold-lamé evening dress and wanted one just like it. She got her wish when she was clad in a gold-lamé gown in a scene in *Gentlemen Prefer Blondes* (1953).

While Rogers was making *Black Widow*, Marilyn was filming *There's No Business Like Show Business* (1954). One day Marilyn wandered over to Rogers's dressing room for a visit. Rogers asked how Joe DiMaggio was. Tears welled up in Marilyn's eyes before she could answer. Rogers guessed that the marriage was on the rocks and asked Marilyn if that was the case. Marilyn nodded her head. Rogers advised Marilyn not to leave Joe and Marilyn did not say a word. She just shrugged her shoulders and returned to her set.

Once, at her church on Sunday morning, Rogers noticed Marilyn sitting in the last pew. Rogers speculated that if Marilyn had been grounded with a religious belief she may have avoided her tragic end (Rogers 348–9, 398).

ROY ROGERS Singing cowboy who starred in movie and televison westerns. Rogers was usually associated with Dale Evans and his trusty horse, Trigger. MM met Roy Rogers in a sporting goods store in Van Nuys, California; they met again in Las Vegas in May 1946. Rogers was making a movie, *Heldorado*, and Marilyn was fulfilling the residency requirement for a divorce from her first husband, James Dougherty. The 34-year-old actor let the 19-year-old model and starlet ride on Trigger, and then invited her to join him and some of cast members of his film for dinner at the Last Frontier Hotel. In a letter Marilyn wrote, "I met most of the studio people including Roy Rogers and I rode his horse, gee he is nice" (Guiles 98).

Other Source: Riese & Hitchens 450; *www.imdb.com*.

MICKEY ROONEY Short-statured actor, a Hollywood fixture for 80 years. Marilyn and Rooney probably met on May 26, 1948, when they attended the premiere of the film *The Emperor Waltz*. In 1950, Rooney was the star of a roller-skating epic called *The Fireball*. In his autobiography Rooney claims to have gotten MM a small part in the film. She had already abandoned her real name, Norma Jeane Baker, but Rooney did not seem to realize that.[61]

> I couldn't help *looking* when a fantastically sexy blonde named Norma Jean [sic] Baker wiggled into my life. A friend wanted me to see if I could wangle her a part in *The Fireball*, a rollerdrome melodrama I was making at United Artists. I had made it a policy never to wangle parts for anybody. If I started that, there'd never be an end to it.
>
> In this case, however, I wanted to do this particular friend a favor, so I took Norma Jean out for drinks early one night to see for myself. Wow! She wasn't wearing a bra, or stockings, or panties either. Her skimpy little frock left nothing to the imagination. She was all there, right in plain sight. And the way she looked at me—with her moist, half-opened eyes and her moist, half-opened mouth! And the way she talked! Every word she uttered seemed to have a sexy subtext. "But Mickey," she said in her precious little voice, "I'm more than a pretty girl. I can do—*anything!*" She reached over and touched my knee.
>
> So I helped Norma Jean Baker get a bit part in *The Fireball*. I remember her having one line: "Honey, I'll be here when you want me" [Rooney 208–9].

For her part, Marilyn was disappointed by Rooney, concluding that he was not as nice as his movies made him out to be. Rooney whispered dirty remarks in her ear, prompting Marilyn to say, "He's really terrible, isn't he?" (Gilmore 109).

In March 1952, Rooney happened to be in the restaurant that Joe DiMaggio and Marilyn went to on their first date. Rooney came over to the table, not to talk to Marilyn but to Joe. That same year bandleader Ray Anthony recorded a song about MM entitled "Marilyn." The song, with Rooney playing drums, was presented to the actress at Anthony's Hollywood home (Riese & Hitchens 453; Schwarz 176–7; Shevey 201–2; *www.cursumperficio.net/biography/1952*).

ELEANOR ROOSEVELT First lady of the United States (1933–1945). After the death of her husband, Franklin, she went on to be a diplomat and human rights activist. She died three months after MM at the age of 78. Surprisingly, there was a time when Eleanor and Marilyn were neighbors. During the last five years of her life, Marilyn maintained an apartment on East 57th Street, New York. Mrs. Roosevelt lived across the street. One day they met at the hairdresser and took a shine to each other. They then arranged to have hair appointments at the same time so they could sit next to each other and talk (Arnold 1987, 23).

JAMES ROOSEVELT Brigadier-general, U.S. Representative and son of President Franklin and Eleanor Roosevelt. James Roosevelt wrote to Marilyn Monroe asking if she could deliver a brief greeting on an October 7, 1960, NBC television program on behalf of the Eleanor Roosevelt Institute for Cancer Research. Marilyn replied, through her agent, Rupert Allan, that she must regretfully decline, as she was hard at work on *The Misfits* in the desert heat of Nevada (Banner 152).

BILLY ROSE   Famous impresario, showman, lyricist, once married to Fanny Brice. Between 1955 and her death seven years later, Marilyn Monroe was a fixture at the home of her acting coaches and mentors, Lee and Paula Strasberg. On at least one occasion she sat around the kitchen table with Billy Rose (Adams 259).

NORMAN ROSTEN   American playwright, novelist and poet. Rosten met Marilyn in 1955 in New York and did not know who she was at first. He and his wife became Marilyn's close friends for the rest of her life. Rosten was one of the few people to whom Marilyn showed her own poetry, and he was always supportive. She always called him "Claude" because of a supposed resemblance to the actor Claude Rains. When Marilyn and Arthur Miller began their affair they often used Rosten's home as a safe haven. Rosten attended Marilyn's funeral, and in her will she left $5,000 for the education of his daughter. After Marilyn's death, Rosten wrote two books about her and the libretto for Edward Lademan's 1993 opera, *Marilyn* (Riese & Hitchens 455, Shaw & Rosten, Victor 256).

GENA ROWLANDS   American actress often teamed with her husband, writer-director John Cassavetes. Rowlands made her Broadway debut as "The Girl" in George Axelrod's *The Seven Year Itch*. Rowlands made an unsuccessful screen test for Billy Wilder (Charity 11).

DAMON RUNYON   Newspaperman and writer. Around 1946, when she was still a struggling Hollywood starlet, MM briefly met Damon Runyon. Nearly ten years later, Marilyn said that what she wanted most was to be in the film version of *Guys and Dolls*, a musical

adaptation of Runyon's short stories (Jordan 84; Victor 107).

JANE RUSSELL   Statuesque leading lady who co-starred with MM in 1953's *Gentlemen Prefer Blondes*. Years before they worked together, Russell had an unusual early connection with Marilyn. She was in a high school play with Jim Dougherty, the man who became Marilyn's first husband. Russell played Dougherty's mother in the play. She was also in a singing competition with Dougherty and lost.

On the set of *Gentlemen Prefer Blondes*, Marilyn and Russell got along extremely well, despite the fact that Marilyn was being paid about 10 percent of what Russell was getting and had to fight to even get a proper dressing room. The press tried (and failed) to create a feud between what the *New York Herald Tribune* called "The Haystack Brunette" and "The Blowtorch Blonde." According to Russell: "Marilyn is a dreamy girl. She's the kind who's liable to show up with one red shoe and one black shoe" (Riese & Hitchens 339).

Russell took an almost maternal interest in Marilyn, helping her decorate her apartment and giving her advice on her professional and personal problems. Marilyn was dating ex-baseball player Joe DiMaggio at the time. She asked Russell, who was married to an ex-football player, what it was like being with a professional athlete. Russell replied: "Well, they're birds of a feather and you'll get to know lots of other athletes—otherwise it's great" (Russell 138).

Marilyn and director Howard Hawks often had disagreements. In retaliation, Marilyn would sometimes not come out of her dressing room. It was left to Russell to ease the situation by saying, "Come on Blondie, let's go,' and she'd say, 'Oh, okay,' in her whispery voice and we'd go on together" (Russell 138).

Russell had several other pet names for Marilyn, including "Baby Doll." Said Marilyn: "We got along nicely—Jane called me the "round one"—I don't know what she means by that, but I assume she means it to be friendly" (Riese & Hitchens 458).

Gentlemen Prefer Blondes was a huge success and the two stars were invited to place their hand- and footprints in cement at Grauman's Chinese Theater, on June 26, 1953. Marilyn joked that they should immortalize the assets that got them to where they were—Russell's ample bosom and Marilyn's buttocks. Russell recalled how Marilyn said, "'This is for all time, isn't it?' 'Yes,' I told her, 'it's for all time or as long as the cement lasts.' She was so thrilled she was beside herself and she told me how she'd come to Grauman's when she was a kid and looked at the prints of everyone, and how she'd dreamed about being a movie star more than anything. It was something precious to me, her saying that" (Gilmore 147–8).

That same year Russell and Marilyn sang a song at a charity event organized by Danny Thomas for the benefit of St. Jude's Hospital. In 1955, Russell got Marilyn to help with WAIF, an organization dedicated to helping homeless children.

Russell was a churchgoer and wanted to share her faith with Marilyn. Marilyn did go along to a prayer meeting but concluded that it was not for her. Said Marilyn: "Jane, who is deeply religious, tried to convert me to her religion and I tried to introduce her to Freud. Neither of us won" (Victor 257).

Russell observed of Marilyn: "Diamonds are the last thing on her mind. That gal would rather have several good books" (Conover 54). She also said: "Marilyn was very shy and very sweet and far more intelligent that people gave her credit for" (Russell 137).

MARGARET RUTHERFORD   Academy Award-winning British actress who seemed to corner the market on dotty aunts and eccentric spinsters. In 1960, Rutherford was in Hollywood working on a Danny Kaye comedy, *On the Double*. At the same studio, MM was putting the finishing touches to *The Misfits*. Marilyn came over to meet Margaret Rutherford in her dressing room. The older woman and the blonde bombshell must have hit it off because Rutherford recalled how Marilyn "lay her sad little face in my lap and was soon asleep." Later, Rutherford described Marilyn as "that dear little waif-child, whom life and Hollywood were destined to destroy" (Simmons 137).

ROBERT RYAN   Hollywood leading man who had a 35-year career in movies, usually playing hard-bitten cops and villains. In 1952, Ryan was one of the stars of *Clash by Night*, which featured MM in a supporting role. As befitting a fast-rising young star, the studio wanted to give Marilyn equal billing with her established co-stars Ryan, Barbara Stanwyck and Paul Douglas. This was the source of some friction, but Ryan stayed out of the conflict. Sensing that Marilyn was emotionally vulnerable and insecure, Ryan felt protective toward her. When the director, Fritz Lang, belittled Marilyn for her chronic lateness, Ryan asked him to go easy on her. Of Marilyn, Ryan said: "This sexy blonde really has something. She's something else" (Shevey 178). He also said, "I got the feeling she was a frightened lonely little girl who was trying awfully hard. She always seemed to be so mournful-looking around the set, and I always tried to cheer her up" (Victor 258).

-S-

MORT SAHL   Canadian-born standup comedian and political satirist. During the shooting of *The Misfits* Sahl came to Reno, Nevada, to entertain at a birthday party for director John Huston. Marilyn took Sahl's hand and put it over her breast and said: "'Don't be afraid, Mr. Sahl.' And I said, 'I'm not afraid.' And she said, 'How wrong you are. We're all afraid.'" After Marilyn's final divorce, Sahl had dinner with her and offered up some advice: "Well, listen, you were married to Joe DiMaggio and Arthur Miller. I think that the only thing left now is to marry Adlai Stevenson" (Sahl 90).

LILI ST. CYR   Competed with Gypsy Rose Lee as the most famous stripper of the 1940s and 1950s. Actor Ted Jordan made a number of unfounded allegations about Marilyn Monroe, one of the most outrageous being that

Marilyn had a lesbian affair with his ex-wife, Lili St. Cyr.

To prepare for an audition as a burlesque queen in *Ladies of the Chorus* (1948), Marilyn convinced a male friend to take her to see St. Cyr. Marilyn sat right up front in the posh club and studied St. Cyr's every sinuous movement. She thought St. Cyr was beautiful, glamorous and that her striptease performance was a work of art. On the strength of her research, Marilyn got the part (Jordan 102–5, 117).

ANTOINE DE SAINT-EXUPÉRY   Saint-Exupéry was a French writer and pilot. During her brief marriage to Joe DiMaggio, MM presented him with a gold medallion for his watch chain. Engraved on the medallion was a quotation from Saint-Exupéry's *The Little Prince*: "True love is visible not to the eyes, but to the heart, for eyes may be deceived." DiMaggio, whose tastes ran more to television Westerns than to modern classics of French literature, was perplexed, and was overheard saying, "What the hell does *that* mean?" (McCann 46).

CARL SANDBURG   American poet and biographer. Early in her relationship with Arthur Miller, MM confided to him that she needed someone to look up to. Miller replied, "If you want someone to admire, why not Abraham Lincoln? Carl Sandburg has written a magnificent biography of him" (Gottfried 2003, 181). Marilyn took Miller's word to heart and hung a framed portrait of Lincoln in her bedroom. She would later obtain a bust of Sandburg to join it.

In 1959, Sandburg was in Hollywood working on a screenplay and Marilyn arranged to meet him. The unlikely duo hit it off immediately. Marilyn considered the elderly poet to be one of the most interesting people she had ever met. She said, "Carl Sandburg, who's in his eighties—you should see his vitality, what he has contributed. Why, he could play the guitar and sing at three in the morning—I like him very much" (Meyers 176). Sandburg wrote of Marilyn: "She was not the usual movie idol. There was something democratic about her. She was the type who would join in and wash up the supper dishes even if you didn't ask her" (Victor 260). He also observed that Marilyn "was a good talker. There were realms of science, politics and economics in which she wasn't at home, but she spoke well on the national scene, the Hollywood scene, and on people who are good to know and people who ain't. We agreed on a number of things. She sometimes threw her arms around me like people do who like each other very much. Too bad I was forty-eight years older— I couldn't play her leading man" (Victor 260).

A close grandfather-granddaughter relationship developed between the two, which lasted until Marilyn's death, in 1962. Sandburg was invited to deliver the eulogy at Marilyn's funeral, but his health would not permit it. A month after her death Sandburg told a magazine reporter, "Marilyn was a good talker and very good company. We did some mock playacting and some pretty good, funny imitations. I asked her a lot of questions. She told me how she came up the hard way, but she would never talk about her husbands" (Meyers 176–7). Despite being nearly a half-century older than Marilyn, Sandburg survived her by almost five years.

GEORGE SANDERS   British actor who enjoyed a 40-year Hollywood career, portraying cads and scoundrels. In 1948, MM encountered a drunken Sanders at a Hollywood party. After introductions he asked her to marry him saying, "Blonde, pneumatic, and full of peasant health. Just the type meant for me" (Monroe & Hecht 67). Sanders then put his glass down and dozed off. In 1950, Sanders played opposite MM in *All About Eve* and won an Oscar for Best Supporting Actor. Sanders became enamored of Marilyn and the two reportedly had an affair. Sanders's wife, Zsa Zsa Gabor, got wind of this and, on her orders, Sanders was not to lunch with Marilyn at the studio commissary, he was also to confine his communication with her to a chaste, "Good morning" and "Good evening."

As Sanders remembered, Marilyn was "very inquiring and unsure—humble, punctual and untemperamental. She wanted people to like her; her conversation had unexpected depths. She showed an interest in intellectual subjects which was, to say the least, disconcerting. In her presence it was hard to concentrate" (Victor 260).

Other sources: Shevey 147; *www.imdb. com*.

WILLIAM SAROYAN   Short story writer and playwright. In 1952, after the breakup of his marriage, Saroyan claimed to have had a one-night stand with MM (Lee 257).

JEAN-PAUL SARTRE   French existentialist philosopher and intellectual. Sartre prepared a screenplay about Sigmund Freud to be directed by John Huston. Sartre wanted MM to star in the film because he judged her to be the finest actress alive. *Freud* was made in 1962, but without Marilyn (Hayman 364–7; Victor 260).

DORE SCHARY   Schary, who succeeded Louis B. Mayer as the MGM studio head, made the biggest mistake of his career when he refused to give MM a contract. This sent her into the arms of MGM's rival Twentieth Century–Fox. Marilyn had undeniable screen presence in MGM's *The Asphalt Jungle* (1950), but Schary did not think she was photogenic or had star quality and was uncomfortable with her reputation as a veteran of the casting couch. In any case, reasoned Schary, MGM already had a plethora of beautiful actresses. Eventually Schary came to regret that he had let Marilyn slip through his fingers: "I was guilty of an egregious error ... for years I blushed with embarrassment each time her name was mentioned" (Schary 213).

Other sources: Riese & Hitchens 266; Victor 261.

JOSEPH SCHILDKRAUT   Austrian stage and film actor who was active in Hollywood, starring in about 30 films. On February 19, 1956, Marilyn Monroe attended a performance of *The Diary of Anne Frank* at the Cort Theater in New York. Schildkraut played Otto Frank. Marilyn was photographed, in the company of Laurence Olivier, chatting with Schildkraut

after the performance (*www.cursumperficio.net /files/Olivier*).

ARTHUR M. SCHLESINGER, JR.   Historian, social critic and White House special assistant during President Kennedy's time in office. On May 19, 1962, after warbling her famous "Happy Birthday, Mr. President" at a Madison Square Garden fundraiser for the Democratic Party, MM attended a party hosted by the president of United Artists. Schlesinger encountered Marilyn there and recorded how he was "enchanted by her manner and her wit, at once so masked, so ingenuous and so penetrating. But one felt a terrible unreality about her—as if talking to someone under water." Schlesinger wrote in his diary how "Bobby [Kennedy] and I engaged in mock competition for her; she was most agreeable to him and pleasant to me—but then she receded into her own glittering mist" (Summers 367).

PAUL SCOFIELD   Acclaimed English actor who was given an Academy Award for his portrayal of Sir Thomas More in *A Man for All Seasons* (1966). Scofield met MM ten years earlier at playwright Terence Rattigan's country house, near London. Scofield had been invited to a gala hosted by Rattigan, Vivien Leigh and Sir Laurence Olivier in honor of Marilyn and her husband, Arthur Miller. Marilyn was in England to make a movie of Rattigan's play, *The Prince and the Showgirl*, with Olivier (Gottfried 2003, 300).

PETER SELLERS   British comic actor who was bumbling Inspector Clouseau in the *Pink Panther* movies. Sellers never knew MM, but he closely identified with her emotional struggles with alienation and self esteem. On August 5, 1962, when Sellers was in Paris, his good spirits were shattered when he heard the news of Marilyn's passing:

> "It was as if it were the death of the closest person to him in the whole world," says Juroe [European press director and Marilyn's publicity director during the filming of *The Prince and the Showgirl*]. "He became very withdrawn and after a little while said he had to leave." Worried, he felt he should go after him but a friend who had

arrived at Juroe's apartment with Sellers urged, "Leave him alone, Jerry. Let him work it out for himself."

It was ... "a moment of real grief" (Evans 182).

Billy Wilder had wanted to do a comedy in which Sellers would play opposite Marilyn, but it was not to be (Sikov 253–4).

DAVID O. SELZNICK Hollywood producer. During the making of *Let's Make Love* (1960) MM and her co-star, Yves Montand, were invited to a buffet supper at the home of Selznick and his actress wife, actress Jennifer Jones (Guiles 396; Shevey 120; Summers 50–1).

MACK SENNETT Canadian actor and producer who created the Keystone Cops and the Bathing Beauties in the silent film era. Early in her career, MM and a friend were invited to dinner with Mack Sennett. He regaled his guests with stories of the industry's early days. The year Marilyn was born—1926—Sennett produced 45 films and wrote five. In 1928, he was involved in the production of the original version of *Gentlemen Prefer Blondes* (Slatzer 103, 106, 269; *www.imdb.com*).

SHAH OF IRAN During filming of *Something's Got to Give* in 1962 the Shah of Iran, on a state visit to the United States, stopped in at Twentieth Century–Fox. Marilyn was asked to put in an appearance. She declined, saying that she was running a fever and that she could not abide the Shah's hostility toward Israel. Although she was divorced from Arthur Miller, Marilyn had converted to Judaism when she married him (Schwarz 582).

ARTIE SHAW Influential bandleader and clarinettist. When MM posed for her famous nude calendar on May 27, 1949, the photographer, Tom Kelley, wanted his model to feel relaxed so he put Artie Shaw's "Begin the Beguine" on the phonograph. As Kelley explained it: "I find it's a good number for getting a naked girl in a sexual mood. In my experience, I know of no other piece of music that can arouse sexual vibrations faster than Artie Shaw's recording of 'Begin the Beguine'" (Riese & Hitchens 478). When the story of

the calendar session erupted three years later, someone asked Marilyn what she had on during the photo shoot. She replied, "The radio."

IRWIN SHAW Playwright, screenwriter and novelist who wrote *The Young Lions* (1949) and *Rich Man, Poor Man* (1970). In 1952, Shaw was living in the Beverly Carlton Hotel in Beverly Hills. A young starlet, who never seemed to get up before five o'clock in the afternoon, lived in one of the other apartments. Shaw never saw her but could not help but notice that flowers were being constantly delivered to her door. The starlet, of course, was MM (Shnayerson 190).

DICK SHAWN Actor and innovative stand-up comedian. Shawn was doing his comedy act at the Mapes Hotel in Reno, Nevada, while *The Misfits* (1961) was being filmed nearby. MM and the cast and crew of the movie were billeted in the hotel at the time, occupying more than half the rooms. Shawn took the opportunity to visit the set of the film (Goode 182).

NORMA SHEARER Academy Award–winning Canadian actress who was one of Hollywood's biggest stars until her retirement in 1942. In the winter of 1961, in a Los Angeles restaurant, Shearer saw a mutual friend, hairdresser and fellow Canadian Sydney Guilaroff, walk in with MM on his arm. Shearer caught Guilaroff's attention and induced him to introduce her to Marilyn (Guilaroff 159–160).

TOOTS SHOR New York crony of Joe DiMaggio who ran a popular bar/restaurant. Toots Shor became famous for operating a manly hangout for hard-drinking sports celebrities, newspaper reporters, public relations men and theatre people. His establishment was once described as "a gymnasium with room service." During her relationship with Joe DiMaggio, Marilyn often accompanied Joe to Toots Shor's. It was there that Joe attempted a reconciliation with his ex-wife when he threw her a surprise birthday party for her on June 1, 1955. The evening ended when the couple had a fight and Marilyn stormed out (Riese & Hitchens 81, 249).

MAX SHOWALTER *see* **CASEY ADAMS**

SARGENT SHRIVER   Politician and director of the Peace Corps, closely associated with the Kennedy family. At the reception after Shriver's 1953 wedding to Eunice Kennedy, the Kennedys interrupted the merriment by singing "Marilyn," a song written about MM the year before. It proved to be a curious song choice given that Shriver's new brother-in-law, John Fitzgerald Kennedy, was to have a brief affair with the actress.

When Marilyn died in 1962, Shriver, on Peace Corps business, was in Indonesia having a meeting with the country's leader, President Sukarno. Shriver was puzzled as to why Sukarno kept bringing the conversation around to Marilyn Monroe, until he realized that he had been mistaken for the President Kennedy's other brother-in-law, actor Peter Lawford. Sukarno had met Marilyn during a visit to the United States and wanted to know how she had died. Shriver looked momentarily alarmed and stammered: "Well, gee, it's hard to say and there's a lot of speculation." Shriver was then taken aback as Sukarno answered his own question. Sukarno dismissed the suicide theory and stated as fact that Marilyn had accidentally overdosed on sleeping pills. Shriver was beginning to despair that anything of substance was going to get accomplished until Sukarno interrupted the flow of his thoughts to say that the Peace Corps would be welcome in his country (Stossel 286–7).

BUGSY SIEGEL   Notorious gangster who became a major player in the development of Las Vegas. When she was still an unknown starlet, Marilyn, clad in a fetching blue bathing suit, decorated a Beverly Hills pool party at Siegel's mansion. This must have been in 1947, shortly before Siegel was shot to death by unknown assailants. Some have alleged that Marilyn and Bugsy had a brief sexual interlude (Jordan 94; Victor 174).

SIMONE SIGNORET   French actress and wife of Yves Montand, MM's co-star in *Let's Make Love* (1960). During the shooting of the film, Marilyn and her husband Arthur Miller, and Signoret and Montand, lived in adjoining bungalows. By all accounts the two couples got on famously. But when Signoret and Miller were called away, Marilyn and Montand began an affair. Signoret genuinely liked Marilyn and took the news of the affair remarkably well. "If Marilyn is in love with my husband," she said, "it proves she has good taste" (Riese & Hitchens 480). Signoret correctly judged the relationship between Montand and Marilyn, at least from Montand's point of view, as nothing more than a passing fancy. Signoret remained married to Montand for the rest of her life.

In her autobiography, Signoret provides a rare description of Marilyn when she was not being "Marilyn."

> She would reappear wearing a blue polka-dotted rayon dressing gown. Without makeup or false eyelashes, her feet bare, which made her quite short, she looked like the most beautiful peasant girl imaginable from the Ile-de-France, as the type has been celebrated for centuries.
> The famous lock of hair that flopped onto her forehead had disappeared; that puffed-up, sophisticated phenomenon was the result of a hairdresser's vigorous teasing between takes. But now her hair had been brushed back. And her widow's peak appeared.
> It was a very pretty widow's peak, which divided her forehead neatly in half. But she detested it, despised it; it was her personal enemy. She hated it because, curiously, the roots of that hair, fluffy as the hair of a small child, didn't take the platinum dye as well as the rest of the hair on her blond head. The lock that fell over her eye so casually and so accidentally was produced by all that teasing, and it was a shield protecting those darker roots, which might be seen when the camera came in for close-ups. She explained it all to me at the very beginning of our neighborly relations. She had also said, "Look, they all think I've got beautiful long legs; I have knobby knees and my legs are too short." That was hardly true in her dressing gown bought at a local Woolworth's, and it was completely untrue as soon as she was in her "Marilyn" getup. I saw her in her "Marilyn" getup only three times in four months [Signoret 330–1].

In 1959, rumors had circulated that Marilyn would receive an Academy Award nomination for Best Actress in *Some Like It Hot*. Marilyn was not nominated and the award went to Signoret for *Room at the Top* (Signoret 285–96; Victor 273–4).

PHIL SILVERS   Comic actor who is best known for his role as the ever-scheming Sergeant Bilko on television's *The Phil Silvers Show* (1955–1959). Silvers, who was one of Marilyn's friends, was cast as an insurance salesman in her unfinished *Something's Got to Give*, in 1962 (*www.imdb.com*).

FRANK SINATRA   Crooner and Academy Award–winning actor. Frank Sinatra was MM's favorite recording artist. The two may have met in late 1953 when Twentieth Century–Fox was trying to bring them together for *The Girl in Pink Tights*. Marilyn was interested in working with Sinatra but not on what she considered to be an inferior project. Sinatra was a friend of Marilyn's second husband, Joe DiMaggio, and through that connection she certainly made Sinatra's acquaintance by 1954.

When Marilyn and DiMaggio divorced, rumors of a romance with Sinatra inevitably started up. The two did date but how far the relationship went is a matter of speculation. This was about the time Sinatra and DiMaggio were involved in an embarrassing fracas known as the "Wrong Door Raid." On November 5, 1954, the two men, accompanied by some private investigators, were alleged to have kicked in the door of a Los Angeles apartment, expecting to catch Marilyn in the arms of another man (some have suggested it was another woman). Marilyn was not there and the occupant of the apartment was understandably livid, and sued everybody involved. Although DiMaggio eventually settled out of court, the evidence against Sinatra was contradictory. He claimed that he was waiting in the car when the raid happened. Sinatra beat the charge but the resulting publicity was not the type he welcomed. DiMaggio was upset over Sinatra's relationship with Marilyn and suspected he deliberately led him to the wrong address. Their friendship was over.

Marilyn and Sinatra continued to be close friends, and she went to his shows whenever she could. At one point she briefly lived in Sinatra's house when he was out of the country. More movies were proposed but somehow the timing was always wrong, or the script was un-

acceptable. Marilyn and Sinatra never did work together. Sinatra gave Marilyn expensive gifts and her last pet, a poodle she named Maf, a joking reference to his supposed Mafia connections. It is widely believed that Marilyn spent her last weekend alive at the Cal-Neva Lodge, a gambling resort in Lake Tahoe, where Sinatra was performing. At least one biographer claims that, by 1962, Sinatra was hoping to marry Marilyn. When Marilyn was found dead, on August 5, 1962, there were, as usual, a pile of Frank Sinatra records on her turntable. Sinatra, like the rest of her Hollywood friends, was not admitted to her funeral (Clarke 146–7; Kelly 264–6; Taraborrelli 249–54, 360–5, 376–80, 463–7).

EDITH SITWELL   Eccentric English poet and biographer. On a visit to Hollywood in February 1954, Sitwell met MM. The meeting was arranged by the editors of *Life* magazine,

> Miss Monroe and I should be brought face to face, since it was obvious that we were born to hate each other, would do so at first sight, and that our subsequent insults to each other would cause a commotion when reported. They never made a greater mistake.
> That afternoon she wore a green dress and, with her yellow hair, looked like a daffodil. We talked mainly, as far as I remember, about Rudolf Steiner, whose works she had just been reading. At one time … I found myself watching what I believe was known as a Nature-Dance (something uniting one, I expect, with Mother Earth) in which ladies of only too certain an age galloped with large bare dusty feet over an uncarpeted floor. I do not know that this exhibition could be ascribed to Dr. Steiner, but is seemed to have something to do with Higher Thought, and I am afraid that Miss Monroe and I could not resist laughing about it.
> In repose her face was at moments strangely, prophetically tragic, like the face of a breathing ghost—a little spring-ghost, an innocent fertility-daemon, the vegetation spirit that was Ophelia [Sitwell 222–3].

Sitwell went on to say the following about Marilyn:

> In private life she was not in the least what her calumniators would have wished her to be. She was very quiet, had great natural dignity (I cannot

imagine anyone who knew her trying to take a liberty with her), and was extremely intelligent. She was also exceedingly sensitive.

What will-power she must have needed in order to remain the human being she was, after the cruelty with which, in the past, she was treated! That is over now, and she is accepted as the fine artist that she was. But that cruelty was completely odious. It arose partly, I think, from the envy of people who are devoid of beauty, and partly from the heartless stupidity of those who have never known a great and terrifying poverty. There are people, also, who cannot believe that beauty and gaiety are a part of goodness [Sitwell 221].

Sitwell met Marilyn again on July 26, 1956, at playwright Terence Rattigan's country house, near London. The event was a ball given in honor of Marilyn and her husband Arthur Miller. After Marilyn's death, Sitwell said: "If anyone had asked me to compile a list of people who I thought might commit suicide, I would have put her name on it"(Summers 225). Marilyn said of Sitwell: "I expected her to be a real English snob, but she wasn't. She was what my mother would have called a Lady. A grand lady, strong enough to stand up to men" (Weatherby 186).

RED SKELTON   Comedian who became a star in radio, film and television. When top Hollywood talent agent Johnny Hyde died suddenly on December 18, 1950, Red Skelton was invited to be an honorary pallbearer at the funeral. Hyde's protégée, starlet Marilyn Monroe, dressed in black, veiled and sobbing, was also at the funeral (Rose 150–1, Victor 147–8).

HOWARD K. SMITH   Respected American journalist and network news broadcaster. In 1954, Smith visited a Hollywood film studio where some of the scenes from *River of No Return*, starring MM and Robert Mitchum, were being reshot. Smith almost met Marilyn. A friend went over to greet Marilyn and ask her if she would be gracious enough to say hello to Mr. Smith, who had come all the way from London for the occasion. Smith recounts, "The lovely creature skipped the length of the studio, shook hands daintily with a man standing near me, and skipped all the way back" (Smith 218).

ROBERT STACK   Actor who was best known for his portrayal of incorruptible G–man Eliot Ness in the television series *The Untouchables* (1959–1962). Stack knew MM at the beginning and end of her career. "I first met Norma Jean [sic] before she changed her name, when a good-looking Hungarian actor named Eric Feldari took her to one of our swimming parties. She wore a white bathing suit, which she filled beautifully, but then so did most of the other pretty girls. I remember only that she appeared to be shy and somehow on the outside of everything taking place at the party. I tried being a good host, and every time I'd ask if she wanted anything, she'd say, 'No, everything is fine'" (Stack & Evans 84).

By the time Marilyn had become a superstar, Stack, in common with many others, observed that she was full of insecurities and suffered from agonizing frustration and doubt every time she stood in front of the camera. Drawing a comparison with Jean Harlow, who died at age 26, Stack concluded: "Poor Marilyn escaped none of the tortures of being a sex symbol but at least she lived long enough to worry about her first wrinkle" (Stack & Evans 84).

KIM STANLEY   Actress who starred on Broadway as Cherie in *Bus Stop*, a role which MM brought to the screen in 1956. The film's director, Josh Logan, sent Marilyn to the theatre to study Kim Stanley's Southern accent. Stanley's first movie was *The Goddess* (1958), the story of an unstable actress named Rita Shawn. It was a thinly disguised portrait of Marilyn. Stanley had met Marilyn at the Actors Studio in New York and witnessed Marilyn's triumphant performance in a scene from Eugene O'Neill's *Anna Christie*. Stanley recalled that Marilyn "was just wonderful. She *was* wonderful. We were taught never to clap at the Actors Studio—it was like we were in church—and it was the first time I'd ever heard applause there. Some of us went to her privately and apologized" (Rollyson 100). Stanley though that Marilyn had a beauty and innocence that others could only dream about but only really came alive when the cameras were rolling. "Anyone who had any largeness of spirit loved Marilyn. And she won us all" (Krampner 105).

Other sources: Gilmore 168–70; Spoto 348; *www.imdb.com*).

BARBARA STANWYCK Screen legend of Hollywood. In 1952, Stanwyck starred in *Clash by Night*, a film which featured a fast-rising new star, MM. Stanwyck said of Marilyn: "She was awkward. She couldn't get out of her own way. She wasn't disciplined, and she was often late, and she drove Bob Ryan, Paul Douglas and myself out of our minds ... but she didn't do it viciously, and there was a sort of magic about her which we all recognized at once. Her phobias, or whatever they were, came later; she seemed just a carefree kid, and she owned the world" (Smith 233).

Stanwyck was extremely patient and understanding with Marilyn. Fritz Lang, the director of *Clash by Night*, recalled a simple scene where Marilyn flubbed her lines eight or ten times and "not once did [Stanwyck] have a bad word for Marilyn. She understood her perfectly." Lang also said that when reporters came around they said, "We don't wanna talk to Barbara, we wanna talk to the girl with the big tits." Even this did not make Stanwyck lose her temper with Marilyn (Madsen 290–1).

MAUREEN STAPLETON Respected film and stage actress. Stapleton met MM in 1956 at Lee Strasberg's Actors Studio in New York. Stapleton recalled:

> I walked into the West 44th Street headquarters of the Actors Studio and noticed a newcomer in the crowd, a really pretty blonde seated way off in the corner. She slouched in her chair and did everything imaginable to keep from calling attention to herself. Fat chance; this broad was immediately recognizable. Let's face it, Marilyn Monroe could *not* not be noticed. The papers were full of stories about Hollywood's megastar. She'd come to live in New York for a while and was dating Arthur Miller and observing classes at the Studio. That day was the first time I ever saw her. After the session someone introduced us. We shook hands and Marilyn spoke.
>
> "I saw you in *27 Wagons Full of Cotton* and I really liked it."
>
> "Why didn't you come backstage and say hello?"
>
> "Oh," she answered in her whispery voice, "I couldn't. I didn't know you."
>
> "Jesus Christ," I said, "you don't have to know anybody to come backstage, you just go back!" I couldn't believe it; the biggest star in Hollywood, for crying out loud, the biggest star in the world, was too shy to come backstage and see me [Stapleton & Scovell 116].

In February 1956, Marilyn was paired with Stapleton to perform a scene. They started rehearsing a scene from Noël Coward's *Fallen Angels* but switched to Eugene O'Neill's *Anna Christie*. The switch was made because Stapleton did not feel she was any good in the Coward role. Marilyn, full of insecurities, thought it was because *she* was no good. When they presented the scene from *Anna Christie*, they scored a triumph. The audience burst into applause, something that was frowned on in the church-like atmosphere of the Actors Studio (Stapleton & Scovell 114–25).

TOMMY STEELE British singer and pop idol. When she was in England making *The Prince and the Showgirl* (1957), someone made appointments in Marilyn's name with five of London's top dressmakers and even booked Steele, who was a fast-rising young star, for a fake party. The prankster was never found (Morgan 193).

LINCOLN STEFFENS An early-20th-century radical muckraking journalist who exposed corruption in big business and government. *The Autobiography of Lincoln Steffens* was published in 1931 and, after MM read the book, it became one of her favorites. Marilyn carried it around with her on the set of *All About Eve* (1950) and was singing its praises. The director, Joseph L. Mankiewicz, saw her with the book and took her aside for a quiet word. He advised Marilyn to tone down her admiration for Steffens. It would not do her career any good, he said, if she got a reputation as a political radical (Monroe & Hecht 118–21).

ROD STEIGER Academy Award–winning character actor. Steiger had met MM at the Actors Studio in New York. He thought Marilyn had a nervous reliance on her intimidating acting coach, Paula Strasberg (Hutchinson 44).

JOHN STEINBECK   Acclaimed writer of such novels as *Of Mice and Men* (1937), *The Grapes of Wrath* (1939), *Cannery Row* (1945), and *East of Eden* (1952). In 1958, when she was living in New York, MM went to a few dinners and parties at which John Steinbeck was also present. Steinbeck was in awe of Marilyn, who was a movie star at the height of her fame and beauty. In return, Marilyn was in awe of Steinbeck because he was a gifted writer; she had even read some of his books. Six years earlier, Steinbeck had been the onscreen narrator of *O'Henry's Full House*, an anthology film in which Marilyn had a small part. On March 9, 1955, Marilyn had acted as an usherette at a benefit screening of *East of Eden*, based on Steinbeck's novel. After Marilyn's death it was discovered that she owned copies of Steinbeck's *Once There Was A War* and *Tortilla Flat* (*www.imdb.com* ; *www.cursumperficio.net* /files/ Marilyn:stuff).

GLORIA STEINEM   American writer and feminist. In 1956, the 22-year-old Steinem briefly attended classes at the Actors Studio in New York, where she encountered MM. Steinem recalled how "confident New York actors seemed to take pleasure in ignoring this great, powerful, unconfident movie star, who had dared to come to learn. She sat by herself, her body hidden in a shapeless black sweater and slacks, her skin luminescent as she put her hands up to her face, as if trying to hide herself, and she gradually became a presence in the room, if only because the rest of the group was trying so hard *not* to look at her. I remember feeling protective toward this famous woman who was older and more experienced than I; a protectiveness explained by the endlessly vulnerable child who looked out of Marilyn Monroe's eyes" (Steinem 22). Steinem asked Marilyn if she could see herself performing before such an accomplished group. Marilyn replied, "I admire all these people so much. I'm just not good enough." Steinem also said that if the feminist movement had existed in her time it might have been able to save Marilyn's life. In

1986, Steinem wrote a book about MM— *Marilyn: Norma Jeane*.

GEORGE STEVENS   Academy Award-winning movie director and producer. Stevens made the list of MM's approved directors. Even so, they never made a film together (Victor 81).

ADLAI STEVENSON   Politician and ambassador to the United Nations. On May 19, 1962, Stevenson was at a party where he encountered MM. Marilyn had just sung her famous rendition of "Happy Birthday, Mr. President" at a Democratic Party fundraiser at Madison Square Garden. Of Marilyn's performance, Stevenson remembered it being "skin and beads—only I didn't see the beads." At the party, Stevenson thought Marilyn was the most beautiful woman he had ever seen. He recalled how he succeeded in reaching Marilyn "only after breaking through the strong defenses established by Robert Kennedy who was dodging around her like a moth around the flame" (Shevey 39).

JIMMY STEWART   Lanky Hollywood actor, an American institution. Stewart attended an exclusive dinner party at Romanoff's Restaurant in Beverly Hills on November 6, 1954. The stated purpose of the evening was to celebrate the completion of *The Seven Year Itch*, it was, in fact, a confirmation of MM's entry into Hollywood's elite. The centerpiece at all the tables, including Stewart's, was a cardboard cutout of Marilyn in her famous skirt-blowing scene from the movie (Leaming 134).

MILBURN STONE   Actor known to television viewers as Doc Adams on the long-running CBS television series *Gunsmoke* (1955–1975). Stone was in *The Fireball* in 1950, one of MM's early films (*www.imdb.com*).

LEE STRASBERG   Academy Award-nominated producer, director, and actor who became the country's foremost acting teacher. Strasberg, who had studied with Konstantin Stanislavsky at the Moscow Art Theatre was the leading proponent of The Method, the intensely introspective process by which an actor plumbs the depths of his or her emotions and life experiences to create a realistic performance. The Method had its legion of devotees as well as critics. Laurence Olivier, for instance, thought it was pretentious nonsense. Marilyn Monroe, however, was one who was smitten and stimulated by The Method.

Strasberg was the artistic director of the prestigious Actors Studio in New York when he first encountered Marilyn in 1955. He said of her, "She is more nervous than any other actress I have ever known. But nervousness, for an actress, is not a handicap. It is a sign of sensitivity" (q. Riese &Hitchens 501). Strasberg and his wife, Paula, became dominant influences on Marilyn for the rest of her life. Marilyn was in awe of Strasberg and, if truth be told, he was equally swept up in Marilyn's fame and glamor. Strasberg was quoted that the two greatest actors he had ever worked with were Marlon Brando and Marilyn Monroe.

Marilyn began taking private lessons with Lee in February 1955, at his Manhattan apartment. To the annoyance of Lee and Paula's children, Marilyn almost became a surrogate family member. Lee became the all-knowing father figure and Marilyn turned to him for guidance and support during her many professional and personal crises. Strasberg encouraged Marilyn in the belief that within her was a great actress. He also got her interested in psychoanalysis as a means to bring out her talent.

Despite her intense relationship with Strasberg, Marilyn never became a full member of the Actors Studio, as only ten members were elected each year. Instead, she began auditing twice a week. Wearing no makeup, she would sit quietly in the back row, so anonymously that most of her classmates did not even recognize her.

Some biographers have claimed that Strasberg exploited Marilyn, trading on her famous name, accepting gifts, and insisting on an exorbitant salary for his wife's services. Paula Strasberg was Lee's proxy on Marilyn's movie sets. It got to the point that if Paula was not on set Marilyn would not leave her dressing room. Understandably, Paula was universally loathed by Marilyn's directors, although some did admit that Mrs. Strasberg was the only one who could keep their temperamental star functioning.

Lee Strasberg gave Marilyn away at her 1956 wedding to Arthur Miller. Six years later he tearfully read the eulogy at her funeral. In her will Marilyn left the bulk of her estate to Strasberg.[62]

The Eulogy (Delivered by Lee Strasberg, August 8, 1962)
Despite the heights and brilliance she attained on the screen, she was planning for the future: she was looking forward to participating in the many exciting things which she planned. In her eyes and in mine, her career was just beginning. The dream of her talent, which she had nurtured as a child, was not a mirage. When she first came to me I was amazed at the startling sensitivity which she possessed and which had remained fresh and undimmed, struggling to express itself despite the life to which she had been subjected. Others were as physically beautiful as she was, but there was obviously something more in her, something that people saw and recognized in her performances and with which they identified. She had a luminous quality—a combination of wistfulness, radiance, yearning—to set her apart and yet made everyone wish to be part of her, to share in the childish naiveté which was at once so shy and yet so vibrant. This quality was even more evident when she was on the stage. I am truly sorry that the public who loved her did not have the opportunity to see her as we did, in many of the roles that foreshadowed what she would have become. Without a doubt she would have been one of the really great actresses on the stage [Riese & Hitchens 142–3].

Other sources: (Adams 253–75; Hirsch; Strasberg 1992).

SUSAN STRASBERG   Film and stage actress who was the daughter of two of the most influential people in MM's life: Paula and Lee Strasberg. The 15-year-old Susan Strasberg met Marilyn in 1954. Susan had been invited to the set of *There's No Business like Show Business* on the day Marilyn was shooting her "Heat Wave" number. Before long, Marilyn became emotionally and professionally dependent on Paula and Lee and was soon a reg-

ular visitor to the Strasberg apartment. Marilyn lived periodically with the family, even sharing a room with Susan. Susan grew so close to Marilyn that she started to think of her as an older sister. Although she loved Marilyn dearly there were times when Susan experienced something akin to sibling rivalry, resenting the attention her parents lavished on Marilyn but withheld from her. For her part, Marilyn gave Susan extravagant presents, such as a valuable drawing by Marc Chagall. When Marilyn died, Susan was in Rome. Although not Catholic, she lit candles for Marilyn in a 1300-year-old church (Strasberg 1992).

JOHN STURGES   Director who made such classics as *Bad Day at Black Rock* (1954), *Gunfight at the O.K. Corral* (1957), *The Magnificent Seven* (1960), and *The Great Escape* (1963). In 1950, Sturges directed *Right Cross*, a boxing melodrama which included MM in an uncredited appearance (Riese & Hitchens 506; *www.imdb.com*).

WILLIAM STYRON   Author of the *Confessions of Nat Turner* (1967) and *Sophie's Choice* (1979). In 1956, Styron was living in Roxbury, Connecticut. Among his neighbors were the recently married Arthur Miller and MM. Styron complained how the marriage of the playwright and sex symbol brought "to these tranquil glens and glades a gawking procession of sportshirted, Pontiac–ensconced, yowling cretins such as you would never have imagined, and leaving dead around an oak tree not _ mile from this house the lady correspondent from *Paris-Match*, who cracked up chasing the couple. The real estate agent who sold us our place, and who also doubles as town constable, told us with Rotarian pride that land values hereabouts have skyrocketed since the event. I wouldn't be surprised." Styron himself had to make do with fleeting glimpses of Marilyn. One afternoon, as he was driving by, Styron saw a remarkable sight: Marilyn Monroe, clad in a bathrobe, putting out empty milk bottles on the back step (West 285).

SUKARNO   Sukarno was the president of Indonesia (1945–1967). A fan of Hollywood movies in general and MM in particular, he wanted to meet Marilyn when he visited the United States. Accordingly, on May 31, 1956, Marilyn attended a reception for President Sukarno given by the Association of American Motion Picture Producers at the Beverly Hills Hilton Hotel.

> Marilyn Monroe entered the reception room rather self-consciously and was at a loss among unfamiliar faces until she caught the eyes of Louella O. Parsons, the famous film columnist, who took the star protectively to a sofa. But no sooner did they sit down than the youngest journalist of the Indonesian press group shouted to his colleagues, and soon Marilyn was surrounded by a dozen correspondents, admiring without restraint the hottest property of Hollywood. It was at this point that President Sukarno entered the reception room and Marilyn was introduced to him. The meeting between the two celebrities was warm and natural, and the President seemed to enjoy this brief encounter. The press, however, made capital news of it, and so a much-publicized picture of President Sukarno looking appreciatively at Marilyn Monroe as she said something demurely with downcast eyes marked the ending of the press coverage of Sukarno's seventeen-day visit [Harsano 139].

Sukarno spoke to Marilyn, saying: "You are a very important person to Indonesia. Your pictures are the most popular of any that have ever played in my country. The entire Indonesian population is interested in my meeting you" (Riese & Hitchens 507). Later, Marilyn commented that Sukarno, even though he had five wives, kept looking down her dress.

The following year Sukarno survived an assassination attempt in his country and Marilyn offered "Prince Sukarno" political asylum in her home in New York. Marilyn's husband Arthur Miller was not keen on this. In any case, Sukarno did not need rescuing. Washington columnist Drew Pearson claimed that Marilyn referred to Sukarno as president of India and that she had never heard of Indonesia.

When Marilyn died, in August 1962, Sargent Shriver, President Kennedy's brother-in-law and director of the Peace Corps, was in Indonesia. At a meeting with Sukarno, Shriver did not understand why the president kept talking about MM. Eventually, Shriver realized that Sukarno had met Marilyn during his visit to the United States and remembered her. Sukarno said: "The actress, Marilyn Monroe, what really happened to her? How did she die?" (Stossel 286). Shriver did not have an answer. Sukarno answered his own question, dismissing the suicide theory. He stated as fact that Marilyn had accidentally overdosed on sleeping pills (Guiles 318).

ED SULLIVAN Newspaperman whose eponymously titled variety show was a staple of Sunday night television from 1948 until 1971. Sullivan was not a great fan of MM and she never appeared on his program, although he did air a clip of himself attending the premiere of one of her movies and chatting with her. Sullivan even adjusted Marilyn's earrings. This is what Sullivan had to say about "Heat Wave," the production number Marilyn did in *There's No Business Like Show Business* (1954): "Miss Monroe has just about worn the Welcome off this observer's mat.... 'Heat Wave' is easily one of the most flagrant violations of good taste this observer has ever witnessed" (q. Riese & Hitchens 275). Even so, Sullivan was keen to have the cast of *The Misfits* (1961) on his show. A script was prepared but Marilyn refused to appear on television. The other "misfits" (Gable and Clift) declined as well (Goode 110; Shaw & Rosten 87).

-T-

LYLE TALBOT Actor who made numerous television and movie appearances. Talbot's film work was usually confined to "B" pictures. In 1954, Talbot played a stage manager in an "A" picture which starred Marilyn Monroe, *There's No Business Like Show Business* (*www.imdb.com*).

NORMA TALMADGE MM was christened Norma Jeane Mortenson in 1926 by her mother, Gladys Baker Mortenson. At that time, Norma Talmadge was one of the top box-office stars of the silent screen. Gladys was a film cutter at Consolidated Film Industries

in Hollywood and worked on some of Talmadge's films. Gladys was such a fan of the actress that she may have named her baby daughter "Norma" after her.[63] Some said that Marilyn's mother resembled Norma Talmadge. In the two decades after her first movie in 1910, Talmadge had feature roles in 250 pictures. In 1916, she met and married movie executive and producer Joseph M. Schenck. Before long, Schenck had set up the Norma Talmadge Film corporation and the couple was producing their own movies. When the talkies came in, Talmadge retired a wealthy woman. Although there is no evidence that MM and Norma Talmadge ever met, their lives were conjoined. Beside sharing the name "Norma," they shared Joseph Schenck. Schenck, who had divorced Talmadge in 1934, was Marilyn's earliest friend and protector in Hollywood. There have been allegations that in return, Marilyn was the, by then, elderly Schenck's mistress. Marilyn also knew Talmadge's second husband, comedian George Jessel. Jessel definitely wanted more from Marilyn than mere friendship, but she was not interested.

When Marilyn was married to Arthur Miller the couple lived in rural Roxbury, Connecticut, and it was there that she had another tangential connection to Norma Talmadge. Many years before, a neighbor's farmhouse had been used as a backdrop in a Talmadge movie. The actress left her white kid gloves on a cider barrel in the coal cellar. When Marilyn visited the house, the gloves, covered in dust, were still on the cider barrel, kept almost as if they were religious relics. The neighbor, who had hoped to add a new treasure, was infuriated when the marks of Marilyn's high heels were inadvertently obliterated.

In 1926, the year of Marilyn's birth, the Norma Talmadge Film Corporation released *Kiki*, with Ronald Colman as Talmadge's co-star. The film was a silly comedy about a Parisian gamin who falls for the manager of a revue (Leaming 1998, 326–7; Spoto 1993, 15).

RUSS TAMBLYN Supporting player in films, best known for his appearance in *West Side Story* (1961). Tamblyn had a small role in

As Young As You Feel (1951) with MM. He was listed in the credits as Rusty Tamblyn (*www.imdb.com*).

BERNIE TAUPIN   Award–winning songwriter who has often worked with Elton John. In 1973, Taupin wrote the lyrics to John's music for "Candle in the Wind," a tribute to MM. Taupin wanted to write a song that expressed sorrow at Marilyn's untimely death and the public's enduring fascination with her. Taupin said, "I wanted to say that it wasn't just a sex thing. That she was somebody everybody could fall in love with, without her being out of reach." With altered lyrics, Elton John sang the song at the funeral of Diana, Princess of Wales in 1997.

ELIZABETH TAYLOR   Superstar screen actress and philanthropist. MM and Elizabeth Taylor knew each other socially but never worked together. Taylor was the only actress with whom Marilyn felt she was in competition. She regretted not getting the lead in *Cat on a Hot Tin Roof* (1958) and *Suddenly, Last Summer* (1959), both of which went to Taylor. Taylor was five years younger and much better paid. In 1962, Marilyn was getting $100,000 for *Something's Got to Give* while Taylor earned $1 million for *Cleopatra*. The budget overruns on *Cleopatra* were a contributing factor to the decision to shut down Marilyn's film. For *Something's Got to Give*, Marilyn posed for some sensational nude photos. She explained why: "Look, fellas, what I want is to push Liz Taylor off the magazine covers around the world. Let me look through the photographs, and take out what I want—and you get me on the covers" (Summers 368).

After Marilyn's death, a magazine piece stated: "Elizabeth Taylor was a legend, but Marilyn Monroe was a myth." Reportedly, Taylor phoned the author and complained: "You have a nerve saying that Marilyn was a 'myth' and I'm just a lousy 'legend.' I'm much more beautiful than Marilyn Monroe ever was, and I'm certainly a much better actress. What the hell do I have to do to be a myth? Die young and at my own hand?" (Riese &

Hitchens 510). For the record, Taylor was kinder to Marilyn's memory saying of her, "She seemed to have a kind of unconscious glow about her physical self that was innocent, like a child. When she posed nude, it was 'Gee, I am kind of, you know, sort of dishy,' like she enjoyed it without being egotistical" (Victor 302). In 1967, Paramount considered Taylor for *After the Fall*, Arthur Miller's drama based on his late wife.

TERRY-THOMAS   British comic actor with a distinctive gap-toothed smile who specialized in portraying upper-class cads. In the early 1960s Terry-Thomas made a few Hollywood films and appeared on American television programs. It was probably then that he encountered Marilyn Monroe. The day he saw her in person he wrote, "I was disappointed, for she seemed almost ugly. Her hair was lank, she was wishy-washy, pale and not in very good shape. Probably she was very ill. I was reminded of a cheap, pink balloon" (Terry-Thomas 56).

DANNY THOMAS   Affable comic actor, seen mostly in television, and a notable philanthropist. In July 1953, Thomas coordinated a charity show for the benefit of St. Jude's Children's Hospital. Jane Russell and MM sang a song at the event held at the Hollywood Bowl. Three years earlier, Thomas and Marilyn had attended the funeral of top Hollywood talent agent Johnny Hyde. Thomas was asked to be an honorary pallbearer while Marilyn's experience was quite different. Reports vary, but either Marilyn threw herself sobbing on the casket or plucked a single white rose from the spray on the coffin and preserved it for years between the pages of a Bible. Marilyn had been Hyde's protégée and his family blamed her for his untimely death (Rose 150–1, Victor 147–8; *www.imdb.com*).

DYLAN THOMAS   Hard-drinking Welsh poet. In 1953, just before his death, Thomas was on an American tour. He accepted a dinner invitation with journalist Sidney Skolsky, actress Shelley Winters and her roommate, MM. For the occasion Marilyn picked wild flowers from an empty lot and decorated their apartment with them and with Japanese lanterns and candles.

Winters described the evening, as well as Marilyn's cooking skills, or lack thereof:

> Marilyn and I spent the entire day cleaning the apartment, and we prepared dinner. The arrangement was that I did the real cooking and she did the dishes and the cleaning up. Not only could Marilyn not cook, if you handed her a leg of lamb she just stared at it. Once I asked her to wash the salad while I went to the store. When I came back an hour later, she was still scrubbing each leaf. Her idea of making a salad was to scrub each lettuce leaf with a Brillo pad....
>
> Mr. Thomas drank practically all his dinner. Marilyn had made a pitcher of gin martinis, and since we didn't have a pitcher, she made it in a milk bottle. She and I had two juice glasses of martini each, Sidney had none and Mr. Thomas drank the rest. To slow him down, Sidney suggested a straw. A bottle of red and a bottle of white wine at his elbow disappeared next, followed by six bottles of beer he had bought in a supermarket [Winters 1989, 32–3].

At the end of the evening, Thomas started singing a traditional folk ballad:

> Come all ye fair and tender maids
> Who flourish in your prime, prime,
> Beware, beware, keep your garden fair,
> Let no man steal your time, time
> Let no man steal your time
>
> 'Cause when your time is past and gone,
> He'll care no more for you, you
> And many a day that your garden is waste,
> 'Twill spread all over with rue, rue
> 'Twill spread all over with rue
>
> A woman is a branch, a tree,
> A man is a clinging vine, vine,
> And from his branches carelessly
> He takes what he can find, find
> He takes what he can find [Tremlett 136].

Marilyn and Winters were nearly in tears when the drunken Welshman left their apartment (Winters 1989, 32–4).

DAME SYBIL THORNDIKE   Acclaimed British stage actress who took occasional film roles. Thorndike as the Queen Dowager appeared opposite MM in *The Prince and the Showgirl* (1957). Before the first rehearsal Thorndike didn't recognize the blonde bombshell and began asking when the star would be arriving. During the filming, Marilyn was tardy and had trouble remembering her lines. Thorndike never complained and was always patient and understanding: "Such a darling girl though always late on the set and terribly unhappy about something." One morning, co-star and director, Sir Laurence Olivier, made Marilyn apologize to Thorndike for keeping her waiting in full costume and makeup. Marilyn offered the apology and Thorndike said, "Not at all, I'm sure we're all very glad to see you. Now that you are here, that is" (Morley 133). Thorndike came to have a high regard for Marilyn as a film actress: "When I started to play scenes with Marilyn I would say to Larry, 'Does that get over, what is it she's doing? I can't hear a word she says. I think it's so underplayed.' 'Do you, dear?' he said; 'well, come and look at the rushes.' And I went to see them and of course she was perfect. I was the old ham. You see, Marilyn knew exactly what to do on the screen. I never did" (Morley 133–4). Thorndike was 75 when she acted with Marilyn and survived her by 14 years.

THE THREE STOOGES   Zany comedy troupe who perfected extreme slapstick in nearly 200 short subjects and a few full-length features. One of the latter was *Snow White and the Three Stooges*, released in 1961 by Twentieth Century–Fox. While that was being made, Marilyn Monroe was finishing up *The Misfits* on an adjoining sound stage. Edson Stroll, the actor who played Prince Charming in the Stooges' film, recalled that Marilyn's "dressing room was next to mine and we were very friendly. I remember her stopping by the stage and watching the Stooges on the set. They really liked her" (Cox & Terry 124).

JAMES THURBER   Humorist and cartoonist who died nine months before MM. Thurber, who was nearly blind, was asked what he would most like to see if his sight was restored for one day. He replied that since he already knew what "Marilyn Miller" looked like he would like to see how his friends and acquaintances had aged. The interviewer then asked Thurber if he accepted the definition of an egghead as someone who refers to Marilyn

Monroe as "Mrs. Arthur Miller" (Fensch 115). After Marilyn's death, a copy of *Thurber Country* was found among her possessions (*www.cursumperficio.net* /files/Marilyn:stuff).

GENE TIERNEY Film and stage actress. When she was still an unknown bit player MM went to a star-studded party at the home of a Hollywood agent. Among the guests was Gene Tierney. In 1954 Marilyn lobbied for a role in *The Egyptian*, but lost out to Tierney. *Laura* (1944) starring Tierney and Dana Andrews, was one of Marilyn's favorite films. She admitted to having seen it at least 15 times (Monroe & Hecht 56; Victor 106).

TINKER BELL Tinker Bell is the mischievous fairy in J. M. Barrie's famous play, *Peter Pan*. The Disney animated film of the story was released in 1953, about the time that MM achieved movie stardom. Almost immediately an urban legend arose that Marilyn was the inspiration and reference model for the little blonde fairy, Tinker Bell. There was an earlier rumor that Marilyn was the model for *Cinderella* (1950) and the Tinker Bell myth was probably derived from that one. In fact, it was actress Margaret Kerry who pantomimed the actions that were animated as Tinker Bell. It is not known if Marilyn saw the movie or was aware of the rumor (Genge 195; *www.tinkerbelltalks.com*).

MIKE TODD Brash Broadway and movie producer known for *Around the World in Eighty Days* (1956) and his marriage to Elizabeth Taylor. MM wanted to be in the film but, despite doing a private audition for Todd, he felt she was not right for the story and turned her down. On March 30, 1955, Todd had staged a benefit performance of the Ringling Brothers Circus at Madison Square Garden, in aid of the Arthritis and Rheumatism Foundation. Marilyn was on a break from her film career, and Todd got her to take part. She became the highlight of the evening. Clad as a showgirl in spangles, sequins and long white gloves, Marilyn led the opening procession perched atop an Indian elephant which was painted pink. The resulting photographs went out to maga-zines and newspapers everywhere. The following week, Marilyn was interviewed by Edward R. Murrow on his *Person to Person* television program. She said of her elephant ride that it meant a lot to her because she had never been taken to a circus when she was a child (Riese & Hitchens 517; Todd 263–4).

MEL TORMÉ Jazz vocalist whose smooth voice earned him the nickname of "The Velvet Fog." It has been alleged that Tormé had an affair with MM in 1954. In his autobiography, Tormé neither confirms nor denies the truth of this. Tormé met Marilyn in 1952 when he was playing the Roxy Theater. Tormé was asked to bring Marilyn out on stage, talk with her about her new movie, *Monkey Business*, and sing a duet with her. Upon meeting Marilyn, Tormé thought: "She was heart-staggeringly gorgeous, eager to work with me, terribly nervous, and possessed of a breathy little singing voice that seemed incapable of rising to more than a whisper" (Tormé 195).

Tormé wrote six minutes of dialogue and a parody of "Oh, Do It Again." Marilyn liked the material and learned it. "I had heard stories about this girl, unflattering gossip about her sexual exploits, her temperament, her flightiness, her undependability. Yet I had worked intensively with her for three solid days. She had been with me at least, a consummate pro, practicing the duet again and again, trying the dialogue I had written this way and that, for maximum effect. She had been outgoing, easy, affectionate, complimentary, diligent—in short, terrific" (Tormé 196). On the night of the performance, however, Marilyn was petrified, slightly tipsy and surrounded by flunkies. Tormé kicked everyone out of the dressing room, calmed Marilyn down and proceeded to get a great performance out of her.

Two years later, in Las Vegas, Tormé and Marilyn resumed their relationship. For two months they were inseparable, seeing movies, going to restaurants and talking. And then it ended. Tormé gave Marilyn a list of fun books to read as an antidote to the highfalutin' Proust and Jung she had been reading. Tormé always called her "Sadie" or "Babe," both of which

Marilyn loved. He wrote: "The 'slovenly,' not-very-bright, temperamental, profligate woman described by so many writers was a Marilyn Monroe I never met. The woman-child I knew for an all-too-brief period of time was a nice, reasonably intelligent, eager-to-better herself individual. She was also insecure, slightly cynical, and opinionated. Her face was always scrubbed, her hair attractively windblown or set. Her language could be salty, but ... her beauty and impishness allowed her to spew forth the most outrageous expletives and get away with them. She was, far and away, the sexiest-looking lady I ever knew" (Tormé 200–1).

SPENCER TRACY   A Hollywood legend, one of the greatest film actors of all time, making 74 films during a 40-year career. In December 1950, Tracy and an unknown starlet named Marilyn Monroe attended the funeral of talent agent Johnny Hyde. Tracy was an honored guest while Marilyn was anything but. Author Frank Rose described the scene: "Leaning against the rough stone wall of the church was an uninvited guest—Marilyn Monroe, dressed entirely in black. Her face was pale, her body racked with sobs. In a voice thick with tears, she called out his name, 'Johnny, Johnny, Johnny.' Had she killed him? Would he still be alive if she hadn't been so selfish?" Marilyn had been Hyde's protégée and his family blamed her for the breakup of his marriage and untimely death at the young age of 53 (Rose 150–1).

TRIGGER   Trigger was a golden Palomino horse ridden by cowboy star, Roy Rogers. Trigger was born in 1932 and died in 1965, three years after Marilyn. In May 1946, MM ran into Roy Rogers in Las Vegas. Marilyn was there to get a divorce from her first husband and Rogers was there to make a movie, *Helldorado*. The two were only slightly acquainted but Rogers gave the unknown model and starlet a signal privilege. In a letter to the head of the modeling agency for which she worked, Marilyn explained: "Las Vegas is really a colorful town with the Helldorado [sic] celebra-

tion and all.... Roy Rogers was in town making a picture. I met him and rode his horse "Trigger" (cross my heart I did)!" (Shevey 106).

Other sources: Guiles 98; Riese & Hitchens 450; Victor 254; *www.imdb.com*

MARGARET TRUMAN   Daughter of President Harry Truman who became a popular writer of mystery novels. On June 1, 1955, Margaret Truman was at the premiere of *The Seven Year Itch*. The event was held at Loew's State Theater in Times Square in New York City (Victor 266).

TOM TRYON   Actor and popular novelist. In 1962, Tryon was in MM's unfinished *Something's Got to Give* as the man stranded on a tropical island with her. Right from the start Tryon could see that something was wrong with his glamorous co-star and he was worried. He recalled that "from the moment she came on set, she looked like a piece of fine crystal about to shatter. All of her moves were tentative and tenuous. In the first take she only had two words to say, which were 'Nick, darling,' but she couldn't get the words correct no matter how many times we tried it. My heart went out to her." After Marilyn's death the film was made under the title *Move Over Darling* (1963), with Chuck Connors taking over for Tryon and Doris Day taking Marilyn's role (Wolfe 414–15; *www.imdb.com*).

SOPHIE TUCKER   Actress and singer known for her comical and risqué songs. Sometime around 1947, when Marilyn Monroe was still an unknown starlet, she was seen as a Beverly Hills pool party at the home of the notorious gangster, Bugsy Siegel. Among the guests was Sophie Tucker (Jordan 94).

LANA TURNER   Glamorous movie star of the 1940s and 1950s. MM considered Lana Turner to be something of a role model. When they met, Turner gave Marilyn advice on makeup, how to walk, and what to say and what not to say. Marilyn sent her a photo inscribed: "I have always been a fan of yours.... I love your style; I love your sophistication; and I love your sex appeal. Teach me these three." Turner said of Marilyn: "She was such a dumb broad when she came to Hollywood, but there was something about her heart and mind that I cared for" (Root, Crawford & Strait 157).

KENNETH TYNAN   British dramatist and critic. Tynan thought MM "was not far from being a madwoman with all her psychoneurotic idiosyncrasies" (Summers 225). Tynan met Marilyn for the first time at a party at Gene Kelly's home in Los Angeles. Marilyn busied herself cooking hot dogs (Tynan 156). They next met in 1956, in London. Marilyn was filming *The Prince and the Showgirl*. After the film wrapped, Tynan and his wife planned to host a dinner for Marilyn and her husband, Arthur Miller.

> There were to be ten guests in addition to the Tynans, Miller and Monroe. Those invited included John Osborne and Mary Ure (Alison Porter in *Look Back in Anger*), Peter Hall and his wife Leslie Caron, Maria St. Just (Britneva at the time) and Cyril Connolly. Elaine decided to get in outside caterers (the Tynans scarcely cooked for themselves, let alone others) and a simple, mouth-watering feast was prepared for serving in the largest Mount Street room: rich paté, pheasant, crème brulée and a cheeseboard. An hour before the starting time, Miller phoned Tynan. Monroe was indisposed, but he would be coming along. A quarter of an hour later, the plan changed: they would both be coming. Five minutes later, the final message: neither would be coming. "My wife," Miller told Tynan "is hysterical." "So is mine," replied Tynan. Miller offered his apologies the following day:
> Dear Kenneth Tynan:
> I beg your forgiveness for not having come to your party. Marilyn is only now getting back on the road to her normal energies and as that evening approached it didn't seem wise to go out. As you know, the movie production hours of work are cruel and she has been doing this almost without a break since last January when she started *Bus Stop*.
> My best regards
> Arthur Miller [Shellard 179–80].

On November 18, 1956, in the Royal Court Theatre, Arthur Miller took part in a serious discussion on the state of British drama. Tynan was also part of the discussion panel. Marilyn took it all in from a seat in the fourth row. The audience was more interested in seeing her than in following the debate.

In the last year of her life, Tynan and Marilyn briefly crossed paths in New York. Tynan cattily joked to a friend that Marilyn was a woman whose "bottom has gone to pot and whose pot has gone to bottom" (Shellard 250).

-U-

LOUIS UNTERMEYER   Acclaimed writer who was appointed poet laureate in 1961. Three years before that, Untermeyer and Marilyn Monroe crossed paths. The event was an awards ceremony at the prestigious National Institute of Arts and Letters in New York City. Marilyn was present because her husband, Arthur Miller, was receiving an award for drama. When Untermeyer offered to introduce fellow poet Dorothy Parker to Marilyn Monroe, Parker jumped at the chance, inserting herself at the head of the receiving line. On December 20, 1958, Untermeyer sent Marilyn a note expressing regret at the news of her recent miscarriage and enjoyment of her appearance in the latest issue of *Life* magazine, in which she impersonated sirens Lillian Russell, Clara Bow, Theda Bara, Marlene Dietrich, and Jean Harlow (Banner 181; Meade 1988, 365).

-V-

ROGER VADIM   French screenwriter and film director. In 1956, Vadim made *And God Created Woman*, which was partially an homage to MM. The story resembled Marilyn's actual life—a poor orphan girl who grows up beautiful and seeks love wherever she can find it. The film starred Vadim's wife and France's answer to Marilyn, Brigitte Bardot (Victor 13).

RUDOLPH VALENTINO   Legendary Latin lover on the silent screen. MM and Jane Russell, stars of *Gentlemen Prefer Blondes,* were invited to put their hand- and footprints and signatures in cement at Grauman's Chinese Theater in 1953. Twenty years earlier Marilyn's mother had taken her there. Marilyn recalled that, "I used to try and fit my hands and feet in the stars' prints. The only ones that fit were Rudolph Valentino's" (Spada & Zeno 74). Marilyn also visited Valentino's grave and noted that he died in 1926, the same year she was born (DeDienes 83).

MAMIE VAN DOREN   Buxom, blonde, "B" movie queen of the 1950s. Along with MM and Jayne Mansfield, Mamie Van Doren was one of the "Three Ms." Sort of a down-market Monroe, Van Doren never achieved the same level of stardom. When Marilyn was in *Some Like It Hot* (1959), Van Doren was in *Sex Kittens Go to College* (1960).

Van Doren was married to bandleader, trumpeter, composer and actor Ray Anthony. In 1953 Anthony wrote "Marilyn" a song in honor of Marilyn Monroe. A gala launch party for the song was held at Anthony's home. Sparing no expense, Twentieth Century–Fox flew Marilyn in by helicopter. Landing on Anthony's lawn, the back draft swept hats and chairs into the swimming pool. Van Doren resented her husband's friendship with Marilyn.

> One day I found out from a columnist that Marilyn Monroe had been in the hospital with exhaustion and a bad cough, and had received two dozen roses from none other that Ray Anthony.
> I was furious.
> "How's Marilyn?" I asked him icily that evening.
> "I don't know. Is there something wrong with her?"
> "Why, there must be, Ray. Otherwise why would you send her two dozen red roses?"
> His face turned red. He muttered, "Roses?"
> "Yes, roses, you son of a bitch! Not only did you send flowers to another woman, but sent them to someone who's my direct competition. It's as if I decided to sleep with Harry James!"
> "I didn't sleep with her!"
> "How do I know that? You gave that big party for her" [Van Doren & Aveilhe 186].

A few months before Marilyn's tragic death, Van Doren ran into her at a fashionable New York restaurant. Van Doren had worked in Italy and claimed that Marilyn had asked her to accept her "David" award, the Italian equivalent of the Academy Award. Marilyn was given the award for her performance in *The Prince and the Showgirl* (1957). Marilyn had just been fired from *Something's Got to Give* and, according to Van Doren, was glum, depressed, tipsy, and not looking her best. Van Doren had overcome her jealousy and Marilyn thanked her for picking up her award.[64] They discussed their movie careers, children, and the men in their lives. Van Doren was aware of the rumors of Marilyn's involvement with the Kennedy brothers but did not bring them up even as Marilyn said, "Do your best, Mamie, not to fall in love with anybody in government. Because after they fuck you—they fuck you."

> A little while later I hurried out of the Russian Tea Room and out onto Fifty-seventh Street. There was a violent thunderstorm under way and a hard, hard rain was pounding down onto the steaming hot pavement. I dashed across the street and into the entrance of the Salisbury Hotel. I would never forget my last sight of Marilyn sitting at that lonely table. In front of her on the white tablecloth were three empty glasses. A fourth stood before her, full of ice and the clear, sharp, characterless vodka that she was using to blot out her private horrors. What I couldn't tell her, because we were never close enough, intimate enough, was that it was what we all faced. When you make your living as a glamour girl, there is always, lurking around the corner, the specter of getting old, and losing your glamour [Van Doren & Aveilhe 189].

JIMMY VAN HEUSEN   Popular American composer and songwriter who won four Oscars and an Emmy. Early one Monday morning, during the production of *Let's Make Love* (1960), Van Heusen and his musical collaborator Sammy Cahn were told to get over to Twentieth Century–Fox's musical department as quickly as possible to run through the songs in the movie for Marilyn Monroe. Van Heusen was told, "No way [you can't come], we'll *never* be able to get her here again" (Cahn 241). Just a few weeks before MM's death, Van Heusen saw her at a party at actor Peter Lawford's beach house. At the end of the evening Van Heusen and singer Nat "King" Cole gave Marilyn a lift home (Epstein 1999, 324).

GLORIA VANDERBILT   Artist, actress and socialite. MM was known to have attended at least one party at Vanderbilt's home. At the beginning of her Hollywood career Marilyn had a slight acquaintance with Pat DeCicco, a Hollywood agent who was Gloria Vanderbillt's first husband. In the last year of her life, Marilyn became friendly with a relative of Gloria's, Frederick Vanderbilt Field, a millionaire who was one of America's foremost communists. Field was living in voluntary exile in Mexico when he met Marilyn, who had traveled there to buy furnishings for her new house. The F.B.I. made note of Marilyn's and Field's association (Howard 227; Taraborrelli 2009, 429; Victor 105).

FRANKIE VAUGHAN   An English pop singer who made a few movies. Despite acting opposite MM in *Let's Make Love* (1960), Vaughan's career in the United States never took off. He returned home and was very successful in his native country. Unlike so many of her co-stars, Vaughan did not have any conflicts with Marilyn. He said of Marilyn: "She was always on time for rehearsals. There were none of those notorious late starts. When she arrived, everybody smartened up, as if her presence was the light that fell on everyone. Certainly she seemed to be very professional" (Wolfe 328).

　　Other sources: (Riese & Hitchens 534; *www.imdb.com*)

GWEN VERDON   Broadway dancer and actress who also appeared in films, notably *Damn Yankees* (1958). In 1953, Verdon was the assistant choreographer on *Gentlemen Prefer Blondes*. It was evident to Verdon that MM was not a natural dancer but that she was willing to work very hard to overcome her deficiencies. Verdon said, "Marilyn, strangely enough, could do almost anything you would ask her to do if you could show it to her" (McCarthy 508). Verdon instructed Marilyn in how to be sexy while singing "I'm Just a Little Girl From Little Rock." As another dancer observed: "Nobody was able to satirize sexiness and be sexy at the same time the way Gwen

could. She was the one who taught it to Monroe" (Gottfried 1990, 92).

CHARLES VIDOR   Hollywood director who made *Gilda* (1946), *The Fountainhead* (1949) and *A Farewell to Arms* (1957) among others. On November 6, 1954, Vidor was on hand to honor MM and the completion of her new film, *The Seven Year Itch* at an elite Hollywood party (Shaw & Rosten 70).

-W-

ROBERT WAGNER   Handsome leading man in film and television who was twice married to Natalie Wood. Wagner got his start in movies as a lowly "test boy." "I was the guy," wrote Wagner, "they always used when the studio was making screen tests of new actresses. And believe me, no job is more dead-end than that. The only interesting thing that came out of it was when they were testing a new kid and asked me to do a couple of scenes with her. Her name was Marilyn Monroe" (Harris 1988, 8). The test, a love scene, was shot on June 14, 1951. On the strength of it Wagner got a part opposite Marilyn in *Let's Make It Legal*. In the following months, Marilyn and Wagner became rising stars and began appearing together in public for the publicity value. The two continued to be friends for the rest of her life. Wagner sent Marilyn a bouquet of flowers on her last birthday, in 1962 (Brown & Barham 22, 175; Riese & Hitchens 318; *www.cursumperficio.net* /biography/1952).

ROBERT F. WAGNER, JR.   Mayor of New York City (1954–1965). On June 13, 1957, at the premiere of *The Prince and the Showgirl*, at Radio City Music Hall, MM was seated between her husband, Arthur Miller, and Mayor Wagner (Verlhac 131; *www.cursumperficio.net* /biography/1957).

NANCY WALKER   Comic actress who achieved her greatest success on television. Walker was a good friend of actor Montgomery Clift. Walker met MM when Clift invited her to go with him to a dinner party at Monroe and Arthur Miller's New York apartment on East 57th Street. Walker and the other guests could not help but notice that Marilyn was two hours late for her own party—in her own home (Bosworth 330; Shevey 318).

IRVING WALLACE Bestselling author and screenwriter. Wallace met MM in 1952 at a dinner party for a visiting New York magazine editor. Wallace recalled: "About a third of the way into the evening, the front door opened, and a ravishing, somewhat shyly nervous blonde entered. She was breathtaking. She was Marilyn Monroe. After a few introductions, she found a chair against a wall and never once moved from it the entire evening. Within minutes after Marilyn had sat down, the men at the party began to move in, surround her, and I confess I was one of them. I sat on the floor, literally at her feet, puffing my pipe and feasting my eyes upon her. All I can recollect of our own conversation was Dostoevski—we were discussing great novelists, and she was deep into Dostoevski, awed and shaken by him."

In his 1974 novel, *The Fan Club*, about a blonde bombshell actress who gets kidnapped by her fans, Wallace modeled the fictional heroine on Marilyn (Leverence 358).

ELI WALLACH Accomplished stage and film actor who worked with MM in *The Misfits* (1961). Wallach was never sure how he came to be cast in the film but suspected that Marilyn had something to do with it. Wallach and Marilyn met in New York in 1955 and became close friends; he was appearing at the time on Broadway in *Teahouse of the August Moon*. Marilyn went to see the play, standing backstage in the wings, the better to observe the stage actor's craft. Thereafter, Marilyn called Wallach "Teahouse." Wallach found Marilyn to be much more intelligent than he had been led to believe, as well as shy, down-to-earth and unlike her glamorous movie-star image. The two of them would often get together for lunch and discuss books and plays. Sometimes they would go out dancing. A tabloid columnist

maintained that Wallach was functioning as a "beard" (Wallach 209) for Arthur Miller but Wallach did not know Miller at the time. Marilyn also became friendly with Wallach's wife, actress Anne Jackson. Marilyn visited the couple's home and even volunteered her services as a baby sitter.

Wallach was studying at the Actors Studio and soon Marilyn started attending biweekly classes as an observer. He remembered Marilyn sitting quietly and inconspicuously in the back row. Wallach was among those who witnessed Marilyn and Maureen Stapleton perform a powerful and moving scene from Eugene O'Neill's *Anna Christie*.

One morning, on the way to the Actors Studio, Marilyn and Wallach passed a huge billboard of Marilyn's famous skirt-billowing scene from *The Seven Year Itch* (1955). Marilyn said, "You see that? That's all they want me to do in films. I told 20th Century–Fox and the press that I want to play Grushenka in Dostoevsky's *Brothers Karamazov*. They all laughed, but none of them have read the book; I call them 19th Century–Fox" (Wallach 210).

Marilyn was a great admirer of Albert Einstein and gave Wallach a book of the great scientist's letters. She had once jokingly prepared a list of her favorite sexy men, and both Einstein and Wallach were included. Wallach replied with a framed photograph of Einstein. Before he gave it to her, Wallach signed it "To Marilyn, with respect and love and thanks. Albert Einstein" (Summers 74). Marilyn was well aware of the deception but she proudly displayed the photograph on her piano.

Marilyn and Wallach's friendship was strained during the filming of *The Misfits*. He thought she had changed from the vibrant woman he had known in New York. She was now distant, isolated, and her self-confidence had nearly evaporated. Wallach could not help but notice that his friend was chronically late, unable to remember her lines, battling health issues, was dependent on barbiturates, and that her marriage to Arthur Miller was on the rocks. During the shooting of a dance sequence, Marilyn felt that Wallach was deliberately maneuvering her face away from the camera. She said: "Well, the public is going to find my rear more interesting to look at than Eli's face anyway" (Guiles 413). Marilyn also felt that Wallach took Miller's side during the breakup of her marriage. When Marilyn died in 1962, Joe DiMaggio made sure that Wallach and her other Hollywood friends were barred from the funeral (Gottfried 2003, 245–6; Summers 175–6; Wallach 207–27).

RAOUL WALSH   Gruff, one-eyed Holly-wood film director. When Soviet leader Nikita Khrushchev visited the United States in September 1959, the Soviet leader was the guest of honor at a luncheon at the Twentieth Century–Fox studio café. Walsh sat beside MM during the event. He remembered how "Marilyn's finely chiseled features added up to the same ethereal beauty that had struck me when I first met her." Reportedly, just days before her death, Marilyn had suggested that Walsh take over the direction of her suspended film, *Something's Got to Give* (Walsh 367).

RAY WALSTON   Character actor who never quite lived down his television series, *My Favorite Martian* (1963–1966). In 1960, Walston was in Billy Wilder's Oscar–winning follow up to *Some Like It Hot* (1959), *The Apartment*. There is a brief scene in the film which features a breathless blonde. Walston turns to Jack Lemmon and says, "Listen, kid, I can't pass this up; she looks just like Marilyn Monroe!" Marilyn attended a screening of the film but did not publicly comment on the reference to her (Riese & Hitchens 16; *www.imdb.com*).

ANDY WARHOL   Eccentric pop artist. Along with his image of Campbell's tomato soup cans, Warhol's most famous work was a series of garishly colored silkscreens of MM's face which he titled, *Colored Marilyns*. Warhol used a black-and-white publicity photo of Marilyn from her 1953 film *Niagara* as his starting point. Warhol said:

> In August '62 I started doing silkscreens. The rubber-stamp method I'd been using to repeat images suddenly seemed too homemade; I wanted something stronger that gave more of an assembly-line effect.
> With silkscreening, you pick a photograph,

blow it up, transfer it in glue onto silk, and then roll ink across it so the ink goes through the silk but not through the glue. That way you get the same image, slightly different each time. It was all so simple—quick and chancy. I was thrilled with it. My first experiments with screens were heads of Troy Donahue and Warren Beatty, and then when Marilyn Monroe happened to die that month, I got the idea to make screens of her beautiful face—the first Marilyns [Warhol & Hackett 22].

Elsewhere Warhol said: "I just see Monroe as another person. I wouldn't have stopped her from killing herself. I think everyone should do whatever they want to do and if it made her happier, then that is what she should have done. As for whether it's symbolic to paint Monroe in such violent colors: It's beauty, and she's beautiful, and if something's beautiful, it's pretty colors, that's all. Or something." He concluded by saying: "She was a fool to kill herself. She could have been the first great woman director because she understood how to make movies" (Bockris 113).

JACK WARNER   Canadian-born movie mogul who ran Warner Bros. Studio. In December 1950, Warner and Marilyn Monroe attended the funeral of talent agent Johnny Hyde. On March 1, 1956, Warner held a press conference with MM to announce a distribution deal for *The Prince and the Showgirl*, a film to be made by Marilyn Monroe Productions. During the filming, Warner was biting his nails with reports of her tardiness and the growing animosity between Marilyn and co-star and director, Laurence Olivier. Marilyn wrote Warner a rambling letter full of complaints, such as "pacing in the first third of the picture slowed ... one comic point after another flattened by inferior takes ... jump-cutting kills the points, as in the pantry scene.... Americans are not as moved by stain-glass windows as the British are and we threaten them with boredom ... much of the movie is without music when the idea was to make a romantic movie" (Thomas 1990, 222). Upon its release the film was considered to be a disaster and a box-office flop although it has come to be better regarded in the decades since it was released, primarily because of Marilyn's performance (Riese & Hitchens 542; Rose 150).

DAVID WAYNE   Mild-mannered Broadway, film and television actor who was usually in a supporting role. In the space of three years, Wayne was in four MM films, more than any other actor: *As Young as You Feel* (1951), *We're Not Married* (1952), *O'Henry's Full House* (1952), and *How to Marry a Millionaire* (1953). Because of Marilyn's chronic lateness, Wayne described his experiences on the last named film as "one of the worst times I've ever had in my life" (Morgan 130).

Other sources: Riese & Hitchens 543; *www.imdb.com*

JOHN WAYNE   Iconic action star; one of Hollywood's biggest names. Wayne knew MM but never worked with her. Wayne's daughter recalled an amusing incident when the two screen legends crossed paths:

> I was only about four years old when my parents took me to a party thrown by the Foreign Press Association. All night long, a pretty, sad-eyed platinum blonde hung all over my father. I was more curious than resentful, until one of the woman's shoulder straps floated off her alabaster shoulder. Her bosom was exposed! Feeling this could not go unreported, I pulled my mother toward a corner. "Mom, you know that pretty blonde who's holding Dad's arm? She has no brassiere on!"
>
> My mother glanced just for an instant. "That's Marilyn Monroe, honey," she said evenly. "She's always been very fond of your daddy" [Wayne 141–2].

CLIFTON WEBB   Elegant stage and film actor known for his snide upper-class roles. Webb knew MM socially but never worked with her except once at the beginning of her career. In 1948 Webb made a movie called *Sitting Pretty*. A photographer from *Life* magazine came to the set and took a series of photos of Webb sitting with pretty starlets on either side and a big box of chocolates in his lap. One of the unknown starlets was Marilyn Monroe. She was not in the film.

At a party at Webb's house several years later, Marilyn's insecurities surfaced and she stuck close to fellow guest Judy Garland for support. Marilyn said, "I don't want to get too far from you. I'm scared." Garland replied, "We're all scared. I'm scared too" (Shipman 421). During her brief second marriage, Webb telephoned a San Francisco psychic on Marilyn's behalf and arranged a consultation for a "Mrs. DiMaggio." In a magazine article, Webb said of Marilyn that she was "very sweet, very serious. She likes to talk about the theater and the kind of thing that makes people tick. She is intense and completely straightforward. She reads all the time. She is in complete earnest towards her career" (Picturegoer 11 June 1955).

Other sources: Edwards 1974, 202; McCann 51; Morgan 141; Shevey 371; www.cursumperficio.net/files/fox-twentieth century

ORSON WELLES   Actor, producer, and director famous for his 1938 *War of the Worlds* radio broadcast, and for the 1941 film *Citizen Kane*. When MM was an unknown 21-year-old starlet, Welles had a short affair with her. Leaving a crowded Hollywood party, the couple went upstairs to a bedroom. Their lovemaking was rudely interrupted when a jealous husband, thinking his wife was with Welles, barged into the room. Welles received a punch to the head before the interloper realized he had made a serious mistake. On January 26, 1956, Marilyn received the award of the "Women's Division of the Jewish Philanthropies of New York City." She was photographed sitting in Orson Welles's lap. Welles had received the men's award.

Other sources: Leaming 349; *www.cursumperficio.net* /biography/1956

MAE WEST   Hourglass-shaped actress, writer and outrageous sex symbol of the 1930s and beyond. On July 27, 1954, Mae West opened a show at the Sahara in Las Vegas. MM had recently married baseball player Joe DiMaggio and West could not resist getting a dig in when she said, "Why marry a ballplayer when you can have the whole team?" (Leonard 289). The press tried to bait her by asking West her opinion of Marilyn. West said that she had never met her. Upon being told that

Marilyn was being called another Mae West, she shrugged and murmured, "Well, if you want imitations..." (Leonard 288). Eventually, West did concede that Marilyn was the best of the blondes who followed in her footsteps. The rest, she observed, only had "big boobs" (Leonard 288). Later, West said how much she regretted never meeting Marilyn and admitted that she was very beautiful and a wonderful actress. West very nearly did meet MM. At a photo shoot on Santa Monica beach, just a few weeks before Marilyn's death, a "mystery woman," her face concealed by a large straw hat, stood silently watching Marilyn pose for the camera. The photographer, George Barris, later learned that the mysterious watcher was none other than Mae West. Of Mae West, Marilyn said, "I learned a few tricks from her—that impression of laughing at, or mocking, her own sexuality" (McCann 87).

JAMES WHITMORE   Character actor who had a long and distinguished career. In 1950, in one of his first film roles, Whitmore landed a meaty supporting role in *The Asphalt Jungle*, a gritty film-noir which featured MM (*www. imdb.com*).

RICHARD WIDMARK   Academy Award-nominated actor who was often seen in film-noir roles. Widmark was in a movie of that type with MM in 1952, *Don't Bother to Knock*. He was so frustrated by Marilyn's chronic lateness that he was reduced to pacing up and down and loudly complaining, "Where is that goddamn lady?" (Shevey 190). For someone who believed that the more takes he did the worse he became, Widmark was as patient as could be with Marilyn. He would say to her, "Come on, Marilyn. For Crissakes: come on baby" (Shevey 194).

Upon first meeting Marilyn, Widmark thought it was unbelievable that such a beautiful girl could be half crazy. Although he acknowledged her astonishing impact on the screen, Widmark did not like the experience of working with Marilyn in *Don't Bother to Knock* because he simply could not relate to her. She had no connection to the other actors,

and Widmark never felt that he was actually acting with her at all. In 1987 Widmark narrated *Marilyn Monroe: Beyond the Legend*, for cable television (Guiles 201–2; Riese & Hitchens 549; Victor 323; *www.imdb.com*).

BILLY WILDER   Brilliant Vienna–born director, screenwriter and producer. Billy Wilder directed two of MM's most famous films, *The Seven Year Itch* (1955) and *Some Like It Hot* (1959). Wilder developed a love-hate relationship with Marilyn. He thought she was a natural genius in front of the camera but not really an actress. In order to capture a luminous three-minute scene, Marilyn drove Wilder crazy with her extreme lateness, inability to learn lines, multiple neuroses, fears, dependence on her pretentious acting coach, and the need for endless takes. But, no matter what Marilyn did to Wilder's blood pressure, it was worth it in the end. Wilder could see that Marilyn had that special something, a magical "flesh impact" (Zolotow 256). He said of Marilyn that "she looks on the screen as if you could reach out and touch her ... she had a quality no one else ever had on the screen except Garbo." Wilder described making a movie with Marilyn as a long, painful session with the dentist. It was a horrible experience at the time but so very much worth it when it was over. For surviving two motion pictures with Marilyn Monroe, Wilder went on record as saying that the Screen Directors Guild should decorate him with a Purple Heart. For her part, Marilyn thought Wilder was a brilliant director but he was too concerned with the box office.

Marilyn was so often late on *The Seven Year Itch* that the shooting went three weeks longer than scheduled. This cost the studio an extra $30,000 per day, a huge sum in 1955. When the movie was finally completed, Wilder did not invite Marilyn to the wrap party at his house and vowed never to work with her again. But, of course, he changed his mind.

On *Some Like it Hot* Marilyn required an incredible 65 takes to complete a simple scene requiring her to open and close drawers and say, "Where's that bourbon?" In desperation,

Wilder wrote the line out and taped it to the bottom of each drawer. Marilyn, who was probably dyslexic, kept saying "Where's the whisky?" "Where's the bon bon?' and "Where's the bottle?" (Zolotow 263). Marilyn felt under such pressure that she would burst into tears after each flubbed take. That would require more lost time as her makeup had to be reapplied. Wilder never knew what to expect from his star. Later in the same film Marilyn went to the other extreme. She completed a scene with three pages of dialogue in one take. After *Some Like It Hot* wrapped, Wilder said, "I am eating better. My back doesn't ache anymore. I am able to sleep for the first time in months. I can look at my wife without wanting to hit her because she's a woman" (Wood 157).

Wilder ridiculed Marilyn's ambition to improve her craft by studying the Method at the Actors Studio. He did not notice any improvement and suggested that Marilyn would be better off studying railroad engineering because then, at least, she would know how to arrive on time. Marilyn heard Wilder's comment and was hurt by it.

At the time of her death, Wilder and Marilyn had reconciled and were discussing making *Irma La Douce*. The movie was made in 1963 with Shirley MacLaine (Crowe 36–8, 84–7, 158–65; Dick 78–91; Wood 109–14, 152–62; Zolotow 1977, 255–72).

GENE WILDER Academy Award–nominated stage and screen actor known for his comic roles. As a young actor in the 1950s, Gene Wilder took classes at the Actors Studio in New York. Marilyn Monroe was one of Wilder's classmates. Marilyn, attending anonymously and looking like "a hayseed country cousin with freckles," was heard to make some mumbled comments about a scene Wilder had presented (Adams 254).

MICHAEL WILDING British actor once married to Elizabeth Taylor. One afternoon while Taylor was at the studio, Wilding was painting in his Hollywood home when the doorbell rang. The paint-splattered actor opened the door to find MM standing there with a pile of clothing draped over her arm. Wilding explains what happened next:

"Would you think it dreadful of me as a perfect stranger to ask you a favor?" I recovered myself sufficiently to reply, "Ask away."

Shyly, she explained that her studio had suggested the exterior of my house as a picturesque background for some publicity stills. Then pointing at the clothes draped over her arm, she blurted out, "You see. I need some place to change my costumes." "Say no more," I said. "Welcome to Chez Wilding." With a mock bow I ushered her into the hall, explaining that, as my wife was out, she was welcome to use her bedroom. "Thank you so very much," she murmured. Then, with a sudden dimpling smile, she added impishly, "Its odd isn't it? I'm more used to taking off my clothes than putting them on."

Half an hour later there were a timid knock and Marilyn, peering through the half-open study door, said, "I just kinda wanted to thank you for your hospitality." I jumped to my feet and said, "Come on in." She swayed toward me and I noticed beads of perspiration trickling down her forehead. Sitting her on the couch, I said, "You look as if you could do with a drink. How about a glass of champagne?" Leaning back wearily, she lisped, "Bliss. Sheer bliss."

When I returned a few minutes later with a bottle and a couple of glasses, she greeted me with a wan smile and asked, "Do you mind if I take my shoes off? I always take my shoes off when I'm feeling kind of all in." "Take off anything you like," I replied, adding quickly, "I meant that only in the nicest way." She gave me that rainbow smile again and murmured, "You Englishmen only ever mean anything in the nicest way." Suddenly she caught sight of her reflection in a mirror on the wall and with a grimace asked plaintively, "Do I look as lousy as I feel?" Before I could reply she said angrily, "It is all right. You can come out with the truth which is more than mirrors ever do! If you follow me? "Not exactly," I confessed. She cupped her face in her hands and, speaking with the intensity of a child trying to make an impression. She burst out, "Haven't you ever known the feeling that inside you were falling to bits, like a cracked egg? I often feel that way and then I look in the mirror and expect to see my face all coming apart. You know, your eyes pointing in the wrong directions and you have two noses? You know what I mean, a face like a Picasso painting? Just by looking at it you know he's painting a person who's crying inside. My doctor tells me that crying is good for one. But, you see, I can't cry. No matter how bad I feel, I can't cry."

"Your doctor's right," I replied gently. "Tears are a way of letting off steam." She drained her glass and announced that she was due back at the studio in half an hour. At the front door, she put her hand in mine. "I'll remember what you said today about crying being good for you. Maybe, if I try hard enough, I'll learn the knack" [Wilding 90–1].

ESTHER WILLIAMS   Top box-office draw who starred in an unusual genre of motion pictures, the swimming musical. During the 1952 Christmas season, Marilyn was photographed at a party talking with Esther Williams. Williams attended the March 9, 1953, awards ceremony at which Marilyn Monroe was voted "Fastest Rising Star." Marilyn commanded everyone's attention in a dress she had to be sewn into. Williams figured that her own champagne-colored strapless evening gown with matching orchids made her a "classy counterpoint" to MM (Williams 222–3; *www.cursumpeficio.net* /biography/1952).

TENNESSEE WILLIAMS   Pulitzer Prize–winning author who wrote *The Glass Menagerie*, *A Streetcar Named Desire*, *Cat on a Hot Tin Roof*, and *Suddenly Last Summer*. MM regretted losing the leads in the film versions of the last two plays to Elizabeth Taylor. Marilyn was introduced to Williams in New York and, next to her husband Arthur Miller, he became her favorite playwright. Williams had expressed a desire to meet Marilyn and she reciprocated, although she was not sure she understood the humor in his plays. Reportedly, Williams teased Marilyn by disparaging Miller. Marilyn went to a couple of opening nights of Williams's plays and they met again in Hollywood, on the set of *Let's Make Love* (1960). The set was closed to visitors but she invited him to watch her do a dance number.

Williams had wanted Marilyn for *Baby Doll* (1956), a movie he had written about a childlike bride in Mississippi. But director Elia Kazan and the studio would not agree, insisting that Carroll Baker be given the lead role. After the movie was made, Williams said Marilyn would have been ideal for the part because she was a child-woman herself.

In the Actors Studio, Marilyn had portrayed Blanche DuBois in a scene from *A*

*Streetca*r *Named Desire* (Brown & Barham 90; Victor 327; Williams & Mead 233–4).

DON WILSON   Jack Benny's rotund announcer on radio and television. Wilson also appeared in a few films, including *Niagara* (1953) (*www.imdb.com*).

EARL WILSON   Syndicated newspaper columnist. He met MM in July 1949 when she was on a cross-country tour promoting *Love Happy*, a rather indifferent Marx Brothers movie in which she had a very small part. In his first interview with Marilyn, on July 24, 1949, Wilson asked her why she was called the MMmmmmmm Girl. (It was, of course, a studio-supplied nickname). Marilyn replied: "It seems some people couldn't whistle so they went 'MMmmmmmm'" (Riese & Hitchens 555).

Wilson became one of Marilyn's press allies and they maintained an association for the rest of her life. Wilson frequently included items about Marilyn in his column and she would sometimes feed him tidbits of information. In September 1955, when she was secretly seeing Arthur Miller, Wilson asked Marilyn if she had any love interests. She quipped: "No serious interests but I'm always interested" (Riese & Hitchens 556). Five years later, Wilson was given the scoop on Marilyn's upcoming divorce from Miller. As a token of their friendship, Marilyn presented Wilson with an autographed copy of her famous nude calendar. "I hope you like the hairdo" (Riese & Hitchens 556) read the inscription. She later suggested a different version, "I hope you don't mind me not wearing earrings."

WALTER WINCHELL   Influential syndicated newspaper columnist who was also the narrator on television's *The Untouchables* (1959–1962). On September 15, 1954, Winchell was on hand to see MM shoot her famous skirt-blowing scene from *The Seven Year Itch*. Winchell witnessed his friend Joe DiMaggio go into a silent rage as the scene was filmed. Winchell was the only member of the press admitted to Marilyn's funeral. He had known about Marilyn's relationship with the

Kennedys, but never revealed it. In his columns, Winchell suggested that the circumstances surrounding Marilyn's death were suspicious. To his cronies, Winchell bragged that he had bedded MM and rated her performance as merely "average" (Klurfeld 119; Shevey 28, 56, 281–2).

DUKE AND DUCHESS OF WINDSOR
When he abdicated to marry American divorcée Wallis Simpson in 1936, the Duke of Windsor had been King Edward VIII of Great Britain for exactly 325 days. In 1957, New York gossip columnist and socialite Elsa Maxwell threw an April-in-Paris charity ball at which the ex-royal couple were the guests of honor. However, when MM arrived, clad in a backless gown with a plunging neckline, she managed to upstage everyone, including the duke and duchess. Maxwell wrote: "Naturally, when Marilyn came in, all the attention was focused on our table; and there was nearly a stampede" (Martin 436).

SHELLEY WINTERS
Academy Award–winning actress. In light of her later screen image it is hard to imagine that at one time Shelley Winters was considered to be a sexy young starlet, but she was. In 1951, Winters shared men, a mink coat, a two-bedroom apartment and a swimsuit with MM. The apartment was rent controlled so they could afford to fill it with second-hand furniture. The two young actresses would play records in their apartment, classical in the morning and Nat King Cole and Frank Sinatra in the afternoon. Winters, who was six years older (and survived her by 43 years) functioned, by her own account, as Marilyn's role model. When Winters cut her blonde hair short and signed up for acting lessons with Charles Laughton, the Actors Lab and the Actors Studio, Marilyn followed suit. Winters even laid claim to Marilyn's signature open-mouth smile. Marilyn observed how her roommate smiled with her mouth open and asked her why she did that. "Well," replied Winters, "I have slightly buck teeth and when I smile with my mouth open, you can't tell" (Winters 1980, 221). Marilyn

thought the smile was sexy and used it thereafter. Winters was gracious enough to say that Marilyn did it better.

During the making of *Some Like It Hot*, in which her co-stars Jack Lemmon and Tony Curtis were disguised as women, Marilyn found it easier to relate to them if she pretended they were both Shelley Winters.

Winters and Marilyn met in the late 1940s. In those days Marilyn would sit quietly at the studio and watch the working actresses eat lunch. "Her name," remembered Winters, "was Norma Jeane Something. She rarely spoke to us, and when she did, she would whisper. We would shout back at her, 'What did you say?' and that would scare her more. She always wore halter dresses one size too small and carried around a big library book like a dictionary or an encyclopaedia" (Winters 1980, 91).

When Marilyn was in the Canadian Rockies making *River of No Return* (1954), Winters was on location nearby making *Saskatchewan*. Winters visited her friend and observed how the dictatorial director Otto Preminger tried to intimidate Marilyn. She also observed Marilyn's revenge. After filming a scene on a raft, Marilyn slipped while coming ashore. "Watch your step," said Winters, "you can break a leg on this slippery pier" (Winters 1980, 451). That was all the inspiration Marilyn needed. In short order, Marilyn announced that she had broken her leg. Too prove it, she started hobbling around with crutches and a plaster cast. Preminger was tamed. Said Winters: "Dumb? Like a fox, was my young friend Marilyn. That night we celebrated at a nightclub, and at one point she was doing a sort of rhumba.... For God's sake, Marilyn, sit down! You're supposed to be crippled!" (Winters 1980, 453).

Other sources: Summers 123–4; Winters 1980, 91–3, 235, 306–9, 445–53; Winters 1989, 32–7, 42–9, 212–17, 269–73

ESTELLE WINWOOD
Character actress who specialized playing ladylike eccentrics. Winwood, who lived to be 101, was born 43 years before MM, yet survived her by nearly

22 years. Winwood had a small part in *The Misfits* (1961) as an eccentric church lady collecting donations in a bar. During the making of that film, a star-struck extra approached Marilyn and asked her if she was really who she appeared to be. Marilyn donned Estelle Winwood's wig and said, "No, I'm Mitzi Gaynor" (Goode 117; *www.imdb.com*).

NORMAN WISDOM   British film comedian, singer and actor. Wisdom was the star of a number of low-budget British film comedies, one of which was being made at Pinewood Studios at the same time Marilyn was making *The Prince and the Showgirl* with Sir Laurence Olivier. Wisdom remembered how Marilyn "came in to watch my work. In fact, she quite unintentionally ruined a couple of takes. Obviously, of course, once the director has said 'Action,' everyone must remain silent, no matter how funny the situation might be, but Marilyn just could not help laughing, and on two occasions she was politely escorted off the set. The nicest thing that happened was that we passed each other in the long hallway one lunchtime. It was crowded, but she still caught hold of me, kissed and hugged me, and walked away laughing. Everybody in the hall could not believe it, and I remember my director, Bob Asher, shouting out, 'You lucky little swine'—I agreed with him" (Morgan 203).

NATALIE WOOD   Former child actress who became a major star as an adult. In 1948, when she was only ten years old, Natalie Wood was in a forgettable movie called *Scudda Hoo! Scudda Hay!* In the film an unknown blonde starlet had a walk-on in a scene with Wood and June Haver. It ended up on the cutting room floor. The blonde was, of course, MM and the movie usually considered to be her first screen appearance. Years later, Wood said: "When you look at Marilyn on the screen, you don't want anything bad to happen to her. You really care that she should be all right ... happy" (Riese & Hitchens 337).

In September 1959, Soviet Premier Nikita Khrushchev, on a state visit to the United States, came for a tour of the Twentieth Century–Fox studio. Among the bevy of celebrities on hand was Marilyn Monroe. When Khrushchev stopped to speak to Marilyn, she was prepared. The Russian–speaking Natalie Wood had taught Marilyn to give Khrushchev a greeting in his own language. Marilyn said: "We, the workers of Twentieth Century–Fox, rejoice that you have come to visit our studio and country" (Winters 1989, 308).

Wood encountered Marilyn the night before she died, at a party at Peter Lawford's beach house. Wood recalled overhearing Marilyn mumbling to herself, "Thirty-six, thirty-six, thirty-six—it's all over" (Finstad 2001, 245). When Marilyn was found dead a few hours later, Wood was shocked and worried that she too would end up dead and alone after taking too many pills.

JOANNE WOODWARD   Accomplished film actress. Six weeks before MM's death, Woodward had this to say about her: "Marilyn is quite a product of our generation and it would be an honor for any girl to emulate her" (*Los Angeles Herald-Examiner* 6/24/62). The occasion was Marilyn's rejection of *The Stripper*. The role was given to Woodward, who made the film the year after Marilyn's death. The film was based on a Broadway play by William Inge, *A Loss of Roses*. In 1956, Marilyn had given an acclaimed performance in Inge's *Bus Stop* and, on the basis of that, was approached to do the latter movie (Godfrey 116; *www.imdb.com*).

MONTY WOOLLEY   Actor whose most famous role was *The Man Who Came to Dinner* (1942). Monty Woolley was in the cast of the 1951 MM movie, *As Young as You Feel* (Riese & Hitchens; *www.imdb.com*).

FRANK LLOYD WRIGHT   Famed architect MM went to see Wright at his New York hotel in 1958. She wanted Wright to design a dream house for her and her husband, Arthur Miller, in Roxbury, Connecticut. Wright was enchanted by the glamorous movie star, although upon being asked how he liked Marilyn Monroe, he simply said, "She carries herself well" (Tafel 68). Although he was 91 years old at the time, Wright came out to the site and, because it was after dark, inspected it with a flashlight. Miller remembered Wright's visit differently: "It was Marilyn's idea to bring Wright up, and one day the three of us drove up. Wright went to sleep in the back seat. I got a speeding ticket for doing 48 in a 45 mph zone. It was a gray afternoon by the time we got up there. We had smoked salmon and a few cold things. Wright warned me against pepper but I had a little anyway. He and I walked up to the high ground where there was an old orchard above a pasture, which faces north but has an endless view over the hills. He took one look and then peed and said, 'Good spot,' and we walked down" (Tafel 68).

For a $100,000, fee Wright provided the Millers with a portfolio of his architectural drawings. These were based on a design he had prepared for a couple in Texas and a Mexican politician, all of whom had failed to build it. Marilyn was thinking of children, so Wright included an elaborate nursery in the plans. *Architectural Digest* described the plan as "a modernist *Xanadu*. It had a circular living room with a domed ceiling sixty feet in diameter supported by fieldstone columns, each five feet thick. A seventy-foot swimming pool was cantilevered into the hillside, and Wright had also imagined a conference room, a chauffeured limousine in the driveway and a pennant flying from the roof ... but there was only one bedroom." The plan proved to be too rich for the Millers, the swimming pool alone would have cost $250,000! In any case, Marilyn and Arthur soon separated.

Frank Lloyd Wright's granddaughter was the actress Anne Baxter. Baxter was in three of Marilyn's early films: *A Ticket to Tomahawk* (1950), *All About Eve* (1950), and *O'Henry's Full House* (1952) (Gill 475; Gottfried 2003, 314; Victor 329).

WILLIAM WYLER   Award–winning director who was on MM's list of approved film makers. Marilyn never worked with him but, at one point, Wyler was considered for the film which became *The Prince and the Showgirl*

(1957). Wyler and Marilyn probably met at a New Year's Eve party in 1948 (*www.cursumperficio.net* /biography/1948).

JANE WYMAN   Academy Award–winning actress who was Ronald Reagan's first wife. It is no understatement to say that MM and Wyman were not close. Wyman had married a man with whom Marilyn had fallen in love, Fred Karger, a musician at Columbia studio. (Wyman was actually married to Karger twice, 1952–1954, and 1961–1965.) On November 1, 1952, Marilyn and columnist Sidney Skolsky happened to be having dinner at the same swank Beverly Hills restaurant at which Wyman and Karger were dining. Skolsky recalled: "The only bitchy thing I ever saw Marilyn do occurred one night at Chasen's restaurant. As we approached the checkroom, there was an event taking place in the large private party room.... Marilyn and I were told that the Fred Karger and Jane Wyman wedding party was in the room. Marilyn said she had to go in and congratulate Fred. She knew this would burn up Jane Wyman. She boldly crashed the reception and congratulated Fred. As Marilyn and Jane were pretending they didn't know the other was in the same room, the tension in the atmosphere would have been as easy to cut as the wedding cake" (Morella & Epstein 1985, 177).

A couple of years later, when *The Seven Year Itch* was playing in Los Angeles, Marilyn played a practical joke on Wyman. In the middle of the night, Marilyn and a couple of friends, one of whom was Karger's first wife, stole a life-size cardboard image of Marilyn in her famous skirt-blowing scene from Grauman's Theater. They stuck the cut-out in the middle of Wyman's front lawn. Wyman was not amused by the prank (Miller 1987, 468–9; Riese & Hitchens 566; Summers 58; Victor 330).

-Y-

SUSANNAH YORK   British–born actress. Director John Huston wanted MM to co-star with Montgomery Clift in his biographical movie, *Freud*, about the life of Sigmund Freud. But Marilyn's analyst advised against it and she did not do it. Susannah York got the part instead (Victor 106; *www.imdb.com*).

ALAN YOUNG   Canadian actor whose claim to fame was being a horse's co-star in television's *Mr. Ed* (1960–1965). In 1946 *The Alan Young Radio Show* sponsored a float in the annual Hollywood Christmas Parade. Twentieth Century–Fox sent over some starlets for the occasion. After the parade, the participants retired to the Brown Derby for refreshments. Young found himself sitting next to one of the starlets, a shy, quiet and very beautiful 20-year-old by the name of Norma Jeane Dougherty. On an impulse, Young asked her to go to a party the following evening. After a moment of hesitation, she agreed. At the time, Norma Jeane was living with a foster parent who was a practitioner of Christian Science. Young realized that he and his date had a mutual connection to the Christian Science Church. On the way to the party, Norma Jeane recalled how much she had enjoyed going to Sunday school. After an uneventful party, the evening ended with a peck on the cheek, and that was that.

Six years later, in 1952, Young was in the makeup chair in the RKO studios for *Androcles and the Lion*, when a stunning blonde walked in.

> "Alan," she said delightedly. "How are you?"
> "Fine," I replied. "How are you?"
> I wanted to say "Who are you?" because I hadn't a clue who she was. We spoke for a few moments in generalities. Then she kissed me on the cheek and took off. My makeup man was impressed. "Wow, you're a friend of Marilyn Monroe?" he said admiringly.
> Now I remembered. On a neighboring sound stage, Marilyn—Norma was shooting *Clash by Night*—a movie that would take her out of fourth or fifth billing and turn her into the world's hottest movie star. I never met her again.
> But I've never forgotten Norma Jean [sic], a little girl who loved her Sunday school [Young & Burt 108].

In 1955, Young was in *Gentlemen Marry Brunettes* the lackluster sequel to MM's *Gen-*

tlemen Prefer Blondes (1953). If Marilyn ever watched Alan Young in *Mr. Ed* there is no record of it (*www.imdb.com*).

LORETTA YOUNG   An Academy Award–winning actress who had a long career in film and television. On November 6, 1954, Young was one of 80 guests at a star-studded dinner party at Romanoff's, a swank Beverly Hills restaurant. The evening was to celebrate the completion of *The Seven Year Itch* and to honor its star, MM. Young was seated at a table which had a cardboard centerpiece of Marilyn in the skirt-blowing scene from the film (Leaming 1998, 134).

-Z-

DARRYL F. ZANUCK   Studio head, screenwriter and producer at Twentieth Century–Fox. For $75 a week, Zanuck signed MM to her first six-month movie contract on August 26, 1946. Even though Marilyn became his studio's biggest box-office draw, Zanuck never supported her.

In 1970, he recalled his first meeting with Marilyn and the nude calendar scandal.

> One day, a great friend of mine, Joseph M. Schenck, brought over to my home in Palm Springs this very beautiful girl who was also on the plump side. I didn't jump up and say, "Oh, this is a great star," or anything like that. Later on, Joe said, "If you can work her in some role or something, some, you know, supporting role, do so." I did, but I didn't think I had found any gold mine.
> Then came the calendar, with pictures of her nude. When it turned up, everybody said, "Oh my God, how can we suppress it?" But one man, Harry Brand, who was in charge of publicity, said, "This isn't going to kill her. It's going to make her. I'd like to get a piece of this business." She ended up on ashtrays and on everything else, and we never got a penny of kickback on any of it. John Huston gave her a hell of a good role in *The Asphalt Jungle*. Jesus, she was good in it. I thought it must have been the magic of Huston, because I didn't think she had all that in her. But then I put her in *All About Eve* as George Sanders' aspiring-actress protégé, and she was an overnight sensation [*Look* 11/3/1970].

Marilyn did not think that Zanuck liked or respected her. She said: "Mr. Zanuck had never seen me as an actress with star quality. He thought I was some kind of freak. Studio bosses are jealous of their power. They are like political bosses. They want to pick out their own candidates for public office. They don't want the public rising up and dumping a girl they consider 'unphotogenic in their laps'" (Riese & Hitchens 568–9). Marilyn's assessment was essentially correct. Although he reluctantly acknowledged her screen appeal, Zanuck thought Marilyn was a jumped-up nobody, with little talent, who got to where she was via the casting couch. He already had Betty Grable so he didn't need another blonde. When asked about the casting couch, Zanuck replied: "Not even Marilyn Monroe. I hated her. I wouldn't have slept with her if she'd paid me" (Churchwell 209).

Zanuck saw Marilyn as a personality, not an actress, and kept trying to put her in pictures that emphasized cleavage over acting skill. After he viewed the rushes of *Gentlemen Prefer Blondes*, Marilyn had to sing privately for Zanuck before he would believe she had done her own singing in the film. Not surprisingly, Marilyn objected to this treatment: "I want to be an artist, not an erotic freak. I don't want to be sold to the public as a celluloid aphrodisiac. It was all right the first few years. But now it's different" (Summers 71).

After the quick successes of *Niagara*, *Gentlemen Prefer Blondes*, and *How to Marry a Millionaire* (all in 1953), Marilyn figured that she deserved some respect and a decent paycheck. Zanuck did not see it that way and refused to renegotiate her contract. After being forced to do two mediocre films, *River of No Return* and *There's No Business Like Show Business* (both 1954), Marilyn rebelled and went into hiding. After a complicated legal fight, Marilyn severed her ties to Fox until she got what she wanted. Marilyn returned to Fox in triumph in February 1956, one month before Zanuck resigned. (Zanuck returned to Fox in 1962, the year Marilyn died.)

Other sources: Riese & Hitchens 568–70; Summers 69, 72, 82

FRANCO ZEFFIRELLI Italian film, theatre and opera director. In the 1950s and 1960s, Zeffirelli established his reputation by mounting stage productions in London and New York. After the New York opening of his version of Shakespeare's *Romeo and Juliet*, Zeffirelli went to a party given by Lee Strasberg of the Actors Studio. He was introduced to Strasberg's most famous student. Zeffirelli wrote: "Rather out of place among them was Marilyn Monroe. Although a Hollywood star, Marilyn was trying to improve her skills as an actress and was sensitive about her image as a scatterbrained sex-goddess—though it must be said that that was the role she adopted most often even off-camera, giving the impression it was the real one for her. She was particularly simpering that night, apologizing for not having been at the performance; it was just impossible for her to go anywhere because of the crowds, so she never got to see anything. She giggled embarrassingly and we all agreed it was an awful destiny for her and I suggested we might put on a special matinee behind locked doors for those deprived stars who otherwise wouldn't get to see Shakespeare" (Zeffirelli 168).

Strasberg wanted Zeffirelli to cast Marilyn in Chekhov's *The Three Sisters*, but the Italian was reluctant. MM and Zeffirelli were never to work together. He was worried about Marilyn's voice and nervousness before a live audience. Nevertheless, he agreed to meet her the next day for lunch. Marilyn arrived incognito and they discussed the play. Zeffirelli found her "very bright in a cuckoo sort of way," but not right for any of the sisters in the play. As a consolation he suggested the part of Natasha, the sister-in-law. Zeffirelli wrote: "I knew she had lost interest. She wanted me to tell her she was great and would be greater, that we'd start rehearsals in forty days and open in Boston before Broadway, but I couldn't. It was five o'clock and dark outside when we parted. As she was getting into her taxi, something seemed to click into place for her, as if what I had said made sense. She told me she would perhaps like to consider Natasha and that maybe I was right" (Zeffirelli 169).

FRED ZINNEMANN   Four-time Academy Award–winner. According to the 1955 list she presented to Twentieth Century–Fox, Zinnemann's name was one of 16 film directors with whom Marilyn was willing to work. Despite her confidence in Zinnemann, a collaboration never occurred (Victor 81).

Notes

Introduction

1. This tiny detail has not deterred Haugensund, the small Norwegian city where Mortensen was born, from erecting a life-sized sculpture of Marilyn Monroe.

2. When Gladys died in 1984, she was 81 years old and had outlived her famous daughter by more than 20 years.

3. Marilyn Monroe would return to RKO for a secondary role in *Clash by Night* (1952).

4. "Carole Lind" and "Jean Monroe" were also considered. Norma Jeane did not legally change her name to Marilyn Monroe until March 12, 1956.

5. Even though it was filmed second, *Dangerous Years* was the first Marilyn Monroe film to be released. It came out five months before *Scudda Hoo! Scudda Hay!*

6. Marilyn's first husband, Jim Dougherty, had joined the Los Angeles Police Department and was assigned to crowd control at Grauman's Egyptian theater the night *The Asphalt Jungle* premiered. Fortunately, Marilyn was a no-show, so Jim did not have to endure an awkward encounter with his ex-wife.

7. Jim Dougherty was one of the first to learn of his former wife's death. The police officer who arrived at Marilyn's home was a friend of Dougherty's and phoned to tell him the tragic news.

Encyclopedia

1. To see Edie Adams impersonate Marilyn Monroe go to www.youtube.com and search "Edie Adams as Marilyn."

2. Television host Jack Paar acted opposite Marilyn in *Love Nest* (1951).

3. After Marilyn Monroe's death, Allen wrote some murder mysteries, at least five of which had passing references to her.

4. The Ambassador Hotel in Los Angeles housed the Blue Book Modeling Studio and Agency, at which the 19-year-old Norma Jeane Dougherty began her modeling career in 1945.

5. Marilyn is reported to have once given an interview (while in the nude) to Wohlander (Summers 44).

6. From 1949–50, Marilyn lived at another address on North Palm Drive.

7. In *Ladies of the Chorus* Marilyn sang "Every Baby Needs a Da-Da Daddy." In 1952, the number was edited into another Columbia feature, *Okinawa*, in which it is viewed by soldiers embarking on a troop ship (www.imdb.com).

8. To see a clip from this episode of *I Love Lucy* go to www.youtube.com and search "I Love Lucy-Lucy being Marilyn Monroe."

9. To see Marilyn Monroe as Theda Bara, go to www.marilynmonroe.ca.

10. To see this photo (mislabeled carnation), go to www.cursumperficio.net /files/B/Beaton Cecil.

11. *The Hostage* contains a brief reference to Marilyn when the character Teresa says, "I'm not Marilyn Monroe or Jayne Mansfield."

12. To see "The Honolulu Trip," go to www.youtube.com and search "Jack Benny and Marilyn Monroe." Ten years later, on November 26, 1963, Benny did the skit again, this time with Jayne Mansfield.

13. The terms of Marilyn's contract with 20th Century–Fox prohibited her from accepting payment for her appearance on the Benny program (Victor 33).

14. Berle had forgotten one later meeting: Marilyn and Berle were at a press conference for *Let's Make Love* on January 16, 1960 (www.cursumperficio.net/files/ Berle).

15. To see Marilyn's impression of Clara Bow, go to www.marilynmonroe.ca.

16. Some say they met in 1951, while Brando was working on *A Streetcar Named Desire* (www.cursumperficio.net biography/1954).

17. *The Asphalt Jungle* was, in fact, Marilyn Monroe's sixth motion picture.

18. Durango, Colorado, not Durango, Mexico.

19. The president's actual birthday was May 29.

20. Sale must have been aware of Marilyn's problems with punctuality as he had directed her the year before in *A Ticket to Tomahawk*.

21. It is interesting to note that Carson was a Canadian and there is no evidence that he ever filed for American citizenship. (www.wikipedia.org)

22. Charisse may not have been aware that, four days before Marilyn's death, Twentieth Century–Fox resigned Marilyn to complete the film (Victor 285).

23. Because of legal complications, Mrs. Chekhov never received any money from Marilyn's estate. She died in 1970 (Victor 53).

24. Sharp-eyed film buffs claim to have spotted Marilyn as an uncredited extra in a third film—*Green Grass of Wyoming* (1948).

25. Marilyn may have been sarcastic here. There were rumors that Crawford was an unfit mother, and Marilyn may have heard them (Guiles 214n).

26. Crawford was mistaken. As anyone who has seen *The Prince and the Showgirl* (1957) can attest, Marilyn knew how to curtsy. She does so several times in the film.

27. Needless to say, the story arose that Marilyn was

responsible for parachutes that life *does* depend on and that one day a pilot was killed because of a parachute she had improperly packed (Guiles 85n).

28. To see Marilyn as Marlene Dietrich, go to and search Gallery-Avedon.

29. The wedding ring was sold at an auction on October 28, 1999, for $772,500.

30. Eban's memory may be faulty here. Other biographers do not record Marilyn Monroe and Senator Kennedy being together at this time. Photographs exist of Marilyn at the game, but not Kennedy.

31. To see the results of Eisenstaedt's work with Marilyn go to /files/E/Eisenstaedt Alfred.

32. Engel has brief mentions of Marilyn Monroe in at least two of his novels, *A City Called July* and *Murder on Location.*

33. Betty Grable was married to bandleader Harry James, and Lauren Bacall was married to Humphrey Bogart.

34. Faulkner was probably unaware that, during this period, Marilyn Monroe and Eleanor Roosevelt were neighbors in New York City (Arnold 1987, 23).

35. The event was dramatized by Bonnie Greer in 2006, as *Marilyn and Ella.*

36. It should be noted that the 59-year-old Gable had been a three-pack-a-day smoker.

37. When the film was finally made, in 1964, it had a different director (Ken Hughes), and Kim Novak was the female lead.

38. Marilyn's "big" scene had her walk down some church steps and say, "Hi, Rad," to Haver. Haver then replies to Marilyn, "Oh, hi, Betty." You can see it on : "Marilyn Monroe Scudda Hoo! Scudda Hay!"

39. Actually, it was Artie Shaw's "Begin the Beguine," on the phonograph.

40. Hellman was one of many who assumed that any blonde who looked like Marilyn Monroe had to be an incompetent in the kitchen. There is evidence that Marilyn became an accomplished cook, and that she even toyed with the notion of writing a cook book (Banner 213, 220–1).

41. To see Marilyn Monroe's F.B.I. file, go to: foia.fbi.gov/foiaindex/monroe,htm.

42. Not to challenge Leachman's veracity, but I can find no other reference to Ted Kennedy and Marilyn Monroe being in the same room at the same time.

43. As it turned out, the book was never adapted as a movie.

44. Although the two women had no direct contact, Wendy Leigh wrote a novel, *The Secret Letters of Marilyn Monroe and Jacqueline Kennedy* (2003), in which they did.

45. President Kennedy's actual birthday was ten days later, on May 29.

46. The dress Marilyn wore that night was sold at auction, on October 26, 1999, for $1,267,500.

47. Mandrax, a powerful sedative.

48. To see Harold Lloyd's photographs of Marilyn Monroe go to /files/L/Lloyd Harold.

49. McMahon must have been mistaken. In 1953, Marilyn had no plans to travel to Korea to entertain the troops; the decision to do so was made at the last minute. In February 1954, while visiting Japan, an Army general asked her to come over to Korea to boost the morale of the troops. Marilyn agreed.

50. Her name was misspelled as Marion Makeba (files/ John F. Kennedy).

51. Upon learning of her conversion to Judaism, the governments of Egypt and Syria banned Marilyn's films.

52. It is generally accepted that Marilyn and Miller met in early 1951. Mitchell provides an alternate scenario.

53. In 1952, Mitchell was in *Okinawa*, which features Marilyn in clips from *Ladies of the Chorus* (1948).

54. Moore was also in *Okinawa* (1952), which features Marilyn in clips from *Ladies of the Chorus* (1948).

55. To see an excerpt from the *Person to Person* interview, go to : "Marilyn Monroe Person to Person."

56. Technically, Pat O'Brien was in a third MM movie, 1952's *Okinawa*, which features Marilyn in clips from *Ladies of the Chorus* (1948).

57. *Ladies of the Chorus* was, in fact, Marilyn's third movie.

58. Preminger and Marilyn probably first met at a New Year's Eve party, in 1948 (www.cursumperficio.net/biography/1948).

59. Puente can be forgiven for believing a popular Hollywood legend. In fact, Lana Turner was discovered at the Top Hat Malt Shop, not Schwab's (Schwarz 312–13).

60. Quinn's memory may have become a little hazy with the passage of time. While Marilyn *did* visit Brando in the studio, there is no other claim that Marilyn Monroe ever set foot in Brownsville, Texas.

61. In a 1998 interview, Rooney claimed to have invented the Marilyn Monroe name. It was, he said, a combination of the stage actress Marilyn Miller and a screenwriter by the name of Monroe Manning (Schwarz 176–7).

62. When Lee Strasberg died, in 1982, the estate of Marilyn Monroe passed into the hands of a woman with whom she was only slightly acquainted: Lee's second wife, Anna. Lee had married Anna a year after the death of his first wife, Paula. Marilyn Monroe did not die a wealthy woman, but her estate earns million in royalties each year.

63. The inspiration for Marilyn Monroe's birth name may be less glamorous. For a time, Marilyn's mother, Gladys, worked for a couple with a daughter named Norma Jeane.

64. Van Doren must be mistaken. On May 13, 1959, Marilyn went to the Italian Cultural Institute in New York to collect her David di Donatello Award in person.

Bibliography

Adams, Cindy. *Lee Strasberg: The Imperfect Genius of the Actors Studio.* Garden City, NY: Doubleday, 1980.

Allyson, June. *June Allyson.* New York: G. P. Putnam's Sons, 1982.

Amburn, Ellis. *The Sexiest Man Alive: A Biography of Warren Beatty.* New York: HarperEntertainment, 2002.

Anderson, Christopher. *Citizen Jane: The Turbulent Life of Jane Fonda.* New York: Henry Holt, 1990.

Anderson, Janice. *Marilyn Monroe.* New York: Crescent, 1983.

Anonymous. *Images of Marilyn Monroe.* Bath, England: Parragon, 2008.

Arce, Hector. *Groucho.* New York: G. P. Putnam's Sons, 1979.

Arnold, Eve. *Flashback! The 50s.* New York: Alfred A. Knopf, 1978.

_____. *Marilyn Monroe: An Appreciation.* New York: Viking, 1987.

_____. *The Unretouched Woman.* London: Jonathan Cape, 1976.

Atlas, James. *Bellow: A Biography.* New York: Random House, 2000.

Bacall, Lauren. *By Myself.* New York: Alfred A. Knopf, 1979.

Baker, Carroll. *Baby Doll: An Autobiography.* New York: Arbor House, 1983.

Baker, Roger. *Marilyn Monroe.* New York: Crescent, 1990.

Baltake, Joe. *The Films of Jack Lemmon.* Secaucus, NJ: The Citadel Press, 1977.

Banner, Lois. *MM—Personal: From the Private Archives of Marilyn Monroe.* New York: Abrams, 2011.

Barra, Allen. *Yogi Berra: Eternal Yankee.* New York: W. W. Norton, 2009.

Beaver, James N. *John Garfield: His Life and Films.* South Brunswick and New York: A. S. Barnes, 1978.

Behlmer, Rudy. *America's Favorite Movies: Behind the Scenes.* New York: Frederick Ungar, 1982.

Ben Cramer, Richard. *Joe Dimaggio: The Hero's Life.* New York: Simon & Schuster, 2000.

Benny, Jack, and Joan Benny. *Sunday Nights at Seven: The Jack Benny Story.* New York: Warner, 1990.

Benson, Jackson J. *The True Adventures of John Steinbeck, Writer.* New York: Viking, 1984.

Bergreen, Lawrence. *As Thousands Cheer: The Life of Irving Berlin.* New York: Viking, 1990.

Berle, Milton, and Haskel Frankel. *Milton Berle: An Autobiography.* New York: Delacorte, 1974.

Bernard, Susan. *Bernard of Hollywood's Marilyn.* New York: St. Martin's Press, 1993.

Bilman, Larry. *Fred Astaire: A Bio-Bibliography.* Westport, CT: Greenwood Press, 1997.

Blotner, Joseph. *Faulkner: A Biography.* New York: Random House, 1984.

Bockris, Victor. *The Life and Death of Andy Warhol.* New York: Bantam, 1989.

Bogdanovich, Peter. *Fritz Lang in America.* New York: Praeger, 1967.

Bogle, Donald. *Dorothy Dandridge: A Biography.* New York: Amistad, 1997.

Bosworth, Patricia. *Montgomery Clift: A Biography.* New York: Harcourt Brace Jovanovich, 1978.

Boyd, Brian. *Vladimir Nabokov: The American Years.* Princeton, NJ: Princeton University Press, 1991.

Brady, Kathleen. *Lucille: The Life of Lucille Ball.* New York: Billboard, 2001.

Braun, Eric. *Doris Day.* London: Weidenfeld and Nicolson, 1991.

Bret, David. *Maria Callas: The Tigress and the Lamb.* New York: Robson/Parkhust, 1998.

Brian, Dennis. *Tallulah Darling: A Biography of Tallulah Bankhead.* New York: Macmillan, 1980.

Brown, Peter Harry, and Pat H. Broeske. *Howard Hughes: The Untold Story.* New York: Dutton, 1996.

Brown, Peter Harry, and Patte B. Barham. *Marilyn: The Last Take.* New York: Dutton, 1992.

Brown, Richard. "Marilyn Monroe Reading Ulysses: Goddess or Post-Cultural Cyborg?" In: Kershner, R. B., ed. *Joyce and Popular Culture.* Gainesville: University Press of Florida, 1996.

Bruccoli, Matthew J., ed. *Conversations with Ernest Hemingway.* Jackson: University Press of Mississippi, 1986.

_____. *Selected Letters of John O'Hara.* New York: Random House, 1978.

Bryer, Jackson R., ed. *Conversations with Lillian Hellman.* Jackson: University Press of Mississippi, 1986.

Buckle, Richard, ed. *Self Portrait with Friends: The Selected Diaries of Cecil Beaton 1926–1974.* London: Book Club Associates, 1980.

169

Buckley, Jr., William F. *A Hymnal: The Controversial Arts*. New York: Berkley, 1981.

Caesar, Sid, and Eddy Friedfeld. *Caesar's Hours: My Life in Comedy, with Love and Laughter*. New York: Public Affairs, 2003.

Cahn, Sammy. *I Should Care: The Sammy Cahn Story*. New York: Arbor House, 1974.

Calhoun, Ward, and Benjamin DeWalt, eds. *Marilyn Monroe: A Photographic Celebration*. Irvington, NY: Hylas, 2008.

Callow, Simon. *Charles Laughton: A Difficult Actor*. New York: Grove Press, 1987.

Capote, Truman. *The Dogs Bark: Public People and Private Places*. New York: Random House, 1973.
_____. *Music for Chameleons*. New York: Random House, 1980.

Capra, Frank. *Frank Capra, the Name Above the Title: An Autobiography*. New York: Macmillan, 1971.

Capua, Michelangelo. *Yul Brynner: A Biography*. Jefferson, NC: McFarland, 2006.

Carey, Gary. *Anita Loos: A Biography*. New York: Alfred A. Knopf, 1988.
_____. *Judy Holliday: An Intimate Life Story*. New York: Seaview, 1982.

Carey, Macdonald. *The Days of My Life*. New York: St. Martin's Press, 1991.

Carr, Virginia Spencer. *The Lonely Hunter: A Biography of Carson McCullers*. Garden City, NY: Doubleday, 1975.

Channing, Carol. *Just Lucky I Guess: A Memoir of Sorts*. New York: Simon & Schuster, 2002.

Charity, Tom. *John Cassavetes: Lifeworks*. London: Omnibus Press, 2001.

Churchill, Sarah. *Keep On Dancing*. New York: Coward, McCann & Geoghegan, 1981.

Churchwell, Sarah. *The Many Lives of Marilyn Monroe*. London: Granta, 2004.

Clarke, Donald. *All or Nothing at All: A Life of Frank Sinatra*. London: Pan, 1997.
_____. *Capote: A Biography*. New York: Simon and Schuster, 1988.

Clooney, Rosemary, and Joan Barthel. *Girl Singer: An Autobiography*. New York: Broadway, 1999.

Collins, Joan. *Past Imperfect: An Autobiography*. New York: Simon and Schuster, 1978.

Conover, David. *Finding Marilyn: A Romance*. New York: Grosset & Dunlap, 1981.

Considine, Shaun. *Bette & Joan: The Divine Feud*. New York: Dell, 1989.
_____. *Mad as Hell: The Life and Work of Paddy Chayefsky*. New York: Random House, 1994.

Cooke, Alistair. *America Discovered: From the 1940s to the 1980s*. New York: Alfred A. Knopf, 1988.

Corliss, Richard. "Marilyn Lost and Found." *Time*, May 25, 2001.

Cotten, Joseph. *Vanity Will Get You Somewhere*. San Francisco: Mercury House, 1987.

Cottrell, John. *Laurence Olivier*. Englewood Cliffs, NJ: Prentice-Hall, 1975.

Coward, Noel. *The Letters of Noel Coward*. New York: Vintage, 2009.

Cox, Stephen, and Jim Terry. *One Fine Stooge: Larry Fine's Frizzy Life in Pictures: An Authorized Biography*. Nashville: Cumberland House, 2006.

Crawley, Tony, ed. *The Wordsworth Dictionary of Film Quotations*. Ware, England: Wordsworth Reference, 1994.

Crist, Judith. *The Private Eye, the Cowboy and the Very Naked Girl: Movies from Cleo to Clyde*. New York: Holt, Rinehart and Winston, 1968.

Cronin, I., and Ben Siegel, eds. *Conversations with Saul Bellow*. Jackson: University Press of Mississippi, 1974.

Crowe, Cameron. *Conversations with Wilder*. New York: Alfred A. Knopf, 1999.

Curtis, Tony. *Tony Curtis: The Autobiography*. New York: William Morrow, 1993.

Dalton, David. *James Dean: The Mutant King*. New York: St. Martin's Press, 1974.

Darlow, Michael. *Terence Rattigan: The Man and His Work*. London: Quartet, 2000.

David, Lester, and Irene David. *Bobby Kennedy: The Making of a Folk Hero*. New York: Dodd, Mead, 1986.

Davis, Sammy, Jr., Jane Boyar, and Burt Boyar. *Why Me?: The Sammy Davis, Jr. Story*. New York: Farrar, Straus and Giroux, 1989.

De Dienes, André. *Marilyn Mon Amour*. New York: St. Martin's Press, 1985.

De La Hoz, Cindy. *Marilyn Monroe: Platinum Fox*. Philadelphia: Running Press, 2007.

DePaulo, Lisa. "The Strange, Still Mysterious Death of Marilyn Monroe," *Playboy*, December 2005.

Dewey, Donald. *Marcello Mastroianni: His Life and Art*. New York: Birch Lane Press, 1993.

Dick, Bernard F. *Billy Wilder*. Boston: Twayne, 1980.

Dietrich, Marlene. *Marlene*. New York: Grove Press, 1987.

Dittman, Michael J. *Jack Kerouac: A Biography*. Westport, CT: Greenwood Press, 2004.

Doll, Susan. *Marilyn: Her Life & Legend*. Lincolnwood, IL: Publications International, 1990.

Douglas, Kirk. *Let's Face It: 90 Years of Living, Loving and Learning*. Hoboken: Wiley, 2007.

Dyer, Richard. *Heavenly Bodies: Film Stars and Society*. 2d. ed. London: Routledge, 1986.

Eban, Abba. *Abba Eban: An Autobiography*. London: Weidenfeld and Nicolson, 1978.

Eden, Barbara, and Wendy Leigh. *Jeannie Out of the Bottle*. New York: Crown Archetype, 2011.

Edwards, Anne. *Judy Garland: A Biography*. New York: Simon and Schuster, 1974.
_____. *Vivien Leigh: A Biography*. New York: Simon and Schuster, 1977.

Eells, George. *Hedda and Louella: A Dual Biography of Hedda Hopper and Louella Parsons.* New York: G. P. Putnam's Sons, 1972.

_____. *Robert Mitchum.* New York: Franklin Watts, 1984.

Eisenstaedt, Alfred, and Arthur A. Goldsmith. *The Eye of Eisenstaedt.* New York: Viking, 1969.

Eisner, Lotte H. *Fritz Lang.* London: Secker & Warburg, 1976.

Eliot, Marc. *Cary Grant.* New York: Harmony, 2004.

Engelberg, Morris, and Marv Schneider. *DiMaggio: Setting the Record Straight.* St. Paul, MN: M.B.I., 2003.

Epstein, Daniel Mark. *Nat King Cole.* New York: Farrar, Straus and Giroux, 1999.

Epstein, Helen. *Joe Papp: An American Life.* Boston: Little, Brown, 1994.

Epstein, Joseph. *Fred Astaire.* New Haven: Yale University Press, 2008.

Evans, Mike. *Marilyn Handbook.* London: MQ Publications, 2004.

Evans, Peter. *Peter Sellers: The Man Behind the Mask.* New York: New American Library, 1980.

Faris, Jocelyn. *Jayne Mansfield: A Bio-Bibliography.* Westport, CT: Greenwood Press, 1994.

Fensch, Thomas, ed. *Conversations with James Thurber.* Jackson: University Press of Mississippi, 1989.

Fetherling, Doug. *The Five Lives of Ben Hecht.* New York: Zoetrope, 1977.

Finch, Christopher. *Rainbow: The Stormy Life of Judy Garland.* New York: Ballantine, 1975.

Finstad, Suzanne. *Natasha: The Biography of Natalie Wood.* New York: Harmony, 2001.

_____. *Warren Beatty: A Private Man.* New York: Random House, 2006.

Fisher, Eddie. *Been There, Done That.* New York: St. Martin's Press, 1999.

Fishgall, Gary. *Gregory Peck: A Biography.* New York: Scribner's, 2002.

Fitzpatrick, Kevin C. *A Journey into Dorothy Parker's New York.* New York: Roaring Forties Press, 2005.

Fleming, Ian. *From Russia, With Love.* London: Jonathan Cape, 1957.

Fonda, Henry, and Howard Teichmann. *Fonda: My Life.* New York: New American Library, 1981.

Fonda, Jane. *My Life So Far.* New York: Random House, 2005.

Fonteyn, Margot. *Autobiography.* London: W. H. Allen, 1975.

Francisco, Charles. *Gentleman: The William Powell Story.* New York: St. Martin's Press, 1985.

Frayling, Christopher. *Sergio Leone: Something to Do With Death.* London: Faber and Faber, 2000.

Freedland, Michael. *Jack Lemmon.* London: Weidenfeld and Nicolson, 1985.

Gargiulo, Suzanne. *Hans Conreid: A Biography, With a Filmography and a Listing of Radio, Television, Stage and Voice Work.* Jefferson, NC: McFarland, 2002.

Gaugh, Harry F. *Willem de Kooning.* New York: Abbeville Press, 1982.

Gavin, James. *Stormy Weather: The Life of Lena Horne.* New York: Atria, 2009.

Gazzara, Ben. *In the Moment: My Life as an Actor.* New York: Carroll & Graf, 2004.

Genge, N. E. *Urban Legends: The As-Complete-As-One-Could-Be Guide to Modern Myths.* New York: Three Rivers Press, 2000.

Gentry, Curt. *J. Edgar Hoover: The Man and the Secrets.* New York: W. W. Norton, 1991.

Gibson, Barbara, and Ted Schwarz. *Rose Kennedy and Her Family: The Best and Worst of Their Lives and Times.* New York: Birch Lane Press, 1995.

Gill, Brendan. *Many Masks: A Life of Frank Lloyd Wright.* New York: G. P. Putnam's Sons, 1987.

Gilliatt, Penelope. *Unholy Fools: Wits, Comics, Disturbers of the Peace: Film & Theater.* New York: Viking, 1973.

Gilmore, John. *Inside Marilyn Monroe.* Los Angeles: Ferine, 2007.

Gingold, Hermione. *How to Grow Old Disgracefully.* New York: St. Martin's Press, 1988.

Glatzer, Jenna. *The Marilyn Monroe Treasures.* New York: Metro, 2008.

Glendinning, Victoria. *Edith Sitwell: A Unicorn Among Lions.* New York: Alfred A. Knopf, 1981.

Godfrey, Lionel. *Paul Newman Superstar: A Critical Biography.* New York: St. Martin's Press, 1978.

Goode, James. *The Making of The Misfits.* New York: Limelight Editions, 1986.

Gossett, Jr., Lou. *An Actor and a Gentleman.* Hoboken: John Wiley & Sons, 2010.

Gottfried, Martin. *Arthur Miller: His Life and Work.* Cambridge, MA: Da Capo Press, 2003.

_____. *The Life and Death of Bob Fosse.* New York: Bantam, 1990.

Graham, Bill. *Bill Graham Presents: My Life Inside Rock and Out.* New York: Doubleday, 1992.

Graham, Sheila. *Confessions of a Hollywood Columnist.* New York: William Morrow, 1969.

_____. *The Rest of the Story.* New York: Bantam, 1965.

Granger, Farley, and Robert Calhoun. *Include Me Out: My Life From Goldwyn to Broadway.* New York: St. Martin's Press, 2007.

Granger, Stewart. *Sparks Fly Upward.* New York: Putnam, 1981.

Grant, Barry Keith, ed. *Fritz Lang: Interviews.* Jackson: University Press of Mississippi, 2003.

Griffin, Merv, and Peter Barsocchini. *Merv: An Autobiography.* New York: Simon and Schuster, 1980.

Griffin, Merv, and David Bender. *Merv: Making the Good Life Last.* New York: Simon and Schuster, 2003.

Grobel, Lawrence. *The Hustons*. New York: Charles Scribner's Sons, 1989.

Grobel, Lawrence, and James A. Michener. *Talking With Michener*. Jackson: University Press of Mississippi, 1999.

Grodin, Charles. *It Would Be So Nice If You Weren't Here: My Journey Through Show Business*. New York: Morrow, 1989.

Gromyko, Andrei. *Memories*. London: Hutchinson, 1989.

Grunes, Dennis. "Two Daughters." In *All the Available Light: A Marilyn Monroe Reader*, edited by Yona Zeldis McDonough, 184–94. New York: Simon & Schuster, 2002.

Guilaroff, Sydney. *Crowning Glory: Reflections of Hollywood's Favorite Confidant*. Los Angeles: General, 1996.

Guiles, Fred Lawrence. *Legend: The Life and Death of Marilyn Monroe*. New York: Stein and Day, 1985.

Guinness, Alec. *Blessings in Disguise*. London: Fontana/Collins, 1986.

Hadleigh, Boze. *Bette Davis Speaks*. New York: Barricade, 1996.

Hagen, Roy, and Laura Wagner. *Killer Tomatoes: Fifteen Tough Film Dames*. Jefferson, NC: McFarland, 2004.

Hall, William. *Raising Caine: The Authorized Biography*. London: Sidgwick & Jackson, 1981.

Haney, Lynn. *Gregory Peck: A Charmed Life*. New York: Carroll & Graf, 2004.

Hart, Dennis. *Monitor: The Last Great Radio Show*. San Jose: Writers Club Press, 2002.

Harris, Warren G. *Audrey Hepburn: A Biography*. New York: Simon & Schuster, 1994.

_____. *Cary Grant: A Touch of Elegance*. New York: Doubleday, 1987.

_____. *Clark Gable: A Biography*. New York: Harmony, 2002.

_____. *Gable & Lombard*. New York: Simon & Schuster, 1974.

_____. *Natalie & R. J.: Hollywood's Star-Crossed Lovers*. New York: Doubleday, 1988.

_____. *Sophia Loren: A Biography*. New York: Simon & Schuster, 1998.

Harsano, Ganis. *Recollections of an Indonesian Diplomat in the Sukarno Era*. St. Lucia, Queensland: University of Queensland Press, 1977.

Hart, Henry. *James Dickey: The World as a Lie*. New York: Picador, 2000.

Haygood, Wil. *In Black and White: The Life of Sammy Davis, Jr.* New York: Alfred A. Knopf, 2003.

Hayman, Ronald. *Sartre: A Biography*. New York: Simon and Schuster, 1987.

Head, Edith, and Paddy Calistro. *Edith Head's Hollywood*. New York: E. P. Dutton, 1983.

Herndon, Venable. *James Dean: A Short Life*. Garden City, NY: Doubleday, 1974.

Hersh, Seymour M. *The Dark Side of Camelot*. Boston: Little, Brown and Co., 1997.

Heston, Charlton. *In the Arena: An Autobiography*. New York: Simon & Schuster, 1995.

Heymann, C. David. *R. F. K.: A Candid Biography of Robert F. Kennedy*. New York: Dutton, 1998.

Hickey, Des; Smith, Gus. *The Prince: Laurence Harvey: His Public and Private Life*. London: W. H. Allen, 1976.

Hirsch, Foster. *Laurence Olivier*. Boston: Twayne, 1979.

_____. *A Method in Their Madness: The History of the Actors Studio*. New York: W. W. Norton, 1984.

Holden, Anthony. *Olivier*. London: Weidenfeld and Nicolson, 1988.

Holtzman, Will. *Judy Holliday*. New York: G. P. Putnam's Sons, 1982.

Howard, Jean. *Jean Howard's Hollywood: A Photo Memoir*. New York: Harry N. Abrams, 1989.

Hunter, Alan. *Walter Matthau*. New York: St. Martin's Press, 1984.

Huston, John. *An Open Book*. New York: Alfred A. Knopf, 1980.

Hutchinson, Tom. *Rod Steiger: Memoirs of a Friendship*. London: Victor Gollancz, 1998.

Inge, M. Thomas. *Truman Capote: Conversations*. Jackson: University Press of Mississippi, 1987.

Isherwood, Christopher. *Christopher Isherwood Diaries: Volume One 1939—1960*. London: Methuen, 1996.

Israel, Lee. *Kilgallen*. New York: Delacorte, 1979.

Jablonski, Edward. *Harold Arlen: Rhythm, Rainbows and Blues*. Evanston: Northwestern University Press, 1996.

Jeremiah, David. *Slaying the Giants in Your Life*. Nashville: Thomas Nelson, 2001.

Johnson, Dorris, and Ellen Leventhal, eds. *The Letters of Nunnally Johnson*. New York: Alfred A. Knopf, 1981.

Jordan, Ted. *Norma Jean: My Secret Life with Marilyn Monroe*. New York: New American Library, 1991.

Kaminsky, Stuart. *John Huston: Maker of Magic*. Boston: Houghton Mifflin, 1978.

Kanin, Garson. *Hollywood: Stars and Starlets, Tycoons and Flesh-Peddlers, Moviemakers and Moneymakers, Frauds and Geniuses, Hopefuls and Has-Beens, Great Lovers and Sex Symbols*. New York: Viking, 1974.

Kashner, Sam. "The Things She Left Behind." *Vanity Fair*, October 2008.

Kazan, Elia. *Elia Kazan: A Life*. New York: Alfred A. Knopf, 1988.

Kelley, Kitty. *His Way: The Unauthorized Biography of Frank Sinatra*. New York: Bantam, 1987.

Kellow, Brian. *The Bennetts: An Acting Family*. Lexington: University Press of Kentucky, 2004.

Kiernan, Thomas. *Sir Larry: The Life of Laurence Olivier*. New York: Times, 1981.

Klein, Edward. *All Too Human: The Love Story of Jack and Jackie Kennedy.* New York: Pocket Books, 1996.

Klurfeld, Herman. *Winchell: His Life and Times.* New York: Praeger, 1976.

Knef, Hildegard. *The Gift Horse.* London: André Deutsch, 1971.

Kobal, John, ed. *Marilyn Monroe: A Life On Film.* London: Hamlyn, 1974.

Korda, Michael. *Another Life: A Memoir of Other People.* New York: Random House, 1999.

_____. *Charmed Lives: A Family Romance.* New York: Random House, 1979.

Krampner, Jon. *Female Brando: The Legend of Kim Stanley.* New York: Back Stage, 2006.

Krohn, Katherine E. *Ella Fitzgerald: First Lady of Song.* Minneapolis: Lerner, 2001.

Lacey, Robert. *Grace.* New York: G. P. Putnam's Sons, 1994.

LaGuardia, Robert. *Monty: A Biography of Montgomery Clift.* New York: Arbor House, 1977.

Lambert, Gavin. *On Cukor.* New York: G. P. Putnam's Sons, 1972.

Leachman, Cloris. *Cloris.* New York: Kensington, 2009.

Leaming, Barbara. *Marilyn Monroe.* New York: Crown, 1998.

_____. *Mrs. Kennedy: The Missing History of the Kennedy Years.* New York: The Free Press, 2001.

_____. *Orson Welles: A Biography.* New York: Viking, 1985.

Lee, Lawrence, and Barry Gifford. *Saroyan: A Biography.* New York: Harper & Row, 1984.

Lee, Peggy. *Miss Peggy Lee: An Autobiography.* New York: Donald I. Fine, 1989.

Leigh, Janet. *There Really Was a Hollywood.* Garden City, NY: Doubleday, 1984.

Leigh, Wendy. *The Secret Letters of Marilyn Monroe and Jacqueline Kennedy.* New York: St. Martin's Press, 2003.

Leonard, Maurice. *Mae West: Empress of Sex.* London: HarperCollins, 1991.

Levant, Oscar. *The Memoirs of an Amnesiac.* New York: G. P. Putnam's Sons, 1965.

Leverence, John. *Irving Wallace: A Writer's Profile.* Bowling Green, OH: The Popular Press, 1974.

Levinson, Peter J. *September in the Rain: The Life of Nelson Riddle.* New York: Billboard, 2001.

Levy, Emanuel. *George Cukor, Master of Elegance: Hollywood's Legendary Director and His Stars.* New York: William Morrow, 1994.

Lewis, Jerry, and James Kaplan. *Dean & Me (A Love Story).* New York: Doubleday, 2005.

Lindfors, Viveca. *Viveka ... Viveca.* New York: Everest House, 1981.

Linet, Beverly. *Ladd: The Life, the Legend, the Legacy of Alan Ladd.* New York: Arbor House, 1979.

_____. *Susan Hayward: Portrait of a Survivor.* New York: Berkley, 1981.

Lodge, Henry Cabot. *The Storm Has Many Eyes: A Personal Narrative.* New York: W. W. Norton, 1973.

Loos, Anita. *The Talmadge Girls: A Memoir.* New York: Viking, 1978.

Lord, Graham. *Niv: The Authorized Biography of David Niven.* London: Orion, 2004.

Luce, Claire Boothe. "The 'Love Goddess' Who Never Found Any Love." (*Life,* August 7, 1964.) In *All the Available Light: A Marilyn Monroe Reader,* edited by Yona Zeldis McDonough, 83– 102. New York: Simon & Schuster, 2002.

MacAdams, William. *Ben Hecht: The Man Behind the Legend.* New York: Charles Scribner's Sons, 1990.

MacRae, Sheila, and H. Paul Jeffers. *Hollywood Mother of the Year.* New York: Birch Lane Press, 1992.

MacShane, Frank. *Into Eternity: The Life of James Jones, American Writer.* Boston: Houghton Mifflin, 1985.

_____. *The Life of Raymond Chandler.* New York: E. P. Dutton, 1976.

Madsen, Axel. *John Huston.* Garden City, NY: Doubleday, 1978.

_____. *Stanwyck.* New York: HarperCollins, 1994.

Mailer, Norman. *Marilyn.* New York: Warner, 1975.

_____. *Of Women and Their Elegance.* New York: Simon & Schuster, 1980.

Mankiewicz, Joseph L., and Gary Carey. *More About All About Eve.* New York: Random House, 1972.

Marill, Alvin H. *Robert Mitchum on the Screen.* South Brunswick and New York: A S. Barnes, 1978.

Marshall, Catherine. *To Live Again.* New York: McGraw Hill, 1957.

Martin, Deana, and Wendy Holder. *Memories are Made of This: Dean Martin Through His Daughter's Eyes.* New York: Harmony, 2004.

Martin, Ralph G. *The Woman He Loved.* New York: Signet, 1975.

Martin, Ricci, and Christopher Smith. *That's Amore: A Son Remembers Dean Martin.* Dallas: Taylor Trade, 2002.

Martinson, Deborah. *Lillian Hellman: A Life with Foxes and Scoundrels.* New York: Counterpoint, 2005.

Mason, James. *Before I Forget.* London: Hamish Hamilton, 1981.

Mast, Gerald. *Howard Hawks, Storyteller.* New York: Oxford University Press, 1982.

Mayo, Virginia. *The Best Years of My Life.* Chesterfield, MO: BeachHouse, 2001.

McBride, Joseph M. *Focus on Howard Hawks.* Englewood Cliffs, NJ: Prentice-Hall, 1972.

McCann, Graham. *Marilyn Monroe.* New Brunswick, NJ: Rutgers University Press, 1988.

McCarthy, Todd. *Howard Hawks: The Grey Fox of*

Hollywood. New York: Grove Press, 1997.

McCombs, Don, and Fred Worth. *World War II: 4139 Strange and Fascinating Facts*. New York: Wing, 1983.

McDonough, Yona Zeldis, ed. "Reliquary." In *All the Available Light: A Marilyn Monroe Reader*, 200–14. New York: Simon & Schuster, 2002.

McGee, Tom. *Betty Grable: The Girl with the Million Dollar Legs*. Vestal, NY: The Vestal Press, 1995.

McMahon, Ed, and David Fisher. *For Laughing Out Loud: My Life and Good Times*. New York: Warner, 1998.

McNulty, Thomas. *Errol Flynn: The Life and Career*. Jefferson, NC: McFarland, 2004.

Meade, Marion. *Buster Keaton: Cut to the Chase*. New York: HarperCollins, 1995.

_____. *Dorothy Parker: What Fresh Hell Is This?* New York: Villard, 1988.

Meadows, Audrey. *Love, Alice: My Life as a Honeymooner*. New York: Crown, 1994.

Mellen, Joan. *Marilyn Monroe*. New York: Galahad, 1973.

Mendelsohn, Michael J. *Clifford Odets: Humane Dramatist*. Deland, FL: Everett/Edwards, 1969.

Meyers, Jeffrey. *The Genius and the Goddess: Arthur Miller and Marilyn Monroe*. Champagne: University of Illinois Press, 2010.

Miller, Arthur. *Timebends: A Life*. New York: Grove Press, 1987.

Miller, Russell. *Bunny: The Real Story of Playboy*. London: Michael Joseph, 1984.

Mills, Hillary. *Mailer: A Biography*. New York: Empire, 1982.

Minnelli, Vincente, and Hector Arce. *I Remember It Well*. London: Angus & Robertson, 1974.

Miracle, Berniece Baker, and Mona Rae Miracle. *My Sister Marilyn: A Memoir of Marilyn Monroe*. New York: Boulevard, 1995.

Mitchell, Glenn. *The Marx Brothers Encyclopedia*. London: B. T. Batsford, 1996.

Mobilio, Albert. "Scratching Tom Ewell's Itch," In *All the Available Light: A Marilyn Monroe Reader*, edited by Yona Zeldis McDonough, 53–59. New York: Simon & Schuster, 2002.

Monroe, Marilyn, and Ben Hecht. *My Story*. New York: Stein & Day, 1974.

Montand, Yves, Hervé Hamon, and Patrick Rotman. *You See, I Haven't Forgotten*. New York: Alfred A. Knopf, 1992.

Morella, Joe, and Edward Z. Epstein. *Jane Wyman: A Biography*. New York: Delacorte, 1985.

_____. *Rita: The Life of Rita Hayworth*. New York: Doubleday, 1983.

Morgan, Michelle. *Marilyn Monroe: Private and Undisclosed*. New York: Carroll & Graf, 2007.

Morley, Sheridan. *Sybil Thorndike: A Life in the Theatre*. London: Weidenfeld & Nicolson, 1977.

Morley, Sheridan, and Ruth Leon. *Marilyn Monroe*. Stroud (U.K.): Sutton, 1997.

Murray, Christopher. *Sean O'Casey Writer at Work: A Biography*. Montreal: McGill-Queen's University Press, 2004.

Nash, Alanna. *Baby, Let's Play House: Elvis Presley and the Women Who Loved Him*. New York: HarperCollins, 2010.

Negulesco, Jean. *Things I did ... and Things I Think I Did*. New York, Linden Press, 1984.

Nicholson, Stuart. *Ella Fitzgerald: A Biography of the First Lady of Jazz*. New York: Da Capo Press, 1995.

Nicosia, Gerald. *Memory Babe: A Critical Biography of Jack Kerouac*. New York: Grove Press, 1983.

Norman, Philip. *Elton John*. New York: Simon & Schuster, 1993.

Oderman, Stuart. *Lillian Gish: A Life on Stage and Screen*. Jefferson, NC: McFarland, 2000.

O' hAodha, Michael. *Siobhan: A Memoir of an Actress*. Dublin: Brandon, 1994.

O'Hara, Maureen, and John Nicolette. *'Tis Herself: A Memoir*. New York: Simon & Schuster, 2004.

Olivier, Laurence. *Confessions of an Actor: An Autobiography*. New York: Simon and Schuster, 1982.

Oppenheimer, Jerry. *The Other Mrs. Kennedy: Ethel Skakel Kennedy: An American Drama of Power, Privilege and Politics*. New York: St. Martin's Press, 1994.

O'Sullivan, Michael. *Brendan Behan: A Life*. Dublin: Blackwater Press, 1997.

Paar, Jack. *P. S. Jack Paar*. Garden City, NY: Doubleday, 1983.

Parsons, Louella O. *Tell It to Louella*. New York: G. P. Putnam's Sons, 1961.

Payn, Graham, and Sheridan Morley, eds. *The Noel Coward Diaries*. Boston: Little, Brown, 1982.

Persico, Joseph E. *Edward R. Murrow: An American Original*. New York: McGraw-Hall, 1988.

Phillips, Gene D. *George Cukor*. Boston: Twayne, 1982.

Pierce, Patricia Jobe. *The Ultimate Elvis: Elvis Presley Day By Day*. New York: Simon & Schuster, 1994.

Pilcher, Jeffrey M. *Cantinflas and the Chaos of Mexican Modernity*. Wilmington, DE: AR, 2001.

Plowright, Joan. *And That's Not All*. London: Weidenfeld & Nicolson, 2001.

Poague, Leland A. *Howard Hawks*. Boston: Twayne, 1982.

Powell, Josephine. *Tito Puente: When the Drums are Dreaming*. Bloomington: AuthorHouse, 2007.

Pratley, Gerald, ed. *The Cinema of John Huston*. South Brunswick and New York: A. S. Barnes, 1977.

Preminger, Otto. *Preminger: An Autobiography*. Garden City, NY: Doubleday, 1977.

Quayle, Anthony. *A Time to Speak*. London: Barrie & Jenkins, 1990.

Quinn, Anthony; Paisner, Daniel. *One Man Tango*. New York: HarperCollins, 1995.

Quirk, Lawrence J. *Claudette Colbert: An Illustrated Biography.* New York: Crown, 1985.

_____. *Fasten Your Seat Belts: The Passionate Life of Bette Davis.* New York: Signet, 1990.

Rampersad, Arnold. *The Life of Langston Hughes: Volume II: 1941—1967: I Dream a World.* Oxford: Oxford University Press, 2002.

Read, Piers Paul. *Alec Guinness: The Authorized Biography.* New York: Simon & Schuster, 2003.

Rebello, Stephen. "Somebody Killed Her," *Playboy,* December 2005.

Rechy, John. "How Marilyn Monroe Profoundly Influenced *The Discrete Charm of the Bourgeoisie.*" In *Luis Buñuel's The Discrete Charm of the Bourgeoisie,* edited by Marsha Kinder, 34–40. Cambridge: Cambridge University Press, 1999.

Redgrave, Vanessa. *Vanessa Redgrave: An Autobiography.* New York: Random House, 1994.

Reed, Philip, ed. *Letters From a Life: The Selected Letters of Benjamin Britten 1913–1976. Volume Four 1952-1957.* Woodbridge: The Boydell Press, 1991.

Reinhardt, Gottfried. *The Genius: A Memoir of Max Reinhardt.* New York: Alfred A. Knopf, 1979.

Reynolds, Debbie, and David Patrick. Columbia. *Debbie: My Life.* New York: William Morrow, 1988.

Ricco, Diana. *Kovacsland: A Biography of Ernie Kovacs.* San Diego: Harcourt Brace Jovanovich, 1990.

Riese, Randall. *The Unabridged James Dean: His Life and Legacy from A to Z.* Chicago: Contemporary, 1991.

Riese, Randall, and Neal Hitchens. *The Unabridged Marilyn: Her Life from A to Z.* New York: Congdon & Weed, 1987.

Rivadue, Barry. *Lee Remick: A Bio-Biography.* Westport, CT: Greenwood Press, 1995.

Robbins, Jhan. *Yul Brynner: The Inscrutable King.* New York: Dodd, Mead, 1987.

Robyns, Gwen. *Princess Grace.* London: W. H. Allen, 1976.

Rogers, Ginger. *Ginger: My Story.* New York: HarperPaperbacks, 1991.

Rollyson, Jr., Carl E. *The Lives of Norman Mailer.* New York: Paragon House, 1991.

_____. *Marilyn Monroe: A Life of the Actress.* New York: Da Capo, 1993.

Rooney, Mickey. *Life is Too Short.* New York: Villard, 1991.

Root, Eric, Dale Crawford, and Raymond Strait. *The Private Diary of My Life with Lana.* Beverly Hills: Dove, 1996.

Rose, Frank. *The Agency: William Morris and the Hidden History of Show Business.* New York: HarperCollins, 1995.

Rubin, Steven Jay. *The Complete James Bond Movie Encyclopedia.* Chicago: Contemporary, 2003.

Russell, Jane. *An Autobiography: My Path & My Detours.* New York: Franklin Watts, 1985.

Sahl, Mort. *Heartland.* New York: Harcourt Brace Jovanovich, 1976.

Schary, Dore. *Heyday: An Autobiography.* Boston: Little, Brown, 1979.

Schechter, Scott. *Judy Garland: The Day-by-Day Chronicle of a Legend.* New York: Cooper Square Press, 2002.

Schickel, Richard. *Elia Kazan: A Biography.* New York: HarperCollins, 2005.

Schlesinger, Arthur M., Jr. *Robert Kennedy and His Times.* Boston: Houghton Mifflin, 1978.

Schwarz, Ted. *Marilyn Revealed: The Ambitious Life of an American Icon.* Lanham, MD: Taylor Trade Publishing, 2009.

Scott, Michael. *Maria Meneghini Callas.* Boston: Northeastern University Press, 1992.

Server, Lee. *Robert Mitchum: Baby, I Don't Care.* New York: St. Martin's Press, 2001.

Shaw, Sam, and Norman Rosten. *Marilyn: Among Friends.* New York: Henry Holt, 1988.

Sheed, Wilfrid. *Clare Boothe Luce.* New York: E. P. Dutton, 1982.

Shellard, Dominic. *Kenneth Tynan: A Life.* New Haven, CT: Yale University Press, 2003.

Shevey, Sandra. *The Marilyn Scandal: The True Story.* London: Arrow, 1989.

Shipman, David. *Judy Garland.* London: Fourth Estate, 1992.

Shnayerson, Michael. *Irwin Shaw: A Biography.* New York: G. P. Putnam's Sons, 1989.

Signoret, Simone. *Nostalgia Isn't What It Used to Be.* Harmondsworth: Penguin, 1979.

Sikov, Ed. *Mr. Strangelove: A Biography of Peter Sellers.* New York: Hyperion, 2002.

Silverman, Stephen M. *The Fox that Got Away: The Last Days of the Zanuck Dynasty at Twentieth Century–Fox.* Secaucus, NJ: Lyle Stuart, 1988.

Simmons, Dawn Langley. *Margaret Rutherford: A Blithe Spirit.* New York: McGraw-Hill, 1983.

Sinyard, Neil. *Marilyn.* London: Bison, 1989.

Sitwell, Edith. *Taken Care Of: The Autobiography of Edith Sitwell.* New York: Athenaeum, 1965.

Slatzer, Robert F. *The Life and Curious Death of Marilyn Monroe.* Los Angeles: Pinnacle, 1975.

Smith, Andrew. *Rescuing the World: The Life and Times of Leo Cherne.* Albany: State University of New York Press, 2002.

Smith, Ella. *Starring Miss Barbara Stanwyck.* New York: Crown, 1985.

Smith, Howard K. *Events Leading Up to My Death: The Life of a Twentieth-Century Reporter.* New York: St. Martin's Press, 1996.

Smith, Matthew. *Victim: The Secret Tapes of Marilyn Monroe.* London: Arrow, 2004.

Spada, James. *Peter Lawford: The Man Who Kept Secrets.* New York: Bantam, 1991.

Spada, James, and George Zeno. *Monroe: Her Life in Pictures.* Garden City, NY: Doubleday, 1982.

Sperber, A. M. *Bogart*. New York: William Morrow, 1997.

Spoto, Donald. *Laurence Olivier: A Biography*. New York: HarperCollins, 1992.

_____. *Marilyn Monroe: The Biography*. New York: HarperCollins, 1993.

Stack, Robert, and Mark Evans. *Straight Shooting*. New York: Macmillan, 1980.

Stapleton, Maureen, and Jane Scovell. *A Hell of a Life: An Autobiography*. New York: Simon & Schuster, 1995.

Starr, Michael Seth. *Mouse in the Rat Pack: The Joey Bishop Story*. New York: Taylor, 2002.

Steinem, Gloria. *Marilyn: Norma Jeane*. New York: Signet, 1986.

Stenn, David. *Clara Bow: Runnin' Wild*. New York: Doubleday, 1988.

Stewart, Wayne. *The Gigantic Book of Baseball Quotations*. New York: Skyhorse, 2007.

Stossel, Scott. *Sarge: The Life and Times of Sargent Shriver*. Washington: Smithsonian, 2004.

Strasberg, Susan. *Marilyn and Me: Sisters, Rivals, Friends*. New York: Warner, 1992.

_____. *Bittersweet*. New York: G. P. Putnam's Sons, 1980.

Sudhalter, Richard M. *Stardust Melody: The Life and Music of Hoagy Carmichael*. Oxford: Oxford University Press, 2002.

Summers, Anthony. *Goddess: The Secret Lives of Marilyn Monroe*. London: Sphere, 1986.

Swindell, Larry. *Charles Boyer: The Reluctant Lover*. Garden City, NY: Doubleday, 1983.

Tafel, Edgar. *About Wright: An Album of Recollections by Those Who Knew Frank Lloyd Wright*. New York: John Wiley & Sons, 1998.

Talese, Gay. *Thy Neighbor's Wife*. Garden City, NY: Doubleday, 1980.

Taraborrelli, J. Randy. *Jackie Ethel Joan*. New York: Warner, 2000.

_____. *The Secret Life of Marilyn Monroe*. New York: Grand Central, 2009.

Taubman, William. *Khrushchev: The Man and His Era*. New York: W. H. Norton, 2003.

Terry-Thomas. *Terry-Thomas Tells Tales: An Autobiography*. London: Robson, 1990.

Theoharis, Athan G., and John Stuart Cox. *J. Edgar Hoover and the Great American Inquisition*. Philadelphia: Temple University Press, 1988.

Thomas, Bob. *Clown Prince of Hollywood: The Antic Life of Jack L. Warner*. New York: McGraw-Hill, 1990.

_____. *I Got Rhythm! The Ethel Merman Story*. New York: G. P. Putnam's Sons, 1985.

_____. *Joan Crawford: A Biography*. New York: Simon and Schuster, 1978.

Thomas, Evan. *Robert Kennedy: His Life*. New York: Simon & Schuster, 2000.

Thompson, Charles. *Bing: The Authorized Biography*. London: W. H. Allen, 1975.

Thurman, Judith. *Isaak Dinesen: The Life of a Storyteller*. New York: St. Martin's Press, 1982.

Todd, Michael, Jr. *A Valuable Property: The Life Story of Michael Todd*. New York: Arbor House, 1983.

Tormé, Mel. *It Wasn't All Velvet*. New York: Viking, 1988.

Tornabene, Lyn. *Long Live the King: A Biography of Clark Gable*. New York: Pocket Books, 1978.

Tosches, Nick. *Dino: Living High in the Dirty Business of Dreams*. New York: Dell, 1992.

Tremlett, George. *Dylan Thomas: In the Mercy of His Means*. London: Constable, 1991.

Truscott, Pamela, and Chuck Ashman. *Cary Grant*. London: W. H. Allen, 1986.

Turan, Kenneth, and Joseph Papp. *Free For All, Joe Papp, the Public and the Greatest Theater Story Ever Told*. New York: Doubleday, 2009.

Tynan, Kathleen. *The Life of Kenneth Tynan*. New York: William Morrow, 1987.

Van Doren, Mamie, and Art Aveilhe. *Playing the Field: My Story*. New York: Berkley, 1988.

Verlhac, Anne. *Marilyn Monroe: A Life in Pictures*. San Francisco: Chronicle, 2007.

Vickers, Hugo. *Cecil Beaton: The Authorized Biography*. London: Weidenfeld and Nicolson, 1985.

Victor, Adam. *The Marilyn Encyclopedia*. Woodstock, NY: The Overlook Press, 1999.

Voss, Ralph F. *A Life of William Inge: The Strains of Triumph*. Lawrence: University Press of Kansas, 1989.

Wagenknecht, Edward. *Marilyn Monroe: A Composite View*. Philadelphia: Chilton, 1969.

_____. *Seven Daughters of the Theater*. Norman: University of Oklahoma Press, 1964.

Wagner, Walter. *You Must Remember This*. New York: G. P. Putnam's Sons, 1975.

Walker, Alexander. *Fatal Charm: The Life of Rex Harrison*. New York: St. Martin's Press, 1992.

_____. *Vivien: The Life of Vivien Leigh*. London: Methuen, 1988.

Wallach, Eli. *The Good, the Bad, and Me: In My Anecdotage*. Orlando: Harcourt, 2005.

Walsh, Raoul. *Each Man in His Time: The Life Story of a Director*. New York: Farrar, Straus and Giroux, 1979.

Wansell, Geoffrey. *Terence Rattigan*. London: Fourth Estate, 1995.

Wapshott, Nicholas. *Rex Harrison: A Biography*. London: Chatto & Windus, 1991.

Warhol, Andy, and Pat Hackett. *POPism: The Warhol '60s*. New York: Harcourt Brace Jovanovish, 1980.

Warren, Doug. *Betty Grable: The Reluctant Movie Queen*. New York: St. Martin's Press, 1981.

Watts, Steve. *The Magic Kingdom: Walt Disney and the American Way of Life*. Boston: Houghton Mifflin, 1997.

Wayne, Aissa, and Steve Delsohn. *John Wayne: My Father*. New York: Random House, 1991.

Wayne, Jane Ellen. *Gable's Women*. New York: Prentice Hall, 1987.

Weatherby, W. J. *Conversations with Marilyn*. London: Sphere, 1977.

Webster, Jack. *Alistair Maclean: A Life*. London: Chapmans, 1991.

West, James L. W. *William Styron: A Life*. New York: Random House, 1998.

Widener, Don. *Lemmon: A Biography*. New York: Macmillan, 1975.

Wilding, Michael. *The Wilding Way: The Story of My Life*. New York: St. Martin's Press, 1982.

Williams, Dakin, and Shepherd Mead. *Tennessee Williams: An Intimate Biography*. New York: Arbor House, 1983.

Williams, Esther. *The Million Dollar Mermaid*. New York: Simon and Schuster, 1999.

Wilson, Earl. *Hot Times: True Tales of Hollywood and Broadway*. Chicago: Contemporary, 1984.

Winecoff, Charles. *Split Image: The Life of Anthony Perkins*. New York: Dutton, 1996.

Winters, Shelley. *Shelley: Also Known as Shirley*. New York: William Morrow, 1980.

_____. *Shirley II: The Middle of My Century*. New York: Simon and Schuster, 1989.

Wolfe, Donald H. *The Last Days of Marilyn Monroe*. New York: William Morrow, 1998.

Wood, Tom. *The Bright Side of Billy Wilder, Primarily*. Garden City, NY: Doubleday, 1970.

Wright, William. *Lillian Hellman: The Image, the Woman*. New York: Ballantine, 1986.

Yablonsky, Lewis. *George Raft*. New York: McGraw-Hill, 1974.

Young, Alan, and Bill Burt. *Mister Ed and Me*. New York: St. Martin's Press, 1994.

Zec, Donald. *Sophia: An Intimate Biography*. London: W. H. Allen, 1975.

Zeffirelli, Franco. *Zeffirelli: The Autobiography of Franco Zeffirelli*. London: Weidenfeld and Nicolson, 1986.

Ziegler, Philip. *Diana Cooper: A Biography*. New York: Alfred A. Knopf, 1982.

Zierold, Norman. *The Moguls*. New York: Coward-McCann, 1969.

Zimroth, Evan. "Marilyn at the Mikvah." In *All the Available Light: A Marilyn Monroe Reader*, edited by Yona Zeldis McDonough, 176–183. New York: Simon & Schuster, 2002.

Zolotow, Maurice. *Billy Wilder in Hollywood*. New York: G. P. Putnam's Sons, 1977.

_____. *Marilyn Monroe*. New York: HarperCollins, 1990.

Internet Resources

www.imdb.com
www.marilynmonroe.ca
www.tinkerbelltalks.com
www.wikipedia.org
www.cursumperficio.net

Index